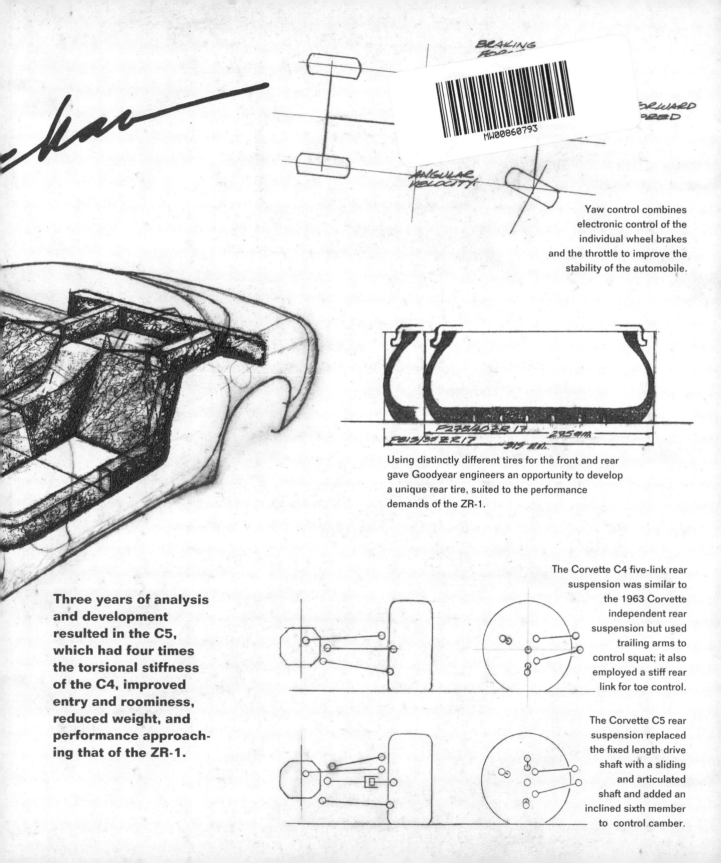

Yaw control combines electronic control of the individual wheel brakes and the throttle to improve the stability of the automobile.

Using distinctly different tires for the front and rear gave Goodyear engineers an opportunity to develop a unique rear tire, suited to the performance demands of the ZR-1.

Three years of analysis and development resulted in the C5, which had four times the torsional stiffness of the C4, improved entry and roominess, reduced weight, and performance approaching that of the ZR-1.

The Corvette C4 five-link rear suspension was similar to the 1963 Corvette independent rear suspension but used trailing arms to control squat; it also employed a stiff rear link for toe control.

The Corvette C5 rear suspension replaced the fixed length drive shaft with a sliding and articulated shaft and added an inclined sixth member to control camber.

CORVETTE
FROM THE INSIDE

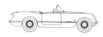

THE 50 YEAR
DEVELOPMENT HISTORY

AS TOLD BY DAVE MCLELLAN,
CORVETTE'S CHIEF ENGINEER 1975–1992

DAVE MCLELLAN

B WWW.
BentleyPublishers
.com

Chapter 1: In 1989 the ZR-1 was introduced on winding and twisting French roads.

Chapter 3: The 1963 Corvette was designed as both a coupe and convertible.

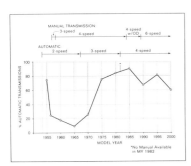

Chapter 5: Replacing the two-speed Powerglide transmission with the three-speed Turbo Hydramatic caused a dramatic shift in buyer preference.

Chapter 5: The 1982 Collector's Edition was the first production Corvette to have a hatchback.

CORVETTE
FROM THE INSIDE

Chapter 10: A Corvette tire being tested in colored water over a glass road.

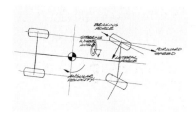

Chapter 10: Yaw control combines electronic control of the individual wheel brakes and the throttle to improve stability.

Chapter 12: The Lotus 4.0 liter V-8 Etna engine was the precursor to the LT5.

Chapter 17: The Mosler MT900 is currently being developed as a road car.

B | **BENTLEY PUBLISHERS** | Automotive Books & Manuals

Bentley Publishers, a division of Robert Bentley, Inc.
1734 Massachusetts Avenue
Cambridge, MA 02138 USA
800-423-4595 / 617-547-4170

Information that makes
the difference®

www.
BentleyPublishers
.com

Copies of this book may be purchased from selected booksellers, or directly from the publisher. The publisher encourages comments from the reader of this book. These communications have been and will be considered in the preparation of this and other books. Please write to Bentley Publishers at the address listed at the top of this page or e-mail us through our web site.

Since this page cannot legibly accommodate all the copyright notices, the Art Credits constitute an extension of the copyright page.

Library of Congress Cataloging-in-Publication Data

McLellan, Dave, 1936–
   Corvette from the inside : the 50 year development history as told by Dave McLellan,
Corvette's chief engineer, 1975–1992 / by Dave McLellan.
     p. cm.
  Includes index.
  ISBN 0-8376-0859-7 (alk. paper)
   1. Corvette automobile--History. 2. General Motors Corporation. Chevrolet Motor
Division--History. I. Title.
  TL215.C6 M37 2002
  629.222'09--dc21   2002020068

ISBN 0-8376-0859-7 (hardcover)
ISBN 0-8376-0191-6 (two-book slipcased set containing leather-bound editions of
                 Corvette from the Inside and *Zora Arkus-Duntov: The Legend Behind Corvette*)

Bentley Stock No. GCMC

05 04 03 02   10 9 8 7 6 5 4 3 2 1

The paper used in this publication is acid free and meets the requirements of the National Standard for Information Sciences-Permanence of Paper for Printed Library Materials. ∞

Corvette from the Inside, by Dave McLellan

Manufactured in the United States of America

Front Cover: Photo of Dave McLellan by Jonathan A. Stein. Illustration of 1989 Corvette ZR-1 by Dave Kimble. Blueprint ©2002 General Motors Corporation. Used with permission. GM Media Archives.

Inside Front Flap: Photo by Mike Mueller.

Back Cover: Drawing by Dave McLellan. Photo of millionth Corvette by D. Randy Riggs. Photo of Portland International Raceway by Rich Chenet.

Inside Back Flap: Top photo courtesy Dave McLellan Archives. Bottom photo by Mike Mueller.

Endleaves: Drawings by Dave McLellan.

Title page: Cutaway illustration of 1989 Corvette ZR-1 by Dave Kimble.

Artwork from GM Media Archives is © 2002 General Motors Corporation. Used with permission.

Dedicated to Jesus Christ my Lord and Savior who has given me my gifts and talents and blessed me with a wonderful family: My wife Glenda, our sons David and Philip, Philip's wife Jeannie and our first grandchild, who will arrive just as this book is being published.

Dave and Glenda in front of their home of 32 years. The house was designed by John Howe, a life-long associate of Frank Lloyd Wright.

Drawing by Carlos Leon-York

Prologue

AFTER MORE THAN THREE DECADES as an engineer for General Motors, I retired at the end of 1992. I could have stayed on, but things were changing at GM, the early retirement package was right, and so was the timing for me to move on.

For those 33 years of my GM career I had been ideally situated to watch some of the industry's most momentous changes. I'd also had a chance to watch some of the General's giants in action, including Bill Mitchell, Ed Cole and Zora Arkus-Duntov. While I was actively pursuing my career, however, there wasn't much time for reflection and introspection about what I was watching unfold or the part that I was playing.

Once I retired, I began making notes for what would become this book. I started writing this in a stream of consciousness style, putting down everything I could remember from a particular era or on a particular subject. Piecing this together led to an order for the book that was more circular than the linear year-by-year flow of most Corvette books. I shared this as an outline with potential publishers, and Michael Bentley and I came together as the best fit. The next step was to begin organizing these notes and dividing them into sections and chapters, followed by several years of writing.

I was determined that this book would be neither my biography nor another Corvette coffee-table book. It would simply be my view of the Corvette from both the inside and the beginning. That meant that the who, what, when, where and why of the Corvette were important to this book. This turned out to be an opportunity for me to re-think the Corvette in the light of these questions from an insider's perspective. My inside view of GM dated back to 1959, and in 1975 I had gained the vantage point of Corvette's chief engineer. Like few others, I knew the characters and had participated in the decisions that shaped the Corvette. In telling this story I know I have left out the names of important contributors to the Corvette. This was unfortunate but a limitation of keeping the story moving. Please know that by your work you will all be remembered as an important part of the Corvette team.

Those of you who have met me and worked with me probably know that whenever I tell a story verbally, I'm always reaching for pencil and paper to illustrate my point. This book is no different, as I was always grabbing that pencil to sketch out visual examples of what I was describing in words. The big difference is that through this book, I hope to reach a much larger audience with my message and my illustrations.

Although I like to think of this story as told from my unique point of view, it's not something that I could have done completely on my own. I want to personally thank my wife, Glenda, for her encouragement and for keeping me focused on the task of writing. And, I want to thank my publisher, Michael Bentley, for his leap of faith that an engineer could actually write. My editor, Jonathan Stein, deserves commendation for his encouragement, guidance and dedication to keeping the book in my voice. There are also a number of friends from my Corvette days who helped to jog my memory or added significantly to the book. I recall sitting with Zora Arkus-Duntov on a golf cart, undisturbed for hours, discussing Allards, Porsches and mid-engined Corvettes. Larry Shinoda and I spent an afternoon exploring his contributions to Corvette design. Extensive interviews with Roy Midgley and Anil Kulkarni brought Corvette engines, past, present and future into focus. Doug Robinson and John Powell helped me sort out the showroom stock racing adventures that helped raise the production Corvette to a new level of performance. And, lastly, a special thanks to Reeves Callaway and Charlie Kenny who each contributed side bars to my discussions of their respective contributions to the Corvette. I hope that you will enjoy reading my story of the Corvette as much as I enjoyed writing it.

Dave McLellan, 2002
Holly, Michigan

The Corvette is Born 1

ALL TOO QUICKLY, THE STEEP CANYON carved out of the French Alps opened up and we were in the quaint bobsled resort village of Villard-de-Lans. In a blink we were out its other side and heading down into the Gorges de la Bourne. Clinging to the face of the mountain, the ZR-1 twisted and turned down another wild road, a road that in the dead of winter is used for the Monte Carlo Rally. My exploration of first and second gear acceleration, braking and handling seemed to go on forever as the gorge continued mile after mile.

The date was March 8, 1989, and I was on the new car press introduction of the 375hp, 180mph ZR-1 Corvette en route from the Geneva auto show to Carcassonne, in the South of France. The earliest production cars had been completed just in time for the introduction and subsequent press trips. Even though I was Corvette Chief Engineer, this was my first real drive of the car that I will always think of as "King of the Hill." It was also one of my best memories of my 17 years as Chief Engineer.

The ZR-1 was made for French roads. Winding and twisting through historic valleys, many of these same roads are used for the Monte Carlo Rally.
Courtesy Goodyear Tire & Rubber Co.

THE HERITAGE OF THE CORVETTE

Every production Corvette that followed the 1953 Motorama car has been evolutionary, building on the version that came before it. One year might see minor adjustments to the body or chassis, while another year would see the introduction of an all-new engine. Not only was the ZR-1 a major refinement and development of the 1984 Corvette, it owed its very existence to each Corvette that preceded it. Even today's C5, which reached production after my tenure as Corvette Chief Engineer, owes much to both the ZR-1 and its antecedents.

1989 ZR-1 Performance	
0–60 mph	4.3 seconds
1/4 mile	12.83 sec. @111 mph
Top speed	178 mph

The Corvette was originally introduced as part of General Motors' Motorama extravaganza in 1952. The overwhelming response to the car reaffirmed Ed Cole's resolve to see that it reached production.

GM Media Archives

The heart of the XK120 Jaguar was the 160bhp 3.4 liter, six-cylinder double overhead cam engine that became the basis for the C and D Type race cars and the E Type sports car.

Courtesy Road & Track Magazine

The MG TC was the quintessential traditional sports car. Its roots are to be found in the first cars of the twentieth century with their flexible frames, stiff suspensions and modest performance.

Photo by Marvin Lyons

Although my personal Corvette journey began in 1974, to put the tale in context I have to start at the beginning—to even before the Motorama show car took center stage in 1952.

The production Corvette was released just 68 years after the invention of the automobile. In those intervening years, between 1885 and 1952, the automobile developed from buggy to serious transportation. Roads that hardly existed at the turn of the twentieth century evolved into intricate networks, and automobile technology advanced to produce road racing cars capable of 200 mph.

In the beginning, all automobiles were sports cars by default. To go anywhere by automobile was a great adventure. As roads, the infrastructure and automotive technology developed over the next two decades, the automobile became a dominant mode of personal transportation, and the sports car became a specialized product. The advancing technologies transferred from auto racing, aircraft racing, and military aircraft design served to redefine the sports car. So by 1952, enthusiasts who were steeped in the mystique of the sports car and who saw the first Corvette on the Motorama stage, questioned whether an American sports car, particularly one produced by Chevrolet, could meet their expectations. Knowing what the sports car enthusiast knew and what the expectations for a sports car were in 1952 will help us to understand what happened when the Corvette was introduced.

When the Corvette was first shown to the public, it was instantly subject to comparison to the leading contemporary sports cars—the Jaguar XK120 and the MG TC. These two cars were vastly different in both performance and appearance, but they were both great fun to drive and exciting to look at. To some degree though, the Corvette was at a disadvantage

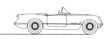

because the United States had very little heritage of nimble, responsive sporting automobiles, without harking back to the Edwardian days of American motoring with cars such as the Stutz Bearcat and Mercer Race-A-Bout. But in 1953, very few drivers or automobile enthusiasts in the United States had experience with these two legendary automobiles.

Without a recent past of small sporting cars capable of carrying two passengers, American automakers and designers had no choice but to look across the Atlantic. In Europe, marques such as Mercedes-Benz, Alfa Romeo, Aston Martin and scores of others had a history of building fast, responsive and exciting automobiles, some of which were equally at home on road or track. Detroit was slow to copy such innovations as double-overhead cam engines, fully independent suspensions and disc brakes. But at General Motors, styling chief Harley Earl was more than willing to pay close attention to European trends and specific designs.

The 646bhp Mercedes-Benz W.125 was nearly invincible during the 1937 Grand Prix season, and it either introduced or included virtually all of the important elements of the modern sports car.
DaimlerChrysler AG

MOTORAMA MADNESS

Every year since 1949, a road show extravaganza called Motorama traveled around the United States, showing off the future as envisioned by GM. In each of those years, GM Styling had contributed show cars to the Motorama stage. Most of those cars were larger than life and were an evolution of Earl's 1938 Y-job, which incorporated influences from such styling icons as the Auburn speedster and the Cord 810. GM's stylists were always working to make their cars look long, low, and sleek.

GM's show cars of the late 1940s and early 1950s drew their inspiration from the military airplanes of World War II and the early jet planes being developed. These cars sported tail fins and intake and exhaust nozzles, themes that the designer used to express speed, power, and aggression. The trend was exemplified by show cars such as the Buick XP 300 and the Le Sabre. Looking back, it is clear that they were a product of their time, not a portent for the future.

Harley Earl, GM's first head of styling, was himself larger than life. Tall and imposing, he drove his stylists with tactics of fear and intimidation. As Vice President of GM Styling, he watched his own boys grow up taking a strong interest in the sports cars

The 1938 Y-job show car incorporated elements from contemporary icons and art deco design, melding them into a car that would signal the next wave of design trends from GM.
GM Design Center

The Le Sabre show car drew its inspiration from the military jet planes developed after World War II.
GM Design Center

3

Trained in his family coach building business, in his three decades as head of GM's Art and Color Section—later GM Styling—Harley Earl turned GM into a design powerhouse.
GM Media Archives

The unsung hero of the Corvette, Bob McLean, designed the car under Harley Earl's direction. McLean was also responsible for the radical turbine-powered Firebird concept cars.
Courtesy Michael Lamm

of the 1950s such as Jaguars and Ferraris. It struck him that he could design sports cars too. Early in 1952, Earl decided that his next Motorama show car would be a sports car. He made some sketches of what he thought it should look like and then tapped young engineer-designer Bob McLean—just hired from Cal Tech—to flesh out his ideas and turn them into a real car. Earl's original sketches have been lost, so we don't know exactly what he defined for McLean, but we do know what they produced—the first Corvette.

Bob McLean was later described by Chuck Jordan, who worked for him and later went on to be Vice President of GM Design Staff, as "very creative and interested in the architecture of the automobile—he knew engineering." McLean later contributed to the Sting Ray Corvette and was responsible for the radical turbine-powered Firebird concept cars.

Earl organized the Corvette project in absolute secrecy, even keeping it away from his other stylists. He set up his studio on the third floor of Plant 8, an old Fisher Body factory about a mile from the General Motors Building where his other studios were located. To deflect the curious he gave the car the code name Opel, the name of GM's German subsidiary.

Bob McLean, fresh from California, was very familiar with the sports car racing scene that was already developing there and knew what it took to make a sports car. He turned his assignment and Harley Earl's sketches into what he thought a real sports car should look like. As the project developed, he and Earl saw an opportunity to produce a show car that could become a sports car for sale to the public.

The car they designed broke the pattern of the larger-than-life show cars that had been coming from Earl's studios. McLean's car was scaled to the people who rode in it and to the mechanical components that would make it a real car. It was at least a foot lower than contemporary cars. With the top down, its form was a simple "one box" design dominated by its flowing fender, its low and wide grille, and a hood that started lower than the fender.

Conventional wisdom credits the XK120 Jaguar, first shown in 1948, as being the inspiration for Earl's new show car. It was certainly the inspiration for the chassis, but it couldn't have been the inspiration for what Earl's car would look like. The XK120 Jaguar was itself a design in transition from the classic sports car. The dominant form of the Jaguar was still its long, tall hood which flared into the cockpit and then fell to the road at the end of a long sloping trunk. The flowing cutaway fenders were still

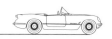

tacked onto the body. The influences behind Harley Earl and Bob McLean's new car are to be found elsewhere.

Since the late 1930s, the Italian bodybuilders had been experimenting with new aerodynamic forms for the sports car. In 1937, Touring designed the special-bodied BMW 328 that would become the inspiration for the XK120. In a series of unplanned steps, cars in general—and sports cars in particular—were becoming lower and wider, with the fender line gradually becoming totally integrated into the form of the body.

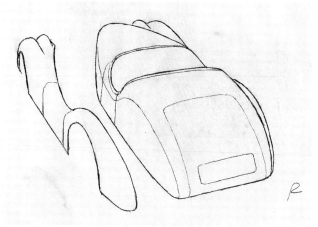

The final expression of this search for a new form was the Cisitalia 202. The initial body design came from aeronautical engineer Giovanni Savonuzzi in 1947, with limited production coupe, convertible, and spider designs refined and built by Pinin Farina. Although production was limited, it is likely that Harley Earl saw a Cisitalia 202 early in its life. If he hadn't seen the Cisitalia at a major European salon or through his friendship with Batista "Pinin" Farina, it is likely he would have seen one in the United States, where it was imported by Max Hoffman. Earl also would have been aware of the car's inclusion in the "Eight Automobiles" exhibit at New York's Museum of Modern Art in 1951.

Was the XK120 Jaguar the design inspiration for Earl and McLean's new car? I don't think so. The Jaguar evolved from designs of the 1930s, which had yet to eliminate separate fenders attached to a body.
Drawing by Dave McLellan

The low, integrated form of the Cisitalia set it apart from its contemporaries and warrants a detailed comparison with the Corvette. One good look clearly supports the theory that the Cisitalia Spider Nuvolari roadster influenced Earl and Bob McLean as they worked out the lines of their first Corvette. Both the Cisitalia and the Corvette were low and wide and featured low hood lines and a fender line fully integrated into the body. Both had front fender lines, which fell only slightly as they

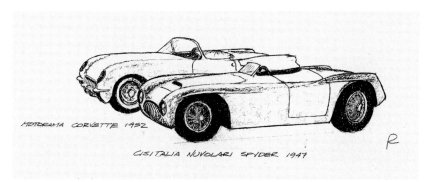

The design similarity between the 1947 Cisitalia 202 Nuvolari roadster and the Corvette (conceived in 1951) are striking even down to the toothed oval grille and the stone guards over the headlights. Two features added by Earl and McLean were the wrap-around windshield and fully-disappearing top.
Drawing by Dave McLellan

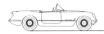

defined the door and then flowed into the rear fender that kicked the line back up again. Other similarities included wide, oval radiator grilles comprised of multiple vertical bars and head lamps integrated into the leading edges of the fenders and protected behind mesh grilles. Though often shown with wire wheels, the Cisitalia 202 also had a streamlined wheel cover detailed with radial slits—similar to the one later used on the Corvette.

COLE ADOPTS THE CORVETTE

Cadillac, GM's luxury car division, had recently been transformed by its Chief Engineer, Ed Cole, who led the development of the new V-8 engine, automatic transmission, power steering, and air-conditioning. Souped-up versions of Cadillac's new V-8 engine were finding their way into Allards and early Cunninghams. Ed Cole often drove to work in his Cadillac-powered Allard or in his XK120 Jaguar. Unfortunately for Cadillac, Cole had just moved to Chevrolet and was in the midst of the most monumental task of his career, turning around GM's low-price, high-volume division. Chevrolet was the most staid and old-fashioned of GM's car divisions. Yet Chevrolet was a famous name with a stellar past. William Durant, ousted as GM President, started Chevrolet with racing driver Louis Chevrolet in 1912. The intention was to produce a car to compete with GM's low priced entries, but Durant was so successful that he was able to buy GM and, together with Chevrolet, form the modern General Motors Corporation. By the late 1920s, Chevrolet had overtaken Ford to lead the low-price market. But by the early 1950s, Chevrolet was in decline and due for an overhaul.

Ed Cole was well on his way to turning Chevrolet around when Harley Earl showed him his Project Opel in May 1952. Cole was excited and wanted the car help to create a new youth and performance image for Chevrolet. The renaissance Cole was planning for 1955 was still a year and a half away from its public unveiling. But if he could assemble this sports car quickly, using available Chevrolet components, he could get out in front of the new 1955 V-8-powered Chevrolets by at least a year.

Cole convinced his boss, Chevrolet General Manager Tom Keating, that they should produce the car. Together with Harley Earl, they tried to convince GM President Harlow "Red" Curtice that their show car should be produced. Curtice was not so easily convinced. He told them not to go ahead with the production project until they had public feedback from the Motorama show, which was still six months away.

GM powerhouse Ed Cole was the consummate engineer—even as president of the giant automaker.
GM Media Archives

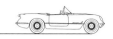

Confident he would get a positive public response, Ed Cole wasn't about to wait for the Motorama presentation to start the production design. Ever the risk-taker, Cole ignored Curtice's cautious direction and forged ahead. In any case, Cole knew he could hide the details in his massive Chevrolet budget, at least until he had to pay for major tools.

Harley Earl's vision was to create an affordable sports car. Once the layout was defined, Chevrolet would select components of proven reliability and modify them only as necessary to fit the styling theme. There was no time to do more.

Ed Cole was fortunate to have Maurice Olley heading Chevrolet's Research and Development Department. Olley began his career at Rolls-Royce and in 1930 joined GM, where his seminal work on vehicle handling led to the adoption by GM of SLA (short-long arm) independent front suspensions on all its cars in 1935 and 1936. During World War II, Olley coordinated the manufacture of the Rolls Royce Merlin aero engine in the United States by the Packard Motor Car Company. Back at GM after the war, he was working on low-investment, inexpensive plastic body panel technology in addition to his favorite suspension projects. Cole asked Olley to work with Bob McLean at Styling and to design the production Opel.

Still without an official name, the Opel project was known within Chevrolet by its EX-122 experimental code. It was an opportunity for Maurice Olley's R & D department to demonstrate its packaging skills, knowledge of ride and handling, and skill at fabricating a body in the new fiberglass reinforced plastic material with which they were experimenting.

To fit the Chevrolet's six-cylinder engine under Bob McLean's hood and to approach a 50/50 weight distribution, Olley moved the engine rear-

Maurice Olley's work on suspension and handling and Chevrolet R & D's development of the plastic car body formed the basis for the first Corvette.
Drawing by Dave McLellan

Bodied entirely in plastic, this 1952 Chevrolet convertible was GM's first use of the new technology for automobile bodies. The body was left unpainted to expose the translucene of the fiberglass construction.
GM Design Center

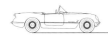

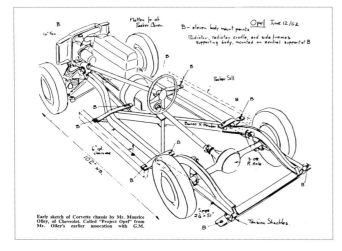

The original Corvette chassis was expeditiously produced from the Chevrolet passenger car parts bin.
Dave McLellan Archives (both)

Triple carbs were the first step in transforming the 106 hp "stove bolt six" sedan engine into a 150 hp sports car engine.
Dave McLellan Archives

ward, behind the front suspension cross-member, and lowered it to the ground-clearance line (an imaginary line six inches above the road). The Corvette's hood was so low that the front of the engine's valve cover had to be skived to clear it. Producing only 106 hp in production form, the straight-six was "hot-rodded" with three side-draft carburetors, a dual exhaust, increased compression ratio and a modified cam to produce 150 gross horsepower.

The production manual steering had to be modified, but there was still room to fit it under the engine. The standard Chevrolet drove the rear wheels through a three-speed manual transmission, which was shifted by levers and rods from a column-mounted lever. For the Corvette, the steering column was drastically lowered, bringing the manual shift linkage into hard interference with the engine. We do not know if Chevrolet attempted to get around this problem before they abandoned the manual transmission and went with only the Powerglide two-speed automatic—which was optional on other Chevrolet models. For both GM and the American public, the manual transmission was by now old technology, while the automatic transmission was new and high tech.

PACKAGING THE CORVETTE

The low height of the car and the use of a conventional frame dictated a seating position with the driver sitting upright on a shallow cushion with his or her legs stretched out in front. Clearance to the driver's seatback located the rear wheels and established the wheelbase. With the engine moved back and the axle moved forward, the much shorter distance between the back of the transmission and the axle negated the use of the Chevrolet sedan's torque tube axle. A short U-jointed prop-shaft was used to connect the transmission to the Hotchkiss-drive rear axle, which was located by longitudinal leaf springs.

The Corvette's chassis was developed around a modified passenger car frame. The fiberglass body provided no structural rigidity, and was required to support only local loads such as the door hinge and lock sys-

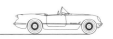

tem. The frame tied everything together and gave the car its torsion and beaming stiffness. Because the closed-body passenger car carried most of its stiffness in its steel body, the frame had to be heavily reinforced for the Corvette. The side rails were boxed and a massive cross-member was added to give the frame as much torsional stiffness as possible.

The front suspension was taken directly from the passenger car without changing spring rates, although the spring height was reduced to reflect the lighter weight of the vehicle. A large front stabilizer bar was added to reduce roll and to control the load transfer distribution as it affected limit-handling. The steering linkage was modified to connect with the steering box and the lowered steering column. Offered only with manual steering, the car was fitted with a big 17-inch steering wheel and slow steering—3.7 turns lock to lock—in order to make the low-speed turning effort acceptable.

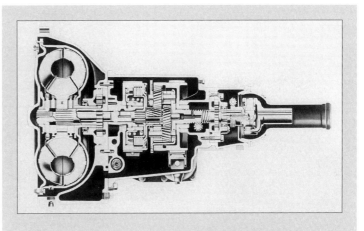

CHEVY'S POWERGLIDE AUTOMATIC TRANSMISSION

GM had introduced the first Hydra-matic, automatic transmission for Oldsmobile in 1939. The transmission consisted of a fluid coupling with four forward speeds automatically shifted by engaging planetary gears with clutches. This was the beginning of a major trend in GM toward automatic transmissions. These transmissions were well accepted by a driving public that was willing to pay a premium for them.

Chevrolet's version of the automatic transmission—the Powerglide—cost much less than the four-speed Hydramatic. The Powerglide used a torque converter with a complex planetary gear set that gave it two forward speeds and reverse with the torque converter effectively providing the additional ratio needed to launch the car.

Drawing courtesy the Detroit Public Library, National Automotive History Collection

With driver and luggage on board, the Corvette featured a 50/50 weight distribution, which left the car with virtually no inherent understeer. To provide the moderate amount of understeer necessary for safe and controllable handling, Olley used the rear axle. As he put it, he "gave tail to the arrow." The axle was located by its leaf springs, which were inclined in the side view so that as the car rolled into a turn, the axle yawed (steered) slightly in a direction that would straighten the car's path or cause it to understeer. For every degree of body roll, the rear axle yawed 0.15 degrees (15 percent roll understeer). Ordinarily, this would have been way too much, but with its high roll stiffness the car kept this steer effect small enough to avoid yaw oscillation.

Standard Chevrolet brakes, completely shrouded by unventilated steel wheels and wheel covers, completed the chassis package. The car was never seriously tested as a sports car. If it had been put through trials, many of the problems inherent in the design, such as lack of brake-cooling, would

have been found early and been fixed. As it was, the first attempts to race this new Chevrolet sports car ended prematurely with faded and failed brakes. Wire wheels were very popular on contemporary sports cars, not just because they looked good but because they allowed cooling air to surround and penetrate the drum brakes.

Harley Earl's Project Opel was very secret, but not so secret that his other stylists didn't get wind of it. Young Chuck Jordan was a summer student in one of the other Styling studios. Hearing that the studio containing the clandestine project was off-limits didn't deter him. He stayed late one night and snuck into the Opel studio to see the car that everybody was talking about. What he saw blew him away. He was most impressed with the completely new way the fenders and the body were integrated. He particularly remembered the wire mesh headlamp detail, which caused the viewer's eye to follow the surface of the fender rather than the notched opening of the headlight.

Chevrolet and GM Styling were excited about the car. The program was moving forward toward production even though they still had no authorization to do so. EX-122, the one-off Motorama show car, would get a plastic body. Olley's Research and Development team also proposed fiberglass-reinforced plastic as the production body material. At the speed the team was moving, fiberglass would have to be used for at least the initial run of production bodies because steel tooling would take too long to produce.

The United States Rubber Company had been touring the automobile manufacturers trying to interest them in the use of a fiberglass and resin body-manufacturing process they were developing. Ed Cole, who always wanted to do things yesterday, agreed. By the time EX-122 arrived on the Motorama stage, it represented a fiberglass-bodied sports car that was being readied for production.

Was fiberglass ready for a production body application? Chevrolet would soon find out. There is real value in responding quickly to an idea car while the excitement of the new design is still fresh in the public's mind. On the other hand, once the assembly line has started, one doesn't want to stop production for a problem, particularly with the dealers primed and the public waiting with cash in hand.

THE CRY FOR PRODUCTION

On the Motorama stage, the Corvette was a sensation. As the hit of the show, it drew enormous crowds, which were captivated by its unique

NAMING THE CORVETTE

Both names and emblems are important to new cars. Chevrolet management and their advertising agency, Campbell-Ewald, got together to name the new car. After rejecting some 300 names, they gave up. Only afterward did one of the participants, Myron Scott, propose the name "Corvette." Corvette was the name of a class of fast naval pursuit ships. It also sounded good as the name for Chevrolet's fast new car, and it started with the letter "C." Myron proposed the name to Ed Cole and the rest is history.

Until the day before the opening of the Motorama show, the Corvette emblem depicted crossed American and checkered flags. At the eleventh hour, GM lawyers rejected this commercial use of the American flag, and a flag with the fleur-de-lis was reluctantly substituted.

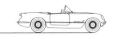

By the time the EX-122 arrived on the Motorama stage, it represented a fiberglass-bodied sports car that was being readied for production.
GM Design Center

styling and low, flowing shape. Chevrolet subsequently received some 7,000 letters from Motorama visitors, who asserted that if Chevrolet would build this totally modern-looking car, they would buy it.

The public's show of interest finally tilted Red Curtice to approve the car for production. Along the way, the decision to use a fiberglass body had been reconsidered, and GM's top management told Chevrolet to body the car in steel. Still wanting to put the car in production quickly, Cole ignored management's direction and proceeded with a fiberglass body. Low investment cost and short lead time won out over high tooling cost and long lead time. In case top management balked, Chevrolet formulated a contingency plan to retool the car in steel using temporary kirksite dies. This plan was never implemented.

The process of building spot-welded, sheet-steel car bodies had been perfected in the 1920s and had become almost universal in the 1930s. These cars could be painted on an assembly line at a speed of almost one per minute, using DuPont's Duco nitrocellulose lacquer. The Corvette was being tooled at only one-tenth of this rate, but it would still need to rely on the techniques of mass production to be successful.

There was no history of building fiberglass car bodies in volume. Before World War II, Henry Ford commissioned an experimental car body from plastic resins derived from soybeans, and by 1953 boats were being built out of fiberglass, but only at very low volume.

Before World War II, Ford experimented with plastic made from soybeans, as evidenced by this 2,250-pound experimental car. The car's builder, Lowell Overly, is seated in the car.
From the Collections of Henry Ford Museum & Greenfield Village

Bob Morrison and his MFG Corporation had more experience than anyone else around, and actively pursued the contract for the Corvette. Chevrolet's vacillation extended into January of 1953, when Morrison was finally awarded the contract. He had only seven months to tool and produce the first bodies.

FROM FLINT TO ST. LOUIS

The first of the production Corvettes were built in Flint, Michigan, in a vacant customer delivery building on Van Sylke Road starting at a rate of one per day. Deliveries began in August 1953 at a sticker price of $3,498. Chevrolet built 300 Corvettes for the 1953 model year and put them into the hands of celebrities as a conscious strategy to influence the market with celebrity endorsement. The idea was to get these powerful and high-profile people to tell their friends what a great car the Corvette was, thus setting the stage for the Corvette's sales success. If Corvette measured up to expectations, it would be great, but if it didn't, word of mouth could have a downside.

Unfortunately for the Corvette, Chevrolet put these first, still imperfect cars into the hands of people who had little tolerance for poor body panel fits, significant water leaks, an awkward and complicated top system, and performance flawed by overly sensitive carburetors. Many of the celebrity drivers soon became annoyed or bored with their Corvettes, parked them, and went back to driving their regular cars. The strategy of funneling the cars to specially selected customers also turned out to be counterproductive because it interfered with supplying cars to those people who really wanted them and who, in their excitement to be the first owners, might have forgiven Chevrolet for the Corvette's shortcomings.

The 1954 Corvette was basically the same car as the 1953 model, although it received slight appearance modifications and upgrades as production moved from Flint to what would become its long-time home in St. Louis. In 1954 Chevrolet built 3,640 Corvettes, but toward the end of the model year, dealers were getting such negative feedback from customers that they refused to accept any more. By the end of the model year there were 1,100 unsold Corvettes sitting in the St. Louis yard as the 1955 model production was supposed to begin. Subtracting the unsold cars from the total number of 1953 and 1954 Corvettes built leaves 2,840 Corvettes that had been sold to dealers—and presumably to customers—before the feeding frenzy turned sour.

THE ORIGINAL FIBERGLASS PROCESS

The plastic system used to build the bodies of the first production Corvettes was quite different from the process that Corvette uses today. The first cars were built in single-sided "female" tools by laying in a mat of chopped fiberglass. The filaments of glass no bigger than a human hair gave the matrix its great strength. The plastic resin was the "glue" that bonded the glass fibers together. By itself, the plastic resin was weak and brittle, but used properly with fiberglass, it formed a tough, durable sheet about one-eighth inch thick.

For the early Corvette panels, the resin was poured into the mold, wetting the fiberglass and filling any voids. A plastic bag was laid over the tool and sealed around its edges. Any trapped air was sucked out with a vacuum pump. Thus the backside of the part was subject to one atmosphere of air pressure, compacting the fiberglass-resin matrix. This was fine in theory, but in practice the fiberglass tended to withdraw from the edges and corners and from the first surface, leaving resin-rich, glass-poor areas that would crack under stress.

The one-sided tools also left the parts with a very rough and irregular second surface. Having no control over thickness made it extremely difficult to control the fit-up of these first parts to their inner reinforcements.

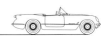

MAURICE OLLEY: ENGINEERING THE FIRST CORVETTE

Maurice Olley unveiled the Corvette to the Detroit engineering community in a paper presented to the Society of Automotive Engineers on October 5, 1953. Olley said, "As a sports car it must have a cruising speed of at least 70 mph, a weight-to-power ratio of better than 25-to-1, ample brakes, and good handling qualities." Olley described the attributes he was aiming for as:

"A quick steering with light handling.

"A low center of gravity.

"Minimum overhang, . . . or low moment of inertia relative to wheelbase.

"Weight distribution front and rear close to 50/50.

"Smooth yet firm suspension.

"Finally, it is a matter of safety that the response of the car should be immediate, but without oversteer."

Olley's "firm suspension" was extremely firm, even by modern Corvette standards, with a rear suspension static deflection of only five inches. Dynamically, this would produce a suspension ride frequency of 1.4 Hz. Equation: $f = 1/2\pi\sqrt{g/\Delta}$.

Olley also gave us his perspective on sports cars and, by inference, the Corvette that he had just completed.

"The sports car is a serious form of transportation. It ranks with the chariot, with the tilbury, and curricle of the 1800's, with the roadster of the 1920's, as a necessary step in providing convenient, lively transportation for two people in a smaller package.

"Also it is a bit of an adventure, fun to drive, fun to build."

Olley expressed no interest in developing the Corvette as a sports car capable of racing and winning. In fact, he threw in his own disclaimer.

"These brief notes should not leave the impression that the General Motors Corporation has lost all sense of decorum and is entering the race car field."

Olley poked fun at the pretentiousness of some sports car enthusiasts and in his own dry way described how he chose the exhaust sound of the Corvette.

"A requirement important in the minds of sports car enthusiasts is that the exhaust should have 'the right note.' They don't agree what this is. Some prefer 'foo-blap' while others go for 'foo-gobble.' It is impossible to please them all. We hope we have achieved a desirable compromise."

Olley was analytically interested in the competition and developed a comparison table and performance figures for the Corvette against an unnamed European competitor. He presented this data as part of his paper.

In the face of criticism, Olley didn't budge on Chevrolet's reasoning for choosing an automatic transmission.

"The use of an automatic transmission has been criticized by those who believe that sports car enthusiasts want nothing but a four speed crash shift. The answer is that the typical sports car enthusiast, like the 'average man,' or the square root of minus one, is an imaginary quantity.

"Also, as the sports car appeals to a wider and wider section of the public, the center of gravity of this theoretical individual is shifting from the austerity of the pioneer towards the luxury of modern ideas.

"The performance curve …shows that there is no need to apologize for the performance of this car with its automatic transmission."

Put in perspective by comparison with contemporary sports cars, as well as automotive writer Ralph Stein's "ideal" sports car, we can see that the automatic transmission Corvette was essentially equal in performance to the XK120 Jaguar and vastly superior to the MG TC.

Acceleration and top speed comparison

	MG TC	XK120 Jaguar	300SL Mercedes	Ralph Stein's Ideal Sports Car	1953 Corvette
0–60mph	21.2 sec	11.7 sec	7.4 sec	6 sec	12 sec
1/4 mile	21.8 sec	18.3 sec	15.1 sec	12–14 sec	19 sec
Top speed	75 mph	122 mph	140 mph	150 mph	—

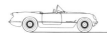

A total of 300 cars were built in Flint at a rate upwards of 3 per day, before production was moved to St. Louis for the 1954 model year.
Dave McLellan Archives

Poor body panel fits were characteristic of all early Corvettes and were indicative of questionable build quality.
Dave McLellan Archives

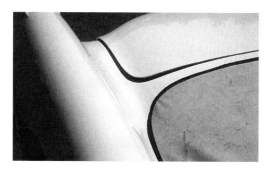

QUALITY TROUBLES

The car's poor body panel build quality and panel fits reminded potential customers that the body was made of fiberglass, not steel. Would it hold up? Could it be repaired? The car's poor showroom appearance and word of mouth from celebrity owners killed the euphoria and market pull that had started as a mad rush when the car was first introduced.

Most Chevy dealers were not prepared to sell Corvettes. Their experience was in selling low-priced cars to people who could just barely afford their first new car. Their typical customer was in no position to buy a two-passenger fun car, even if he or she wanted one. The people who might have bought a Corvette had never been to a Chevrolet dealership and had no intention of starting now. Finally, the car did not have the respect of the sports car community. Enthusiasts who would have sought it out were turned off because it didn't have the "right stuff" to make it a sports car.

Chevrolet walked into major problems. On the assembly line, the fiberglass couldn't be handled like a steel body, which could be "adjusted" with a hammer and a two-by-four. Resin-rich edges tended to crack and craze, while air entrained in the fiberglass left the top surface porous. When these air bubbles were heated in the paint-drying process, they would burst through the wet paint, leaving craters that had to be repaired.

The most serious error Chevrolet made was allowing the cars to go to the dealership with body panel fits that were, to put it mildly, awful. Doors were out of flush by as much as three-eighths to one-half inch, and there was no way to seal such a gap from severe water intrusion. One problem resulted from the front-hinged hood, which required a pop-up spring mechanism so that the hood would clear the front header before it started to rotate forward. This system didn't work well and wasn't adjustable, so the front of most hoods rode high. Deck lid gaps and fits were very open, and the top

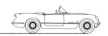

stowage lid fit badly. Even though the body was painted white, making it hard to read irregularities, a customer was likely to sense that this car was not built to acceptable quality standards.

The fiberglass body was made up of 62 separate pieces bonded together. Every inch of bond seams had to be ground down and smoothed for painting. Between the porosity inherent in the finished bond seams and in the early fiberglass panels themselves, painting was a nightmare! Even at the low production rate of the Corvette, the lacquer paint required drying ovens that heated the freshly painted body to about 250°F. Heating the air that was trapped in the pores of the panels caused it to expand and blow holes in the skinned over but still wet paint. The plant had to dig out the hole, fill it, sand it down and then repaint the car. We'll never know how many times some of these cars were repainted. Cars restored years later show evidence of several repainting attempts. Lacquer applied too thickly also tended to crack and craze after only a few years. Taken altogether, with a price tag of $3,498, the showroom appearance of the Corvette gave customers pause as to whether they should buy one.

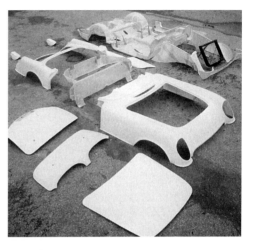

The fiberglass body was made up of 62 separate pieces bonded together. Every inch of visible bond seam had to be ground down and smoothed for painting.
Dave McLellan Archives

The decision to produce the body in fiberglass was Chevrolet's worst mistake, and it became its worst nightmare. It almost killed the car as the public came to reject the use of this new material. The only good news of this early attempt to use fiberglass was that the tooling was inexpensive and could be quickly redone. Its cost was low because there was only one low-pressure die set per part, compared with the four or five tool steel die sets needed to press each steel part.

Chevrolet took a major risk by being the first major automaker in production using a body made entirely of fiberglass. Even though Chevrolet had experimented with fiberglass, the process and the results were quite untested. The first two years of production would become the test. So little was known about the material and the process that virtually everything was being invented on the fly.

WHAT WENT WRONG IN PARADISE?

Why did Chevrolet get its new sports car so wrong and have such a difficult time trying to fix it? In today's organization, the engineering and manufacturing teams work together from the start of a program to process a car so it can be built economically and at top quality. It wasn't always this way. I joined Chevrolet Engineering in 1967, some 14 years

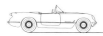

after the problems with those first Corvettes. Although the people had changed, Chevrolet was much the same hierarchical organization as it had been in 1953—engineering engineered and manufacturing manufactured. There was little cooperation or commitment to work together at the middle levels, where cooperation is essential to success.

It is telling that the Chevrolet organization was often described using a smokestack analogy: decisions had to rise all the way to the top to be rammed down the throats of the other departments. Manufacturing was very protective of its turf and often resisted help as if it were an incursion. Engineering found it easier and less confrontational to literally throw their designs over the wall.

Manufacturing was led by hard-driving executives who often rose through the ranks to lead. They were responsible for output at any cost and the cost was often high. These were the same bosses that—15 years before—had driven workers into sit-down strikes and into organizing themselves as the United Auto Workers union. Few of them were engineers, so they had little idea what engineers could do to help them. When engineering did help, because manufacturing didn't understand what engineering had done, manufacturing would undo it at the first opportunity. Middle manufacturing management, with the support of their top brass, had also learned to play the "blame game." They could always find someone else to blame for their mistakes. It became institutionalized as the "GM salute."

But in this case, engineering was just as much to blame as manufacturing. Because of the educated technical nature of the team, engineering developed into a much more collegial, professional organization. It's not surprising that the two organizations didn't communicate well. Engineering management tried to avoid conflict and confrontation with manufacturing management, who had learned to use bluster to keep engineering off balance. Only years later did engineering management finally negotiate engineering's relationship and responsibilities with manufacturing.

Corvette production went very wrong, and nobody stepped forward to fix it. After having finished the car once, Maurice Olley and Chevrolet Research and Development moved on to other projects. Maintaining the car was now the responsibility of the Production Design departments for engine, drivetrain, chassis, and body. Nobody seemed to be responsible for the overall car, short of the General Manager. It took his intervention to make anything happen.

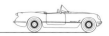

Even taking into account how dysfunctional the system was, it is still surprising that Chevrolet released the cars to the dealerships in the condition they were in, setting themselves up for the subsequent sales indignities. Chevrolet dealers were in no position to fix the poor body fit and leak problems that Chevrolet had shipped to them. Dealership body shops were trained to fix steel. Their salesmen had no clue how to sell a sporty car. Most of the big dealerships, intent on turning a profit, never ordered or sold a Corvette. Fortunately, there were a few maverick dealers, like Bob Rosenthal, who took on the Corvette because it was new and innovative. Under Ed Cole, Chevrolet would test its dealers' ability to sell innovative products by introducing a flurry of new models such as the Corvette, Chevelle, Corvair, Camaro, and Chevy II. But this was still 1953 and Chevrolet dealers were enjoying the postwar sellers' market. They were still a year away from the introduction of Ed Cole's 1955 Chevrolet which would start the revolution in the Chevrolet product line and wake up the dealer organization.

In the same line of questioning, why didn't Harley Earl insist that the technical package under the skins be competitive as a sports car? After all, his son was an avid sports car racer, and his close friend General Curtis LeMay was a strong supporter of such racing. Why didn't Ed Cole, who was a hot-rodder and drove high-performance cars, insist that the car be produced with the Cadillac V-8 engine until the Chevrolet V-8 was available. Although the Cadillac engine was 100 pounds heavier than the Chevrolet six-cylinder, it would have produced over 200 hp in a Corvette installation. When used in Allard or Cunningham sports cars, that same engine was hot-rodded to over 300 hp. Unfortunately, we will never know the answers to these questions because neither Earl nor Cole ever explained themselves.

When *Road & Track* reviewed the first Corvette, the magazine was guardedly positive about the car, commenting negatively only about the brakes and the automatic transmission. The writers found the performance and handling acceptable. They knew that there were body fit and water leak problems because they commented on their test car's minimal body leaks and good panel fits. The editors tried to encourage Chevrolet by suggesting that the company or an owner could add finned aluminum rings to the brake drums and replace the steel wheels with Kelsey-Hayes wire wheels to dramatically improve brake cooling. *Road & Track* quoted Olley's justification for the automatic transmission, and commented that

his "statement from Chevrolet should get a rise from 100,000 *Road & Track* readers."

The automatic transmission made driving so much easier that more people could comfortably drive the automobile. However, if the car was a sports car and was to be driven not only on the road but on the track, an automatic transmission was not suitable. The manual transmission gave precise and predictable control of the engine-road relationship; the automatic did not. Downshifting would also have allowed engine braking to supplement the drum brakes, which were marginal by sports car standards. Chevrolet could have hedged its bet by releasing Corvettes with a choice of automatic or manual transmissions. Yet, it elected to release only the automatic, suggesting that the company's marketers didn't perceive that there was a problem in selling a sports car without a manual transmission.

The *Road & Track* article also commented that:

"The amazing thing about the Corvette is that it comes so close to being a really interesting, worthwhile and genuine sports car—yet misses the mark almost entirely. Last June we said, 'The outstanding characteristic of the Corvette is probably its deceptive performance. The second most outstanding characteristic of the Corvette is its really good combination of riding and handling qualities.'"

They added:

"It may not be suitable for road-racing as it comes from the factory—but …it should be easy enough to strip the car down to a better weight. Watching a Corvette in an airport race coming into a corner with fast company, we have observed that the brakes show up poorly, but the actual cornering is done just as fast, flat and comfortably as several imported sports cars we could name."

Road & Track even made Chevrolet aware of an adapter plate that would mate a Lincoln three-speed manual transmission with overdrive to the Chevrolet engine. But the car-buying public would have to wait another two years for Chevrolet to introduce a Corvette with a manual transmission.

Corvette racer and performance-part producer Dick Guldstrand remembers a whisper campaign attacking the safety and repairability of these early Corvettes. Apparently started by competitors, it questioned the safety of the fiberglass body—suggesting that in a crash the body would

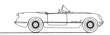

DRIVING A 1954 CORVETTE

In the early 1990s at the National Corvette Restorers Society (NCRS) convention in Seven Springs, Pennsylvania, I had the opportunity to drive Joe Stern's beautifully restored 1954 Corvette. Before driving it, we removed the plastic side windows and lowered the top.

The side windows were held in place by two fasteners, a knurled nut and a toothed bar. Once removed, the plastic windows were stowed in bags that snapped into the forward bulkhead of the trunk. The top was easy to unlatch at the front and back, but there was another knurled nut above the side window. Unscrewing this on both sides allowed the header bar to be folded inward so that the top could fold onto itself in a scissors action. The top folded into the stowage space under the deck lid, but as the top was folded, care had to be taken not to pinch the canvas. Once the top was tightly packed, the deck lid was lowered and latched.

Even as an agile 180 lb six footer, I had to squeeze under the steering wheel. At best, this is a space you crawl into even with the top down. Once in the seat, the steering wheel loomed large right in front of me.

Starting the cold engine required full manual choke and very little throttle. The six-cylinder engine cranked slowly on its six-volt starter before coming to life. It idled smoothly with a loud and sporty burble. As the engine warmed, a small amount of choke was required to prevent the engine from stalling as the accelerator was depressed. Lacking an accelerator pump for transient enrichment, the throttle had to be eased open if engine stalling was to be avoided.

I pulled the gear selector of the automatic rearward to shift from Park into gear. I knew I was out of Park but I didn't know what gear I was in. Both Joe and I fiddled with it for a while and we finally found the drive detent. Because reverse was located behind low gear, there was no way to downshift without the risk of engaging reverse.

Looking forward, I was immediately aware that I was seeing through the very top of the windshield just below the header. There were no sun visors. This "wraparound" windshield curved down at the sides, so I was often looking over the windshield—which would be a problem if the top were up.

As we took off down the road, the engine flared quickly on the loose torque converter with a low-frequency throatiness that was very pleasant and distinctive. It wasn't a particularly racy sound but it had its own unique character. Driving away, I became quickly aware of the slow, but light, steering. The brakes worked in a very normal manner.

After the engine was warm, I stopped on a clear stretch of road and made a full-throttle acceleration run. The acceleration performance of the car from a standstill was pretty good. The engine flared as we started to move, and then as road speed built up the engine speed and road speed started to rise together. The transmission upshifted at 45 mph, but I couldn't read the low, centrally-mounted tachometer. Joe read the tachometer on the next try and found we were upshifting at 4,500 rpm. Driving along as slowly as 25 mph and punching full throttle produced no downshift. The speed had to be very slow before the transmission would shift into low gear. After finding reverse so easily, I was reluctant to pull the lever into low.

At speed, I became very aware of the lash in the steering—as much as four to five inches. The bias ply replica tires tugged and pulled across every irregularity in the road. There was nothing precise about tracking this car on these curving roads. The best tracking strategy I found was to let the car wander a little and then pull it back across the path I was trying to maintain.

Driving on Pennsylvania's curving mountain roads in a 40-year-old car made me a more conservative evaluator than usual. The gravel shoulders, ditches, trees, and other obstacles reminded me that I needed to keep some margin in hand. Yet, trying to be conservative and driving on dry asphalt, I still found myself squealing the tires and approaching the handling limit unexpectedly.

My impression of the 1954 Corvette was that I was driving the car, not the road. I was continuously paying attention to the car and trying to stay within its limits. The following day, I drove the same route in a 1994 Corvette convertible and found that I was concentrating on the road ahead and not worrying about the car. The Corvette had come a long way in 40 years.

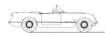

fly apart and leave the occupants totally exposed to the elements. Dick cannot remember ever seeing a crash picture of a Corvette in which the body had disappeared. The fiberglass was, however, expensive to fix until proper repair techniques had been worked out and disseminated to the field.

When Chevrolet established the first Corvette power train, they actually met the performance of their target competitor, the XK120 Jaguar. The performance comparison on page 13 shows this. It also shows the danger of matching what your competitor did two years ago. The 1953 Corvette's performance below 100 mph closely approached that of the 1951 Jaguar XK120, but by 1954, Jaguar had moved on with the faster XK140.

MUSCLE FOR THE CORVETTE

Although the 1955 Corvette may have looked very much like the 1953 and 1954 models, it was really a very different car, thanks to Chevrolet's new 265 cid V-8 engine, which was available as an option. The four-barrel Corvette version of the V-8 produced a healthy 195 gross hp at 4,600 rpm. Orders for the 1955 Corvette trickled in, but the sales department would not authorize production until the inventory of unsold 1954s had been whittled down. As a result, 1955 production started very late and through the entire model year they built only 700 cars—all but six of them V-8's. By any standard, this was a dismal sales experience and far from the 10,000-unit planned production. Chevrolet decided to cancel the Corvette at the end of the 1955 model when providence— by way of Ford—intervened.

Chevrolet and arch rival Ford competed for dominance in the low-price field, with each company selling about two million cars and trucks a year. Their dealer networks were about the same size, and in any one year, one could outsell the other, simply by virtue of the products available. In the fall of 1954, Ford introduced the two-passenger Thunderbird. If Chevrolet had quit the field—as sales performance justified—it would have been a great embarrassment, so the company had to make the Corvette successful. The simple fact that Ford sold 16,155 Thunderbirds in that first year—1955— showed that there was hope for successful sales in the market segment.

The 1955 Thunderbird saved the Corvette from extinction, although it only survived for three years before being replaced by the much larger four-passenger Thunderbird.
Photo by Mike Mueller

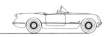

Like the Corvette, the Thunderbird was a two-passenger convertible. Its design was a scaled-down version of Ford's razor-edged sedan styling. Though quite different, each car carried popular styling themes. The Thunderbird was powered by Ford's post war overhead-valve V-8 engine mated to either a three-speed manual transmission or the more popular three-speed torque converter automatic transmission. Although it had excellent acceleration, it remained a second slower 0-60 mph than the V-8 Corvette. Where the cars differed was in the body design. The Thunderbird had roll-up side windows and an easily erected convertible top. Most importantly, though, the body of the all-steel Thunderbird was of a very high quality, the panels fit well, and the body gaps were even.

Although sales figures for 1955 did not reflect it, the V-8 engine dramatically improved the Corvette's acceleration and drivability. The 12-volt starter and automatic choke made starting easy and the four-barrel carburetor made driving a pleasure. The car still had the same body with its quirks and maladies. Unfortunately, because the 1955 looked the same as the earlier cars, it played no part in undoing the damage the first two model years had caused to Corvette's reputation.

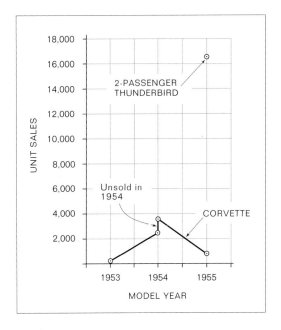

From the very beginning Thunderbird outsold Corvette.

CORVETTE TRIES THE TRACK

Road & Track magazine tested the 1955 Corvette and declared that "The V-8-powered version gives truly startling performance, as might be expected, but the transmission and brake deficiencies still will not satisfy the demands of either competition or of the true sports car enthusiast, no matter how loyal he may be to American engineering know-how." The journalists complimented the car, again, for its "good combination of ride and handling." They did mention that they had received a number of letters from owners of 1954 Corvettes complaining of water leaks during heavy rain and the lack of bumper protection.

Chevrolet could talk about the Corvette being a sports car all they wanted, but the proof would come only on the racetrack. Racing enthusiasts doubted that the Corvette could stand up to the stresses of racing, and they were right. Dr. Dick Thompson, who would eventually become famous as a Corvette racer, was one of the first to test a Corvette on the track. He was driving a Jaguar XK120 in a race at Andrews Air Force Base

outside of Washington DC when local Chevrolet dealer Bob Rosenthal asked him to sample a new Corvette during a practice session. Although both the brakes and the automatic transmission failed during the test, before they gave out, Thompson demonstrated that the car had potential, lapping almost as fast as with his Jaguar.

SCCA rules classified production sports cars by displacement. The Corvette's L-6 3.6-liter engine put it in the C-production class along with the Jaguar XK120, the Allard J2X and the Mercedes-Benz 300 SL. Without a massive effort aimed at reducing weight, increasing power, upgrading the brakes, and making it reliable enough to finish, there was no way the Corvette could be competitive in this class. The racing development required was so major that only Chevrolet could tackle it. But Chevrolet did nothing. Meanwhile, the V-8 Powerglide 1955 Corvette saw limited amateur racing action in the hands of Chevrolet dealer Addison Austin, who by the fall of 1955 finished tenth overall at Watkins Glen, then third in class and first in class in subsequent SCCA regional races.

This dismal tale of the first Corvette and its failure in the marketplace is in sharp contrast to the value of these same cars now. Today, these earliest Corvettes trade for more than new Corvettes. They are valuable because they are rare and because they were the first Corvettes. The 1953 through 1955 models are the earliest examples of what would become the longest running and most successful sports car on the planet.

With these first Corvettes, the marketplace spoke, as it always does, rewarding manufacturers who produce what buyers want and punishing those who produce what buyers don't want. By all accounts, those who saw the Motorama show car were touched by it in some way. Sports car enthusiasts saw a car that looked like a sports car but, because of its Chevrolet sedan component base, could not live up to the promise of its appearance. The less sophisticated public, looking at the car without all the pre-conceived notions that the enthusiast has, saw a car like no other car ever seen before. It was low, sleek, and flowing in its lines, and its open cockpit with no visible top brought visions of open-air wind-in-the-face motoring. This was a car to take to the open road. Quite simply, this looked like a car that made driving an end in itself.

It probably didn't matter that the first Corvette had a six-cylinder engine. The four-cylinder Mazda Miata is popular today with only marginally better performance. That the Corvette had an automatic transmission probably didn't matter either—except to the enthusiast. Chevrolet was probably right in thinking that the automatic would broaden the

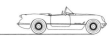

appeal of the car. And, automatics were high tech. It probably didn't matter that the Corvette didn't have the brakes to make it a sports car suitable for the racetrack. But it did matter that when the cars arrived on the showroom floor the panels simply didn't fit properly. The terrible fits turned off potential customers and reminded them that the car was made of a new and untried body material called fiberglass. Those who drove Corvettes soon became disenchanted as the rain poured in and they could hardly see out with the top up. On top of all this, the drivability of the three-carburetor intake was touchy at best.

The first owners never became Chevrolet's best spokespeople as had been hoped. Chevrolet sold only 2,840 Corvettes before the initial euphoria turned to disappointment. Customer complaints about problems that the dealers could not resolve reached such a pitch that the dealers refused to take any more cars. The 1955 Corvette only served to highlight the problems.

While Americans rejected the Corvette outright, they bought 20 times as many Thunderbirds, even though the two dealer organizations were comparable and were slugging it out one-for-one in every other market segment. It would take Chevrolet several years, and a new look for the Corvette, to undo the negative market they had created.

Duntov Develops the Corvette

2

WHEN ZORA ARKUS-DUNTOV visited the 1953 Motorama show at the Waldorf Astoria Hotel in New York City, he was very impressed with the beautifully proportioned and detailed Corvette show car. At the same time, Zora, with his European-trained racer's eye, doubted that the car was really a sports car, given its standard "Detroit" chassis fitted with a prewar six-cylinder Chevrolet engine and a Powerglide two-speed automatic transmission.

JOINING GM

Zora was impressed enough to write Ed Cole a letter saying that he would like to work on the Corvette. He was looking for work anyway and here was a chance to get involved with a company that was at least trying to produce a sports car. One of Cole's lieutenants responded by letter suggesting that Zora should stop in for a talk when he was in Detroit. Although the letter clearly showed some interest, it was not a job offer. Needing employment, Zora took a job with Fairchild Aviation and began a very short career in aviation.

Zora's insatiable interest in sports cars led him to present a paper to the Society of Automotive Engineers (SAE) that spelled out his prescription for a production sports car, including the importance of racing to its success. He sent Ed Cole a copy of the paper and almost immediately received an offer to come to Detroit. This paper is not known to exist, but a paper presented to the SAE Mid-Michigan Section meeting in Lansing on September 28, 1953, has survived. This version probably contains the same material and identifies the author, Z. Arkus-Duntov, as employed by Chevrolet Motor Division, General Motors Corporation.

ZORA ARKUS - DUNTOV

Zora Arkus-Duntov was hired by Ed Cole and initially worked for Maurice Olley in Chevrolet R&D doing V-8 engine development. Zora's focus and determination played a great part in making the Corvette an icon.
Drawing by Dave McLellan

Cole hired Zora, but for V-8 engine development. From a Chevrolet perspective, this was much more important than working on the Corvette because of the significance of the new V-8 engine to the entire Chevrolet product line. Zora came to Detroit and began work in the Chevrolet Research and Development Department under Maurice Olley. In between his projects on the V-8 engine, he started testing the Corvette. Nobody asked him to, but he couldn't keep his hands off it.

WORKING ON THE CORVETTE

Zora's first project on the Corvette was to solve a staining problem on the rear end of the car. The exhaust, which had been styled to exit through cutouts in the rear valence of the car, was staining the white paint. Zora made the exhaust visible by injecting kerosene into it. He then took motion pictures of the moving car to show Chevrolet management what was happening. When moving, the car carried an attached wake of air along with it. The exhaust from the twin pipes was exiting directly into this wake, filling it with exhaust fumes, which then contaminated the painted surface exposed to the wake. More importantly, Zora found that driving with the top up and the side windows removed, caused the exhaust contaminants to migrate forward into the passenger compart-

ZORA'S VIEW OF A SPORTS CAR

In a paper delivered at the SAE Mid-Michigan meeting, Zora summarized his view of the first half century of the sports car as:

"The sports car as derivative of [the] racing car flourished from 1910 but died in the early thirties.

"From the mid-thirties up to the present day, the sports cars we have are derivative of the passenger cars or conceived as such.

"All successful sellers among the sports cars were endowed with a racing halo provided by [a] few specialized machines of the same make.

"The interests and volume sales of sports cars can exist only in the economics of prosperity.

"The concept of the sports car varies with geographic boundaries, road system, traffic laws and national character.

"As far as the American market is concerned, it is still an unknown quantity since an American sports car catering to American tastes, roads, way of living and national character has not yet been on the market.

"If Mr. Ford, prior to his decision to launch the Model T, would have consulted statistics instead of his imagination, the world today would have a very different shape. When he took his visionary step, the market for volume sales of automobiles did not exist. He created the market by giving the American public what they wanted at a price they could afford.

"The Corvette is the first American sports car offered to the public. It is Chevrolet's concept of a sports car which the American public will want. The results of this bold decision to bring out the American sports car may be an experiment with high engineering and promotional value or a visionary move which will open for the American automobile industry a new market and will affect our way of life by providing a gayer existence.

"The automobile started as an instrument of pleasure for a few became a transportation for all, was made to reply to a requirement beyond utility and maybe now in a particular form as a sports automobile will become a source of joy for many—the answer lies with the American public and we will know it in the not too distant future."

ment. Among the many changes that were made for the 1956 model, was moving the exhaust outboard into the ends of the fenders.

Though Maurice Olley's Chevrolet Research and Development Department laid out the first Corvette, the ongoing production design was the responsibility of the respective production design departments responsible for the body, chassis and powertrain of Chevrolet's sedans and light trucks. R&D could influence the Corvette's design but no longer had direct control over it. Zora wrote a letter to Carl Jacust, Chevrolet's Chief Body Engineer, outlining redesigns that were needed to solve the Corvette's worst shortcomings. Among other things, Zora argued that the side curtains and the cranky top system had to go.

In 1955, Chevrolet was still a top-down organization in management style. Chief Engineer Ed Cole or General Manager Tom Keating made all important product decisions. Duntov was acting like a "product champion" although he had no authority to do so, and in the process he ruffled a lot of feathers. Years later, as their product line grew too complex to manage from the top down, Chevrolet instituted a system of Product Program Managers to act across all division activity as product champions for each car and truck line. Duntov was the role model for these product champions.

Late in the 1955 model year, Chevrolet introduced the three-speed manual transmission as an option in the 1955 Corvette with the V-8 engine. Only 60 to 70 of these were built before the end of the model year. However, it was a first sign that Chevrolet was starting to respond to the issues that had been raised by *Road & Track* magazine and sports car enthusiasts in general. Unfortunately, the Corvette was virtually on its deathbed before management responded.

ZORA MAKES HIS MARK

Even though the 1956 Corvette had the same general form as the 1955, the body was almost all new. The most useful changes came in the passenger compartment where the windshield header had been raised to improve driver visibility, roll-up side windows replaced the snap and bolt-in plastic windows and the convertible top was redesigned to fold without having to first unbolt the header bar. From the outside, the sculptured, concave side of the car and many graphic detail changes were enough to signal that this was a new car.

The chassis was modified as a result of Zora's development work. Even though *Road & Track* magazine's John Bond had given the Corvette

The 1956 Corvette had a new body, a modified chassis and V-8 engines producing upwards of 225 hp.

Courtesy the Detroit Public Library, National Automotive History Collection

high marks for handling, Duntov found the car difficult to drive smoothly at the limit. The rear suspension, with its 15 percent roll understeer, was coupling roll and yaw. Any roll oscillation that the driver induced by quickly steering the car also caused a corresponding yaw oscillation, giving the car a corkscrew motion. To counter this, Duntov raised the rear leaf spring front attachment points to reduce the rear roll understeer. Meanwhile, understeer was added in the front suspension by increasing caster. (Caster increases the steering's self-aligning tendency, itself an understeer effect.) With the steering arms behind the wheel center, increasing caster by rotating the steering knuckle also changes the steering geometry in a direction to increase front roll understeer. With those changes, Duntov found the car a pleasure to drift through a turn.

COMPETITION AND THE CORVETTE

Looking for ways to quickly establish the Corvette's performance credentials, Duntov continued to follow the strategy that he had outlined in his SAE paper. Winning races would, of course, establish the car, but the chassis was nowhere near ready for the stresses of competition. Just as important, getting the car ready would take months. The quickest way to gain notice would be to set a speed record. He promoted the idea with Ed Cole and won his approval to attempt a production speed record of 150 mph with a Corvette V-8 on the sands of Daytona Beach, Florida.

Daytona Beach had been the site of many record-breaking attempts early in the century and was also—by July 1949—the home of some of the earliest NASCAR races, which used the beach and the adjacent local road for stock car racing.

Duntov wanted to break 150 mph. He rightly guessed that he would need to go 160 mph on pavement in order to go 150 mph on the high-rolling-resistance wet beach sand. Working in the privacy of GM's Desert Proving Grounds, he removed the windshield from a 1955 V-8 manual transmission test car and installed the hot new 2-4 barrel, 225 hp engine. This was fast, but still not fast enough, Duntov calculated he would need another 30 hp to reach 160 mph. On the phone back to Chevrolet Engineering, Duntov invented the "Duntov Cam" as his solution to gain the needed 30 hp. Going strictly for top-speed horsepower, Duntov left the cam

profiles (opening and closing rates) alone and simply increased the duration that the exhaust and the intake valves were held open, thus improving exhaust evacuation and intake filling at high rpms.

In February of 1956, Duntov went 150.583 mph on the sands of Daytona in a streamlined 1956 Corvette. This was the first of the many records that would be set by the Corvette. It was also a start toward establishing the Corvette as an honest-to-goodness performance sports car.

Ed Cole was so enamored with the performance of his new V-8 engine and its 150 mph speed record that he ordered Duntov to begin testing at Sebring for the 12-hour international endurance race. Simultaneously, at a New York luncheon, Cole announced to the press that Chevrolet would enter the Corvette in that spring's Sebring race, which was now only a little more than a month away. Without even testing it, Duntov knew that the Corvette was nowhere near ready for the racetrack. In fact, he considered its drum brakes dangerous and refused to even drive the Corvette on the Sebring racetrack. Sebring was known to be one of the hardest tracks on brakes in the world. It was hopeless to expect a good showing against the sports racing cars that would be competing. Even though the Corvette was a powerful car, it was too heavy, had no proven reliability and lacked adequate brakes. Cole would hear none of Duntov's arguments. He told Duntov to come home and then hired John Fitch—one of the best sports car racing drivers of the day—to get the car ready.

Preparing the Corvette for Sebring proved to be an enormous task. Production class rules dictated that everything that went into the car to make it race-worthy had to be available from a Chevrolet parts counter. When they started track-testing at Sebring, the car could not go a full lap without failing. After a great deal of effort, they were able to get the car to run with a modest level of performance, although the brakes remained an Achilles heel. Chevrolet entered four cars: three in the production class and one in the prototype class. The production cars used 265cid engines to the same specification as Duntov's record car. The fourth car was bored out to 307cid and used a ZF four-speed instead of the stock three-speed. All four entries were fitted with oversized fuel tanks, limited-slip differentials, Halibrand knock-off magnesium wheels, and cerametallic brake linings and driving lights.

Internationally renowned sports car racer, John Fitch, in one of the three Corvettes used to set the NASCAR sanctioned speed records.
GM Media Archives

One of the production class cars, driven by Ray Crawford and Max Goodman, finished fifteenth, while the other two broke. The prototype, driven by Walt Hansgen and John Fitch himself, finished a respectable ninth overall. After the race, Fitch summed up their monumental effort: "Our performance was less than we had hoped but more than we deserved." That the Corvette could compete and finish a race was now established. It was now time to unleash a flood of private-entry activity.

SCCA racers were amateurs; they had to own the cars they raced. John Fitch approached Dick Thompson with a deal: If you'll buy the car, we'll take it back after every race and Duntov will rebuild it. With Thompson living on the East Coast and racing much of the time on the West Coast and with Duntov in Detroit, this was a potentially impossible logistics problem. They surreptitiously built several identical race cars for Thompson. To the SCCA scrutineers they were one car, carrying identical serial numbers and the same California license number, BXL-190. To Chevrolet's credit, the company took what was learned from this effort and made the improved parts available to all Corvette racers as RPO 684. Of course, those close to the factory still had an edge: They were one generation ahead in race component development.

ZORA'S DREAM—THE CORVETTE SS

Back in Detroit, Bill Mitchell—Harley Earl's right hand in GM Styling—was very impressed with Chevrolet's new V-8 engine and talked Ed Cole into installing one in the engineless D-Type Jaguar that Mitchell had acquired. Duntov was given the assignment of installing the V-8 engine but went to Cole arguing that it wouldn't be right for Chevrolet to install its new engine in a Jaguar chassis. In fact, he asserted, GM should produce a special Corvette to demonstrate the V-8's potential. Cole agreed and the Corvette SS was born. With all the resources of Chevrolet Research and Development behind him, Duntov targeted the SS for the 1957 Sebring race. He produced two race cars—the Corvette SS and its "mule" test bed.

Duntov dipped into his European racing experience to incorporate the best features that had already been proven in European Grand Prix and sports car racing. He designed the SS, his first race car, around the Chevrolet V-8 engine with its still experimental fuel injection and a four-speed, close-ratio, manual transmission. The rear axle was chassis-mounted and incorporated a quick-change gear set to adapt the drive ratios to each track's requirements. The de Dion rear suspension was a much-simpli-

fied version of the rear suspension proven by Mercedes in its W.125 Grand Prix car before World War II. The unique feature that allowed it to be much simpler than the Mercedes, was the four rubber-bushed trailing arms, on which the suspension was mounted. This mounting also proved to be an Achilles heel because the bushings were prone to failure. The SLA (short-long arm) front suspension was quite conventional. The 12 in. x 2-1/2 in. aluminum-finned drum brakes were borrowed from a Chrysler application and were mounted outboard at the front and inboard on the differential at the rear. The front brakes used two leading shoes with cerametallic linings. Brake balance was adjustable front to rear and used a "Mickey Mouse" mercury switch and solenoid deceleration cutoff for the rear brakes.

The SS had another weakness. In order to make the car as light as possible, its wheelbase had been shortened to 92 inches, and this was accomplished by moving the driver's feet and the pedal box forward to a location beside the engine. The exhaust, which normally exited through this area, was diverted sharply up and over the pedal box, then down the outboard side of the box. Even with much insulation, the heat was inescapable and—in a long race—unbearable for the driver's feet.

The D-Type Jaguar, a proven, internationally competitive race car, had a solid rear axle and spot disc brakes, incorporating 20 separate pistons pressing 20 separate pads against the four discs. The D-Type Jaguar structure was a mixture of a stressed aluminum body tub and a trussed tubular front subframe. With no time for an involved test program to develop a stressed skin structure, Duntov borrowed the structure concept from the contemporary Mercedes 300 SL, producing a multi-tube, three-dimensional space frame that was both stiff and strong. Duntov stripped down a 300 SL to its space frame and copied the space frame as closely as possible, modifying it for the wider V-8 engine and for his different rear suspension. While GM Styling was installing the magnesium body and detailing the SS, Duntov cobbled up the test mule from spare parts, gave it a crude plastic body and went testing.

Top: The Corvette SS was a ground-up race car from GM Styling and Chevrolet R&D.
Zora Arkus-Duntov Collection

Bottom: As part of its development, the Corvette SS was tested in a wind tunnel.
GM Media Archives

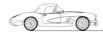

It was fortunate that Duntov had the mule because he was able to log about 2000 miles of track time and sort out many of the chassis details. Juan Manuel Fangio and Stirling Moss, the world's top two racing drivers, were contracted to drive the SS in the 1957 Sebring 12-hour race. Fangio drove the mule in practice and set a lap record in the process. But this car would not race; its appearance was not up to GM's standards.

The SS was delayed repeatedly because GM Styling was still painting and detailing it to show car standards, including a heavy grille and a bullet-shaped headrest. John Fitch, who was responsible to Chevrolet as the racing team manager for the SS, started calling Ed Cole to try to get the car moving. Cole assured him that the car would be ready to race. The continuing delays, however, forced Fitch to release Fangio and Moss from their contract. The SS finally arrived the day before the race, with the touch-up crew still working on it. However, Harley Earl would not even let the car practice for fear its paint would be chipped. So, on race day, it sat on the grid, waiting to be sorted out in the race by its new drivers, John Fitch and Piero Taruffi.

At the start, the SS out-dragged the competition but was soon passed by the Ferraris and Maseratis. After only three laps, Fitch pitted the SS to replace a front tire, flat spotted by an erratic brake that had not been properly bedded in. Next, the engine began to run sporadically. A shorting ignition condenser was replaced. Then the car stopped out on the course. Fortunately, Fitch had a spare coil, which solved the problem. Taruffi replaced Fitch on lap 21 during the first scheduled fuel stop. On the twenty-third lap the rear suspension lateral control link bushing failed, allowing the tires to rub on the fenders as the axle swung from side to side. Without lateral control, the car's handling at speed was impossible. Hopelessly out of the running, the car was mercifully retired. Fangio was the overall winner in a 4.5-liter Maserati, with production-based Corvettes finishing a respectable twelfth, fifteenth and sixteenth overall.

Fitch recounted, years later, that Cole and he had very different ideas of "ready-to-race." Cole seemed to be operating on the naive assumption that Chevrolet R&D could design and build a race car and then just show up and win against the world's most seasoned race

At the start, the SS out dragged the competition but was soon passed by the Ferraris and Maseratis. On the 23rd lap the rear suspension lateral control link bushing failed and the car had to retire.

GM Design Center

teams. Fitch (and Duntov) knew that it took much more than just show-ing up to win.

CHANGES FOR CHEVROLET AND CORVETTE

After Sebring there was an ambitious plan to develop the SS and to field a three-car team for the Le Mans 24-hour race on June 10. However, the Automobile Manufacturer's Association (AMA), which included GM, announced an agreement on June 7, 1957, to cease all involvement with racing. GM's President Harlow "Red" Curtice, told Chevrolet to discon-tinue all racing activity. He enforced the decree through financial controls and the threat that he would fire the General Manager if he had to. Dun-tov had no choice but to put his two cars and all their parts in storage and go back to working on the production Corvette. The AMA ban on rac-ing was a terrible blow to Duntov and Cole, whose strategy to establish the Corvette's credentials with a strong racing program was well under way and now had to be suspended.

With the introduction of the four-speed manual transmission and fuel injection, 1957 was an important year for the production Corvette. Ten percent of Corvettes were sold with the four-speed manual transmission, and 16 percent were sold with the optional fuel injection system.

Most Chevy dealers did not understand Ed Cole's introduction of innovative technology in the Chevrolet line, and, unfortunately, dealers didn't order what they didn't understand. And most Chevy customers were not sophis-ticated enough to demand high-tech options like fuel injection. Consequently, there was little market pull to help the sales of these options. Additionally, most Chevy dealers were ill-equipped to support these new options, giving the dealers a bad reputation for service.

By 1957 Corvette sales were starting to take off, yet they were still far short of Chevrolet's original projec-tion of 10,000/year and even further short of Thunderbird's sales.

Corvette sales were starting to make a comeback. From the dismal 700 Corvettes of 1955, by 1956 production was up to 3,467, and in 1957 production almost doubled to 6,339 Corvettes. This was still nowhere near the sales performance of the Thunderbird, which was selling upwards of 15,000 cars a

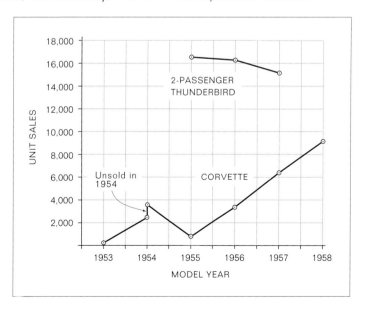

year, but it was a vast improvement. The advances in quality and performance of the production car and Chevrolet's involvement in racing were starting to pay off.

The formula for a sports car that the public would buy was now starting to become clearer. Not only did the car have to perform as well as the competition, it had to demonstrate that it could sustain that performance on the racetrack. Simultaneously, it had to offer its civilian owner reasonable creature comforts. Customers would not put up with water pouring in during a rainstorm, and they wanted a car that had adequate weather sealing and an effective heater.

Bill Mitchell was Harley Earl's hand-picked successor as Vice President of Styling. Bill had an ego every bit as big as Earl's and felt that he needed to give the Corvette a distinctive "Mitchell" personality. Although still working for Earl, Mitchell was involved in the modest styling change that was made for the 1956 Corvette. His next move—after he assumed the helm of Styling in December 1958—would establish the Corvette styling direction for the next decade.

Bill Mitchell bought the Corvette SS mule race car from Chevrolet for one dollar. Chevrolet, banned from racing and under close corporate scrutiny, stipulated that the car had to be rebodied to hide its Corvette identity. Whatever Mitchell did with the car had to be done at his own expense. Mitchell could go racing if he wanted to—but only as a private citizen. For his new Corvette shape, Mitchell went back to Bob McLean's

Bill Mitchell (center) was the hand-picked replacement of Harley Earl (left), seen here with GM boss Harlow Curtis.

From the Collections of Henry Ford Museum & Greenfield Village

Corvette design team. With Studio Engineer Ed Heinzman, McLean came up with the bright idea that a car shaped like an inverted airfoil would hug the road better. They sketched a shape that gave expression to this idea and applied it to their Corvette SS mule, which they renamed the "Sting Ray."

In its first outings as a race car, the Sting Ray tried to tell them how wrong they were regarding the inverted airfoil shape. At speed, the car didn't hug the road; it wanted to fly! The front of the car went to full rebound, becoming so light that it was almost uncontrollable. The car was totally erratic on the track, yet at first no one recognized that it was the car's fault! The SCCA officials assumed it was Dr. Dick Thompson's erratic driving. They banned him from racing for three months so he could go home and think about driving in a more

responsible manner. Mitchell's team finally solved the problem by adding huge grilles to the hood, venting enough of the lift pressure to keep the front end down. Unfortunately, by then Mitchell had become so enamored with the high razor-edged shape that he couldn't be talked out of it.

When the Sting Ray was finally tested in a wind tunnel to measure lift and drag forces, McLean had confirmation that he had gotten it wrong and that the shape generated lift. The wind tunnel results also confirmed what the Sting Ray race car was trying to tell them. Again, they ignored the numbers and kept going. After all, they were stylists and styling was everything.

When Mitchell had the mule rebodied as the Sting Ray, he saw it as the precursor of Corvettes to come. Always the engineer, Duntov saw it as an aerodynamic headache.

Dave McLellan Archives

The high razor-edged shape was next applied to the Corvette "Q" car, which was being conceived as the next-generation Corvette. The late 1950's were heady times for the GM engineering teams. Chevrolet was developing its rear-engine Corvair, and Pontiac was developing the rope-shaft, transaxle Tempest. The Tempest rope-shaft, transaxle driveline concept was actually developed first for a full family of V-8 passenger cars, the "Q" cars. Duntov reasoned that he could use the "Q" transaxle, planned in both automatic and manual versions, with a mid-ship V-8 engine in the first mid-engine Corvette. Ultimately, the passenger car applications fell through because of their high cost and marginal increase in interior roominess. While they reduced the transmission and driveline hump to the level of a modern front-wheel drive car, this benefited only the fifth and sixth passengers, who were otherwise forced to straddle the hump. There was no way that the Corvette could go it alone with something as expensive to tool as an automatic transmission transaxle, so the mid-engine car was stillborn.

At about this time, I remember attending an Engineering Society of Detroit lecture by Zora Arkus-Duntov in which he talked about his race car design experiences. When he got to talking about the body, he left me with the impression that, to him, the body simply added weight and made the car go slower. He commented on aerodynamics, but mostly talked about reducing its negative effects.

Today, Bill Mitchell, Bob McLean and Ed Heintzman are chastised for their dumb idea regarding the inverted airfoil. It was not a dumb idea; they just had it wrong because they were unaware of the unique physics for objects running close to the ground. If they had pursued the physics of

the phenomenon in the wind tunnel and had designed shapes accordingly, they would now be credited with the aerodynamic revolution that overtook automobile racing. Unfortunately for them, they fell in love with the first design theme that their inverted airfoil idea suggested and stuck with it. Fortunately, though, they were vocal enough about their idea that it reached the ears of Frank Winchell and Jim Hall, who got it right.

THE SMALL BLOCK PLAYS ITS PART

The Chevrolet V-8 engine began to show its muscle as it was being developed. It was known within Chevrolet as the "small block" because of the minimalist design strategy pushed by Ed Cole. In order to be the leader in the low-priced field, Chevrolet had to design smart and put complexity into the design process, not into the hardware. It is a tribute to engine designer Al Colby and his team that they crowded more engine into less space than had ever been done before. Every detail was mathematically analyzed and then trial-and-error tested until the minimum that would do the job had been achieved.

AERODYNAMIC DISCOVERY AND THE CHAPARRAL

In 1960, Chevrolet R&D, now headed by Frank Winchell, began a long and fruitful relationship with Jim Hall, who was building a series of race cars to compete in prototype sports car racing and in the Canadian-American Challenge Cup (the Can Am). Hall was told of McLean's idea that an inverted airfoil would act like an inverted wing and suck the car onto the road. He reshaped the nose of his next race car, the Chaparral 2, to give it this effect. Midway through his next test session, satisfied with the performance of his car with no nose at all, he added the inverted airfoil nose and retested the car. The front wheels lifted right off the road at 120 mph. Hall immediately called Winchell for help. They obviously didn't know what was causing the lift effect, so they started inventing on the fly. They decided to try a shovel nose, so Hall cobbled one onto the car. On the track, this had the opposite effect: The front end was now sucked down so hard that the suspension went to full bump! Hall cut away part of the nose of the car and got it back to near neutral lift and went racing. But Winchell got to thinking about what had just happened. The car was trying to tell him something—and he would listen.

Frank Winchell recounted years later in a tongue-in-cheek footnote in *Race Car Vehicle Dynamics* by William F. Milliken and Douglas F. Milliken that, "In any event, his

[Mitchell's and McLean's] idea of an 'inverted airfoil' profile for a racing car would have worked out well if the CG had been high enough, say 50 feet [off the ground]." In other words, an inverted airfoil free of the ground effect would have behaved as expected. They were about to discover the unique aerodynamic behavior of bodies speeding close to the ground.

Winchell next tried a real wing mounted over the rear suspension. By the time the wing idea appeared on Hall's Chaparral, they had thought through the problem of applying down force through the body, and realized that they could generate so much aerodynamic down force, that the suspension would bottom out. So they applied their wing's down force directly to the wheels through the rear suspension uprights. Hall was now developing his car with

Frank Winchell and Zora Arkus-Duntov were contemporaries in Chevrolet R&D, although they never got along.
GM Media Archives

continued on next page

AERODYNAMIC DISCOVERY AND THE CHAPARRAL *(continued)*

Chevrolet R&D's clandestine help and using a Chevrolet-supplied torque converter automatic transmission. Two-pedal driving presented the opportunity to install a third pedal that controlled wing attitude with two positions: a go-fast, low-drag setting and a maximum down-force setting to use during cornering. With his shovel nose and rear wing, Hall achieved lateral accelerations approaching twice gravity (two g) in skid pad tests on his private racetrack in remote west Texas.

When he went racing Hall was invincible—until his wing broke. A wing failure, while cornering at two gs, is devastating. The car, suddenly back in a one g world, was so far over its limits that serious crashes were inevitable. Hall's (and Chevrolet's) mistake was in not designing the wing for the high-energy vibration field (ten g) that exists on a suspension upright. Driver-adjustable, suspension-mounted wings were soon outlawed, forcing race car designers to stiffen their suspensions dramatically as they applied wings and ground effect devices directly to the body.

Winchell's ultimate idea for generating down force appeared as the Chaparral 2J, the vacuum suction car. Almost the entire underbody was skirted to within a fraction of an inch of the ground with suspension-controlled Lexan skirts. Two large, snowmobile-engine-driven fans sucked the air out from under the car, achieving 1.7 g down force with ease. Unfortunately, the fans, which were aimed to the rear, picked up everything on the road and blew it at the following competition. In its first outing at Riverside, the Chaparrel 2J set a new track record, but

the fan system was unreliable and failed within only a few laps. Hall demonstrated to the SCCA officials that, unlike the early wing failures, a failure of the suction fan system posed no threat to the safety of the driver, because the vacuum diminished slowly enough that the driver could control the situation. But, before the next race, the sucker car was banned, not for its unreliable suction system, but for its technological threat to the "sport" of motor racing.

In spite of certain designs being quickly banned, the idea of using aerodynamic down force spread quickly. Colin Chapman and Peter Wright of Lotus were soon experimenting with wings on their Formula One Grand Prix car. Their work, by 1980, led to the rule bending Lotus 86, which had its aerodynamic body suspended separately from the conventional chassis that carried driver and powertrain. This was done in order to isolate the driver from the violent ride of a too-stiff suspension. This too was banned, but not for any technical flaw. To take advantage of what was still legal, and to fully exploit the newly discovered ground effects, Peter Wright and other Formula One designers began using moving ground-plane wind tunnels specifically designed to explore the effects of running in close proximity to the ground. Wright also set about solving the too-stiff ride vs. down-force problem. As a result, he designed a car with an active, height-controlled suspension that allowed some amount of normal ride dynamics but compensated for the aerodynamic down-loading with fast-acting height adjustment. Called "hydraulic active suspension," it was introduced into Formula One Grand Prix racing in 1980 on the Lotus 92.

The Chaparral 2C was the first embodiment of all that Hall had learned in this first round of aerodynamic development. Here Hall drives the 2C at Riverside in 1965.

Photo by Bob Tronolone

The Chaparral 2J vacuum suction car was the obvious way to generate downforce. Vic Elford drives the 2J at the Monterey Grand Prix in 1970.

Photo by Bob Tronolone

The heart of the engine was its wedge-shaped combustion chamber with its inclined intake and exhaust valves and a spark plug located close to the hot exhaust valve. At the time, Pete Estes, later a general manager of Chevrolet and ultimately the president of General Motors, was a test engineer at the GM Research Laboratories and helped develop the wedge-shaped combustion chamber. He then wrote the definitive report on fundamental combustion chamber design, which would be referred to and quoted for decades within GM. Developed in conjunction with tetraethyl lead, GM's wedge-shaped chamber, with its turbulence-generating squish area and spark plugs located as close as possible to the hottest surface in the chamber, allowed higher compression ratios and gave increased power and efficiency compared to all previous combustion chambers examined.

The valve mechanism in Chevrolet's V-8 was unique and typified Chevrolet's minimalist strategy. Its use of a single camshaft in the V of the engine and mechanical or hydraulic lifters driving pushrods was conventional. Replacing the rocker shaft with individual ball studs that acted as the pivot for stamped rocker arms was unique. The shaftless stamped rocker concept had actually been invented at Pontiac, but Chevrolet was not embarrassed to adopt a good idea. The stamped rocker was used to good advantage. It produced a very light and stiff valvetrain, which allowed camshaft designs that are able to operate the valves at the high accelerations needed for good cylinder-filling at high engine speeds.

The relatively large displacement of the engine and its compact exterior size demanded the most precision iron castings that had been made up to that time. For the engine block and head castings the negative of the exterior form and all the interior voids would be formed in a reusable resin-sand mixture, with molten iron poured into the void. The inner cores had to be very precisely located in order to ensure that minimum wall thickness was maintained, yet the tight overall packaging allowed little room for error as the engine was cast. The result was an engine that was lighter and much more powerful than the smaller displacement six-cylinder unit it replaced. Even though it was more powerful, the efficient combustion chamber design and the short exhaust passage within the head allowed less heat to reach the cooling system, which in turn allowed for a smaller radiator.

The shaftless stamped rocker was classic Chevrolet—an elegant yet inexpensive solution to a problem.

Illustration by Dave Kimble

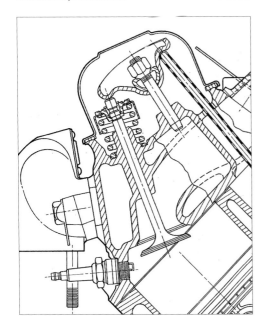

The engine was originally developed around two-barrel and four-barrel carburetors. The Corvette never used less than the four-barrel and followed it with fuel injection and multiple 4-barrel carburetors as performance and airflow requirements escalated.

As the Corvette continually raised its standards for cornering, braking and accelerating, it pushed the limits of carburetor-metering, which caused it to run lean in an acceleration environment. This required a redesign of the float chamber so that the metered fuel level was more constant and fuel was extracted from the chamber as close to the center of the fuel volume as possible.

PERFORMANCE BUILDS

In the years 1958 through 1962, largely because of the small-block V-8 and continued development of fuel systems, Duntov and Chevrolet continued to refine the Corvette and to support it in racing. Unfortunately, official racing involvement was out of the question because of the AMA ban on participation and its strict enforcement within GM. Thanks to earlier racing involvement, by 1957 the RPO 684 had been developed, including special front and rear springs and shocks, heavier front stabilizer bar, a quick steering adapter, segmented sintered-metallic brake linings, finned cast-iron brake drums, fresh ducting to the rear brakes, and front air scoops (known affectionately as "elephant ears"). Positraction was available for the manual transmission axles, and horsepower continued to increase, as did engine displacement. By 1957, the Corvette engine measured 283cid and was rated as high as 283 gross horsepower (ghp) with fuel injection, which was increased to 290 ghp the following year.

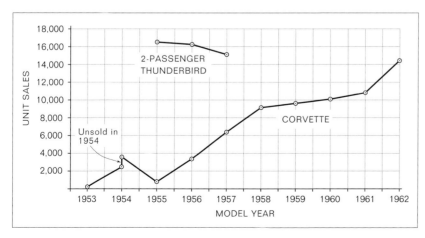

Corvette production to 1962. The Corvette had come a long way from its feeble beginnings but it still had a ways to go to catch the 3-year performance of the 2-place Thunderbird.

By 1962, Corvette production had increased to 14,531 per year. The 327cid V-8 engine was rated as high as 340 ghp with carburetors and 360 ghp with fuel injection. The cars still were available with only manual steering and manual brakes, and there was no air-conditioning. Manual steering meant that the large steering wheel remained, although it had slowly been redesigned to be located farther away from the driver's gut to give him a little more maneuvering room. Handling was still compromised by the narrow, low-cornering stiffness of the bias ply tires , which made the car feel very "loose" in cornering. Every parallel tar strip and ridge in the pavement tugged at the tires, requiring continual steering correction.

The manual drum brakes, particularly in racing applications, used sintered, ceramic-metallic linings. Compared to the asbestos-organic brake materials, ceramic-metallics tended to make the brakes more erratic. When cold, their coefficient of friction was so low that the driver had to

ROCHESTER MECHANICAL FUEL INJECTION

One of Duntov's projects in Chevrolet R&D was to help John Dolza and Rochester Products Division adapt their mechanical fuel injection system to the Corvette. Direct, high-pressure mechanical fuel injection had made the diesel engine possible. Bosch, in Germany, was the first to successfully adapt direct mechanical injection to gasoline injection for the Mercedes-Benz V-12 aero engine used in the Messerschmitt Bf 109. After the war, Mercedes used direct cylinder injection in their W.196 Grand Prix car, their 300 SLR sports racing car, and on their 300 SL sports car. Chevrolet took a different approach to fuel injection: injecting the fuel in a continuous spray into each of the intake ports just upstream of the intake valves.

The advantage of port fuel injection in 1957 was the same as it is today—a dry manifold. With a carburetor, the manifold has to transport fuel vapor, suspended fuel droplets and liquid flowing along the surfaces of the manifold passages. The vapor and suspended phases travel with the airstream and arrive at the cylinders much sooner than the slower-traveling liquid phase. The liquid phase, moving along the walls of the manifold, follows paths like a river and winds up arriving later and with a different distribution, cylinder to cylinder, than the vapor flow, aggravating the cylinder-to-cylinder variation in air-fuel ratio. Furthermore, a manifold filled with a combustible air-fuel mixture can be ignited, resulting in an explosive backfire.

Rapidly opening the throttle in an acceleration, causes the manifold vacuum to drop, also increasing fuel wetting. The resulting, momentary, lean air-fuel ratio ingested into the cylinders may not fire at all, resulting in the engine hesitating when it should be producing full power. To compensate, an accelerator pump adds a slug of fuel during every throttle transient. Add to this the pulsating effects of the intake gas dynamics on fuel delivery and one begins to wonder why the carbureted engine runs at all. Fuel injection was seen as a better way to go, bypassing the wet manifold distribution problem and putting the right amount of fuel at each intake valve as a function of engine speed and load.

Dolza's system was entirely mechanical. The electronic fuel injection systems of today would have to wait for the digital microprocessor in order to be viable. Still, it was a complex jewel of a system that Dolza developed and Rochester Products Division manufactured for the Corvette. Dolza's fuel injection system began by measuring the mass flow of air through a venturi. The venturi restriction produces a pressure-drop signal that is mathematically related to the mass flow of air. Using a control diaphragm, similar to one used in an aneroid barometer, the pressure-drop signal acts on the control diaphragm to create a force.

After the fuel is delivered from the tank and admitted into the float chamber by a float valve, a small gear pump delivers the fuel to the metering cavity. As stated in an SAE paper Duntov and Dolza prepared, "Some of the fuel delivered to the metering cavity flows directly to the eight continuous spray nozzles; the remainder of the fuel flows through the spill ports back to the float chamber. The

continued on next page

push very hard, and they were also terribly noisy and wore out quickly, but on the track they made up for all their shortcomings by providing stopping power long after the asbestos-organic brakes would have faded away. However, Chevrolet recommended the use of sintered, ceramic-metallic shoes only on the racetrack, suggesting "that for ordinary driving between meets . . . it may be desirable to replace the ceramic-metallic linings with conventional components."

One of the Corvette's major performance developments was the availability, in 1957, of the four-speed manual transmission. The very tight shift pattern worked well as a four-speed because the driver simply had to go for the corners of the square to find the right gear. I never did understand the close ratio spreads that Duntov preferred. A small peaky engine needs gear ratios that are close together so the driver can stay in the power band, but a big V-8 has such a broad, flat torque curve, that you can relax the ratio spread a little.

ROCHESTER MECHANICAL FUEL INJECTION *(continued)*

amount of fuel spill (and consequently the fuel delivered to the injectors) is regulated by the spill plunger."

An ingeniously simple pivoting control arm transmits the force created by the airside control diaphragm to the spill plunger. According to the SAE paper:

"An increase in air flow through the venturi causes an increase in the venturi signal which, acting on the control diaphragm, results in an increase in the force acting on the top of the spill plunger. The spill plunger then moves to a new balanced position to obtain a fuel pressure increase proportional to the venturi signal increase. Since the increased fuel pressure results in a fuel flow proportional to the increase in air flow indicated by the venturi signal, a constant air fuel ratio will be maintained as long as the linkage ratio is not changed."

The air-fuel ratio was changed between power (12.5:1) and economy (15.5:1) by shifting the pivot point on the control arm.

Dolza had worked this all out mathematically, ultimately relating air velocity to fuel flow. The equation that expressed the constant relationship between venturi pressure drop and fuel flow was reproduced in the mechanical analog system by forces transmitted through the control arm lever. Though the system was in reality more complex than described above, this was its essence as a typical analog control system in the days before digital electronics.

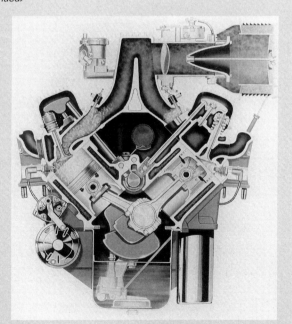

Fuel injection, previously seen only in military aircraft and race cars, was a startling development for 1957.
Courtesy the Detroit Public Library, National Automotive History Collection

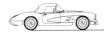

Four gears have a wide speed range to cover. First gear launches the car and with its axle ratio needs to produce an overall ratio of about 9:1. Any more than that and the tires light up too easily; any less than that and the clutch gets overworked as you try to avoid bogging the engine during a launch. Thus the 2.20:1 first gear preferred the 4.11:1 axle (9.08:1 overall). With the 4.11:1 axle and a direct fourth gear (1:1), the engine was turning almost 5,500 rpms at 100 mph, and top speed was limited to about 120 mph by running out of revs. You could, of course, select alternative axle ratios of 3.7:1 or 4.56:1, which moved the engine-speed-to-road-speed relationship up or down by about 10 percent.

The solid rear axle, technically called a "Hotchkiss drive," was the same compromised leaf spring suspension found in the classic prewar sports car. The flexing leaf springs located the axle and controlled its steer geometry. The leaf springs also had to react against the effects of accelerating and braking torque. Engine torque, particularly when it is multiplied by the transmission's first-gear ratio, applies a sufficient moment to the axle to lift the right wheel almost completely off the ground. The usual open differential can transmit only as much torque as the least loaded wheel can generate. Positraction was introduced to solve the lightly loaded wheel-spinning problem.

Dropping the hammer, as you would in a serious acceleration run, not only sets the tires spinning, it starts a complex vibration at about 3 Hz that is dominated by the tire-axle system. Seen in the side view, the axle moves in an elliptical path and imparts violence to the car. As much as three inches of fore-and-aft motion—with the tire leaving the road—has been observed during this cycle. Just watch an early Corvette trying to launch at the drag strip and you'll see what I mean. Adding dampers that are active in each of the modes would have been an elegant solution to the problem. For the 1959

DRIVING A 1957 FUELIE

What were these later solid axle Corvettes like to drive? I drove Mike McCagh's, 1957 fuel injection, 4.56:1 positraction axle, four-speed car on my Pennsylvania mountain route. Mike's car had been through the NCRS's most critical judging and was the winner of both Top Flight and Duntov awards. I drove it in as original a condition as it could be—right down to replica bias ply tires—37 years after it was built. With an engine that has been internally "hot rodded" (NCRS doesn't look inside the motor) and with modern tires, the car has turned a 13.5 second elapsed time at the Milan Dragways outside of Detroit.

The 1956 redesign was evident everywhere. Visibility was much improved, although the top still restricted visibility to the side. The steering wheel, still too large and spindly, was moved forward, but the tachometer remained in its awkward center spot (serious racers added their own steering-column-mounted

tach). Compared to the first Corvettes, this car benefited greatly from the racing development that was going on around it. The car was still crude by the most sophisticated sports car standards, but it got the job done. The ladder frame was not very rigid, and with the stiffened suspension it produced a loose and shaky-feeling platform. Precise handling control was nonexistent due to the bias ply tires, the steering lash and all the flexibility, including the leaf-spring-located rear axle. The fuel-injected engine, the car's best feature, was eager to accelerate and sounded pleasantly loud, sharp and penetrating, even with the factory exhaust. The car was a hoot to drive—for a short distance—but I suspect that high-speed touring with the 4.56:1 axle ratio would be wearing. In Duntov's hands the Corvette had become a racer. It would take a while to round out its personality so that it was competent on both road and track.

Corvette, Duntov stiffened the axle in its wind-up mode (pitch) by adding fore-and-aft radius rods. This helped but was still no solution.

The final year of the solid-axle Corvette was in 1962. From an appearance standpoint, 1961 and 1962 were a transition to the new Sting Ray appearance. The Corvette carried a rear end that had the razor-edged styling that would characterize the look of the all-new 1963 Corvette.

By 1962, the Corvette had established itself. It was now successful to the point of selling 14,531 cars per year. For several years, Corvette owners had been banding together in Corvette clubs, which Chevrolet recognized and supported. Joe Pike was the Corvette merchandising manager and directly supported the clubs and racing activities, from a marketing perspective. With the product appreciably improved, a growing loyal following, and modest competition success, the Corvette was ready for its next great leap forward.

During his 18 years as the merchandising manager of the Corvette, Joe Pike went far beyond what the organization asked of him to make the Corvette a success.

GM Media Archives

The Second Generation Corvette—C2 1963–1967 3

ZORA ARKUS-DUNTOV WAS CONSTRAINED by cost as he tried to maneuver the Corvette into becoming a more sophisticated sports car. General Motors' major Q-car program—with the transaxle needed for Duntov's first mid-engine proposal—was killed because of cost. As a result, the mid-engine Q Corvette could not stand alone, so it too was rejected. The Corvette's low sales, about 10,000 per year, mostly with manual transmissions, made it very expensive to amortize the tools for anything so complicated as an automatic transmission. This left Zora walking the fine line between designing the next-generation Corvette as an affordable but unsophisticated sports car and a costly state-of-the-art sports car that would meet the demands of the sports car enthusiast. Against this background, the all-new body and frame and the advanced rear suspension of the 1963 Corvette were an extraordinary accomplishment.

Chevrolet now had an excellent powertrain for the Corvette in its "small block" V-8 engine, which was available with either carburetors or fuel injection and a four-speed manual transmission. Duntov threw away the rest of the Corvette design and rethought it from the ground up. Always aiming for a Corvette with the highest possible performance, Duntov tried to design a sports car for the street that was also at home on the racetrack. Acceleration, braking, cornering and ride as it affected car control were all important to Zora, and with increasing skill he embodied these attributes in his Corvettes. Ride was important for passenger comfort but was never allowed to take precedence over handling.

Although the original 1963 "split-window" Sting Ray is coveted today, both Duntov and the automotive press denounced the visibility-impairing divided rear window.
Drawing by Dave McLellan

THE NEW CORVETTE TAKES SHAPE

Although Zora was actively working on the chassis concept for the 1963 Corvette, he was still formally assigned to the Chevrolet Research and

Development Department. Simultaneously, he was also designing the Chevrolet Experimental Research Vehicle I (CERV I). In order to finish the CERV I, Zora took on the project full time while Walt Zeyte was assigned to complete the production Corvette. Zeyte produced a series of pretest cars that were used to demonstrate proof of concept before the program was turned over to the Production Department. Walt's 25-year association with the Corvette and Zora had started with work on the 1953 and culminated with him ultimately becoming Zora's chassis engineer.

Zora recognized the necessity of an independent rear suspension in a high-performance sports car. He had experienced enough of the problems with the solid-axle, first-generation Corvette. A number of car companies—including Chevrolet with the 1960 Corvair—were continuing to use swing axles in their sports cars and sedans. Duntov had raced Porsches with swing axles and had tested the various Mercedes swing-axle cars. He had personally seen the treacherous handling of the high-powered mid-engine Auto-Union type C Grand Prix car. Both Auto-Union and Mercedes, after using swing axles in their grand prix cars, reverted to de Dion axles as a better solution. After World War II, Mercedes reverted to the swing axle for the 300 SL because it was less costly than a de Dion system. The German company then gravitated to a low-pivot swing axle for the 300 SL roadster, the racing 300 SLR and the W.196 Grand Prix car.

INDEPENDENT REAR SUSPENSION FOR CORVETTE

Chevrolet R&D's solution to the question of the rear suspension problem was clever: They used a fixed-length, U-jointed shaft as both the drive shaft and as a lateral suspension link. Wheel camber was controlled with an inclined lower link, and wheel toe and fore and aft were controlled with a trailing arm. This concept was first tested in the powerful, mid-engined CERV I and proved to be such a good rear suspension that it was used in the 1963 Corvette. It was elegant for its simplicity and low cost. Compared with a swing axle, it gave reduced camber change with ride and had a low roll center that made it easy to tailor the limit-handling with stabilizer bars. Aggressive launches were remarkably free of power hop but the simple trailing arm design gave the car an annoying pitch under hard acceleration.

The 1965 Corvair adopted this rear suspension in response to criticism of its earlier swing axle. The 1984 Corvette used a variant on this concept, introducing a controllable antisquat characteristic achieved by replacing the trailing arm with trailing links inclined upward in the side view.

INDEPENDENT REAR SUSPENSION PRIMER

An independent rear suspension provides ride isolation by letting each wheel move up and down independently of the other and provides engine torque isolation by mounting the differential directly to the chassis. If a bump is encountered under hard cornering, the wheel moves up and down, but it also changes camber. For a given ride travel, this camber change is most severe with the short swing-axle suspension. The high-pivot center of the swing axle also induces a significant net lift force on the rear of the vehicle, tending to jack the rear end and further exaggerate the camber change. Also, the cornering force generated by the tire changes with camber. A dip encountered under hard cornering causes a significant and rapid loss in lateral force, giving the driver a major path-control problem. Add to that the power and braking forces the driver induces, and path control in limit-handling maneuvers on undulating roads becomes a task reserved for only the most skilled drivers. The influence of camber change can be covered up with very stiff springs, which will not let the wheels move as much, but only at the expense of acceptable ride isolation.

Mounting the differential directly to the chassis isolates the tire loading from the torque reaction of the engine, which with a solid axle tries to lift the right tire off the road while pushing the left tire into the road.

The ultimate objective is to design a rear suspension that lets the tire generate the highest possible cornering force yet be insensitive to ride motions and controllable in response to engine torque and braking. In 1963, all known independent rear suspensions other than the swing axle required axle drive shafts that changed length as well as angularity. This required a complicated sliding joint that, today, is inexpensively mass-produced for front-wheel-drive cars, but this was not the case at that time.

Chevrolet R&D had designed a simplified de Dion rear suspension for the 1957 Corvette SS that demonstrated again that the de Dion axle used by Mercedes in their W.125 and later by Auto-Union in their type D Grand Prix racing cars would do the job. Even simplified it was still considered too expensive by Chevrolet because it required complicated axle drive shafts that could freely change length under torque as the suspension went through its ride travel. The de Dion tube location scheme used in the Corvette SS had proven unreliable, although I suspect this could have been resolved.

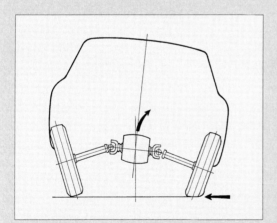

The simple swing axle offers an excellent ride and isolates the suspension from engine torque, but extreme camber changes can make the car's handling unpredictable when cornering on undulating roads.

Courtesy Road & Track Magazine

The de Dion rear axle—as used on the Corvette SS—retained the best features of the solid axle, and kept the wheels upright under cornering and always running parallel. It also isolated the suspension from engine torque.

Zora Arkus-Duntov Collection

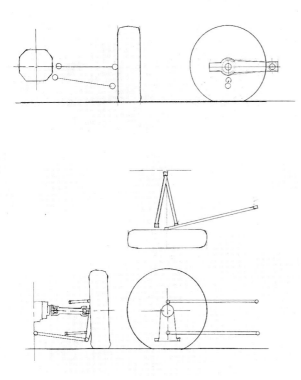

Top: The CERV I and the 1963 Corvette shared an independent rear suspension that used a fixed length, u-jointed shaft, as both the drive shaft and as one of the lateral suspension links.

Bottom: Lotus Cars introduced a similar, double-transverse-link rear suspension in its 1960 Lotus Eighteen Formula One and Formula Junior cars, as well as in its Lotus Nineteen sports racer.

Drawings by Dave McLellan

CERV I was first exposed publicly during tire tests in Riverside, California, during the winter of 1960. Earlier that same year, Lotus Cars introduced a similar, double transverse link rear suspension in its 1960 Lotus Eighteen Formula One and Formula Junior cars, as well as in its Lotus Nineteen sports racer. It's hard to say who should get credit for the concept. Both design groups were working out the details in secret at least a year earlier, with the results surfacing in cars in different parts of the world within months of one another, with Lotus first. The Lotus design was different in that it used a pair of parallel trailing links where the 1963 Corvette used a trailing arm.

Derived from Chevrolet production hardware, the SLA front suspension was conventional by comparison. It included a linkage for power steering or, in the case of manual steering, a steering damper to control wheel kick.

The car was put together with a boxed frame structure that surrounded the driver and allowed the seating space to nestle down inside the frame almost to the ground clearance line. The result was a lower seating position and, consequently, a profile lower than any previous Corvette. The body was available both as a convertible and as a coupe. In both cases, considerable steel reinforcement was used in the body. In fact, the reinforcements formed a cage over the passenger compartment, and was dubbed the "birdcage."

STYLING RUNS THE SHOW

Bill Mitchell and his stylists were still enamored with the 1960 Sting Ray race car's high razor-edged shape. They had grafted it onto the "Q" Corvette, and they now adapted it to Zora's new chassis, giving the 1963 Corvette the distinctive appearance that the Sting Ray race car had popularized. Zora recognized the lift problem that flawed the shape and planned to use large grilles in the hood—as had been done on the Sting Ray race car—to minimize the aerodynamic lift of the front end. At the last minute he realized that engine vapors exiting these grilles would contaminate the windshield and the cabin ventilation system. The plan

was abandoned, and the 1963 Sting Ray Corvette was introduced with dummy grilles in the hood and a full-blown lift problem.

Mitchell was also enamored of a razor-edged feature line down the middle of the car that led him to impose the split-rear-window theme. He and Duntov fought over this detail. It cost Duntov his access to Styling for a while but Duntov had the final say because the split rear window lasted only one year. Today, it's the defining feature of the 1963 Corvette, which makes the car even more valuable because of the limited volume of coupes that were built. (Moving the inside rearview mirror slightly to the right could have solved the rear visibility problem that had everyone complaining.)

The 1963 Corvette was designed as both a coupe and convertible. The coupe had a "birdcage" body struc-ture that surrounded the passengers and supported the plastic panels.
Dave McLellan Archives

What kind of relationship did Duntov have with GM Styling? At best, they tolerated each other. Both Earl and Mitchell kicked Duntov out of Styling. Fortunately, their temper tantrums were short-lived, and Dun-tov was soon allowed back in. Duntov had little patience for stylists who ignored engineering principles and designed purely for appearance, pro-ducing flamboyant sports cars that did not meet the requirements of an aerodynamic, high-speed road car.

The underlying question was, whose car was it? After all, Harley Earl and GM Styling had conceived the Corvette and now Bill Mitchell was in charge and was carrying on in that great tradition of Styling reigning supreme. Yes, Duntov through his persistence had given the Corvette much of its success as a sports car. And Chevrolet—which was responsi-ble for selling the Corvette—was yet another voice to be heard. It wasn't always clear who was in charge, although the balance was still weighted toward Styling. These competing power centers within GM were a major source of tension and conflict in the Corvette program. As Bill Mitchell moved beyond the Sting Ray, his designers produced even more flam-boyant and exaggerated show cars they continued to call Corvettes. Styling used the Corvette as a way of exploring design ideas and concepts that would later find their way into production Corvettes and even into mainstream GM passenger cars. The Mako Shark I and Mako Shark II helped Mitchell explore themes that would ultimately become the 1968 Corvette. The 1968 styling, with its "Coke bottle" exaggeration, was derived from the Mako Shark II show car and was to last through the 1982 model year.

Frank Winchell as GM's Vice President of Engineering Staff, and Mitchell's engineering peer, put a positive spin on Mitchell's contribution as GM's Chief Stylist. In *Race Car Vehicle Dynamics* by William F. Milliken and Douglas L. Milliken, Winchell observed:

> "Bill Mitchell probably sold more cars for GM than anybody in its history but he didn't know, or care, if F = ma or not. He was, at the time, the most powerful executive in the corporation. He scared almost everybody, Shinoda and I [sic] excepted. He liked big toothy grills, fake portholes and big airscoops that were hooked up to nothing. If chrome had not been invented by the time he got there, nobody would have ever heard of him. He had no idea at all what a car wanted to look like. He tried to make them look like sharks and P-38's. He didn't like anything that looked functional. If he couldn't disguise it, he covered it up, particularly if it was a screw, any screw. But he was bananas for horsepower. If it was big and shiny, smoked the tires and made lots of noise, it was a car. Americans agreed—in droves. His 'designs' were the paragon of the industry. Everybody tried to make theirs look like his. I was in his corner, I just didn't think it was going to last forever."

Top: The Mako Shark I show car was Bill Mitchell's next exploration of themes that would ultimately lead to the 1968 Corvette.

Bottom: The Mako Shark II show car explored a body having an exaggerated "Coke bottle" shape and sharp-edged raised fenders. With lower front fenders and more restrained details, it became the 1968 Corvette.

Dave McLellan Archives (both)

Chevrolet's production departments were responsible for preparing the 1963 for the manufacturing process, but they left it with lots of loose ends. Bob Vogelei was assigned to clean up the production design and would stay with the Corvette for the next twenty-one years. Vogelei soon became responsible for all Corvette body engineering and led the teams that did late 1960's mid-engine prototypes and the entire body, exterior, interior and structure of the all-new 1984 Corvette.

MORE SALES, BUT NOT ENOUGH

In 1963, the marketplace rewarded Chevrolet for its all-new Corvette with a 50 percent increase in Corvette sales over the previous year's record sales. Corvette's 1963 record of 21,513 sales was continually eclipsed every year, with a little upheaval between 1967 and 1973. Sales finally peaked in 1979, when Chevrolet sold 53,807 Corvettes.

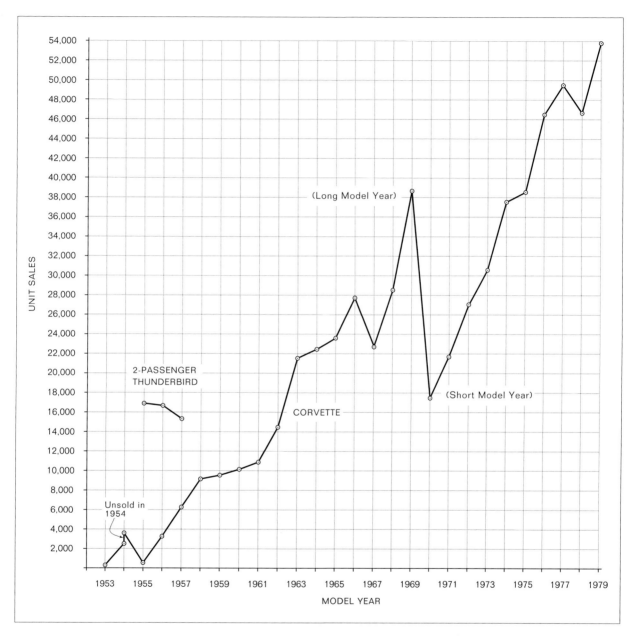

1963 was the first year that Corvette production surpassed the benchmark set by the 1955–1957 passenger Thunderbird.

Ed Cole couldn't stand to see Ford selling 80,000 Thunderbirds a year, even if it had evolved into a car very different from the original 1955 two-seat T-Bird that had trounced the original Corvette in the sales contest. Chasing after Thunderbird sales with a four-seat Corvette was all Cole's idea. Duntov was against it and Joe Pike (Corvette's Merchandising Manager) was against it, but Cole was for it and he was the boss. So, who killed it? Cole had Styling do a complete mock-up of the four-seat car. They added several inches to the Corvette's wheelbase and ballooned the roofline in order to achieve a small back seat. On the day it was ready, Cole arrived at Styling with GM's President, John Gordon in tow. Mitchell had strategically parked the four-seat Corvette in his executive garage, where Cole and Gordon couldn't miss it. Gordon took the bait and muscled his way into the back seat. It was a tight fit—so tight that he couldn't get out.

The hapless Gordon was stuck. With lots of pulling and tugging they finally extricated him, but that ended all talk of a four-seat Corvette. Was this a setup by Mitchell to kill the car? He never told, so you can decide....

Ed Cole advanced from Chevrolet Chief Engineer to General Manager and, ultimately, to President of GM. When Cole moved on from Chevrolet, Pete Estes (whose combustion chamber research was the foundation of the Chevrolet small-block V-8) replaced him as General Manager. Chevrolet and GM were flush with cash and Estes, in asserting control and intending to put his mark on Chevrolet, had the organization redesign and retool all Chevrolet products in the next two years, 1967 and 1968. The Corvette was originally intended to be changed in 1967, but was delayed while Styling's Mako Shark II derived fenders were cut down so you could see over them. The "toned down" 1968 was still so rushed into production that the first year was a disaster for fits, function and cooling.

The long, sloped nose of the 1968 left too little area in the nose for a cooling intake,

SHELBY'S SNAKE

Carroll Shelby's Ford Cobra was an excellent example of a British hybrid racing car. The genesis of the car was the AC Ace, which used either the prewar AC straight six, or the BMW 328-derived Bristol six-cylinder engine. The large diameter tube chassis and four-wheel independent suspension of the AC Ace was recognized by Carroll Shelby as the possible basis for a V-8 powered sports car. He interested Ford in it and worked with AC to produce a powerful and competitive hybrid. One thing the Cobra had going for it was that it weighed approximately 900 pounds less than the Corvette. It didn't meet any of the requirements that the Corvette met as a street machine, such as providing reasonable creature comfort, and its sales performance showed it. Over all the years of Cobra production, Ford and Shelby sold less than 1,000 Cobras, but on the racetrack none of that mattered. The lightweight Cobra completely frustrated the Corvette's racing in production classes. As the Cobra increased in power and performance, the problem only became worse.

The Ford V-8-powered AC Cobra was to become Corvette's nemesis on the racetrack. Ken Miles drives a 289 Cobra at Mosport in Canada.

Photo by Don Markle

particularly after bumpers and lights were accommodated. The majority of the cooling air had to come from underneath, because Styling wouldn't budge on their design. Chevrolet had no experience with bottom-breathing intakes so they did the best they could and let the car go into production undercooled. The 1968 cooling fiasco demonstrated how little Styling had learned from the 1963 front lift fiasco. Bob Vogelei's small Body Design Group was all Chevrolet had working on the 1968 until the proverbial "shit hit the fan" and Vogelei got more help than he needed. Walt Zetye's group, doing chassis, had a little better time of it because their changes were not nearly so extensive.

Both teams were also responsible for their respective parts of the mid-engine Corvette that Duntov was pushing so hard for. This was not the last time that Chevrolet tried to do too much with too little. Unfortunately, the good soldiers, caught in the middle trying to do the impossible, also took the blame for what was really management's failure.

A STING RAY WITH REAL STING

As soon as Chevrolet introduced the 1963 Sting Ray Corvette, Duntov planned to take it racing and clean up. In its first outing in California, to Duntov's surprise, Ford and Carroll Shelby showed up with a car that was to become Corvette's nemesis, the Ford V-8 powered AC Cobra.

Duntov countered with the special production Grand Sport (GS) Corvette, which had a planned build of 125 cars, sufficient to qualify it as a "production car" by the SCCA rules. The powertrain was derived from the production Corvette but most of the components were unique. Back at Chevrolet R&D, Duntov was developing engines for the GS as exotic as four-valve, four-cam V-8 race motors. The car was tied together by a large diameter tubular frame and wrapped in a body that looked like the production Corvette but was much lighter.

Actually, the GS looked like a clumsy version of the production Corvette. Larry Shinoda, who was responsible for adapting the inverted air foil, high razor-edged shape to the production Corvette, relates that by the time the GS Corvettes were being built, Duntov had been barred from Styling, in the aftermath of one of Mitchell's many temper tantrums. The design of the GS was bootlegged out of Shinoda's studio by Dun-

Duntov's response to the AC Cobra was the lightweight Grand Sport (GS) Corvette.
Dave McLellan Archives

Top: Larry Shinoda contributed to the design of the Corvette throughout the 1960s. His curiosity about the technical aspects of design is seen in the scale model-wind tunnel he built.

Photo Courtesy Larry Shinoda Collection

Bottom: Gib Hufstader (right) was a member of Zora's inner circle of engineers who labored to make the Corvette a better car.

Dave McLellan Archives

tov's engineer, Gib Hufstader, who hand-carried sketches on scraps of paper.

In the initial build, five cars were started, but the bean counters soon discovered them and put a halt to the project. Chevrolet was able to finish the five cars and sell them to several potential racers, although they left the factory untested and lacking race motors. With only five cars built, the Corvette Grand Sport would have to race in the prototype class against Ferrari and Maserati. The strategy of going head to head with the Ford AC Cobra, a "production sports car," was blunted, and Ford didn't have to lift a finger.

Between Winchell's support of Jim Hall's Chaparral race cars, and Mitchell racing the Sting Ray as a privateer, GM and Chevrolet were building a strong relationship with the sports racing community despite the enforced AMA ban on racing. The sale of the Grand Sports also brought Roger Penske into a direct relationship with Chevrolet. Penske was racing and trying to build a business career at the same time. With Mark Donohue, Penske would go on to success in the Trans Am with the Z28 Camaro and ultimately would build a racing and business dynasty that would extend from race car building to seemingly effortless wins at Indianapolis, to businesses as diverse as rental trucks and diesel engines.

STOPPING POWER TO MATCH THE HORSEPOWER

Duntov, once again frustrated by the AMA ban on racing, continued to probe for solutions to beating the AC Ford Cobra and decided to put the new Chevrolet "big block" into the Corvette. The first year for the big-block Corvette was 1965, when it was introduced in 396cid, 425 horsepower manual transmission form.

That same year was also the first time that disc brakes were available on the Corvette. Disc brakes were first developed by Dunlop for the D Type Jaguar and were first proven in the 1953 Le Mans 24-hour race. Driving for Allard, Duntov had a ring-side seat to see the utter superiority of the disc brakes. As Zora recounts, Stirling Moss came up to him before the race and cautioned him not to follow his Jaguar when braking. In the race Duntov learned why. Moss' disc brake-equipped Jaguar reliably slowed from 170 mph for the 24 hours of the race, something that no contemporary drum-braked car could do. Since that first experience at Le

Mans, development work on disc brakes accelerated, producing a brake system that was far superior to the mature drum brake.

I asked Zora why he didn't introduce disc brakes sooner on the Corvette? He told me that he had tried to contact Dunlop, who was the manufacturer of the disc brakes for the Jaguar, but was unable to get a response. Although he never used the Dunlop disc brakes on the production Corvette, Duntov did use them on the CERV cars, so he ultimately did have some contact with Dunlop. Ultimately, he put together a production program to develop a ventilated disc brake system for the Corvette with Kelsey-Hayes, an American manufacturer of wheels and brakes. At the last moment, the business was given to Delco Moraine, GM's own brake subsidiary, with the understanding that if they could produce the disc brake system for the same cost, the job was theirs. Delco had ignored the initial program, and had let Kelsey-Hayes do all the work. Realizing that Duntov was serious, Delco nosed back into the program by playing corporate politics at the highest level. Except for a seal-induced corrosion problem that took a long time to solve, the resulting four-wheel ventilated disc brake system was state of the art.

The big block gave the Corvette chassis all the power it could handle. It also gave the Corvette a sense of effortless performance because the mid-range torque of the big-block engine was so great that, in the manual transmission version, the driver hardly had to shift to a lower gear to achieve exciting passing performance. To its disadvantage, the big block was considerably heavier than the small block, and the added weight was concentrated up front. The power had to be carefully modulated during a launch or the tires would easily light up. With too much wheel spin, standing-start performance was blunted, so the full difference between the small block and the big block couldn't be seen in its acceleration times. Fortunately, by the time this startling big block performance was available, so too were four-wheel disc brakes, without which the chassis surely would have been overpowered. In 1965, in its big-block, disc-brake form, the Corvette Sting Ray was a formidable sports car that gave very little away to the competition—at any price.

THE AUTOMATIC CHOICE

Although the 1953 Corvette was introduced with only the Powerglide automatic transmission, manual transmissions were introduced soon after—the three-speed in 1955, and the four-speed in 1957—and Corvette buyers fell in love with manual transmission. Through the late 1950s and 1960s, the manual transmission option dominated Corvette sales, reaching 80 percent by 1967.

In 1968 the three-speed Turbo Hydramatic automatic transmission was introduced. Its two-speed Powerglide predecessor had been an acceptable low-cost transmission but gave away performance to the manual. The new Turbo Hydramatic gave away nothing; it had sufficient torque multiplication to light up the tires on a start, and its three ratios left no gaps in performance all the way to top speed. You could still beat it with the manual, but you had to make a full drag strip start to do it. It took several more years, but the Corvette market ultimately rediscovered the automatic transmission. The automatic rose to 75 percent of Corvette sales and remains there today.

The Mid-Engine Corvette 4

IN SO MANY WAYS ZORA ARKUS-DUNTOV was an engineer of exceptional talent and energy. The Corvette SS—designed in 1957—verified for Zora that a race car with a very stiff structure and a de Dion rear suspension could easily handle the power of a race-prepared Chevrolet V-8 engine. It taught him that GM Styling neither thought nor cared much about aerodynamic lift and drag. The dictum that form follows function was not yet in Styling's vocabulary. As Zora drove the SS, the long bulging hood that covered the fuel injected V-8 and obstructed his forward vision, and the sweltering heat in the cockpit, got him thinking about putting the engine behind the driver.

ZORA'S INFLUENCES

A quarter of a century earlier, Dr. Ferdinand Porsche had conceived and developed the mid-engine Auto Union type C Grand Prix car. As a young engineer in Germany, Zora had watched as Auto Union struggled to develop the car and to find drivers who could master its handling quirks. He knew that the type C, with its rearward weight bias, swing-axle rear suspension and lack of stabilizer bars to trim load-transfer distribution, was a treacherous car to drive at the limit. He had also seen the car com-

Dr. Ferdinand Porsche designed the mid-engine Auto Union type D, which is the precursor of all modern mid-engine race cars.

Courtesy Road & Track Magazine

pletely reengineered by Auto Union for the 1938 season. Designated the type D, it solved the handling problems of the type C and demonstrated the viability of the mid-engine race car.

The first inkling that Zora was thinking about a mid-engine Corvette was the stillborn "Q" Corvette proposal. Zora followed this with a pair of experimental cars that allowed him to test his concept of a mid-engine car. With a ban on racing and the bean counters snooping everywhere within General Motors to enforce it, Zora had to be clever with his

reasoning behind these cars. It was the early 1960s and GM and Ralph Nader were going at it over the Corvair, which had been designed with a swing-axle rear suspension and was being criticized for its limit-handling. But Chevrolet R&D would explore rear suspension designs for rear engine cars with a pair of Chevrolet Experimental Research Vehicles (CERV).

ZORA'S FIRST MID-ENGINE CAR

This was enough cover for Zora. CERV I was an open-wheeled, mid-engine 550 hp V-8 race car designed to showcase the Chevrolet V-8 as a stock block capable of winning the Indianapolis 500. This car was conceived two years before Jack Brabham drove an under-powered, mid-engine 2.7 liter Cooper Climax to a ninth place finish at Indy. Brabham finished just eight minutes behind the winner, touching off the mid-engined race car invasion from Europe. CERV I was also Zora's first exploration of the independent rear suspension that he was to use on the all-new 1963 Corvette. With literally twice the power and a much more rearward weight bias than the production car, CERV I was an excellent "stress test" of the suspension concept.

Top: Chevrolet Experimental Research Vehicle number 1 (CERV I) was an open-wheel, mid-engine 550 hp, V-8 race car designed to showcase the Chevrolet V-8 as a stock block capable of winning the Indianapolis 500.

GM Media Archives

Bottom: Two years after the CERV I was built, Jack Brabham drove a mid-engined 2.7 liter Cooper Climax to a ninth place finish at Indy. On pit lane, Brabham passes A. J. Foyt's roadster.

Photo ExxonMobil Corp., courtesy Road & Track Magazine

The CERV II of several years later was an exciting concept that some saw as a thinly veiled Le Mans prototype. Duntov placed the Chevrolet V-8 engine longitudinally behind the driver. Instead of simply powering the rear wheels, he used two automatic transaxles, one ahead of the engine and one behind the engine, to power all four wheels. The high-performance torque converters and the two-speed transaxles came out of the same Chevrolet R&D program that would lead to the automatic transmission Chaparral. By picking different torque converter characteristics for the front and the rear, Zora was able to compensate for weight distribution and give the car excellent power-on handling. With the engine behind the driver, the intake system, carbureted or injected, could employ the long, tuned inlet runners that would peak the power without obscuring the driver's field of vision. Additionally, the exhaust could use long tuned runners, without compromising the driver's comfort.

With the possibility of power outputs in excess of 400 horsepower in a production version, CERV I

demonstrated the benefit of having 60 percent of the vehicle's weight on the driving wheels. Meanwhile, CERV II demonstrated the potential of four-wheel drive for an ultimate performance Corvette.

The CERVs were designed on narrow tires, and though fitted with wide racing tires during their development phase, they were originally conceived on the premise that narrow tires and the continued escalation in horsepower would characterize the future for the production Corvette. Race car tires were already in transition toward the wide-bias ply tire construction.

OPTIONS FOR THE FUTURE

Even as the all-new 1963 Corvette was taking the enthusiast market by storm, Zora was moving on. The two concept vehicle experiments, CERV I and CERV II, led him to propose a mid-engine production Corvette that was presented to Chevrolet in 1964 as one of a series of future option strategies. The first proposal, which I suspect was presented as a straw man, was to face-lift the 1963 car for the 1966 model year on the current chassis. Proposal number two was a new light-weight, front-engine car using a structural steel backbone underbody with fiberglass body panels that would appear as a 1967 model. The current chassis and powertrain would be used in modified form. The third proposal was for a new rear-engine (actually mid-engine) car that would also appear as a 1967 model. It too would use a structural steel backbone underbody with fiberglass body panels. The Chevrolet V-8 was mounted longitudinally and combined with a new transaxle.

When I reviewed these drawings years later, I was surprised that they were considering a backbone design. A backbone, supplemented with adequate rockers, is the only way that sufficient structure stiffness can be achieved through the passenger compartment of a convertible Corvette. Executing a backbone is fairly straightforward with the engine behind the driver, but almost impossible to implement when the engine is in front and is driving the rear wheels. The automatic transmission completely blocks the possibility of running a closed structural box through the center of the car and of being able to tie it into the rest of the structure. If Proposal Number 2 had been approved, they would have been as stymied as we were 25 years later. It took us two years and a major reconfiguring of the driveline

CERV II was a thinly veiled Le Mans prototype with its Chevrolet V-8 engine located longitudinally behind the driver. It used two automatic transaxles to power all four wheels.
Photo by Bob D'Olivo

Chevrolet Proposals for the Corvette:

Proposal No. 1 was to face-lift the 1963 car for the 1966 model year on the existing chassis.

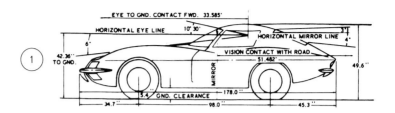

Curb Weight 2200 lb.

Proposal No. 2 was a new light-weight, front-engine car using a structural steel backbone under-body with fiberglass body panels that would appear as a 1967 model.

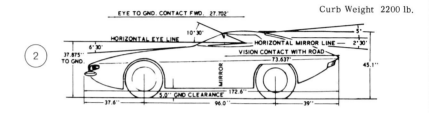

Curb Weight 2475 lb.

Proposal No. 3 was a new rear-engine (actually mid-engine) car that would appear as a 1967 model.

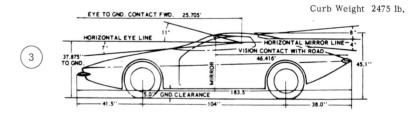

Curb Weight 1650 lb.

GS3: R&D's proposals to Chevrolet included an open cock-pit, mid-engine, four-wheel drive race car known as the Competition Grand Sport, or GS 3.

Dave McLellan Archives (all)

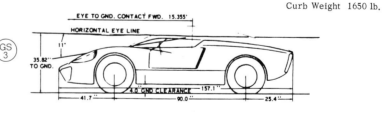

to integrate the backbone into the front-engine rear-drive car. The current C5 generation Corvette is the beneficiary of this solution.

R&D's proposal to Chevrolet included a competition Grand Sport (GS 3). This was described as a "newly styled, lightweight performance vehicle with modified body-frame integral, using structural 'high rocker' steel platform construction with fiberglass outer panels. New chassis with rear mounted engine." From an inspection of the drawings that accompanied the proposal, this was an open cockpit, mid-engine, four-wheel-drive race car.

Chevrolet ultimately face-lifted the Corvette as in Proposal Number 1, but it wasn't ready until the 1968 model year. However, those who worked on it wished that the introduction had been delayed until 1969. A modified Proposal 3 mid-engine car was also built, but it was controversial, causing a battle royal within the organization. Never have I seen such a heated or polarized controversy within GM. When it was no longer a serious production proposal, management decided to show it off at the 1969 New York Auto Show as a running concept vehicle, not a full-fledged prototype. The automotive press did a wonderful job of hyping this mid-engine Corvette to the motoring public, suggesting that it would arrive as the 1973 Corvette. Chevrolet was not so easily convinced. Joe Pike, an early advocate of the mid-engine Corvette, rethought his position and came to the conclusion that Corvette buyers would find the cockpit too cramped and that the engine, buried in the central body work, would be almost impossible to service. This became the official position of the Chevrolet Sales Department and earned Joe the enmity of both Zora Arkus-Duntov and Bill Mitchell.

Throughout this period, Chevrolet was in the enviable position of being able to sell every Corvette it could build. Though willing to show the mid-engine Corvette as a concept vehicle on the auto show circuit, market wisdom told Chevrolet management that the front-engine Corvette had turned on the Corvette enthusiasts. The Sales Department had no interest in screwing up what was finally working well.

The mid-engine Corvette, as it was finally built, was different from the 1964 proposal and different from either of the CERV vehicles. A total departure from the construction of the production Corvette, the car had an integral steel body, with steel skin panels. The V-8 engine was mounted transversely behind the driver and drove through an Oldsmobile Toronado transaxle mated to a unique final drive. There was also a manual transmission version, but it was never tested. The rear suspension used the

U-jointed axle shafts as a lateral link, as Duntov had pioneered with CERV I and used in the 1963 production car.

The Toronado was a V-8 powered front-wheel-drive car with its engine located longitudinally. The torque converter was at the back of the engine and drove the transmission—located beside the engine—through a silent chain. The final drive was on the end of the transmission, with one axle shaft having to pass through the engine sump.

ALL-WHEEL-DRIVE

Why did Zora turn the engine east-west? The V-8 engine is essentially square, taking up roughly the same space whether it is mounted north-south or east-west. He could have mounted the engine longitudinally and used the Toronado transaxle intact, but he consciously made the final drive more complicated by mounting the engine transversely. I asked Zora, years later, if the reason was to accommodate four-wheel drive. With a twinkle in his eye, he admitted it was. In Zora's design the Toronado final drive would become the intermediate differential in a four-wheel-drive system. This was never talked about publicly and no car was ever built with this feature, but there is no doubt that if the mid-engine program had been approved we would have seen an ultimate performance four-wheel-drive version. Zora also designed the mid-engine Corvette to accept the big block, though this was never pursued either.

The mid-engine car was Zora's ultimate vision for the Corvette. It embodied all the ideas he had developed over a lifetime of racing and of designing automobiles. Over the next few years, the mid-engine Corvette was to consume most of Zora's energies, with the front-engine rear-drive production car receiving less and less of his and his team's attention. The understaffed and overworked engineering team, having to design the production and the experimental mid-engine car simultaneously, presided over a deterioration in quality that became obvious with the 1968 and later models.

After a meteoric career at the Pontiac Motor Division, John DeLorean came to Chevrolet as General Manager in 1970. John saw the potential of the mid-engine Corvette but had no data to

How the transverse V-8 mid-engine driveline would adapt to four-wheel drive.

Drawing by Dave McLellan

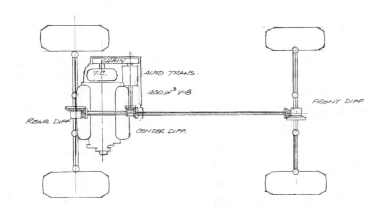

counter the objections of the Sales Department other than his own gut instinct. And he couldn't sell the program to corporate financial management on the decrease in sales volume that the Sales guys were predicting. To keep the program alive and moving, he authorized the fabrication of an all-aluminum version of the car. This car was ultimately constructed in conjunction with Reynolds Aluminum, anticipating the Honda NSX by almost twenty years. New styling forced Bob Robinson, who did the car for Zora, to make many new tools, but the car was generally based on the steel integral-body-frame car. In fabricating the aluminum panels, they found that aluminum couldn't be stretched like steel, so many of the panels had to be hot-formed to keep them from cracking. This car still exists today as a running show car.

If the mid-engine Corvette had been approved for production, it would have required an all-new detailed design, a situation that was not unusual for a car at this stage in its development. These first-generation cars were 7/8 scale models. Interior room was at a minimum; there was virtually no luggage space; the gas tank capacity was inadequate; and the steel structure was patched and cobbled.

After a meteoric career at the Pontiac Motor Division, John DeLorean came to Chevrolet as General Manager in 1970, where he championed the ill-fated mid-engine Corvette.
GM Media Archives

WANKEL TO THE FOREFRONT

Ed Cole, by now, had become President of GM. Cole, an engineer by training and avocation, continued to dominate GM's advanced engineering and was accepted as the de facto chief engineer of the corporation. Cole was driven to bring the Wankel rotary engine into production at GM. The rotary engine was very compact for its power output. Dr. Felix Wankel, its inventor and initial developer, first sold his engine to German automaker NSU, which designed the advanced four-door RO-80 around the Wankel engine. The engine's complex rotor sealing system was not yet reliable and proved the undoing of the car and a disaster to the company. NSU replaced all the engines in all RO-80s, two and sometimes three times, bankrupting the company.

Ed Cole saw the potential of the rotary engine for GM and believed that with GM's technical might behind him he could overcome the engine's problems. Cole turned the advanced engineering and manufacturing capabilities of GM loose on the rotor seal problem. He was in such a hurry and was so confident of success that he set in motion a parallel car program so that there would be a new vehicle ready for the engine. As the engine entered the development stage, he decided to give the engine a high

public profile by featuring it in a mid-engine Corvette. Ed Cole was again acting in his role as the Corvette's mentor.

Zora saw in Cole's Corvette proposal, both an opportunity and a curse. The opportunity was that Zora's dream, the mid-engine Corvette, would be produced. The curse was that the engine was totally underpowered for a Corvette and as yet unproven. GM was developing a two-rotor Wankel, that was producing about 200 hp. Contemporary Corvettes were producing upwards of 400 hp.

To prove to Cole that the two-rotor Wankel engine didn't offer sufficient performance for a Corvette, Zora built a demonstrator from a Porsche 914 that was rebodied to look like a junior version of the mid-engine Corvette. Because of the lackluster performance of its two-rotor Wankel engine, the car convinced Cole that this wasn't a Corvette. Cole bit the bullet and authorized the fabrication of a unique four-rotor Wankel engine for the Corvette.

Gib Hufstader built just one four-rotor Wankel engine, cobbling it together from a pair of two-rotor test units. The four-rotor Wankel was installed in one of the mid-engine Corvettes that had been completely rebodied by Styling to include a very distinctive double-ended theme and bi-fold gull-wing doors. Dubbed the "Four-Rotor Corvette," it was designed by Henry Haga and Jerry Palmer. In my estimation, it was the most elegantly beautiful Corvette prototype ever designed. Its forms would reemerge years later in Palmer's C4 generation Corvette.

The car met Zora's requirements for performance and Cole decreed that this would be the mid-engine Corvette. From his own brief drive in the Four-Rotor, Zora felt that "the engine had the performance of the big block, but that it needed more axle [ratio]." Unfortunately, neither horsepower nor acceleration was ever measured before the engine began to deteriorate in performance. Zora remembered the number, 500 hp, although it was never dynamometer-tested, so we can only estimate its power.

The Arab oil shock of 1973–1974 was a wake-up call for fuel economy and, with the emerging

Top: Using a Porsche 914 rebodied to look like a junior version of the mid-engine Corvette, Duntov proved that the two-rotor Wankel engine didn't offer sufficient performance for a Corvette.

GM Design Center

Bottom: Henry Haga and Jerry Palmer styled the timeless and elegant Four-Rotor Corvette.

Dave McLellan Archives

emission standards, struck at the heart of the Wankel rotary engine development. Along with seal durability, poor fuel economy and high emissions were unsolved problems with little prospect of an early solution, given the underlying physics of the situation.

Ed Cole was taking a great risk, pushing the Wankel engine as the future strategic direction for GM. If the engine succeeded, it would produce a very compact power plant for a new line of much more package-efficient GM cars. If it failed, it would leave GM without future direction at a time of increasing regulatory incursion.

The Wankel engine was not successful at GM. As GM looked to the future, it saw ever-increasing emission and fuel economy standards that could only be met by conventional piston engines with catalytic converters. The Wankel engine, because of its very elongated combustion chamber with its high surface-to-volume ratio, was the worst possible shape to meet the requirements for reducing hydrocarbons. The complex sealing of the rotor within the combustion chamber made it doubly difficult to control oil consumption. Metallic additives in the oil would contaminate and "poison" the soon-to-be introduced catalytic converters.

GM's Hydramatic automatic transmission division had been given the assignment of building the rotary engine. As hard as they tried to make the manufacturing process efficient and as creative as they got with the financials, the expected cost was still hundreds of dollars more than its piston engine equivalent.

The rotary engine program continued into 1974, but it became more and more obvious that it would be impossible to meet the pending emission requirements. They might be able to meet 1975 standards, but as the standards became more stringent going forward, the problem would simply get worse. With Ed Cole's retirement at the beginning of 1975, the rotary engine program was terminated, much like a range officer pushes the button to blow up a rocket that has gone out of control. In the end, reason and the cost accountants prevailed. Unfortunately, another casualty was the mid-engine Corvette program, which had become tied to the rotary engine. The Corvette would have to survive on its carry-over chassis, which was already eleven years old.

THE PRODUCT PLANNERS SPEAK

From the time the first mid-engine concept Corvette was shown to the public in 1969, the enthusiast automobile magazines positively salivated over the idea of Chevrolet producing a mid-engine Corvette. Chevrolet,

on the other hand, by then selling 30,000 to 40,000 Corvettes a year, couldn't see how they could sell any more Corvettes by putting the engine behind the driver. In fact, their analysis indicated that they would sell fewer Corvettes if they were mid-engined, so quite naturally they were against the idea.

Market research in the early 1970s was not what it is today, but by all indications, most Corvette enthusiasts had already settled in their minds as to what a Corvette was—and it had an engine up front and driven rear wheels. As late as 1990, in conjunction with professionally conducted Corvette market research, we asked Corvette owners and enthusiasts about the mid-engine Corvette. What we found was two extremes: There were those who were strongly in favor of the mid-engine Corvette and those who were equally vocal that the front-engine was the only Corvette. Despite 20 years of automobile magazine hype, there has still not been a unanimous groundswell for the mid-engine Corvette.

In all of his years working with the Corvette, Zora had two important visions. The first one, the 1963 Corvette, was put into production and, with its solid axle predecessors, defined the Corvette for its owner group. The second vision culminated in the mid-engine car proposals, first with a V-8 and then with the Wankel engine. Corvette enthusiasts never responded to this dream. In some ways that's unfortunate because Duntov was technically correct in proposing a mid-engine Corvette, which would have given the car some very positive performance benefits. On the other hand, the Corvette has become more than the styling or technical dream of any one man. By the early 1970s, it had become the dream car of some 300,000 Corvette owners—and many more who hoped to own a Corvette in their lifetime. The car had already started down the path of becoming an icon and, in that sense, had gone beyond the point where one could make major changes in the concept without destroying the bond that had been built up over those first two decades.

By 1970, the only way that the Corvette could have gone forward as a mid-engine configuration would have been by management fiat. The Chevrolet Sales Department, sensitive to the Corvette market, realized that the enthusiasts would have to be dragged into a mid-engine car. Without a strong promise of improved sales, there was no reason to change an already successful formula. And that's the way the Corvette mid-engine story ended—with the sales saying no and styling and engineering having gone completely around the horn with a V-8 and then a

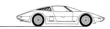

Wankel engine concept. When the Wankel engine failed, Chevrolet lost its only opportunity to make the mid-engine Corvette a reality.

GM made the correct decision in canceling the Wankel engine. At about that same time, Mazda introduced the rotary engine into all but one of its models, with the RX7 sports car coming several years later. The Japanese company virtually went out of business when the oil shock hit, as buyers flocked to more fuel-efficient piston engine cars. Mazda continued to develop the rotary engine for the RX7, but all their other products were switched over, in literally a wartime effort, to conventional piston engines, and they continue that way today.

Zora's dream for a mid-engine Corvette was manifested only in the prototypes: CERV I and CERV II, the aluminum mid-engine Corvette and the Four-Rotor Corvette (which was reengined and renamed the Aero-Vette). The CERVs were loaned to the Briggs Cunningham Automobile Museum in Costa Mesa, California, in order to get them out of sight and out of mind of the GM crusher. When the museum closed and sold off its cars, the CERVs were sold as well, in spite of GM's claim that it had title to them. Today the CERV I is in Mike Yager's Mid America Design Museum in Effingham, Illinois, and the CERV II is in the Indy Speedway Museum in Indianapolis, Indiana. The Four-Rotor, bi-fold-door Corvette is still owned by GM and resides in the National Corvette Museum in Bowling Green, Kentucky. Its four-rotor Wankel engine is there as well. This engine quickly deteriorated and, as there were no replacement parts to make the car run, the engine was replaced with a small-block V-8. The two-rotor Wankel-powered car that was built from a Porsche 914 was for a long time thought to be lost. The 914 that it was built from was one of the first German cars and not yet certified for the United States. It was brought into this country on a customs bond that required that it be taken out again, and it was. It has resurfaced, without its rotary engine, in England. The all-aluminum mid-engine Corvette found a home in Chevrolet R&D and is still displayed by GM on special occasions as part of the history of the Corvette.

My educated guess is that a rotary mid-engine Corvette would have been a disaster. It would have performed well but, subjected to the rigors of racing, it would have succumbed. The mid-engine Corvette program never lost the option of reverting to V-8 power, which would have produced devastatingly powerful two- and four-wheel-drive road cars. The V-8 powered, mid-engine car would have cost about the same as a front-engine Corvette as long as the critical powertrain components were avail-

able from high-volume production. The Toronado transaxle is no longer in production, but today GM has a four-speed transaxle—the 4T80E that is used with the Cadillac Northstar V-8 engine—that could be used for a two-wheel-drive mid-engine Corvette. This transaxle can handle an engine of about 300 hp with a redline of 6,000 rpm.

Finding an engine and an automatic transmission from high-volume production is crucial to the Corvette's hybrid strategy. As a result, the cost is driven by the low-volume components that define the Corvette architecture. These costs are the same whether the engine is in the front or the rear. We will never know if a Corvette as revolutionary as the mid-engine concept cars—V-8 or rotary-powered—would have been more successful than the Corvettes that we did produce over the next three decades.

As part of a competitive car evaluation we put together at the Milford Proving Grounds in 1980, I drove the aluminum mid-engine Corvette. Although it overheated quickly, I'm sure that it could have been developed into an excellent sports car. I saw the Four-Rotor Corvette run just once. Bill Mitchell had it trailered to Road America, where he drove it on a special one-car parade lap of the track. An embarrassment to GM, it smoked badly and barely ran. It was so low on power that we wondered if it would make it around the 4.5 mile track. The final embarrassment was that it didn't even have enough power to climb the ramp into the enclosed truck. Soon after, the engine was replaced with the V-8. In this form, I drove it at Laguna Seca in 1987 during a celebration of Chevrolet's racing successes. I had to drive it with the bi-fold gull-wing door open in order to keep myself from cooking in the California sun. There was no ventilation or air-conditioning, and the side glass was fixed.

An issue that was ignored by Styling as they hyped the mid-engine Corvette was how do you make a car with gull-wing doors into a convertible? At the time, 40 percent of Corvettes were still convertibles, a market the Sales Department would not ignore. The answer was, you didn't offer a convertible version. You couldn't even turn the gull-wing car into a T-top or a targa. Would Mitchell have decreed that this was the design if a mid-engine Corvette had been approved? If you go by his track record with the inverted air foil Sting Ray, you would have to say yes.

In the end, Zora sorely regretted that he never had the opportunity to bring a mid-engine Corvette to production. When he retired in 1975, several years after the mid-engine Wankel Corvette was killed, he still had regrets. In fact, Zora's advice to me upon assuming the role of Corvette Chief Engineer was; "Dave, you must do the mid-engine Corvette."

JOHN Z. DELOREAN AND THE DELOREAN DMC-12

John DeLorean, a supporter of the mid-engine Corvette when he was General Manager of Chevrolet, was elevated to Group Vice President and went through a personal crisis of his own. He ultimately left GM. A few years later he built his own rear-engine sports car. I'm convinced that DeLorean thought that the mid-engine Corvette was an opportunity missed. His gull-wing-door, stainless steel clad, V-6 sports car capitalized on the opportunity he saw. When driven, his car told a different story: It didn't sound, feel or drive like a mid-engine Corvette at all. He had reinvented the Corvair. DeLorean produced about 2,500 cars, ran out of money and had to quit.

The Corvette Ages Through the 1970s

5

THROUGH THE LATE 1960S AND EARLY 1970S, Corvette engineering's focus was on the mid-engine car. Appropriately, much energy was exerted in an effort to get management's approval for a radical redesign of the Corvette. While that effort was going on, the production car, which had begun life in 1963, was slowly aging and going out of style. It was quickly given a tamed-down Mako Shark II look in 1968. Then 1969 was consumed with trying to fix the problems that had been caused by the hasty body redesign of 1968.

Corvette performance reached its last high point in 1969–70. The small block was expanded to 350cid and given new life as the solid lifter LT1 engine rated at 370 gross horsepower (ghp) at 6,000 rpm. The big block was enlarged to 454 cubic inches and rated as high as 390 ghp. These were to be the last high-output, high-compression engines that a Corvette would see for the next 20 years.

In 1970, as the Development Engineer for the new 1970 1/2 Camaro, I was excited with the way the LT1 engine made the Camaro Z-28 come alive. The 350cid engine had pulling torque that the original 302cid Z-28 never had, and it had horsepower as well. I remember the LT1 Corvette as an even more rapacious car. While in Los Angeles on a press mission in 1970, I borrowed an LT1 Corvette convertible from the Chevrolet Public Relations pool. Driving that car, top down, all over the Los Angeles basin for a weekend was an experience I have never forgotten. The rough idle, the high-frequency clatter of the mechanical lifters and the unbridled sense of exhilaration as the car accelerated hard gave a sense of being in control of an almost uncontrollable beast. Too soon, cars like the 1970 LT1 Corvette would be gone, as environmental regulations descended on us.

The '70 LT1 Corvette would be the last high in small block performance for the next two decades.
Photo by Mike Mueller

Chevrolet also introduced the ZR1 option package in 1970. It included the LT1 engine, close-ratio M22 transmission, heavy-duty power brakes, transistorized ignition, aluminum radiator, special springs and shocks, and front and rear stabilizer bars. Apparently never merchandised, only 25 Corvettes with the ZR1 option packages were sold. The thirst of these engines for hard-to-find and expensive ultra-high-octane gasoline made them difficult to drive any distance in their day, and today it is virtually impossible to find fuel of sufficient octane. The fuel situation would have been just as bad had the still-born ZR2 option come to market with a 460 ghp 454cid engine.

PERFORMANCE BEGINS TO SLIDE

General Motors led the industry in support of low lead gasoline as the first step toward the unleaded gasoline that was required with catalytic converters. Initially, low lead meant low octane, so in 1971 GM reduced all their compression ratios to 9.0:1, to make their cars compatible with the new 91 research octane, low-lead gasoline. This particularly hurt the optional 11.0:1 compression ratio Corvette engines, which demanded the highest octane leaded fuel then available. Power increases with compression ratio, so these engines had been pushed until they demanded a diet of 103 octane leaded gasoline.

In 1971, GM also switched its engine ratings from gross horsepower (ghp) to net horsepower (nhp). Corvette enthusiasts, calibrated to the ghp scale and demanding bigger and bigger numbers as their bragging right, were confused and disappointed. They didn't know what "net" horsepower meant, but they did know that smaller numbers meant less power and fewer bragging rights. They didn't know it yet, but this was only the beginning of a decade-long decline in both Corvette's rated horsepower and in Corvette performance as well.

In the 1970-to-1971 transition, the LT1 went from 370 to 330 ghp, or as we would advertise, 275 nhp. By 1972, the last year for the LT1, it was detuned again to 255 nhp. The high-performance big-block LS6, rated at 425 ghp or 325 nhp, was gone within a year, leaving only the LS5, now rated at 270 nhp. However, installed performance, because it relied on torque and the area under the power curve, didn't fall as much as the peak horsepower numbers would suggest.

Pass-by noise laws—beginning in California—necessitated further engine redesigns. Mechanical lifter engines were out, as they were too noisy. Open-element air cleaners were also out, again they were too noisy.

GROSS VS. NET HORSEPOWER

Performance is the lifeblood of the Corvette. When Corvette enthusiasts get together, they talk in shorthand about the performance of their cars: "I have a 350, 370 horse," means I have a 350 cubic inch displacement, 370 gross horsepower engine. Through 1970, horsepower was always reported as gross horsepower because auto manufacturers were in a fierce power race and wanted to hype their products with the biggest numbers they could report.

Gross horsepower is measured according to a procedure defined by the Society of Automobile Engineers (SAE). Basically, the engine is run on an engine dynamometer with all power-robbing accessories removed. There is no air cleaner and no muffled exhaust system. The engine exhaust is dumped right into the room.

As the horsepower race heated up, the engineers started getting clever with the rules. They could get a higher "flash" reading if they started the engine cold and ran it quickly to the horsepower peak. They could get higher corrected power if they ran the engine in a test cell where the ambient temperature was elevated to 130° F and the humidity was 100 percent. The SAE procedure rightly corrects the actual reading to standard conditions for ambient temperature, pressure and humidity. Ignition timing and air-fuel ratio could be tweaked to achieve the maximum horsepower. When all this fiddling was over, the engine was installed in the car, and the accessories were hooked up, the intake had to suffer the indignities of breathing preheated underhood air through an air cleaner and the exhaust had to run through muffled pipes.

Starting in 1971, the advertised power was changed to "net" horsepower, a rating that better reflects the installed conditions. Net horsepower was still measured on a dynamometer, but the engine had all accessories in place, the intake and exhaust systems were complete, and the timing and air-fuel ratio were set as they would be in the car.

At the same time, automakers lowered compression ratios in order to make low lead gasoline work acceptably. The effect of all this was that we now had two different horsepower measurements that didn't correlate well with one another. When we did have data for both systems, the difference was about 20 percent. A reading of 370 ghp equalled no more than 300 nhp. When Corvette finally reported net horsepower in 1972, the low compression LT1 was rated at only 255 nhp.

When we introduced the new LT1 in 1992, we gave it its historically important designation only because it outperformed the original LT1, both on the dynamometer and in the car. A heavier car rated at 300 nhp would beat a lighter car rated at 370 ghp.

THE SHARED CORVETTE-CAMARO PLATFORM CONCEPT

My first direct involvement with Zora came in 1971. John DeLorean, Chevrolet's General Manager, was continuing his probe for a solution to the Corvette dilemma. The mid-engine Corvette was all but dead, although he and Zora were still fighting to keep it alive. The front engine car was costly to build and required a unique and dedicated assembly plant. DeLorean asked if the Corvette could be combined with the Camaro into a new platform that would benefit both cars. The Camaro would gain access to an independent rear suspension, and the Corvette would share an underbody and components and an assembly factory that would allow it to be built at a much lower cost. Zora was vehemently against even pursuing the idea. It would take focus off the mid-engine Corvette (and it might work). I was charged with making it work.

In the end it didn't work, and I demonstrated why. It all came down to engine placement. Even though both cars are front-engine, the Camaro, like most front-engine cars, had its engine located forward between the front wheels. In the Corvette, the engine is located almost twelve inches rearward and down, making it essentially a mid-front engine. This led to a lower cowl height, a longer wheelbase, a lower center of gravity, and a more rearward weight distribution. The Corvette would have been compromised in all these respects if it shared its platform with the Camaro. Conversely, to design a Camaro from the Corvette architecture would have produced a strange-looking, long-wheel-base pony car.

By the time catalytic converters were imposed in 1975, the most powerful Corvette engine was a quieted hydraulic lifter, single-exhaust L82, rated at 205 nhp. But the redesigns due to noise laws affected perceived performance more than actual engine performance. We never had to reduce the efficiency of the engine, other than to reduce some axle ratios. The cars were just so much quieter at full throttle that it seemed like they were way down on power.

A NEW ERA FOR CORVETTE

In addition to the end of the horsepower era, 1972 was the end of an era in another way: It was the last year for chrome bumpers. The 1973 Corvette was distinguished for its soft, dent-resistant front bumper. Thanks to the government, you could now drive your new Corvette into a wall at 5 mph without major damage. However, if you backed into a wall at the same speed, you'd sustain damage to both the chrome rear bumpers and the rear fascia—until the soft rear bumper was added for 1974.

Although 1975 was the end of an era for Corvette, it was also a new beginning. Midway through the model year, on December 31, 1974, Zora

TRAINING FOR CHANGE

Starting in July 1973, my family and I spent a year in Boston. Chevrolet sent me to a year-long study program at MIT (Massachusetts Institute of Technology) as a Sloan Fellow at the Sloan School of Management. The school had been endowed by Alfred P. Sloan, who had led GM through boom and bust cycles, and through the Second World War.

A mid-career experience like this is life-changing. I was thrust into a peer group consisting of 50 highly-competitive individuals, from both the public and private sectors, and from all over the world. First, we had to learn to cooperate and then we amazed ourselves with how much we could learn from one another. This was a third of the value of the program. The next third was the instruction, which was well taught in all areas of business management. The final third was the opportunity we had to interact with business and government leaders. Nearly every week we attended seminars with leaders who came to MIT. Just before Christmas of 1973, we traveled to New York and held a week-long series of seminars with leaders of the financial community. In early spring we traveled to Washington DC and met with Federal Government leaders.

Politically and socially, 1973-1974 was a wild time. The Arab oil embargo had caused a panic that led to long lines at gasoline stations; Spiro Agnew resigned as Nixon's Vice President; and John DeLorean was going through a mid-life crisis that would remove him from the ranks of GM management. During all this excitement, we had the good fortune of meeting Vice President Gerald Ford and Senator Ted Kennedy in seminars. My thesis, *The Automobile Industry and Government—Their Perception of One Another and the Influence This Has on Air Pollution Policy*, explored the hostile climate of vehicle emission regulation.

After I finished my thesis, our class and faculty took a three-week trip around the world. Using our seminar format, we met with business, financial and government leaders in London, Paris, Frankfurt, Moscow and Tokyo. Along the way, we traveled to West Berlin, crossed the Wall into East Berlin, flew on a Russian Illiutian-82 to Leningrad and took the midnight train to Moscow. We were so far north that by two o'clock in the morning it was light enough to see. We passed through birch forests and villages with mud streets and red-starred locomotives steaming up for their day's work. There was virtually no evidence of civilization until we reached the outskirts of Moscow. In Japan our bullet train sped us to Kyoto—at over 180 mph—to an older Japan that is now almost gone.

Arkus-Duntov retired and I took over as the Chief Engineer of the Corvette. We gave Zora a wonderful retirement party at the GM Training Center on the Tech Center site. Over 300 people came. It seemed as though everyone who was important at GM was at the party—from Ed Cole to Bill Mitchell. Zora's many friends in the automobile industry, racing, and the press made the evening a total tribute to Zora and the work he had done to make the Corvette a success.

THE NEW CHALLENGE

In the summer of 1974, I returned to Chevrolet Engineering with a Master of Science in Management from MIT and I was pumped. I had no idea what my next assignment would be, but I felt prepared for anything. When I arrived in July 1974, I was assigned to Zora Arkus-Duntov and was promoted to Staff Engineer. Bob Stempel, Chevrolet's Vice President and General Manager, also gave me a special assignment to work directly for him as he carried out his special assignment from Ed Cole: to manage the introduction of catalytic converters into all of GM's 1975 passenger cars and to make sure that they were safe under all conditions.

Early that spring, Zora and his Corvette team had been testing catalytic converter-equipped Corvettes in the western United States. On one test, the Corvette that Duntov was driving hadn't been filled with gas before they started up Pikes Peak, and the fuel gauge was reading empty as they approached the top. On the way down, Zora shut the engine off to conserve fuel and coasted much of the distance, engaging the engine when he needed its braking capabilities. When he got to the toll gate at the bottom of the mountain the car began to smolder and then burst into flames. Before they could find a fire truck, the car was a total loss.

Although Zora was not aware of it at the time, his car was not out of fuel. The long coast down the hill in gear with the ignition off pumped raw fuel and air through the already heated catalytic converter. The catalytic converter did its job—but one that it was never designed for—all the way down the mountain. Fed with fuel and air, it converted all the fuel's

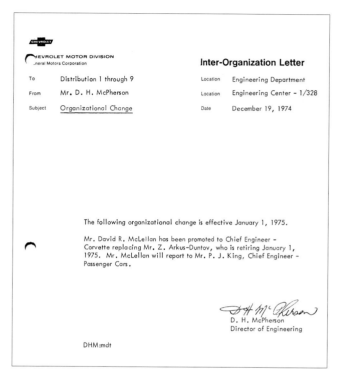

This letter from Don McPherson, Director of Engineering, announced my promotion to Chief Engineer—Corvette.

Dave McLellan Archives

energy into heat, reaching a bed temperature of well over 2,400° F, turning white hot in the process. Because the down-flow bed was hottest on top, the upper shell of the converter literally melted, exposing the car's underbody to the full radiant heat energy of the white-hot converter bed. Over the next few months we came to fully understand this failure mode, and recognized its rarity. We accepted it as an unlikely consequence of catalytic converters and moved on.

SALES STILL SOARED

A situation analysis of the Corvette at the beginning of 1975 would have acknowledged that the car was selling better than ever, even though the small block had been seemingly strangled by a catalytic converter and the big block had been dropped. Corvette performance had taken a big hit, but so had the performance of every other car sold in America. On top of this, customers were consistently complaining about the fit and finish coming out of the St. Louis assembly plant. But because Chevrolet was selling every Corvette it could build, the St. Louis plant didn't want to hear about complaints.

The C3 was a tough body design to build, having been literally thrown together late and implemented with inadequate resources. The plant built the bodies, but in order to make things fit, they kept adjusting their fixtures until the body parts were as much as 1/4 inch to 1/2 inch out of position. The design called for bonding the front and rear fenders together just below their peak line and then grinding some 15 feet of seams to produce a finished surface. These seams introduced grinding irregularities and porosity into a highly visible area.

The paint process included 300° F bake temperature, which brought many body imperfections to the surface.

Photo by P. H. Rezanka

Painters dealt with these surface problems to the best of their abilities but, at the line speed they were running the Corvette plant, the 300° F bake temperature required for the lacquer paint job left the body with craters and pits, particularly in the bond seam area. The plant would sometimes put repair on top of repair until frustration set in and the car was finally shipped.

In the mid-1970s, the dealers were repainting lots of Corvettes. You could even buy a Corvette with only a primer coat. Supposedly, this was to allow the customer to have the car painted a special color without having to first strip off the factory color. However, I suspect that more often than not this was done out of frustration due to the quality of the factory paint job.

On a positive safety note, 1975 also saw the introduction of the first rubber bladder fuel cell in the Corvette.

FIGHTING FOR SURVIVAL

Chevrolet financial was convinced that the Corvette was losing money. They were a strong voice from within the division to not spend any more money than necessary on the Corvette. So to get the Corvette future started again, we raised its price. Over the next nine years, accounting for inflation, we doubled the price of the car. This ultimately hurt sales, but we had little choice: The car's very future was at stake. We were walking a tightrope between not raising the price and selling more Corvettes, or raising the price sufficiently to satisfy financial's demand for profitability—in which case, sales would dwindle.

By 1975, Corvette convertible sales had dropped to 12 percent of production, so the convertible was targeted for cancellation. Since Corvette coupes, with their removable T-tops, were open-air, it was easy to

THE FIRST HATCHBACK

Around 1973, Duntov prototyped a hatchback version of the 1968 car, with the gas tank moved forward right behind the seats. This gave the car a small but easily accessible deep trunk space, but eliminated the contiguous passenger space right behind the seats, and made the cockpit configuration much more like the mid-engine cars. This interesting proposal was deemed to have too high an investment cost and was killed by the financial department.

The experimental hatchback Corvette was an interesting concept that would have to wait until the 1982 model year to become a reality.
Dave McLellan Archives

'76 STEERING WHEEL

When I took over the Corvette, we were starved for capital to do anything. To their credit, the engineers often found ways of getting things done and saving sufficient costs to pay for them. One such project was an elegant leather-wrapped steering wheel for the 1976 Corvette. There was so much cost associated with the 1975 brushed stainless steel, three-spoke wheel that Bob Vogelei, our Chief Body Engineer, was able to commission a completely leather-wrapped wheel that cost enough less to pay for its tooling.

In a cost-cutting meeting, Chevrolet's Engineering Director, Don McPherson, discovered that we were working on a new steering wheel for the Corvette. Don directed me to save even more money by substituting the four-spoke molded-vinyl Vega steering wheel. If you've ever wondered how this cheap steering wheel found its way into Chevrolet's most expensive car, now you know. Fortu-

nately, the economy turned around the next year and we were able to sneak in a steering wheel that wouldn't embarrass Corvette drivers.

In a fit of cost-cutting we were forced to use the four-spoke molded-vinyl Vega steering wheel on the '76 Corvette.

Photo by Mike Mueller

rationalize canceling the convertible. As it turned out, the cancellation allowed a more efficient production of coupes, so the production output of the plant increased, and this in turn boosted sales.

CELEBRATING CORVETTE

The 25th anniversary of the Corvette was upon us with the 1978 model. It prompted us to do what we could to respond to this seminal moment. We had figured out a much lower-cost way of achieving the shape, if not the function, of the hatchback—with a fastback. The fastback left the gas tank in its rear position and gave access to the luggage only from the inside. However, it dramatically increased the luggage space and also gave the cockpit a more open feeling with that big piece of glass behind the seats.

To celebrate the 25th anniversary, Jerry Palmer—who had become Design Staff's Corvette designer—came up with a silver anniversary model that was finished in silver with red stripes. At the last minute, Chevrolet decided that the Corvette would be its entry for Indianapolis 500 Pace car. Fortunately, we had just completed a session in the wind tunnel exploring strategies that would reduce lift and drag for both improved high-speed stability and better fuel economy. The drag coefficient (Cd) of the Corvette was over 0.50 when we started. Adding a front chin and a rear deck spoiler brought the Cd down to 0.42 and reduced front and rear lift as well. The all black Corvette Indy Pace car, with its prominent front air dam and its tall rear-deck spoiler, was the final result.

Chevrolet argued incessantly about how many of these pace cars should be built. The original intention was to build a limited edition, and quantities of 1,500 and 2,500 were considered. In the end, after consulting with the Legal Department, it was decided that a pace car should to be offered to every American and Canadian Chevrolet dealer. That meant that Chevy had to build 6,502 pace cars.

I never understood why the pace car excited the public beyond all expectations. When it was announced, late in the fall of 1977, a feeding frenzy for Indy pace car Corvettes ensued. Most pace car programs are lucky to sell 200 replicas. Here we were with people breaking past security to personally deliver checks to Chevrolet's General Manager in hopes of getting on the list to

Wind tunnel testing helped drop the Corvette's drag coefficient (Cd) from 0.50 to 0.42 while spoilers reduced front and rear lift as well.

Dave McLellan Archives

buy one. We heard stories of pace cars going for several times the sticker price, which made little sense, but feeding frenzies seldom do. When the flag dropped on May 26, 1978, for the start of the Indianapolis 500 mile race, interest in the pace car fell off precipitously, and the speculators who had been instrumental in driving the market to dizzying heights, were now confronted with pace cars selling at a discount.

Just as the Indy pace cars became startlingly popular, so too did automatic transmissions, which had earned the original Corvette such derision. Starting in the late 1950s, when the manual transmission was first available in the Corvette without any restrictions, manual sales quickly climbed to about 75 percent of production. This continued in the 1960s until 1968, when the two-speed Powerglide was replaced with the three-speed Turbo Hydramatic. The Turbo Hydramatic was a superior automatic transmission and, along with a shift in driver preferences, enabled the automatic to become the dominant transmission, with 75 percent of Corvette sales.

As part of the 1978 Indy Pace Car program, 6,502 replicas were built. Less practical than the hatchback, this fixed rear window fastback was approved as the 25th anniversary model for the 1978 Corvette.
Dave McLellan Archives

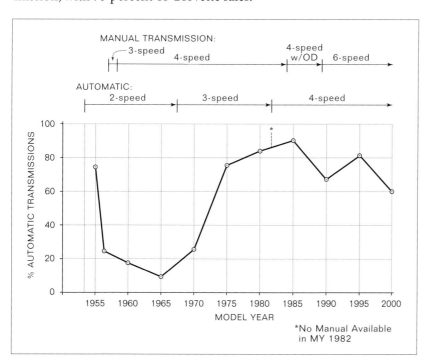

Replacing the two-speed Powerglide with the three-speed Turbo Hydramatic caused a dramatic shift in buyer preference. Over the next several years, the Turbo Hydramatic became the dominant Corvette transmission.

77

ENGINES AND TRANSMISIONS IN TRANSITION

Up to 1974, when the emissions issue intervened, the split between manual and automatic transmissions was determined totally by buyer preference. The 1975 Corvette's catalytic converter was our next response to the ever-tightening emission standards. Due to the stringent standards, and with the primitive emission control technology available to us, it was difficult to certify the manual transmission at all. Compounding this, Chevrolet had so many different engine families to certify that priority demanded that the automatic transmission L48 be certified first. Only after the start of production—when we were assured that we had a car to sell—would the engine certification guys go back and certify the automatic L82 and the manual transmissions for both the L48 and the L82.

The high demand for Corvettes continued during this period—the late 1970s—and left the dealers starved for cars. The uncertainty of ever getting a manual transmission Corvette quickly taught the dealers not to order them at all. At best, the dealers could fill their last orders of the model year with manual transmission Corvettes. As a result, manual transmission sales became sporadic and were suppressed to approximately half the level they should have been if buyer preference had been the only determining factor.

In 1974, Chevrolet had exited the manual transmission business, and had turned it over to Borg-Warner, which was running its production line exclusively for the Corvette. Demand was so low that, as the 1980s dawned, the plant was running way below capacity—and for only half the year. Borg-Warner was so poorly treated as a supplier, by our emission certification program, that the company finally informed us that it was not going to supply manual transmissions to Corvette after 1981. The entire 1982 model year and the first full year of the 1984 model went by before we recovered with a new source for the manual transmission.

As the emission regulations continued to tighten, 1980 was the last year for the 230 nhp L82. In California we shared a 180 nhp, 305cid engine with other Chevrolets. If

TESTING THE COOLING SYSTEM

As we continued to develop the 1978 Corvette through the summer of 1976, we spent several days in the heat of Death Valley testing the cooling and air-conditioning system. On a typical test day we would repeatedly drive from the valley floor at Stovepipe Wells (at sea level) until we crested the 4,000 foot pass that led into the Panamint Valley. Going up, we started in 120° F ambient and climbed at a steady 60 mph toward the pass with the passenger taking data continuously. The run was full of curves and large amplitude swells that could be driven easily at 60 mph. There was so little traffic that we were seldom hindered during a test run. On the downhill return run we were supposed to cool the car down so it could be worked on for the next run. Being invariably bored, from test-driving all day long, we made the return run as fast as we could. Cresting several of these swells at 90 mph launched the car airborne for several hundred feet. As long as we launched the car straight, and held the steering wheel level while we were air borne, the road came up to meet us with little fuss.

On one downhill return we came up behind a Cadillac sedan full of family. It looked like a dad and mom in the front and children and grandparents in the back, with boxes loaded on the package shelf. When we came to a passing zone I pulled out to overtake, but the driver sped up and I backed off. So here we were, going downhill at over 80 mph behind a Cadillac. We knew what we were doing, but did he? On the next swell we watched the Cadillac go airborne with passengers and boxes floating at zero gs. When it returned to earth the driver braked hard and we sped past.

1980 wasn't bad enough, in 1981 we had to develop an even more restrictive catalytic converter and design a computer-controlled carburetor. This dual-bed catalytic converter oxidized hydrocarbons and CO and reduced nitrous oxides all in the same unit. The carburetor was a strange but pragmatic marriage of the old analog carburetor technology and the new digital fuel injection technology. It was largely unchanged in its operation, although it was calibrated to run lean under all cruise conditions. An oxygen sensor measured the residual oxygen in the exhaust and, through the computer program, told a single pulsed injector in the carburetor to add enough fuel to achieve the stoichiometric ideal air-fuel ratio, which is the "sweet spot" for minimum emissions.

This engine would prove to be our las low in performance (except for California), at 190 nhp, and also a crude beginning for the technology that would ultimately make it possible for us to recover all of our performance loss. With this engine, the 1981 car was the slowest Corvette in about two decades.

The first small step in recovering from 1981 was the use of two throttle body injectors for 1982. These were mounted on a plate and fed a single-plane open manifold. The manifold was inspired by a Trans Am racing manifold that had been used with two 4-bbl carburetors on the 302cid engine a decade earlier. We quickly and naively committed to the single-plane manifold and compact injectors because we saw that it gave us an opportunity to lower the hood line of the all-new, next-generation Corvette by almost two inches. We soon realized what a bad idea it was, but it was too late to back out, so the engine guys had to make it work.

Our first problem was injector sticking. Cadillac solved the problem for us before the 1982 Corvette reached production, but not before the 1981 Cadillac—with cylinder cutoff and the same injectors—shut down a number of customers. Their innovative, fuel-economy-improving cylinder shutoff, called 8-6-4, took the rap, becoming known as the "8-6-4-0," for what was really an injector problem. If each injector had fueled half of the engine, a stuck injector would only shut down that half of the engine, and the car could limp home with four cylinders firing. Unfortunately, both injectors fueled a common manifold, so the result of one failed injector was to double the air-fuel ratio to 28:1—a mixture too lean to burn.

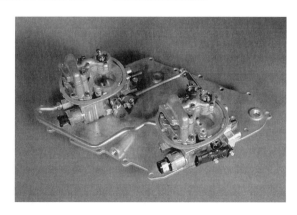

For 1982, Corvette received a new throttle body fuel injection system.
Dave McLellan Archives

Our other problem was with the single-plane manifold itself. Carburetor manifolds for V-8 engines had evolved as tall and complex distribution pipes in an attempt to minimize the air-fuel ratio variations that occurred between cylinders. Why were we so naive as to think that we could flatten the manifold without penalty? The flat Trans Am-style manifold gave such poor cylinder distribution that we had to compensate with extra fuel. When we showed the fuel-injected 1982 model to the press, we pointed to the racing manifold and fuel injection as the identifiable reasons for the horsepower increase to 200 nhp. In reality, the greater power was due to the new low-back-pressure underfloor monolith catalytic converter. But who would equate catalytic converters with improving performance?

The other real performance gain for the 1982 came from the introduction of the 700 R4 four-speed automatic transmission. Its 3.07:1 first gear gave 21 percent more starting ratio than the three-speed it replaced, and it also had a 0.70:1 fourth gear for cruising. In that first year, because the transmission was not programmed to hold itself in fourth gear at full throttle, the 700 R4 was limited to third gear for top-speed running. This meant that top speed was held back to an rpm-limited 128 mph. For the 1984 model, the automatic transmission was modified to run in fourth gear at full throttle, giving the new car a top speed of just over 140 mph with only 205 hp.

It was surprising that our customers didn't desert us during this period. The Corvette was growing old, with some grace and dignity, but it was definitely growing old. Year by year our performance was degraded from the 1970 high point. Fortunately, the competition was still very weak, and the Corvette had a strong "flywheel-effect" in its sales performance. In 1979, our best sales year ever, we sold 53,807 coupes.

I've often wondered if we would have been better off with real head-to-head competition. Chevrolet thrived on its product rivalry with Ford in other markets. A similar rivalry could have done wonders for the Corvette. Selling all they could build, with no real competition in sight, Chevrolet was lulled into a false sense of security. You don't need a new car when you're already selling all you can manufacture. If there is no market pressure to improve performance—don't bother—meet emissions and move on. Customers may complain about quality, but they're still buying them, so what's the problem?

I feel I should apologize for bringing up the dark side of the Corvette, but I don't think you can understand why we let ourselves slip so far if you don't understand our mindset. We just got sloppy when we were the only game in town, and there was no competition prodding us. I personally think that competition would have changed everything for the better, and stimulated the organization to move much faster. Racing creates the same kind of stimulus. You win or you lose. Winning is everything; losing feels awful.

INCREMENTAL IMPROVEMENT

The same period that saw us losing performance and gaining emissions restrictions also saw us facing a major tire problem. Firestone was the dominant tire supplier for Corvette and had taken us into the steel-belted radial age in 1973. A processing problem with the steel wire in the belt of the tire caused Firestone a major warranty problem that ultimately led to a recall of all their steel-belted radial tires in 1977. Any road hazard, such as a nail or a sharp rock, that cut the tread and exposed the steel belt, initiated a progressive corrosion of the steel wire in the belt and ultimately led to tread separation. A monumental recall, with lots of unhappy and vocal customers, not only put Firestone in financial trouble but it let their rival get its nose under the tent.

Firestone's plight gave Goodyear its opening. The 1978 Corvette was delivered with Goodyear tires only. This started a long and productive relationship with Goodyear that took Corvette down in tire aspect ratio, from 70, to 60, to 50, to 45, to 40, and even to 35, with the ZR-1 rear tire. The aspect ratio is the ratio of height to width in the tire cross-section. A 35 aspect tire has a section height that is 35 percent of the width of the tire. As the profile of the tires became lower, we needed to ensure that they continued to be safe at the Corvette's increasing top-speeds. Prior to 1984, the Corvette had been loosely speed-limited, by the axle ratio and engine rpm, to around 130 mph. But the 1984 Corvette was speed-limited only

---

AUDI BEATS CORVETTE; CORVETTE BEATS AUDI

It was in this same period that competitors began taking potshots at us because of our vulnerability. Audi, which was importing the small Audi Fox sedan, took a shot at us with their ad "Audi Fox beats Corvette". They actually ran a competitive slalom test between a Porsche 911 Turbo, an Audi Fox, and a Corvette. The test was essentially *Road & Track* magazine's seven-cone, 100-foot-spacing slalom. As they ran the test, their skilled drivers were able to achieve the highest speeds with the Porsche Turbo; then came the Audi Fox; and last the Corvette. The results were initially reported in print and TV ads as "Turbo Porsche beats Audi Fox beats Corvette" but they soon fell into just saying "Audi Fox beats Corvette."

Beating Corvette was not going to get many Corvette intenders to switch to the Audi Fox, since the two customer bases had such different priorities, but it was embarrassing to Corvette owners to be bested. Our response, as Chevrolet, was to do nothing. Ignore it and it might go away. It didn't—they were persistent.

Actually, a shorter and narrower car like the Fox has an advantage in a slalom: It doesn't have to move as far laterally and it's easier to rotate, so we weren't sure who would win if we decided to challenged the test. Finally, our good friend, Dick Guldstrand, got mad and gathered up some of his race car driver buddies and reran the test with cameras rolling. Switching drivers and cars often, his drivers went faster and faster with both the Corvette and the Audi Fox, and the Corvette was always a little bit faster. They shared this result with Audi and the ads ceased.

by engine power, and topped 140 mph. Beginning with the 1984 model, we would certify our tires to the new top speed.

One of the projects that Zora had under way when I arrived at Corvette in 1974 was an aluminum wheel. It had been several years since Corvette offered an aluminum wheel. We quit selling aluminum wheels because the suppliers wouldn't make them round enough and the castings were too porous to hold air. There still seemed to be some customer interest in an alloy wheel, although we had no way of gauging the extent of it, and had to resort to guessing. The aluminum wheel project had gone through many starts and stops with potential suppliers, and finally landed with a subsidiary of Kelsey-Hayes in Mexico City. They met our standards and put us back into the aluminum wheel business.

Once introduced, the aluminum wheel (RPO YJ8) turned into our worst nightmare. Everyone wanted it. Marketing had predicted a 10 percent penetration for the RPO. How could they have known otherwise? The dealers immediately began ordering them on all their Corvettes and then found that over 90 percent of their orders were rejected because there were so few wheels available. This was still the time of high demand for Corvettes, and dealers were fighting to get them. A rejected order cost dealers their positions in the order queue and soon taught them not to order alloy wheels, so demand plummeted and Chevrolet backed down on their order to Kelsey-Hayes for more capacity. It was over two years before manufacturing capacity began to catch up with the demand for aluminum wheels.

We were still soldiering on with the third-generation Corvette (C3) when, early in 1979, we were finally turned loose to define the long overdue, latest all-new Corvette. This was still not a "go"; it was a "let's think about it." Styling kept the Four-Rotor Corvette in drivable condition, to remind the staff of where it had been and where it should be going. We kept the aluminum mid-engine prototype tucked away in Chevrolet R&D. We started a design project in R&D to define ways of improving the layout and function of the front mid-engine car and to support Jerry Palmer at Styling, who was already starting to sketch the future Corvette. Once under way, we defined several projects that could be transferred to the current-production Corvette. We handed them off to the engineering team, who could then introduce them into production on the current car, and gain design and manufacturing experience.

The Corvette aluminum wheel project went through many starts and stops, finally landing with a subsidiary of Kelsey-Hayes in Mexico City.

Dave McLellan Archives

The Chevrolet Warren plant wanted to discontinue producing the Corvette axle. This was becoming typical of many of our suppliers. The Corvette component base was so old that our parts were no longer shared, or even related to, the high-volume low-cost parts used by other cars. Dana, a major supplier of axles, was selected to supply its 8-1/2 inch Model 44 axle in a new Corvette housing. We asked Dana to make the housing in aluminum instead of cast iron, which was a new experience for both of us. This proved to be an excellent first project because it gave us experience with alloy castings in a high-stress, high-corrosion environment.

The higher coefficient of thermal expansion and greater elasticity of aluminum, compared to iron, made this application challenging. The axle housing must be able to maintain a precise relationship between the pinion and the ring gear, in order to produce an accurate and quiet gear mesh yet still be able to take the gear-separating loads of a Woodward Avenue hole shot without yielding.

The project gave us an opportunity to instrument the driveline to measure torque under various loading conditions. The results surprised us. A smoothly executed, manual transmission hole shot generated a peak dynamic torque no more than 130 percent of what one would predict from the engine output torque multiplied by the first-gear ratio. But a poorly executed, clutch dumping hole shot turned out to be the worst thing you could do to the driveline. Dynamic torque values during the moment of engagement were three times the predicted value. It was a testament to the Corvette's driveline that it had been designed to take such abuse.

We developed the axle to take this abuse, but we also got to thinking about how we could reduce such loads without degrading the system. We reasoned that if we could make all hole shots behave like a good one, we would have the answer. Controlling the engagement rate with an orificed, hydraulically-actuated clutch was the answer. Although the 1984 Corvette would have such a clutch, the 1980 Corvette would have to survive with its mechanical clutch linkage.

The aluminum alloys used in cars are highly corrosion-resistant until they come in contact with a material that has a higher galvanic potential, such as steel. Add an electrolyte, and the aluminum becomes the sacrificial anode, with devastating consequences. Developing the proper coatings for the steel fasteners was an important learning process in the progression toward the extensive use of alu-

Dana adapted its 8-1/2 inch Model 44 axle to an aluminum Corvette-specific housing.
Dave McLellan Archives

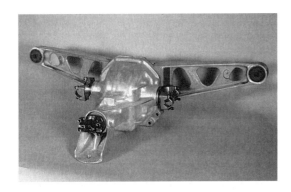

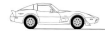

minum in the chassis. The aluminum Dana axle was thoroughly tested and put into production with the 1980 Corvette.

When I took charge of the Corvette, I found engineers who prided themselves on their thorough durability test program and the resulting robustness of the car. However, we had reports of customer problems that we couldn't reconcile with our durability testing. Disc brake caliper corrosion had become endemic in the field, even spawning a cottage industry which rebuilt calipers with stainless steel sleeves. It took us a while to understand the problem, but it taught us a valuable lesson.

The cause of the problem was traced to an outer boot seal—of which there were sixteen—that could leak, allowing moisture to enter and corrode the cylinder wall of the caliper, outboard of the piston's primary hydraulic seal. Brake pad wear was taken up by the piston and its primary seal moving outboard across the now corroded and pitted region of the cylinder. The primary hydraulic brake fluid-to-air seal was being asked to maintain its seal integrity against the pitted surface. Actually, it still did a pretty fair job, but even minute quantities of air entering the hydraulic system were sufficient to give the car a soft brake pedal.

We next found that the outer boot seal's metal retainer was not being pressed into place as firmly as originally intended. That was easy to fix. But even when it was installed correctly there was still a possibility of moisture penetrating the metal-to-metal interface between the retainer and the cylinder bore. Delco Moraine redesigned the molded rubber boot to totally encapsulate the retainer in rubber, and added a rubber lip that would bottom out as the retainer was pressed into place.

The lesson for us was that the aggressive stress-testing of a few cars, as important as it was, wasn't going to find problems that were characterized by low probability of occurrence, or worst of all, easy driving and long months of storage. Corvette's high performance disc brakes have so much capacity that normal driving will not heat the brakes enough to boil off the moisture. When the car is then parked for long months, the corrosion can progress, and subsequent pad wear will produce noticeable symptoms.

In a similar way, after deciding to continue the use of the U-jointed half shaft as a rear suspension member in the next generation Corvette, we started a

A valuable lesson was learned from diagnosing and solving brake caliper corrosion caused by the outer boot seal.

Drawing by Dave McLellan

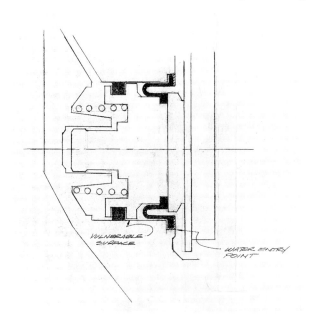

review to thoroughly requalify the reliability of the U-joint. With three drive shafts between the transmission and the rear wheels, the Corvette uses six U-joint assemblies and 24 needle-bearing cups. Each of these cups is sealed and lubricated for life. Every so often we would find a U-joint cup that was dry and rusted, and with all of its needles missing. Fortunately, the U-joint, itself, is such a robust component that even in this state it continued to work, while giving the driver lots of clunking and roughness. But, how does just one out of the 24 cups become afflicted with such a condition in the first place? This had the makings of a good mystery.

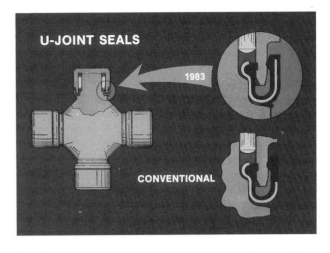

A new seal design solved the problem of dry and rusty needle-bearing cups.
Dave McLellan Archives

The "whodunit" failure mechanism starts with the fact that grease, as thick and heavy as it may seem, floats on water. The needle-bearing cup, spinning around inside the U-joint, is essentially a small centrifuge, pulling everything inside the cup toward the bearings. In the case of a failed seal, water leaks into the cup. The grease seems so viscous and insoluble, one would expect it to be able to protect the bearing. However, since water is even denser than grease, and because the centrifuge is exerting a force several-hundred times gravity, the water is pulled toward the bearings and the grease floats away. Ultimately, the joint is left without any grease, and corrosion siezes it up.

The solution was again in the seal design. The seal had originally been designed with a stamped metal retainer that pressed into the lip of the cup. Any imperfection in this metal-to-metal interface allowed moisture to enter the greased cup. So, again, encapsulating the metal retainer in rubber provided a solid contact and eliminated the possibility of a leak.

A NEW HOME FOR CORVETTE

Throughout the late 1960s, the motor divisions of GM had considerable autonomy. They each made their own engines, and assembled their own cars, most of them in concert with Fisher Body, which provided all of the company's passenger car bodies. However, Chevrolet built its light trucks and the Corvette without any input from Fisher Body. In the early 1960s, GM started a separate Assembly Division (GMAD), which initially assembled a few Buick, Oldsmobile, and Cadillac models. In the process, GMAD assumed responsibility for the content from both the motor divisions and Fisher Body.

There was a continuing power struggle, with the motor divisions and Fisher Body on one side, and the more efficient GMAD on the other. Over several years, the motor divisions and Fisher Body lost ground, and were ultimately reduced to running only their home plants. In 1971, the St. Louis assembly plant was taken over entirely by GMAD.

By the late 1970s, GMAD was planning a complete renovation of the paint shop, in order to meet newly imposed EPA emission regulations. Unfortunately, the St. Louis plant was landlocked in an older section of the city. Such a major renovation would be impossible without shutting down production for a year. The only way to avoid suspending production was to build a new paint shop while the old one continued to run. To make the plan work something had to give, and GMAD decided that Corvette production had to move.

GMAD found an empty 550,000 square-foot factory in Bowling Green, Kentucky, that had been used by Chrysler's Air Temp division to make air-conditioners. GM's manufacturing arm took it over and expanded it into a one-million square-foot, air-conditioned facility with a three-story paint

The Bowling Green plant required extensive reconstruction to be ready to assemble the Corvette.

Dave McLellan Archives

shop. During construction, all the sides were removed from the building and the roof was stabilized with diagonal cables. The paint shop required excavation under the entire north end of the building, which was resting on bedrock. The bedrock was "surgically" blasted to a depth of 20 feet, leaving the local portions of the roof supported on temporary rock pillars.

The building having been finished, and the production line installed, the first Corvette rolled off the line June 1, 1981. For the next three months, both plants produced Corvettes. Then on August 1, 1981, Corvette production at St. Louis ceased, forever. It is ironic that the St. Louis renovation never took place. Bowling Green was not even finished when GMAD made the decision to close the St. Louis plant and replace it with the new "green field" assembly plant at Wentzville, Missouri, about 70 miles to the north. In the end, Corvette was the winner, with its own state-of-the-art assembly factory.

In 1981, Corvette, with GM's Inland Division, introduced the largest, single weight savings I have ever witnessed. A seven-pound fiberglass spring replaced a 48-pound steel spring. We planned to use this emerging

fiberglass leaf spring technology at both ends of the new Corvette, but needed to prove its function and reliability in an application where we had a fall-back option. So, we developed it first as a direct replacement for the steel leaf spring of the existing 1981 Corvette.

It took Lockheed Aircraft Company's development of analysis techniques, that characterize the laminated graphite-filament structure of a graphite-epoxy component, to make our fiberglass spring design calculation possible. When we were through

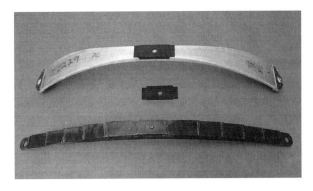

Fiberglass leaf springs replaced the steel components for the 1981 Corvette.
Dave McLellan Archives

we had a spring that was one-seventh the weight of the steel spring that it replaced. The fiberglass spring also had dramatically better fatigue life and would not corrode. Del Schroeder, of GM Manufacturing Development (MD), has to be given credit as the "spark plug" that got us started. Dr. Gordon Warner, a member of the Corvette Chassis Design Group who had also been in MD, brought analysis and manufacturing together to make a working spring practical. Pat De Vincent, of Inland Division, led the team that developed the manufacturing processes that would make the spring.

Pat wore out all of Inland's fatigue-testing machines in the process of thoroughly testing the fiberglass spring prototypes. These machines were designed to test steel leaf springs, which would fail in as few as 200,000 full-amplitude cycles. The fiberglass spring breezed past 200,000 cycles. So, in order to understand how the fiberglass spring would ultimately fail, we continued the test, finally giving up at 2 million cycles with the spring

A FIBERGLASS SPRING PRIMER

A spring stores energy, through the action of being bent or twisted. That's all a spring does. The amount of energy that can be stored is limited by the tensile strain that can be safely imposed on the outer surface. In the Corvette's leaf spring the center of each leaf is essentially unstressed and is going along for the ride, adding weight but contributing little to storing strain energy.

With a spring made of steel, only the most highly-stressed surface matters in an engineering calculation, because steel is isotropic—it has the same strength in all directions. On the other hand, a spring made of glass filaments and epoxy resin is anisotropic, and behaves in a much more complex way. The glass filaments have greater elasticity, allowing them to stretch 30 times more than steel, for a given load. This makes it possible to design a leaf spring without all of the separate leaves. The tensile strength of the glass filaments is so high that it is no longer the controlling parameter. In fact, a fiberglass spring designed to the tensile limit of the glass fibers will fail in shear. So, with fiberglass, the design calculation is based on the tensile and shear strains in the epoxy resin.

still working normally. At this level of stress, the springs often showed some fraying or delamination of the outer fibers, but we could not measure the effect of this on spring rate or load capacity.

Our final uncertainty with the fiberglass leaf spring was the car environment. Our physical chemists told us that filament glass was notorious for absorbing water and losing strength, and that the epoxy resin was good for no more than 220° F before it would start to lose strength. Extensive car tests ensued, and gave us the assurance that there were, in fact, no hidden failure modes. The spring proved to be a total success. The Inland team ultimately learned to make the springs with such efficiency and at such low cost that they could compete with conventional coil springs. The fiberglass leaf spring is now used in millions of GM cars and trucks each year.

From within the GM manufacturing organization, the Corvette is often seen as little more than an annoyance, because of its low sales volume. But the Corvette offers the engineering and manufacturing teams the opportunity to learn how to make new ideas work at low volume, without having to commit to impossible cost and performance goals even before they start. This is the right use of the Corvette.

CHANGING OF THE GUARD

As seemingly wrecked as the Corvette program was in 1975, the engineering team that Zora had trained was still largely in place in the early 1980s. They would be an invaluable asset to getting an all-new Corvette started. Bob Vogelei, since joining the Corvette to clean up the 1963, had led the body and structure team. Bob stayed with the Corvette through the finish of the all-new 1984 program, when he was tapped for a bigger assignment in Chevrolet. Bob was supported by Ron Burns and Paul Huzzard. Ron, a strong production engineer, would design the structure of the 1984 car and develop much of its manufacturing process. Ron would then go on to do the body structure for the newest-generation Camaro and Firebird. Paul took the interior and, with the 1984 in production, graduated to Bob Vogelei's job as Corvette's Chief Body Engineer. He later moved on and, in a recent assignment, was the body chief for GM's aluminium-bodied electric car, the Impact. Gib Hufstader, who cobbled together two rotary engines to make the Four-Rotor Corvette, continued as our powertrain systems engineer. Gib later played a major role in the LT5 development. Walt Zetye, Zora's long-time chassis engineer, was to stay with us until we started the 1984, when he was tapped for a major

chassis assignment in the Truck Group. Ash Torosion, who had designed the original Grand Sport chassis, stayed with us and took responsibility for the new Corvette's brakes.

Before Bill Mitchell retired in 1978, he promoted Henry Haga, who had designed the Four-Rotor Corvette, and sent him to head the Opel design studio in Russelsheim, Germany. Mitchell handpicked Jerry Palmer, who had trained under Haga on the Four-Rotor Corvette, to lead the production studio that would do the next all-new Corvette.

Joe Pike, who was the Chevrolet Sales Department champion for the Corvette, had retired in 1978. We were now supported in the Chevrolet Planning Department by Bob Emerick and Don Runkle. Emerick would solve the profitability dilemma, by arguing successfully for an increase in price. And Don would oversee the 1984 Corvette throughout the entire production process, from its planning stages, to its approval at top of the corporation, and on through the Product Policy Group reviews. Later, as Chief Engineer of Chevrolet, Don would be a leading advocate for the LT5 engine and the ZR-1.

As trained and ready as our styling and engineering teams were, the Corvette cabal within GM's top management had retired by 1978, leaving us with no visible support at the top. Cars like the Corvette are of little importance to the big picture of a corporation like GM with over 100 billion dollars in annual sales. And, to many, the Corvette was just another model that rose or fell on its sales performance. In reality, GM and the Corvette needed each other. The Corvette gave a lot back to GM, in the vision and reach it allowed the stylists and engineers. It also served as a constant reminder of what could be achieved if GM really stretched itself.

Shortly after Zora retired, Ed Cole, by then President of GM, also retired. Three years later in 1978, Bill Mitchell, who had been the head of GM Styling and was responsible for giving the Corvette the style and flair that had helped to turn it into an American icon, retired as well.

Even though Ed Cole had different priorities as the President of GM, he was a consummate engineer. As he rose to the top he never let go of his hobby—engineering. In his last years, he was the de facto chief engineer for all of GM. After the demise of the rotary engine program, he devoted his final days to, among many other things, finding a solution to the problem of putting a catalytic converter in all GM cars. Ed Cole's retirement left a great gulf in engineering management within the company. He had been such a dominant personality that there was no one who

could quite fill his shoes. GM fell into chaos, engineering by committee, as its response to Ed Cole's retirement.

Bill Mitchell, in his last year with GM before retirement, produced a clay model which was based on the 1977 Corvette and had wide strips of chrome outlining all of its feature lines. The chrome outlined the car's windows and doors, and highlighted the fenders. Was he seriously re-exploring chrome or was he simply making the point with corporate management that you could not continue to refresh the Corvette and expect it to go on forever? Bill never explained himself, so we will never know if he was serious or simply making a point.

With all of the changes within the company, we knew that the 1982 Corvette would signify the end of an era. So, we designed a Collector's Edition as a final tribute to the Sting Ray and Mako Shark II generations of Corvette. This car was produced as a hatchback, painted a special gold color with a graded tone, was gold striped, and had a leather interior. This car not only celebrated the end of an era, it signaled that a new era was about to begin.

The 1982 Collector's Edition was the first production Corvette to have a hatchback.

Drawing by Dave McLellan

The Next Generation Corvette

6

BY THE LATE 1970s, TO THE AUTOMOTIVE PRESS and to many of the Corvette enthusiasts who were watching us, it surely seemed as if Corvette Engineering was resting on its oars. We were still not designing a new Corvette, though we should have started years before. Fortunately, the car was selling better than ever, even with our price increases. Unfortunately, the car's sales success lulled management into thinking there was still plenty of time before we had to get started. Given the three- to four-year lead-time needed to design a new car from scratch, we should have had the new Corvette design well under way. Waiting until the demand fell off to start the process was a dangerous gamble. Four years of slack sales could ruin the market for the car. On top of that, it would be incredibly expensive to put manufacturing on a half-time schedule.

The fact of the matter is that, for several years, all of our engineering energy had been focused on surviving the onslaught of regulations. Emission and safety regulations were coming at us from the Federal level and noise regulations were coming at us from several states. Until the onslaught subsided, and we had developed adequate technical responses to them, we were in no position to start a new car design.

From attending Corvette club meetings and talking with Corvette owners and enthusiasts, it became obvious that, whatever we did, we needed to get the Corvette back to the performance level of 1970. Corvette enthusiasts made this clear by their constant talk about performance and their total inattention and even disinterest when I told them how hard we were working to meet the emission and safety regulations, the noise laws, and the impending fuel economy standards. They didn't care and they didn't want to hear about it.

What Corvette enthusiasts complained about most were the reduced horsepower ratings. Gross horsepower numbers had given them bragging rights that we had taken away. They equated their horsepower numbers with performance and were incensed that we were decimating the accel-

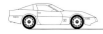

BOB STEMPEL

Bob Stempel was a Corvette owner even during his early career at Oldsmobile. He became Engineering Director of Chevrolet in 1977, moved to Pontiac Motor Division as General Manager in 1980, and then back to Chevrolet as General Manager in 1983. After a very successful tour with Opel in Europe, Bob returned to Michigan to become President, and ultimately Chairman of the Board of General Motors.

Bob Stempel (left), seen with Chevy PR chief Ralph Kramer and Dave McLellan, was a major supporter of the Corvette.

P. H. Cahier Photography

eration and top-speed potential of their cars. It became evident that we had never adequately explained the ratings change to net horsepower. And, now that we were reducing net horsepower with the imposition of a catalytic converter, we really turned off the power-hungry enthusiasts. More than anything they wanted their bragging rights back and they wanted to be able to buy Corvettes that made loud sports car noises. It was finally clear to me that, within the bounds of what was legal, it was engineering's job to recapture the Corvette of 1969–70.

The late 1970s were also a time for reestablishing the top management team that supported the Corvette. After Ed Cole's retirement, it took some time for new leadership to emerge within both GM and Chevrolet. Two key players in this leadership were Bob Stempel and Lloyd Reuss.

FOCUS ON EMISSIONS

The complex and rapidly changing emissions regulations forced the engine group to concentrate almost exclusively on solving emissions problems. Through the late 1970s and early 1980s, Russ Gee and his team became magicians, pulling rabbits out of hats. They struggled, often up until the last moment, to meet each year's increasingly stringent emission standards to obtain the legal certifications that we needed to be able to sell cars.

At first, emission control strategies were developed mostly on the fly. The struggle had to be tempered by the realization that a mistake, or

LLOYD REUSS

On his way to becoming president of GM, Lloyd Reuss crisscrossed paths with Bob Stemple. A long-time Chevrolet transmission engineer, Lloyd moved into program management, heading the Camaro program and then the Vega program. He then moved over to Buick Motor Division, first as Chief Engineer and then as General Manager. Back at Chevrolet, as General Manager after Stemple's departure for Europe, Lloyd rose to Group Vice President and then president of GM. Lloyd can take credit for the 1984 Corvette becoming a targa, the resurrection of the convertible in 1986, and the ZR-1.

Lloyd Reuss helped us with "the big picture" of the Corvette and only occasionally interfered with the details. I appreciated his

help, but because he was so far up in the chain of command, intermediate management often perceived his help as meddling. Thus, his inputs would arrive filtered and delayed, and with all the accompanying trauma of "this is what the boss wants." The most charismatic and enthusiastic person that I have ever worked with, Lloyd sometimes came across as too enthusiastic, losing credibility with the troops in the process. Nevertheless, it was always uplifting to get a pep talk from Lloyd.

On his way to the presidency of GM, Lloyd Reuss was responsible for the 1984 Corvette becoming a targa, the resurrection of the convertible in 1986, and the ZR-1.

Drawing by Dave McLellan

overzealousness, could land the engineers, and GM, in court—they were dealing with the Federal Government.

Russ and his team get credit for the reduced horsepower of the Corvette as we ended the 1970s and moved into the early 1980s. With the 1980 California Corvette, we reached our power nadir. Pressed to the limit for new certifications, Chevrolet could manage only a 180 net horsepower (nhp) 305cid V-8, for all automatic-transmission passenger car applications. Our 49-state version reached its power lowpoint the following year, with only a 190 nhp 350cid engine certified nationwide. It was little consolation to us that this power rating exceeded the first V-8 Corvette's 195 gross horsepower (ghp).

Given the state of emission control technology available for a carbureted engine, the engineers were doing about as well as anybody else. In the end, Russ and his Engine Group would be credited for the restoration of horsepower in the Corvette, starting with the 1982 car, and our first application of fuel injection.

With most of the Corvette team members in place, Styling maintained continuity with Jerry Palmer. As Chief Engineer, I rounded out the group of people who would have the greatest influence over the direction of the Corvette. Though I am writing this narrative mostly from an engineering point of view, there is no more important piece of the Corvette puzzle than styling. It was in the imagination of Harley Earl, that the car was conceived in the first place. Later on, it was the styling direction of Jerry Palmer that would determine the Corvette's future. With his contribution to the Four-Rotor Corvette and his love for sports cars (mostly Ferraris and Corvettes), we couldn't have had a better stylist.

There is no more important relationship in the concept phase of a new car program than the one between styling and engineering. Either department can cause a project to fail, but it takes both, working together, to make it succeed. Unfortunately, Styling management was still in love with the mid-engine Corvette, because it gave them the opportunity to radically change the proportions of the car. A mid-engine car could also be made lower than the front-engine car, because there was no engine to obstruct forward vision. Throughout the concept phase of the new Corvette, I had to deal with a Styling management that wanted a mid-engine car and gave only grudging support to the front-engine design. On the other hand, Chevrolet management, though committed to the front-engine design, would not confront Styling management or come to an agreement with them. So, Chevrolet sent me to do battle with Styling,

PAUL KING

After Bob Stempel left for Pontiac, Paul King moved up to Engineering Director of Chevrolet. Like Lloyd Reuss and Frank Winchell, Paul King began his engineering career assisting in the development of the new automatic transmissions that GM was pioneering. He then gained overall vehicle experience heading Chevrolet's Vehicle Development at the Proving Ground, where my boss's boss reported to him back when I started with Chevrolet. Paul then headed Chevrolet's passenger car body engineering before being promoted to Engineering Director. As Engineering Director, he was my direct boss and the guiding hand on programs, as he controlled all the resources of Chevrolet Engineering. I would never characterize him as a Corvette enthusiast, but he was great to work for, thanks to his salt-of-the-earth approach to tasks.

RUSS GEE

Thanks to new regulations, engine certification had become so complex and legalistic that there was no longer any possibility of the Corvette team certifying its own engines. For everything, from power development to emission development, the testing and certification had to be done within the Engine Group. For the Corvette team this was, at times, like pushing on a rope. However, within the Engine Group, one man had the responsibility for Corvette engines and transmissions, and that was Russ Gee.

Paul King brought in Russ Gee from the Pontiac Motor Division to be his Powertrain Chief Engineer. The demands of meeting the new emission laws that were descending on us year after year made this the most critical job in Chevrolet.

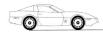
DON RUNKLE

Don Runkle was a Corvette enthusiast who followed me as a Sloan Fellow at MIT. By the late 1970s, he was Director of Chevrolet Market Planning and was in a key position to influence the direction of the Corvette. Don brought his enthusiasm for cars and, especially, his love for Corvettes to Chevrolet Market Planning. As its director, he was responsible for the planning of all Chevrolet's cars and trucks. The Corvette received far more of his group's attention than its one percent of Chevrolet sales could justify.

As Director of Chevrolet Market Planning, Don Runkle was in a key position to influence the direction of the Corvette.

Courtesy Delphi Automotive Systems

armed with instructions that we were not to support any mid-engine proposals. As it was, Styling modeled several more mid-engine concepts and we in Corvette Engineering had to be the bad guys.

DOWNSIZING AT GM

With its increased fuel prices and long gas lines, the oil embargo of 1973-1974 caused a dramatic change in the automobile business. The public responded predictably, and the sales of big, gas-guzzling cars plummeted. Car makers, with their long lead times, responded as fast as they could, implementing downsized strategies—such as rebodying the compact Chevrolet Nova as the Cadillac Seville.

Cadillac, Buick and Oldsmobile had come to own the specialty luxury market with their E-K platform nameplates of Eldorado, Riviera and Toronado. The E-K platform was due for a major change in 1978. Unfortunately, the planning phase of this updating occurred at the peak of the oil crisis, so the cars received a full dose of downsizing for their 1979 introduction. Normally, GM could expect that the introduction of new models would increase sales by as much as 50 percent. Instead, sales came in at 50 percent below the long-in-the-tooth cars they replaced.

The consequence of canceling the old cars and replacing them with cars that customers didn't want was catastrophic to GM's market share in the luxury segment. Previously loyal buyers started looking elsewhere, and they found cars that suited their needs and tastes just fine. Almost a decade went by before GM responded with specialty luxury cars that were the right size. By then, once-loyal GM buyers had discovered the alternatives, making it impossible for GM to regain the market dominance it once had. The ultimate irony of this debacle was that the market research people knew that they were headed for disaster but did not (or could not) communicate this to senior GM management.

GM rushed headlong into the 1980s, downsizing everything in sight and creating the all new transverse V-6 drives, the 1980 X-cars, and the 1982 J-car. In its panic, management even ordered Cadillac to market a derivative of the J-car as the Cadillac Cimarron. For a time, even Corvette was pulled into this downsizing mania. Jerry Palmer had his designers and studio engineers resize the mid-engine Four-Rotor Corvette around the Corporation's new 2.8 liter V-6, "GM's engine of the future." Up to this point, we had avoided studying a V-6 front-engine Corvette, even though influential members of top management considered the V-8 socially irre-

JERRY PALMER

Through its size, form, and details of execution, the Corvette makes a powerful statement about itself as a special car and about its owner as a special person. Building on the heritage of its first 30 years, the next new Corvette needed to be fresh yet recognizable, and familiar to Corvette enthusiasts. Jerry Palmer knew intrinsically what to do, having immersed himself in the Corvette ideology and having aligned himself with its enthusiastic supporters.

Under Harley Earl and Bill Mitchell, it was impossible for a stylist who didn't pay close attention to their direction to get ahead. They both had bigger-than-life egos and treated their stylists as extensions of themselves. Frankly, it's amazing that great stylists grew up under this umbrella. Jerry not only survived, he prospered—possibly as a result of his particular style in dealing with management. Fundamen-

tally, Jerry knew what to do, yet he would listen to the ideas of others. He would then try out suggestions on his designs, work with them, incorporate them, or explain why they wouldn't work. Through this, Jerry always knew where he wanted to take the car design, but, by his personality and low-key approach, he was often able to improve on his best ideas by being open to input.

Many of Styling's designers were not as lucky as Jerry Palmer. Even if they started with good ideas, they could get sidetracked by management's meddling and end up with a muddled design-by-committee. Jerry and I worked closely together during this period and focused on making the new front-engine Corvette the best ever. We never let the mid-engine controversy get in the way of our making progress on the real Corvette.

Jerry Palmer was heavily involved with Corvette design, beginning with the four-rotor Corvette.

Northrop Grumman Corp.

sponsible. Even the next redesign of the Camaro-Firebird F-car platform was being planned as a front-drive V-6.

In parallel with Styling, and in spite of the direction of our own management, we started an engineering study of a mid-engine V-6 Corvette in Chevrolet Research and Development. GM's 2.8 liter engine produced about 130 nhp and less than 200 ft-lbs of torque. If, with its transaxle, the engine saved us some packaging volume and 300 pounds, it would only reduce the mass of the car by about 10 percent, while producing 30 percent less torque and horsepower than the already weak V-8. Although this was clearly not yet a formula for a successful Corvette, we could turbocharge the engine. Because engines have to absorb the huge reciprocating inertial loads of pistons and connecting rods moving up and down at high revs, they are sized by their mechanical loads, not by their gas pressure loads. Thus, naturally aspirated engines can be turbocharged to the point where thermal or emission limitations dominate. Unfortunately, the new manual and automatic transaxles that were being developed for the V-6 applications had no torque capacity margin and would be the primary weakness of a V-6 engine strategy for the Corvette.

Corvette engineering rejected the mid-engine V-6 proposal on performance grounds. Chevrolet management rejected the mid-engine V-6

Design Staff management proposed a V-6 mid-engine Corvette, which was rejected by Chevrolet but soon resurfaced as the Fiero.

Dave McLellan Archives

because there was still no clamor for a mid-engine Corvette among the owner group. Absolutely nobody was asking for a V-6 Corvette. We were not yet doing formal market research but, years later, when we did ask Corvette owners about a V-6 version, they gave us a predictable and resounding NO! Styling, always pushing for a mid-engine sports car, would keep this proposal alive until it re-emerged as the Pontiac Fiero.

THE CORVETTE AS AN ICON

What was this car—the Corvette? Over nearly three decades, Zora Arkus-Duntov and Design Staff had worked to define it. By the end of the 1979 model year, as we were starting work on the next-generation Corvette, Chevrolet had sold 616,711 Corvettes and had been enjoying record sales throughout the late 1970s in spite of the car's reduced power. The Corvette was one of the most recognized, the most aspired to, and the most dreamed about cars in American history. It's influence reached far beyond those who owned one.

At the time, there was already a loyal Corvette following that probably totaled well over a million and, possibly, as many as two million individuals. This loyal group had come to know what a Corvette was and had adopted the car. The question for Chevrolet was: Were we going to drastically change a successful formula or were we going to keep doing what worked? Chevrolet was very reluctant to shake up what was finally working well by trying something that was totally new and unproven—like a V-6 powered mid-engine car.

Market research, in those days, was still very shoot-from-the-hip and it was no different for us, except that we could go out and talk with the Corvette owners and enthusiasts who had banded together in Corvette clubs. To the extent that they could speak for future Corvette buyers, we were conducting valuable—though non-scientific—market research. As a result, we had enough chutzpah to think that we knew what a Corvette was and what it took to make a successful sports car.

Duntov and the press had spent a decade trying to convince Corvette enthusiasts that the next new Corvette should be mid-engined. Yet, when we interviewed Corvette fans, they were quite split in their opinions about the mid-engine Corvette. Some were in favor of it, and some were very vocal against it, but there appeared to be very few who were neutral.

The answer was clear—the only thing that made sense was to continue doing what we knew worked and make it perform even better.

I'm convinced that Chevrolet allowed the mid-engine car to be exhibited because they simply needed a show car. Their history with major new model introductions such as the Corvair was one of great secrecy. Having been unable to garner enthusiast support for a mid-engine Corvette, Duntov's final attempt was to tie the mid-engine Corvette to Cole's rotary engine program. If the rotary engine had succeeded, we wouldn't have been discussing this prior to starting work on the C4 concept—we would have already been working on a mid-engine Wankel-powered car. And that would have been an example of a program decided on by top management fiat rather than by the desires of the customer. That's the way GM too often worked.

Although the decision would have been made at the top, that's not to say that it might not have worked or that Corvette customers wouldn't have descended on their Chevrolet showrooms in droves. But, the public had seen the car in auto shows and in magazine articles and was still ambivalent about it, so it's doubtful that the mid-engine car would have excited the customers any more than did the front-engine car. Chevrolet management knew this and, even though they didn't have hard research to prove it, they were adamant that the next new Corvette should follow in the tradition of the previous Corvettes, with an engine up front and rear-wheel drive.

It continues to amaze me that Styling—which invented the Corvette, and got its way with top management more often than not—couldn't sell the mid-engine Corvette in any of its forms. The Corvette's sales volume and investment cost were inconsequential on a corporate scale. It would have been far less confrontational for management to let Styling have its way than to create rancor each time the mid-engined car was blocked. Styling's responsibility for new product concepts put its work at least four years ahead of the market. At best, the organization set new styling trends, or at least produced designs that were consistent with the direction the market was heading. At worst, or when driven by poor management direction, Styling could misread trends and produce designs that too few people wanted to buy. The mid-engine Corvette, particularly the V-6, was a fundamental mis-reading of the Corvette market.

Styling could make or break a car division general manager. The divisional general manager's success, while rising through the corporate

IRV RYBICKI

With Bill Mitchell's retirement as the Vice President of GM Styling in 1978, the talk was that corporate management was tired of being bullied by strong styling leadership. The next Styling VP was going to be a more malleable "team player," in order to give GM top brass greater control of the styling of its new cars. Management succeeded in placing a team player, Irv Rybicki, in Styling's top spot but, ultimately, GM paid the price—with a generation of lackluster designs that, for the most part, failed to capture the public's imagination.

Irv was a conservative big car designer who had never worked on the Corvette, knew very little about it, and took little interest in it. He had a debilitating back problem during his years as Styling's Vice President and never enjoyed getting into or out of Corvettes. But, through his position, he would influence the next generation Corvette—and not always in ways we would have liked. We were fortunate that we had a strong designer in Jerry Palmer and that Chuck Jordan—Jerry's boss—was there as a buffer to Irv.

As the Styling Vice President who followed Bill Mitchell, Irv Rybicki had considerable influence over the new Corvette.

GM Design Center

ranks, was highly dependent on his or her ability to sell cars. Arguably, the most successful general managers were the ones with the best car designs. Conversely, if saddled with poor designs, a general manager could look like a loser. So, arguing with Styling could be a dangerous game.

It was the E-K platform debacle that finally brought management out of their downsizing funk. Lloyd Reuss revisited the Camaro-Firebird decision and, against the advice of almost everyone involved, stopped the V-6 program. He gave direction to redo these "pony cars" with traditional rear drive, keeping the V-8 in the lineup. The Corvette, too, would be V-8 powered, but management didn't want to hear about any more mid-engine proposals. With help from Chevrolet Research and Development, we had already begun to look closely at the V-8 front-engine layout to see what we could do to improve it.

THE COMPETITION

There were a number of sports cars that we acquired or inherited in the course of conceiving the next Corvette, and many of them came to market during the decade of the 1970s. These cars presented us with a unique opportunity to explore the work of other sports car and exotic car makers and to get to know and drive their products in our daily routine. At their best, sports cars can provide a very personal and passionate bond with their owners. They also reminded us, by their unique characteristics, that there was more than one definition of what makes a great sports car. Analyzed down to their elements, these cars also gave us some good ideas—exemplifying traits worth emulating, as well as reminding us of attributes to avoid. The cars we evaluated included the Porsche 928, Ferrari 330 GT, Maserati Ghibli, and Lamborghini Muira. We also looked at some past GM development vehicles, to give us ideas and help us learn from our own history.

PORSCHE 928

Introduced in 1978, the Porsche 928 was an excellent grand touring car and a benchmark for us in several ways. With its water-cooled, front-mounted V-8 engine, rear transaxle, and two-plus-two seating, it represented Porsche's direction for the future. Unfortunately, it had none of the nimble, sharp, and aggressive feel of the 911, which had propelled Porsche to a position of eminence in the sports car market.

As a touring car, the 928 was excellent, with its driveline and suspension isolation, but judged as a sports car, the 928 was too slick and too smooth. We studied its driveline, however, as a solution to interior accommodation and, although we couldn't afford a rear mounted transaxle, we did adopt a torque tube, to eliminate an intrusive crossmember. We were also impressed by the revolutionary P225/50R-16 low-profile tire from Pirelli, which gave excellent handling but at the expense of tire wear. We were determined to take advantage of this development but felt we first needed to solve the tire wear problem.

While the 928's 4.5 liter, 250 hp V-8 engine promised excellent performance, its curb weight of almost 3,700 pounds slowed it down and made the car feel massive. This was aggravated by its high belt line, massive windshield pillars, and dark interior, which all conspired to make the driver feel closeted.

In several areas, the Porsche 928 served as a benchmark for the C4.
Dave McLellan Archives

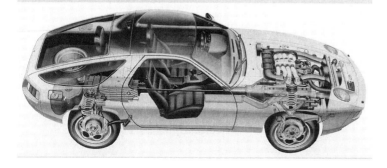

LOOKING TO CORVETTE'S PAST

In addition to evaluating sports cars from other manufacturers, we also looked back at earlier GM concept cars. However, of all the experimental mid-engine Corvettes that had been built, only the aluminum-bodied Corvette was drivable by 1979. We had the aluminum Corvette rebuilt in Chevrolet R&D, and spent some time driving it at the Proving Grounds. The cramped cockpit reminded me of the Muira, but it did have a small rear trunk, which could hold about two gym bags. The front compartment was filled with the radiator, fuel tank, spare tire, and air-conditioning. Its performance and sound cues were typical of an automatic pre-emission small-block, but I was surprised by its soft ride, which gave the car a heavy, lumbering feel on the road.

We also went back and reminded ourselves of our own production Corvette heritage, picking the high-point 1970 LS5 and LT1 Corvette powertrains as benchmarks. These cars were still a lot like contemporary production Corvettes, except for their power and noise. One quarter of all Corvettes sold that year were LS5s. This powertrain is remembered fondly for its huge, effortless mid-range torque and throaty, big-bore V-8 sound. In contrast, the more expensive LT1 did not sell nearly as well, accounting for only 7 percent of production. This engine gave the Corvette a totally different character. High-spirited, with a great, screaming, mechanical V-8 sound, it was what the 1979 Corvette could have been if it weren't for the emission and noise laws that reprioritized engine design.

MASERATI GHIBLI

The Maserati Ghibli was a front-engine V-8 coupe from Italy's second most famous name in racing. While the Ghibli had a conventional driveline, with a live rear axle, it was a delight to drive. Although similar in size and performance to the Porsche 928, it had a completely different feel, characterized by its light and airy two-plus-two cockpit—a feature we would try to capture with the new Corvette.

The Ghibli's only serious flaw was its habit of swapping ends. Closing the throttle in a hard, high-speed corner would cause it to spin so fast we couldn't catch it. After several incidents, we did some tire development on the car and found that switching the Pirelli radials for a glass-belted Uniroyal tire from the Z-28 Camaro tamed its behavior. However, with its harsh ride and sensitivity to parallel tar strips, we were reminded of why the glass-belted tire was not going to be the tire of the future.

The Maserati Ghibli is a delightful car worth emulating in many respects.

Courtesy Road & Track Magazine

FERRARI 330 GT

The Ferrari 330 GT was the smaller of the two Ferrari V-12 front-engine two-plus-two coupes that offered spirited performance. The manual steering was great, once the car was rolling, and it gave excellent feedback and precise control to this live rear-axle car. The 330 GT had all the sensual cues you would expect of a Ferrari as well as the typical Ferrari idiosyncrasies, such as the gated shifter and a radio between the seats.

The Ferrari 330 GT was the first of several Ferraris that influenced future Corvettes.

Photo by Harold Pace

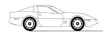
EMISSIONS ROBBING PERFORMANCE

By the time we were seriously developing the concept for the new Corvette, the big block was gone, as was the 370 ghp LT1. Although we didn't know it, by 1981 we would only have a 190 nhp Corvette left. As late as 1979, we still had no idea as to the performance potential of the emission- and noise-controlled Chevrolet small-block. We knew that with a single catalytic converter and a carburetor, we were restricted to 190 nhp. Could we improve that by 10 percent or even 25 percent and still meet regulations? Was a performance cam out of the question? Was fuel injection a mandatory part of the strategy? How big would the engine be? How many catalytic converters did we need, and how large would they have to be, to get the engine back-pressure down to an acceptable level? How large would the intake and exhaust silencers need to be to meet the future noise laws? Could we package this kind of engine, along with its ancillaries, and still have a Corvette?

Porsche had reportedly gone to the front-engine, water-cooled layout to separate the engine and exhaust noise sources, making the job of meeting future noise laws feasible. The rear-engine, air-cooled 911 was an inherently noisy layout, and was further penalized because the proximity of the engine and exhaust tailpipe compounded the noise.

Porsche's emission-controlled 928 gave us a real benchmark. Its 4.5 liter (276 cid), single overhead cam, port-fuel-injected engine produced 250 DIN hp (a DIN hp is 1.37 percent smaller than an SAE hp), even with a catalytic converter. Scaled to the Corvette's displacement, if all other things were equal (which they were not), that would be 316 nhp. Obviously, we had been there in the past. The biggest change was the imposition of the catalytic converter.

LAMBORGHINI MUIRA

The only truly exotic sports car in our comparison group was the Lamborghini Muira. From it we learned how uncompromising, unreliable, and poorly constructed exotic cars could be.

This was an exciting and sensuous-looking, mid-engine V-12 coupe designed by Marcello Gandini, the same designer who later designed the Lamborghini Countach. From the moment I fired up the engine, the Muira was a cacophony of engine noises that screamed with tense excitement. It made no pretense of being practical, or of accommodating the driver and passenger, and it was totally unreliable.

The Muira's mid-engine layout, severe front wheelhouse intrusion, and ultra low roofline were uncompromising as automotive art. (It was also the perfect reminder of where Styling was heading with the mid-engine Corvette.) The front wheelhouse intrusion pushed the foot pedals to the car's centerline, forcing the driver to sit side-saddle. There was no place for the driver's left foot, except over the clutch or on the back side of the wheelhouse, forcing the driver's knee awkwardly up into the air. While sitting in a reclined position, one's head still pushed into the roof. The car accommodated no one except on its own terms, and totally lacked any storage space. But, as an exciting, and expensive toy that could give ten seconds of exhilarating motoring, it had no equal until the Ferrari F-40 a decade later.

The Lamborghini Muira offered exhilarating performance, but the high noise level and limited creature comforts made long trips tiring.

Dave McLellan Archives

THE CATALYTIC CONVERTER DILEMMA

GM's first catalytic converter was approximately 18 inches long, 12 inches wide, and 3 inches deep. Inside, a bed of 1/16 inch ceramic beads was sandwiched between perforated stainless steel plates. The hot exhaust gas flowed from top to bottom: through the first plate, then through the tiny spaces between the ceramic beads, and finally through the second plate. The beads were coated with trace amounts of noble metals, such as platinum, which acted as catalysts when heated.

The exhaust gas leaving the combustion chamber contained minute, but important, quantities of unburned hydrocarbons and carbon monoxide. Air was injected into the exhaust manifold, which ensured that there was sufficient oxygen present to convert the hydrocarbons and carbon monoxide into water and carbon dioxide, both inert chemicals that are not poisonous. If exhaust gases are hot enough, the oxidizing chemical reactions take place naturally. The problem was that during startup and periods of light throttle running, the exhaust was only a few hundred degrees Fahrenheit—not nearly hot enough to drive the oxidization reactions. This is why a converter is needed, as it can catalyze the reactions at temperatures as low as 400 degrees.

Yet another problem was caused when exhaust gas entered the catalytic converter at high temperatures— around 1,700 degrees—with the exothermic catalyzing reaction pushing the temperature even higher by several hundred degrees. The insulated metal shell of the converter was designed to survive this extreme heat, but this added another inch to the clearance required for the underbody of the car. These first converters had to be located far enough away from the engine to protect them from the extremes of engine exhaust heat, but still had to be close enough that they would light off rapidly dur-

ing a cold start. This placed the converter, ideally, about three feet from the engine, which was the space ordinarily occupied by the passenger's feet, in the Corvette.

The dilemma was that the bead converter was too big for the car and too small for the engine. It added more than half an atmosphere of back-pressure, which was greater than three times the back-pressure of the rest of the system put together. Could we make the catalytic converter smaller while reducing its back-pressure, or did the car have to get bigger to accommodate larger multiple converters?

The down-flow bed, bead catalytic converter was notable for its high back pressure due to the turbulent flow around the individual beads.

Drawing by Dave McLellan

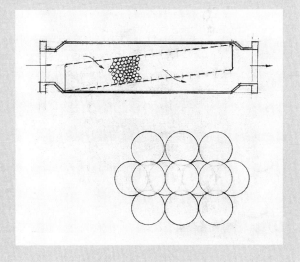

Porsche was using a monolith converter that was quite small. Its one-piece ceramic substrate looked like a nest of tiny soda straws, which achieved the necessary surface area for the catalytic reaction but avoided the turbulent flow that caused such high back pressure in a bead converter. The question we asked ourselves was: How soon could we adopt this technology?

Bosch port fuel-injection allowed Porsche to tune the air intake runners for performance, and at the same time, squeeze out better fuel economy. Cadillac had recently used a Bendix port fuel-injection—licensed from Bosch—on the V-8 Seville. We eyed this technology, but the busi-

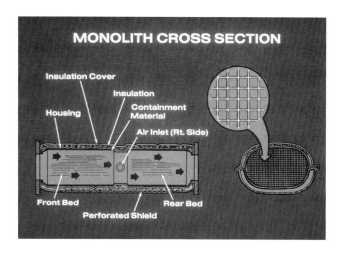

MONOLITH CROSS SECTION

Insulation Cover
Insulation
Containment Material
Housing
Air Inlet (Rt. Side)
Front Bed
Rear Bed
Perforated Shield

The monolith converter, with either a ceramic or metal substrate, solved the back pressure problem and became a crucial element in our strategy to reintroduce performance.
Dave McLellan Archives

ness side of the project, between Bendix and Cadillac, wasn't going well and Bob Stempel didn't want us to further confuse the issue, so the topic—and the technology—was off-limits. Unfortunately at the time, Bendix controlled the North American rights to all Bosch fuel-injection. That left us with our own Rochester port fuel-injection, abandoned 15 years earlier. So, for the time being, we adopted the less efficient throttle-body fuel-injection, and we introduced it in the 1982 Corvette.

Porsche's single overhead-cam per bank may also have been helping to raise the horsepower and torque numbers. Putting the cam in the head eliminates the blockage effect the push rods have on the intake ports, and potentially lightens and stiffens the valve train, all of which contribute to increasing the engine's capacity as an air pump. On the other hand, the small block was producing over 700 hp at 8,500 rpm, in racing configurations. If we could harness even a small portion of this air-breathing technology, we could be back on top.

All these questions were on the table, and many of them were as yet unanswerable because the emissions, fuel economy, and noise regulations were continuing to tighten at a pace that we never expected. Whatever the answers, we knew we needed to keep the pressure on, to recover our power. The Corvette was nothing if it couldn't offer the customer extraordinary performance.

Soon after the 1973–1974 oil crisis, the Environmental Protection Agency (EPA) realized that their emission tests, because they measured the carbon-containing products of combustion, generated data that could also infer fuel economy. With the authorization of Congress, the EPA began to regulate fuel economy, creating the Corporate Average Fuel Economy (CAFE) requirement, and later the Gas Guzzler Tax, as well. Being under the huge corporate umbrella of GM, we didn't have to worry about CAFE, since it was based on the average rating for all of a manufacturer's vehicles taken as a whole. But the Gas Guzzler tax was a different story. The Corvette had a very low fuel economy rating, and this was a penalty that affected individual cars. The Gas Guzzler Tax assessed a fine of $500 for each car sold that missed the threshold, and it kicked in at rat-

ings below 19 miles per gallon. The tax then increased with each mile per gallon missed.

The four-speed automatic transmission scheduled for introduction in 1982 was expected to improve Corvette fuel economy dramatically. This transmission had a 0.7:1 fourth gear and a 3.07:1 first gear. When compared with its three-speed predecessor, the new transmission had 74 percent more ratio range that could be used—with the appropriate selection of axle ratio—to improve performance or economy or both. Yet with our unit injectors combined into a single plane manifold concept, even the four-speed automatic could barely pass the Gas Guzzler minimums. The manual version was expected to be 2 mpg lower, in large part because of the EPA-imposed shift schedule.

The Porsche 928, the 330 GT Ferrari, and the Lamborghini Muira all had five-speed manual transmissions. Corvettes, since 1957, had used four-speed manuals. With their emphasis on power and their high numerical axles, these Corvettes had the first four gears of a five-speed. Driving them, I was always reaching for a fifth gear that wasn't there. In any case, the four-speed was ill-suited to our fuel economy needs, and we were about to lose our production source as well.

Achieving fuel economy with a manual transmission should have been easy: Just shift to keep the car in the highest gear that would move the car forward. Unfortunately, quite early in the EPA fuel economy test program, several car makers had figured this out and pushed it to unrealistic limits, to get fuel economy numbers they could tout in their advertising. When the EPA realized what these manufacturers were doing, it adopted new rules regulating shift speeds, removing this loophole for all of us. With the new rules, we weren't allowed to skip-shift, and there were minimum speeds set for each gear. However, the EPA gave us a loophole in the rule that plugged the loophole: Using an extensive driver survey, if we could prove that drivers were consistently shifting at speeds below 15, 25, 40, and 45 mph then the EPA would let us modify the shift rules. But, because this was quite an unlikely prospect with a performance car, we never even tried.

The obvious "play by the rules" transmission would be a wide-ratio three-speed, with ratios the same as the five-speed's first, third and fifth gears. With a big, powerful V-8 engine, shifting into top gear at 25 mph was the best thing you could do for fuel economy, but a three-speed was a lousy transmission for a performance car.

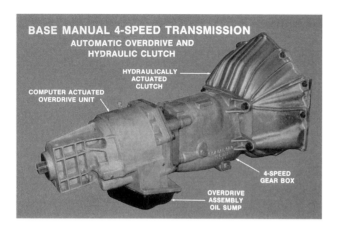

BASE MANUAL 4-SPEED TRANSMISSION
AUTOMATIC OVERDRIVE AND
HYDRAULIC CLUTCH

HYDRAULICALLY
ACTUATED
CLUTCH

COMPUTER ACTUATED
OVERDRIVE UNIT

4-SPEED
GEAR BOX

OVERDRIVE
ASSEMBLY
OIL SUMP

The Doug Nash 4 + 3 manual transmission consisted of the Borg Warner-designed four-speed, mated to an overdrive that functioned on the three top gears.

Dave McLellan Archives

The 4 + 3 transmission became our response to the EPA's rule. A shift from first to second at 15 mph would engage the second overdrive, and subsequent up-shifts would engage the third and fourth overdrives. With the conservative cam timing of the V-8 engine, this strategy provided adequate torque for normal heavy-traffic driving, and improved our fuel economy by about 1.5 mpg—sufficient to meet the Gas Guzzler threshold. Flooring the accelerator pedal, when in any overdrive ratio, induced a computer controlled downshift out of overdrive.

When we first came up with this strategy, even our own people were in disbelief that it would work, and that anybody—much less the EPA—would buy into it. But, not having a better idea and wanting to maximize power, we persisted. So, we secured the backing of the Chevrolet organization and ultimately, the approval of the EPA, to use this as a shift strategy. While using the 4 + 3 transmission worked well as a fuel economy strategy, the car was always confusing to drive and the strategy came to be looked on as an inferior solution, by those who simply wanted a five-speed and didn't care about fuel economy.

The manual overdrive required a planetary gear set, clutches, a hydraulic pump, and an electrohydraulic control system, all the elements of an automatic transmission, which was essentially what it was. Fortunately, Doug Nash Inc. was trying to sell the industry such an overdrive at the time. We ultimately contracted with them to produce the four-speed manual transmission, using Borg Warner's tooling along with a highly-modified version of their original overdrive. Unfortunately, Doug Nash Inc. wasn't very far along with their development of the overdrive, and the project was so complicated, that we were not ready for production until the 1984 model year was half over. Fortunately, time gave us the opportunity to work together to produce a far better transmission.

THINKING THROUGH THE CHASSIS

While we were sorting out this powertrain mess, Brian Decker, recruited out of Chevrolet R&D's analysis group, was reassembling the chassis team that would develop the all-new suspension and brakes for the car. He also took on the assignment of developing the concept for the structure of the new Corvette. We needed to improve the structural stiffness,

particularly in torsion, while meeting crash worthiness requirements, reducing mass, and improving interior roominess—all of which were conflicting goals. Brian started two projects to help us sort this out. The first was with GM Research laboratories (GMR), which applied newly developed analytical optimization techniques to the strength and stiffness problem. The second was with Grumman Aircraft Company, which applied its plastic deformation analysis techniques to the crash-worthiness problem.

The question we posed to GMR was: Define the minimum size and mass of the structure which meets our goals for strength and dynamic stiffness, and falls within the restrictions of the overall body design. Even assuming that the bonded fiberglass floor contributed nothing to the stiffness of the structure, there were so many possible solutions that the conventional trial and error analysis would take far too long, and could still leave us without any assurance that we had found the optimum solution. The GMR approach was to mathematically work its way through all of the possible solutions, applying its decision rules in order to find optimums.

With GMR, we applied their findings to the finite-element model of the structure we had constructed. This modeling technique defined the most mass-efficient structure, including all of its local cross-sections and metal gauge. The final optimized structure consisted of two rails through the engine compartment, transitioning into the two rocker sills and a hinge pillar to the T-bar roof connection. These three structural elements passed through the passenger compartment then transitioned back into the two rear rails. Cross-members stabilized the structure ahead of the engine, behind the seats, and over the rear suspension.

The model revealed to us that we could eliminate the traditional cross-member that supported the tail of the transmission, which we were glad to do because it interfered with the seating and presented a barrier to the exhaust. With such a low car, we wanted to use the entire body height, from the ground-clearance line to the roof, for passenger accommodation. We still had to support the transmission, so we adopted a longitudinal support, similar to the Porsche 928's backbone.

Unfortunately, when we were done, much of this optimization work was for naught. The finite-element model, though it accurately predicted stress and strain, was a poor indicator of the stiffness through the curved sections that transitioned between the two-rail and three-rail structures.

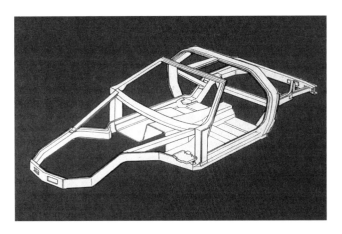

The new car began to take shape, as seen by this drawing of the preprototype structure.
Dave McLellan Archives

The model did not adequately predict the hinge-like behavior of these sections. Even worse, at the last hour, Lloyd Reuss vetoed the use of the T-bar, insisting that the car should be a targa configuration. Without the T-bar, all our calculations were moot.

Brian Decker's second project was a companion analysis of the crash-worthiness of the structure. In a severe crash, the buckling deformation of the structure is the principal means by which the kinetic energy of the collision is absorbed. At the time, we were stretched to compute the linear stresses and strains in the finite-element model. The complexity of analyzing this sort of deformation was beyond our capability. For help with the problem, Brian turned to the Grumman Aircraft Company.

Under contracts with the military, Grumman had been studying the problem of a helicopter crashing vertically. The sudden stop, as it hit the ground, could leave the helicopter's structure relatively undamaged but do great harm to the pilot and passengers. Such an analysis involves a large-scale computation of the behavior of nonlinear elements that could buckle or collapse to absorb the energy of a collision. To manage the massive parallel computations that were required, Grumman invested in a state-of-the-art, multi-million-dollar Cray I computer. Still, it took several days of continuous computing to simulate an event that took less than a tenth of a second in the real world.

Due to a quirk of Grumman's internal billing procedure, the fee for the use of the Cray was priced as if it were a normal mainframe—and far less expensive—computer. As a result, whenever military work was slack, the Cray analysts were encouraged to go looking for civilian jobs that were interesting and that could take advantage of this practical giveaway of Cray computer time.

The first automotive job for the Cray I was an analysis of the crash integrity of the original DeLorean car for Bill Collins, John DeLorean's Chief Engineer. The car, styled by Giorgetto Giugiaro, was announced with much fanfare as the car that would show the industry how to design safer cars. Its composite structure was the crucial element that would make it the world's safest car. This structure was an innovative sandwich of Kevlar and fiberglass, on a foam core that would be saturated with resin, in the "resin transfer" molding process, to form a complete and rigid

underbody. The same process would be used to make the upper structure, including the hoods and signature gull-wing doors.

De Lorean, having built only one show car, which he could not afford to crash, had nothing on which to base his claim of designing the world's safest car. Grumman crushed test sections of the structure and used the resulting data to construct a crash simulation model of the entire car. They then ran the simulated car into a simulated wall at 30 mph, just as would happen in a real-world crash test. The normal dynamic in this event is that the car decelerates at 10 to 40 g, as the front structure buckles and collapses. (At 40 g, a 3000 lb car impacts with a force of 120,000 lb.) The Grumman engineers were horrified by the performance of their DeLorean model. After crushing three feet, the model was still proceeding at 29 mph, and had absorbed only 9 percent of its own kinetic energy. The car was going to use itself up completely in the crash, crushing from one end to the other and making a pancake out of anyone who might be inside. To continue testing the car was a waste of valuable computer time, so the Grumman engineers stopped the simulations.

What to do next? The DeLorean's structure behaved so poorly in a violent crash situation, that a complete and separate safety structure would have to be added. Longitudinal steel tubes were added to the model to give it crash integrity. However, it was never retested because DeLorean fired Chief Engineer Bill Collins, and turned to Colin Chapman, of Lotus Cars, for the eventual production car. With no time left to play around with esoteric ways of rebuilding the car, Chapman simply reengineered the DeLorean with a steel backbone structure, similar to what he used in his own cars.

The Grumman testers used the same modeling approach for the Corvette structure that they had used for the helicopter study and the DeLorean. The Corvette was modeled as if it was a series of sticks. Each stick had detailed bending and compression properties, first as a linear beam and then as a buckling and collapsing beam. As we had expected, the model indicated that the front rails, the principal collapsing elements, would meet our requirements.

Completing the analysis before the finished design was started dramatically increased our confidence in the design and avoided much of the cut-and-try back-tracking that normally goes on in the testing of expensive prototype hardware. It would take us several more months to design the structure in enough detail that it could be prototyped and tested in a

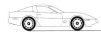

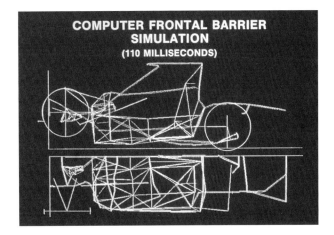

Top: The nonlinear crash model of the Corvette that Grumman engineers ran on their Cray computer.

Bottom: This scale metal crash model was used to verify the Cray computer results.

Dave McLellan Archives (both)

real, full-scale crash test. We also backed up the simulation with a steel scale-model crash test program. The model included scale sheet-steel rails, a honeycomb radiator, and a cast metal engine to simulate the mass of the real engine. This model was drop-tested to simulate a 30 mph crash into a barrier.

TESTING BEGINS

In late 1979 we built our first component test car to evaluate the concept of a torque tube driveline, which would allow us to eliminate the cross-member under the seat. Al Bodnar, of Chevrolet R&D, designed it using a one-inch solid drive shaft to transmit the transmission output torque to the axle. Because the shaft ran without joints, we had to design a stiff, tubular housing to maintain the alignment between the transmission and the axle. At this point, we had no idea how we would service the driveline, other than by disassembling it from the rear, which would require a massive teardown even for minor servicing.

In testing, we discovered that the driveline, as solid as it looked, vibrated in sympathy with the engine's firing frequency. This produced an annoying vibration that was felt in the car, at normal driving speeds. We now knew why Porsche had gone to all the trouble of mounting the 928's battery on the end of the transaxle—and provided a trap door in the body floor for servicing—rather than mounting it in the body, itself. It was because they were using the battery as a tuned absorber for the vibration of their torque tube driveline. We had three possible solutions to our own dilemma: Make the driveline stiffer, and chase the vibration up and out of the driving range; mount a tuned absorber on the driveline; or make the torque tube so soft that the offending vibration would be driven below the running range. It didn't make sense to make the driveline stiffer, as this would dramatically add mass and would still be limited by the stiffness of the transmission itself. Adding a tuned absorber would also add mass and complexity. So, we tried the easy route—cutting the stiffness—and hit the jackpot. Simply slitting the tube over its length—creating an open "C" sec-

THE F-14A TOMCAT AND CORVETTE DESIGN

Our work with Grumman involved several trips to Beth-page, New York, as well as trips by the Grumman engineers to Corvette Engineering at the GM Technical Center in Warren, Michigan. In one of our meetings the Grumman project manager, Arty (Arthur) August, asked us if we would like to take a trip to Calverton, Grumman's flight test center at the far tip of Long Island, to see an F-14A Tomcat. We sure would! The trip turned out to be extra-special because we invited the Corvette stylists Jerry Palmer and Bill Scott and their chain of command Stan Wilen and Chuck Jordan.

As exterior stylists, Palmer and Jordan were captivated by the awesome beauty, yet purposeful shape, of the warbird. As a result of having experienced this airplane up close, Palmer's Corvette designs would be more aggressive, yet flowingly, beautiful. Bill Scott was struck by the incredible complexity of the cockpits. The pilot and his NFO were completely surrounded by switches and controls that they needed to be able to access without looking and while wearing heavy gloves. The total purposefulness of the cockpit displays prompted Bill to think about new ways to present information in future Corvettes. He would return to his studio and, over several iterations, design the most innovative and non-traditional Corvette cockpit ever. Bill's exploration of flat panel displays, with bar graphs and numerical readouts, was carried into the production car as a defining feature. Unfortunately, the automotive press wanted conventional round dials and said so over and over again. Ironically, Bill's graphic and numerical display would be duplicated a decade later in the instrument panels used in Formula I and in Indy-CART racecars.

Bill Scott (right), Corvette's Interior Studio Chief, being briefed in the pilot's cockpit of the Grumman F-14.

Brian Decker (right), Corvette chassis chief engineer in the pilot's seat of the Grumman F-14.

Northrop Grumman Corp. (both)

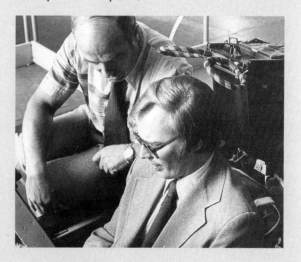

tion—dropped the driveline's bending and torsion frequencies enough to drive the problem out of the running range of the engine.

This also solved our service problem, as we could now revert to a conventional propshaft, and design a C-beam that was less susceptible to angular misalignment. With the shaft U-jointed, we designed one degree of angularity across the joints, so that their needles would always be processing.

We showed the car to top corporate management early the next spring at the Desert Proving Ground. To show them exactly how we were proceeding, we took the body right off the car, leaving the frame, sans crossmember, and the complete driveline exposed. We backed up the display with Jerry Palmer's early drawings of the new car. The management group was a mix of Chevrolet sales executives and corporate executives led by Howard Kehrl, the Group Vice President in charge of Engineering Staff, Styling, and Research, and they had no idea what we were doing. They pulled up to the display in a large van. They got out with Howard in the lead and crowded around the chassis. I was introduced to the group and then began my presentation. When I finished, I asked if there were any questions. I was fully prepared to answer any and all questions they could put to me, even having gone so far as to produce backup charts in anticipation of some of the better and more probing questions.

Howard Kerhl, who had been central to the disastrous E-K downsizing strategy, had the only question, "Can you fit a four-cylinder engine?" I remember being dumbstruck, and gave him a lame answer that I had no time to think through. I could tell by the way he asked the question that he was so deadly serious that a flippant answer was out of the question. The right answer to the question was, of course, "Absolutely not! You should retire the Corvette with grace and dignity before subjecting it to the humiliation of a four-cylinder engine." But this wasn't the time or place for the right answer. I let it pass, writing off Howard Kehrl as part of the problem not part of the solution.

THE CORVETTE TAKES SHAPE

Jerry Palmer's sketches for the new Corvette had progressed to the point where he was ready to move into clay—full size to get visual feedback from his ideas, and 1/4 scale to investigate the influence of several possible shapes on aerodynamic drag. He would then bring these two programs together with a full-scale aerodynamic clay model.

Jerry had designed the Four-Rotor Corvette, a car that, in spite of all of its impracticalities, I still consider to be the most elegant and beautiful Corvette ever conceived. Great automotive designers learn from their creations and move forward. Jerry kept the Four-Rotor in his studio for reference during much of the new Corvette's development phase. He would reuse much of its surface flow, reproportioning everything to the front engine layout. However, he would not repeat it's double-endedness, instead, the new Corvette received a blunt "Kamm" tail.

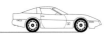
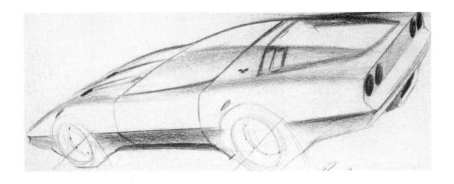

The new Corvette was emerging
from Jerry Palmer's sketch pad.
Dave McLellan Archives

Dr. Wunibald Kamm, an aerodynamics pioneer, investigated the aerodynamic drag of a long, tapered aft body, which kept the airflow attached all the way to the pointed end of the body. He found that the surface drag due to the aft body was greater than the form drag due to bluntly cutting off the tail.

At the time, aerodynamics was becoming important at GM Design Staff, and Jerry was determined not to repeat the mistakes of past Corvette designs that ignored aerodynamics until the design was cast. Two years earlier, GM had started to build a full scale wind tunnel, right next to Design Staff at the Technical Center. A recession, and slumping sales, had caused the facility to be mothballed before it was completed, so it wasn't ready to help us design the new Corvette. We would end up using the Harrison tunnel, on the Tech Center site, for scale model testing and Lockheed's subsonic wind tunnel, in Marietta, Georgia, for full scale testing.

To establish the overall shape (within fairly narrow limits), Design Staff built several 1/4 scale models, each representing major variations in form, with inserts for various backlight slopes that were expected to have an effect on lift and drag. Once the designers and aerodynamicists had used the tunnel as a coarse sieve, they continued, adding clay to try to find the minimum drag configuration. We were a little disappointed that the scale-model testing could only get down to a drag coefficient of 0.365, and we hadn't even dealt with the airflow through the radiator, which was expected to increase drag by at least 50 counts (0.050). We pressed on.

Once Jerry Palmer's full-size model had absorbed the changes from the scale-model wind tunnel testing, and he had reached a design he was happy with, he had his modelers transfer the design to the full-scale wind-tunnel armature. Underneath the surface of this armature was a simulated Corvette, complete with engine, cooling system, and the portions of the chassis and underbody that were exposed. This wood, steel,

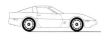

Styrofoam and clay "car," with its simulated engine compartment, weighed more than a real car and had to be made tough enough to withstand being transported to the Lockheed wind tunnel without breaking apart.

Jerry and his team of modelers and aerodynamicists descended upon the Lockheed tunnel and proceeded to conduct a series of over 100 tests. During these tests, they implemented detail changes to the nose and radiator inlet, windshield to side glass form, backlight shape, and Kamm tail cutoff. They eventually got the drag coefficient, including the cooling flow, as low as 0.340. In this configuration, there was still aerodynamic lift at the front and rear, but it was slight. Moving the front chin spoiler down and forward would eliminate front lift, but there was no practical way we could take the front spoiler further than we did, given the trade-off between bumper requirements and cooling flow. Adding a rear deck lip or spoiler changed the rear lift into downforce, but significantly increased drag. They also found that pitching the car slightly nose-down reduced lift, and when they lowered it to the bottom of the height-tolerance band they further reduced the drag coefficient to 0.330. We would remember these last subtle moves when we set up the new Corvette for top speed runs.

The full-scale wind tunnel armature included a radiator, adjustable for pitch. With anemometers mounted on the radiator, we found that the flow through the radiator was maximized if we tilted it forward as little as 15°. This was consistent with another requirement we had set for the car, a minimum cross-section when viewed with radar. Jim Ingle, a.k.a. Jingles, had been experimenting at the Proving Ground with a police radar gun and had verified what we knew from casual observation—the Corvette had a very low radar cross-section.

Jingles measured the maximum distance at which the radar signal, reflecting off the production Corvette and other cars, would produce a speed signal. Most cars would produce a speed signal as far out as 3,000 feet. But, the radar gun wouldn't pick up the Corvette until it was within 1,500 feet. This was a bonus for the speed-hungry Corvette driver, and we wanted to keep it that way. We guessed that the plastic body was transparent to radar, and that it was the metallic components under the skin that were the dominant reflectors. Normally, the radiator (and the air-conditioning condenser mounted in front of it) was the single largest reflector, at radar frequencies. We wondered if the radiator in our new production Corvette, tilted rearward as it was, could be reflecting the radar signal toward the sky. Jingles modified his Corvette test car so he could

tilt the radiator to various angles and reran his radar capture distance test. And he found that a Corvette with its radiator vertical reflected radar just like other cars, but when the radiator was tilted as little as 15 degrees, either forward or backward, it no longer contributed to the capture distance. As a result of this, along with the cooling tests, the radiator of the new Corvette would be tilted forward 15 degrees.

We also put Jingles' learning into our informal design guide and, whenever possible, we aimed metal parts of the car slightly toward the sky or toward the ground. Years later we would see the F-117A stealth airplane and recognize, in its radar-reflecting faceted skins, its kinship to the Corvette.

Jim Ingle, better known as Jingles, has been a major contributor to Corvette development for almost three decades.
Carol Gould Photography

As Irv Rybicki, Jerry's ultimate boss as Vice President of Design Staff, watched the Corvette clay model develop in the studio, he kept complaining that the car was too big. We struggled with that one. Design Staff wanted the car so low that we had cleared everything out of the space between the ground clearance line and the roof, allocating its 42 inches entirely for the driver and passenger. To improve the sight line over the hood, we had lowered the induction system by two inches and pitched the engine down, in front, and dropped it until the starter ring gear was resting on the ground-clearance line. The low hood line trapped us into making the crossfire induction system work. Falling back to the four-barrel carburetor and dual-plane intake manifold was out of the question.

The Corvette is made up of a certain amount of stuff that has to go somewhere, so as we lowered the car it had to get wider. In addition, we had chosen a very wide tire, which significantly increased the width of the car, as its aerodynamic body enveloped the tires. Irv was reacting to the visual consequences of all these decisions. Personally, I thought the car was sized correctly but I felt that the aerodynamics of the car made it look too soft. (Jerry's continual development of its lines would restore the aggressive look.) Making the car physically smaller would cause problems, so Irv kept on us about making the car at least appear smaller. Packaging a production car that is as tightly-packed as the Corvette involves creating several critical paths through the car. We had by now gone down all of these paths—longitudinal, lateral, and vertical—and worked the details enough that we thought we knew how big the car had to be.

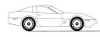

The preprototype, our first design, is distinguished by its forward-raked B-pillar and sharper edges than the production car.

Dave McLellan Archives

The longitudinal critical path starts with the steering rack, located ahead of the engine. The steering-arm ratio then sets up the front-wheel centerline. Replacing the multiple v-belts with a single serpentine flat belt shortened the engine. The path continued rearward, jumping from the engine, with its exhaust manifold, to the driver's right foot on the accelerator pedal. We used a 90th percentile male mannequin as a model to establish the seat-back, which, along with the carpet and intervening structure, determined the location of the rear tire.

The lateral and vertical critical paths were combined, and involved the driver. The exhaust catalytic converter, a smaller monolith type, was located between the seats with the prop shaft and the longitudinal driveline C-beam on top of it. Clearance through the underbody and into the seat and the driver's hips set up the lateral centerline of the driver and the inboard side of the rocker rail structure. The driver's centerline, translated to the roof area, established the side glass and roof header, by their clearance to the driver's head. We shaved a little out of each clearance, but knew we would pay for it in the long run. These clearances were there for a reason—either to accommodate for variations during assembly or to keep heat from penetrating the cockpit.

In a sports car, developing the driver's space requires a balance of space. The driver wants everything at his or her fingertips, yet doesn't want to feel confined, or worse, downright uncomfortable. We had established our goals early on, in terms of percentile accommodation, planning that the car would be adequate for a 90th percentile sized adult male. We would discover years later that the mannequin templates that the Design Staff used to establish this model were ten years out of date, and no longer reflected the actual average adult male's size. As a result, we overestimated the amount we could comfortably shave off the car, in our effort to appease Irv.

In the engineering department, we felt as though we had worked out enough details, between the Design Staff and ourselves, that we could now build a complete car. We planned to build six preprototype cars that would incorporate the then-current styling—the T-bar roof and structure, the C-beam driveline, and the aluminum suspension with fiberglass leaf springs. These cars would serve as our first test-beds for ride and handling, and for structural development, and would ultimately be used in

barrier crash tests to validate the design for crash integrity. We built only three cars before budgetary constraints, and the decision to make the car a targa, brought the preprototype program to a halt.

Designing a complete car, not just chasing cross-sections, forced us to make everything fit together at the same time: power train, structure, suspension, and occupant packaging. Building these cars helped us weed out a lot of mistakes, and trained the engineers and draftspeople on the details of execution that would be repeated when we did the actual production design. The preprototype cars were almost as complicated to design and build as the production car itself. Every part had to be designed in detail, mocked up in cardboard, wood and styrofoam, and then tooled so that the finished part was representative of the actual production processes. Though Bowling Green Assembly was looking over our shoulder, these cars would, in fact, be assembled on a hoist at the Engineering Center. As they began to take shape on their hoists, they were truly a sight to behold.

PASSING THE TEST FOR PRODUCTION

The ultimate test of a new car program was: Could the design stand up to the intense scrutiny of corporate management and their bean counters? Don Runkle, as head of the Chevrolet Planning Department, coordinated the critical, final presentation we would make to the Product Policy Group (PPG). The PPG consisted of all the top officers, from the Chairman on down, who met together to decide the future product strategy of the corporation. Very early on the morning of April 22, 1980, they began to wander through the studios at Design Staff, which were set up to display current new product proposals. The 1983 Corvette was set up for their review in Jerry Palmer's Chev III Studio. Jerry showed them the clay model of the new Corvette; Bill Scott presented his interior design, with its liquid crystal flat panel display; and I showed them the backbone chassis, with its aluminum suspension and fiberglass springs, and answered questions about weight and fuel economy.

The meeting began at 9 o'clock in the Library Conference Room. Waiting in the anteroom, we ran into Bob Stempel, who had just been made General Manager of Pontiac Motor Division. Bob was there to present Pontiac's proposal for a two-seat commuter car, the Fiero. After Bob's presentation, all the Corvette presenters were ushered into the meeting room as a group. As we entered, it was very dark except for the bright screen at the front. I remember stumbling around the podium as we were

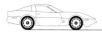
SPY PHOTOGRAPHER

Soon after the preprototypes were being tested at the Proving Grounds, we were surprised to find one of them on the cover of *Car and Driver* magazine! Spy photographers, such as Jim Dunne, would stalk the perimeter of the Proving Grounds hoping to get shots of the new cars. The southwest corner, because of its high hill and trees on the adjacent private land, was particularly vulnerable. Photographers would be willing to spend long hours in a tree, with a long telephoto lens, waiting for a future design to appear on the Belgian Block Road or the North-South Straightaway.

Sales management was rightfully paranoid about showing a new car before introduction. This sort of thing can ruin sales for the current car. So, Jingles scrounged the Proving Grounds boneyard, finding old grilles and chrome moldings that he could use to camouflage the cars. Our handsome preprototype Corvettes were made ugly, with fake front and rear grills and chrome moldings. *Car and Driver* may have had their spy cover of the new Corvette, but we had the last laugh.

Top: Jingles had camouflaged the preprototype, knowing that it was going to have its picture taken. This shot by Jim Dunne made the cover of Car and Driver *magazine.*

Photo by Jim Dunne

Bottom: The preprototype sans camouflage.

Dave McLellan Archives

being introduced, and hearing conversations in the back of the room, where we knew Chairman Roger Smith was sitting.

Don Runkle opened the presentation of the 1983 Corvette with a multiscreen slide show, set to music, which reminded the executives of past Corvette accomplishments and of the Corvette club activity that had come to surround the car. Don then explained Chevrolet's rationale for a new Corvette, and the marketing plan for selling the car. Corporate Marketing Staff presented the increased volume projections for the new car (they were surprisingly and wonderfully optimistic); I presented the technical highlights, including the car's projected fuel economy and performance; and the Financial Department closed the presentation by saying that the car's unit cost and investment, along with marketing's price and volume projections, would produce an acceptable return on investment. We then answered a few questions, the Chairman thanked us for coming, and we left. Then we waited anxiously. No new Corvette program had been approved by the corporation in over 20 years.

Hammering Out the Details of an All New Corvette

7

THE WORD CAME DOWN THROUGH THE BACK DOOR, from the guys who were working behind the scenes with the Product Policy Group (PPH). They had demonstrated their commitment, to helping us get the Corvette approved, by steering our presentations to meet—head on—the issues the PPG wanted to hear about. The 1983 Corvette program was approved as presented.

Up until then, we had been playing in the Chevrolet Research and Development sandbox to define the car well enough for us to make a concrete proposal to the PPG. Now we had to get serious. It was going to take almost $80 million to design the car, develop the processes that we would need to build it, and produce a fleet of experimental cars for testing. It would then cost nearly twice that amount to tool the new Corvette for production.

Each step in this process is critical. Done well, it makes the next step proceed smoothly. Done poorly, or if the results are late, the succeeding steps suffer. For years, the Corvette had been designed on the outside, with contract designers. We had extensive experience trying to make this work well, but contract design was a poor way to design a car, particularly an all-new car. Though there were exceptions, contract designers as a group were not as capable as the in-house designers, which Chevrolet had trained over many passenger car and truck programs. Yet contract designers were periodically in great demand, to handle the overflow of design work that occurred whenever the economy turned positive and the automobile industry released new car programs. Unfortunately, purchasing's management of the outside design process was fundamentally flawed, and we had no control over the process to fix it.

Cash flow is the engine that drives the car industry. The huge up-front cost, of designing and tooling a new car for production, is paid for out of the cash reserves that an automobile company builds up from profits made during an economic boom. Recessions, with their attendant sales

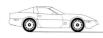

slumps, make each car built cost a lot more, and eat down the company's cash reserves. While car companies like to keep a flow of new products coming, in spite of the economic climate, they have to ultimately hunker down and protect their dwindling cash reserves. The boom-bust nature of the new product cycle was unlikely to change for the Corvette.

In the boom phase of the cycle, the expanding cash reserves could fuel more new products than we had the resources to deliver. Once we had saturated our in-house body design capacity, we looked to the outside contract design houses, for their additional capacity. This put contract body designers in great demand. Technically, we paid these contract designers by the hour for drawing lines. But more importantly, their output represented their skill in analyzing and visualizing a complex three-dimensional product, and committing that design to a two-dimensional representation—a drawing—that could be understood by others. In the aggregate, every hour of designer time led to 100 hours in the tool-and-die shops, as the tools and fixtures were produced to make a real car from the designer's drawings. Given the tremendous leverage associated with their work, we paid the neophyte designer way too much and the skilled designer way too little.

The best designers knew their worth, and were bombarded with job offers from other programs offering as little as 50 cents per hour more. Quite often, GM programs were competing with one another, and stealing one another's designers. Designers had learned that jumping from one program to another was the fastest way to get ahead. So they did, with disastrous consequences to the program they left behind. We could handle a few losses, but when the turnover was wholesale, the quality and timing of the program suffered.

I argued that the new Corvette was too important to Chevrolet to design it in this same manner. But Chevrolet wasn't listening. They had too many new programs for their limited in-house body design resources. Over our objections, the decision was made to leave the Corvette on the outside.

WORK BEGINS

Fortunately, because the chassis does not change with every body cycle, we could have all the Chevrolet chassis designers we needed to do what would be the most innovative Corvette chassis in two decades. It was Brian Decker's brilliant idea to do the Corvette-specific parts of the suspension in aluminum. This gave us the opportunity to optimize our suspension

geometry without having to compromise around the use of existing high-volume tooled components, yet at the same time we could use ball joints and bearings that were already well developed, and available at low cost. Aluminum also gave us the lowest possible unsprung weight.

At this point, with our engine performance and fuel economy constrained by the "Crossfire" induction system to 205 net horsepower and barely exceeding the 19 mpg Gas Guzzler tax threshold, the new Corvette needed all the help it could get to be viable in the future. The most important contributions we could make to the car itself were to lower weight, reduce chassis rolling friction, and improve aerodynamics. By the time we were finished with the chassis, we would use 350 lb of aluminum for control arms, wheels, brake calipers, axle housings, and rear subframes. If we had used iron and steel in these applications, these components would have weighed at least twice as much. This was in addition to the 82 lb savings achieved by adopting fiberglass leaf springs. Reducing weight also gave us the best chance of regaining our pre-emission-control performance edge.

Chassis friction was found in many places but was dominated by tire-rolling resistance, brake pad drag, and seal friction. Each of these had to be tackled one at a time, to make progress. Aerodynamic drag was being dealt with by Jerry Palmer at Design Staff, as he worked to keep the new Corvette's cross section as small as possible and to minimize its drag coefficient.

When we finished with the 1983 Corvette we had the curb weight (with a full tank of gas but without the driver) down to 3,192 lb, compared to the 3,342 lb of the 1982 car. This was as close as we would get to, and within 7 percent of our goal of, 3,000 lb. The drag coefficient, at 0.34, was as low as any car we knew of, and we had not compromised the aggressive styling for aero benefits. This translated into improved performance, with a 0-60 time breaking back into the high 6-second range, and low 15-second quarter-mile times. Thanks to the improved aerodynamics and correct transmission gearing, the top speed was an impressive 142 mph—in spite of only 205 net horsepower.

This new high in top speed led to our decision to raise the tire speed rating to the "Z" level. The "Z" rating, seldom used before, indicated that the tire construction has been tested and is safe beyond the top speed of the car for which it was designed.

Before we were done we would also overachieve on handling. Good handling and ride start with good tires. Although we had a 15-inch tire

The use of aluminum in automotive suspension was pioneered by the new Corvette. Today its use is quite common.

Dave McLellan Archives

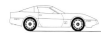

The directional tread pattern of the P255/50VR16 was taken directly from the contemporary Goodyear Formula I rain tire.

Courtesy Goodyear Tire & Rubber Co.

carried over from the pre-prototype program, we were determined to design the 1983 production car around an all-new 16-inch P255/50R16 steel-belted radial tire that Goodyear was developing exclusively for us. The baseline for this tire was the P7 Pirelli P225/50R16, which had been introduced on the Porsche 928. But, unlike the Pirelli, the Goodyear would be a full-tread-depth tire to bring the wear life up to normal passenger car expectations. With the ultimate development of the production car suspension, this tire achieved 0.93g cornering. When shaved to half-tread depth and with a little suspension camber tweaking we broke 1.0g!

The tire developed for the 1983 Corvette is what we call a high-cornering-stiffness tire. Steering the tire just one degree will generate over 350 pounds of cornering force per tire, and produce a 0.1g lateral acceleration, which is half again the cornering stiffness of a normal passenger car tire. These tires demand special attention in suspension design to keep the tire as upright as possible and to precisely control the direction of the tire while giving the needed ride movement and flexibility.

As a platform for the tires, the car was planned to be stiff in roll, rolling no more than 3.5 degrees per g. This was accomplished by using relatively stiff ride springs and roll bars in the front and rear, and in spite of the low roll centers needed to minimize tire camber. The car was also planned to be stiff in pitch, but this was accomplished with antidive and antisquat suspension geometry. No longer would the Corvette pitch down in front under hard braking—using up precious ride travel in the process—nor would it squat in the rear under hard acceleration.

These geometry effects tend to dominate the low lateral acceleration handling. As the tire contact patch approaches its handling limit, it begins to slip on the road, first at its trailing edge and then progressively moving forward, ultimately sliding over its entire area. Under these conditions the lateral force that is generated is affected less by steering the tire with geometry effects and more by the load pressing on the tire. The adjustable element that controls the load on an individual tire is the stabilizer or roll bar. We planned to use a massive front bar to achieve the roll stiffness we were after.

We found, however, that by spreading the body attachment of the front suspension fiberglass spring into two separate attachments 18 inches apart, we could achieve a major portion of the roll stiffness contribution of the front roll bar for free. We still used a massive front bar, but it would have been even bigger and heavier if it had not been supplemented by the

leaf spring. The small rear bar, when it was used, gave us a fine trim on the limit handling.

The front suspension was designed to produce the strongest possible self-aligning torque in the steering, with 6 degrees of caster plus 1/2 inch of pure trail. These combined to move the steer center one inch forward of the center of the tire contact patch. In its front view, the short upper control arm and the long lower control arm (SLA) were laid out geometrically to put the roll center of the body on its suspension at the ground plane. This minimizes the lateral motion of the tire as it goes over a bump and also keeps the outside tire as upright as possible in a turn. Unfortunately, because the suspension had to accommodate the base 15-inch wheel and tire, the brake rotor diameter was limited to 11 1/2 inches and the ball joint span and its kingpin axis were compromised by leaving almost 3 inches of lateral offset (scrub) in the intersection of the ball joint axis with the tire contact patch. Since this amount of scrub was typical of contemporary cars—including the previous Corvette—we thought little of it until we began exploring limits of braking control with antilock brakes the following year and saw the potential of using zero or even negative scrub.

Although the suspension and steering geometry are used to control the steer and camber of the tire, the forces that the tire generates also act on the suspension and cause elastic steer effects. The recognition that everything is elastic, and that it is better to control these elastic movements and put them to work, has led to the development of complex computer programs that predict the elastic behavior of the suspension. As a result, through the choice of geometry and bushing rates, the engineer is able to introduce controlled under- and oversteer effects due to the compliance in the suspension.

This is precisely why we configured the rear suspension with a laterally stiff rear toe link in conjunction with the U-jointed shaft upper link. It not only controlled the roll steer geometry, it moved the steer stiffness center of the rear suspension as far rearward as possible to minimize steer deflection, due to the tire-induced lateral forces.

The virtual side-view geometry of the rear suspension was that of a long arm inclined up and to the front and pointing above the center of gravity. This produced a counter-moment on the body

The new Corvette's rear suspension was an evolution of Duntov's independent rear suspension from the 1963 Sting Ray.

Dave McLellan Archives

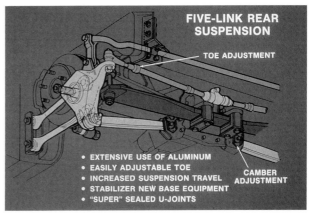

FIVE-LINK REAR SUSPENSION

TOE ADJUSTMENT

CAMBER ADJUSTMENT

- EXTENSIVE USE OF ALUMINUM
- EASILY ADJUSTABLE TOE
- INCREASED SUSPENSION TRAVEL
- STABILIZER NEW BASE EQUIPMENT
- "SUPER" SEALED U-JOINTS

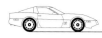

under acceleration that countered the pitch of the body due to its center-of-gravity height. Such an arm would be impossibly long, so it was represented by two arms whose virtual intersection produced the same result.

PUTTING THE BRAKES ON

For 17 years the Corvette had used a four-piston disc brake caliper that gave excellent stopping performance. We had solved the corrosion problem, so the principal reasons for updating the system were to make it smaller to reflect the reduced weight of the new car, make it lighter, and—as a fuel economy measure—eliminate the parasitic loss resulting from disc brake pad drag. We resized the vented brake rotors to the expected 3,150 curb weight of the new car by reducing both their diameter and thickness to 11 1/2 and 7/8 inches respectively.

The previous four-piston caliper (16 pistons per car) used the piston as the floating element between the caliper and the brake pad. However, with this much total piston area, any compliance or clearance in the brake pedal apply system was greatly exaggerated in increased pedal travel. Thus, it was considered impractical to allow the pads to retract away from the

A PRIMER ON ALUMINUM

The decision to produce the suspension knuckles, control arms and links in forged aluminum made the complex new geometry possible. We started with the 1982 Corvette with its rear suspension lower link in forged aluminum. This gave us the opportunity to fully validate the application and take it to production. The driving force behind the use of aluminum was its low investment cost. With a plastic-forming temperature much lower than steel, aluminum could be precision-forged in a progressive series of steel dies. Aluminum forgings were routinely used in aircraft for landing gear and engine supports, and had found their way into the heavy truck and trailer market, where load limits imposed on highways made weight savings pay off. As we investigated these applications, we saw that every aspect of aluminum's use, except for prevention of corrosion, had been thoroughly addressed. Tractor trailers operated in the same corrosion environment as Corvettes, but they had such a short life that their makers didn't worry about corrosion.

In some ways aluminum is very corrosion-resistant. There is no need to paint aluminum because it will form a natural oxide coating, although it is often painted purely for cosmetic reasons. Unfortunately, because of its position in the chart of galvanic potentials, it is the sacrificial anode when it comes in contact with iron and steel in the presence of an electrolyte. In particular, steel washers, bolts, and nuts will corrode their aluminum surroundings. A strategy to minimize this is to have large areas of aluminum in contact with small areas of steel. An even better solution is to coat the steel so it doesn't participate in the chemical reaction.

After many trials, an epoxy paint coating that could be spray- or dip-coated was found to be the robust coating we were looking for. Virtually all of the suspension attachments in contact with aluminum would be coated: fasteners, washers, nuts, and bushing housings. The only exceptions were tapered stud ball joint shanks, where the interface was protected by the rubber seal and applied grease.

The other aspect of dealing with aluminum is its indefinite fatigue limit. Steel has a well-defined fatigue limit at 10 million cycles. Design for fatigue stresses below this point, and the part will function forever. Aluminum, however, has an ever decreasing slope to its fatigue curve. Our suspension load case turned out to be dominated by potholes and curbs, and unless the car hit millions of them, fatigue would not be the limiting load case.

rotors to reduce drag, and they were held in light contact with coil springs behind each piston. This was a non-issue when horsepower was plentiful, and fuel economy was not even considered. But for us, it was important.

The disc brake calipers, developed by Girlock, an Australian joint venture of Girling and Lockheed, were a careful study in design and material application. They took advantage of aluminum to reduce the weight of the single-piston cylinder housing. However, they were designed with a thick bridge as a way to compensate for the higher elasticity of aluminum.

To eliminate pad drag, we had to first reduce the hydraulic volume and compliance of the system. This led us to a single piston, where there had been four, and to floating the caliper on sealed greased pins. The single piston minimized the hydraulic volume within what was considered a normal pedal travel. This left us with enough travel to first bring the pad into contact with the rotor. The inboard brake pad was retracted slightly by the rock-back action of its piston seal. The outer pad and caliper, no longer pressed by the inner piston, were then capable of being knocked back by the next road-induced lateral motion of the rotor.

With the caliper floating on its greased pins, the much larger pad braking reaction forces acted directly on a cast-iron frame that was bolted to the knuckle. This frame also supported the caliper pins and, through its stiffness, contributed to minimizing pad taper wear.

REFINING THE STRUCTURE

All our hard work, to define a more efficient structure, was essentially thrown out when Lloyd Reuss "requested" that we configure the car as a targa without the structural tie of the T-top. His directive came so late that we had no time to rethink the structure to find an efficient solution. In retrospect, having solved the same problem for the succeeding generation Corvette, we should have delayed the car for at least two years to find an appropriate solution.

To give ourselves the best chance of making the structure work with a targa configuration, we took the rocker sill that was tapered from low at the front to high at the rear and made it high all along its length. Tests on the first prototype proved that the car was still too flexible and showed us where the flexibility was concentrated in the structure. We added rein-

The disc brake calipers took advantage of aluminum to reduce the weight of the single-piston cylinder housing.

Dave McLellan Archives

The targa structure became the foundation for the C4 Corvette.
Drawing by Dave McLellan

forcements to stiffen the front rails and to tie them together better. In the end, we were successful in raising all the roof-on structural frequencies above wheel hop—but not as much as we would have liked. Our objective was to have the structure frequencies well above wheel hop, which was the highest frequency road input. With the roof off, the first torsion mode of the structure was still below wheel hop, and there was nothing we could do about it. Raising it a little bit only moved it closer to wheel hop and made the dynamic coupling worse. Actually, we had made our frequency-domain-juggling more difficult as a result of the stiff tires and lightweight suspension. Wheel hop, normally at 12 Hz, was now at 14.5 Hz, 2.5 Hz closer to our roof on structural frequencies.

Shock absorbers are used to dampen and control wheel and body motions. And, in a car with structural body vibration frequencies close to wheel hop, they also play a role in damping the structural modes. To the extent we could, we aimed the tubular shocks at the tire contact patch and made the intervening bushings as stiff as possible, so as to avoid twisting or steering the suspension in response to shock absorber loads. We succeeded best in the front, where the shock absorber was attached to the lower control arm, just inboard of the ball joint. Our original plan was to use the Delco dual-tube gas-bag shock, similar to those used on previous Corvettes. As we got into our development program, we found that a Bilstein high-pressure monotube gave us a better tradeoff among the competing control needs and didn't lose effectiveness in the extreme conditions of the racetrack.

INSIDE THE C4

As Bill Scott developed the interior at Design Staff, two features stood out: The "loaf of bread" in front of the passenger and the flat panel liquid crystal display (LCD) in front of the driver. The "loaf of bread" description came from the observation that an unbelted driver was better protected

BUILDING THE STRUCTURE

The decision to make the structure last as long as the plastic body panels required that we make it from two-side hot-dipped galvanized steel. It became Ron Burns' job to define the processes that would weld this coated steel, bond the plastic panels to it, and guarantee its precision manufacture.

Steel sheet, even in the relatively thick 2 mm gauge that we were planning to use, is typically spot-welded together. In addition, there is some arc welding involved, but if too much arc welding is used heat distortion becomes a problem. A spot-weld is produced by clamping the sheets between electrodes and applying a low-voltage, high-amperage current that fuses the steel sheets together. When they tried to weld through the thick zinc-galvanized coating, the current required to fuse the steel melted the zinc explosively. After many trials, they found they needed to apply a low current to melt the zinc and, using the pressure of the electrodes, squeeze the zinc out of the weld, then zap the weld with a high-current pulse to fuse the steel together.

Building every uni-frame to be dimensionally accurate (and of course the same) was the key to precision-building the car. We had had enough of a "custom built" car and were intent on building the new Corvette with a process that would guarantee the controlled fit of every part. Ron's strategy started with an axis system from which all dimensions were referenced. This axis system was carefully chosen to minimize the possibility that small dimensional errors would cascade into big ones. The design of the detailed parts also allowed for slip at interfaces rather than simply butting together. Each detailed part had its own set of precision gauge holes that related the part to the dimensional axis system. Each part as it was welded to the next was fixture-located by its gauge holes so that it would be welded in the correct design relationship. This dimensional management strategy carried through to the finished uni-frame.

The same gauging and fixturing strategy was applied to the tooling, manufacture, and assembly of the plastic body panels. Unfortunately, the strategy was not well understood, and it was lost on the body panel tooling, as toolmakers did their own thing. As a result, the first weeks of production were a nightmare, as we tried to get panels to fit without even having a common axis system from which to measure discrepancies. Several years later we sorted it all out and, as we had the money to implement the changes, we retooled the gauges and bonding fixtures for the body panels so that they would conform with Ron's original plan.

The dimensional axis and gauging system worked out on the new Corvette would ultimately benefit the C5.

Dave McLellan Archives

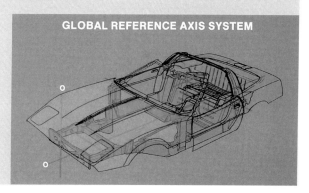

GLOBAL REFERENCE AXIS SYSTEM

in a frontal collision than a passenger, because of the energy-absorbing steering column. An unbelted passenger had to travel much farther before running into the dashboard, so the car could stop before the passenger even made contact. The sooner the passenger contacted the dash, the lower the velocity, and the lower the likelihood of serious injury.

With the new LCD cluster, we would become the guinea pig for AC Spark Plug Division, which developed this technology. Fortunately, we designed and tooled a conventional air-core gauge backup. Unfortunately, Bill was so enamored of the flat panel look that he applied it to the backup as well, leaving it with no anti-reflective lens, a serious problem when you have to see into an unlit piece of instrumentation. This encour-

THE DIGITAL INSTRUMENT PANEL

The small LCDs that are used in watches and calculators are usually reflective and depend on incidental ambient light to illuminate the display. We had the opportunity to do a transmission LCD, in which light bulbs behind the display uniformly illuminate the display through a light pipe. A color mask, using green, yellow, and red filters, would color code the display, making it easier for the driver to differentiate functions at a glance. The actual numbers or bar graphs were produced in much the same manner as in a watch display, but on a much larger scale. The polarized organic liquid crystal material was sandwiched between sealed glass plates. With the cross-polarized overlay, the design allowed very little light to pass through. The glass plates were coated with an almost invisible metal conducting layer that represented each and every element of the display. Applying a micro-current through the grid elements would rotate the liquid crystal molecules, aligning their polarization with the second polarizer and letting light pass through. AC Spark Plug Division described the cells as "negative image, transmissive, twisted nematic LCD's having a dark background and active areas that change from dark to clear like a shutter when energized."

Several pieces of the information we wanted to display on the instrument panel were already available as digitally encoded signals in the engine computer, so the two computers were tied together with a serial-data link. With this link, the instrument panel had access to all the information that was coursing around inside the engine computer. Speed, rpm, temperature, and pressure signals could not only be displayed, but they could also be continually monitored. If they exceeded a limit, a warning light could be turned on, producing a "smart" idiot light. The engine computer drove the pulse-width-modulated fuel injectors. The "on" time of this signal was directly proportional to fuel flow. Using this data and a few calculations, we had miles per gallon, or its metric reciprocal, liters/100 km. We could also calculate average mpg.

Since all the data was processed and displayed digitally, accuracy was limited only by the sensors, Many sensors were being used to manage the engine, and they had already been picked for accuracy. Speed was calculated by counting pulses on a toothed wheel. When the LCD read 140 mph it was correct within one mph. Inaccuracy crept in only as the tires wore. In contrast, conventional air core gauges are highly nonlinear and can be calibrated to be accurate at only one test point. If the reading must always err on the high side, as with speed, one seldom reads high speeds that are less than 5-percent optimistic.

From this project we learned a great deal about making reliable electrical systems, and about producing useful driver displays. As a final step in making this complex display reliable, every production display was electrically and thermally burned in for eight hours before it was shipped to Bowling Green to be installed in a car.

The press saw the LCD instrument panel as glitzy; we saw it as an unambiguous display of information. Shown is an interesting variation on what would become the final production design.

Dave McLellan Archives

aged us to work even harder to make the LCD work, because we knew the backup's shortcomings.

Much to our chagrin, the sports car enthusiast press never liked the digital instrument display. After the euphoria of the new car introduction diminished, the press started complaining that we had traded their familiar and traditional sports car analog gauges for a glitzy Las Vegas Mickey Mouse digital display. But, as we learned to use the display, we found that we could read digital numbers with only a momentary glance away from the road, which was far faster than with the analog version. In showroom stock racing, we would discover just how useful the panel was for the driver who had no time to read gauges.

It is ironic that Corvette, after pioneering precision LCD instrumentation, made the decision to return to primitive analog gauges because of the negative response from the press. Around the time that Corvette was reverting to analog gauges, Formula I and Indy-CART racing embraced LCD technology with instrument panels similar to the original Corvette LCD panel.

Never controversial, but just as high tech, was the Bose sound system destined for the new Corvette. Dr. Amar Bose—an MIT professor of electrical engineering—a leader in acoustics and a developer of home and theater sound systems, came to Delco Electronics with a proposal for a high-performance automotive sound system. When I heard about it, I told Delco that the Corvette had to be first to receive it.

Although the Bose system was a $1,000 option, it quickly became a required part of a new Corvette. Dealers who ordered cars without the Bose audio package couldn't sell them. Customers would ask specifically for Bose, leather and the Z-51 suspension.

Formula I drivers have long relied on digital instruments.
Courtesy the GP Library

The concept of Bose speaker placement achieved a concert hall experience for both driver and passenger. It was so successful that Chevrolet dealers couldn't sell a Corvette if it didn't have a Bose audio system.
Drawing by Dave McLellan

PROTOTYPES AND TESTING

The prototype program greatly expanded the scope of our test and development activity. As development and durability test cars proliferated, Jim Ingle and his small Proving Grounds crew became overwhelmed. Fred Schaafsma, who had just finished managing a similar major test and development program on the 1982 Camaro and Firebird, was asked to take on the new Corvette assignment, mixing our

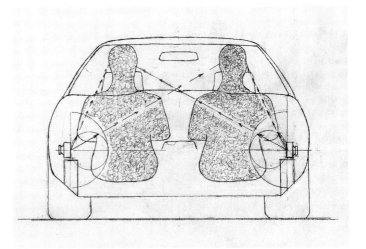

DEVELOPING THE BOSE AUDIO SYSTEM

Dr. Bose was turned off by car sound systems with their thin-sounding paper speakers, distorted base, and limited stereo effect. His first thought was that it would be easy to develop concert hall acoustics in the confined space of a car interior. "A concert hall in a phone booth," he called it. Dr. Bose became enamored of the incredible potential of having a controlled environment where everything was known. He described it as an opportunity to do something even better than what was theoretically possible with home stereo. It turned out to be much more complicated than that, but with perseverance we succeeded.

If a concert performance is properly recorded on tape, the recording contains enough information to reproduce the listening experience of sitting in the auditorium's best seat. The recording contains the slight differences in loudness and time delay which the ear and brain process to tell you where the sound is coming from.

There were a few innate difficulties in developing a sound system for an automobile. Cars are symmetrical along their centerline, as is the typical car stereo installation. However, because the drivers and passengers are off-center, the balance controls are often used to compensate. The driver has to adjust the stereo effect to the left to perceive it in his location. The passenger would adjust the stereo effect to the right. Unfortunately, there is no way to simultaneously give both the driver and passenger the stereo effect using the balance control. Additionally, in order to locate the sound in front of the driver, speakers were usually mounted in the top pad of the instrument panel, and aimed to reflect off the windshield. But, the instrument panel is so packed with instrumentation, wiring, air conditioning, and structural elements that there is no room for a large speaker enclosure that would enhance the acoustics.

To simulate a concert hall within a car requires an understanding of psychoacoustics, which is the study of how the ear hears and the brain processes acoustical signals. Dr. Bose developed a unique and methodical approach to developing a car's interior as a listening space. Unfortunately, it required a car and several weeks of testing to develop the details. For the Corvette, we had neither a pre-prototype nor a prototype car that we could spare. So we built Bose a mock-up of the interior, using a spare uniframe mounted on casters and including the doors,

glass, roof, carpet, seats, and some plywood (to simulate the instrument panel and floors that we had no parts for).

A Bose team, led by Joe Veranth, came to Chevrolet Engineering with a huge quantity of speakers, test equipment and "Morgan," their simulated listener. Seated in the driver's seat, Morgan accurately simulated a human listener, in the physical sense, but it was not as easy to simulate the processing that a real brain goes through when listening. This analysis required a live feed back to Bose's research facility in Framingham, Massachusetts, and the processing capability of their computer lab.

Speaker locations were, at first, an educated guess. Then, as engineers processed the results, they homed in on locations that met all of their criteria. The process began with Morgan listening to a series of tones and pings. From the mathematical analysis of the loudness and time delays of these sounds experienced by Morgan, the Bose engineers would assess ideal speaker location and develop the electrical weighting network that was needed to put the concert in front of the listener.

In the final result, the best stereo effect came from locating the speakers on the doors, facing across the car, at approximately knee level. At the higher frequencies that control the stereo effect, the driver hears the powerful direct main lobe of the right-hand speaker and a less powerful side lobe of the nearby left speaker, creating a balanced stereo effect. The passenger hears the mirror image of this effect, and can enjoy the balanced acoustics as well.

Each front speaker was essentially a high-performance Bose 901 speaker. To it, an electronic weighting network and a power amplifier were added. This was then enclosed in a plastic housing which gave it volume and, with a tuned port, its low-frequency performance. But, front speakers alone could not produce the all-enveloping sound of a concert hall. Rear speakers were needed to fill in the sound. Because there is more space in the rear for large enclosure volumes, these speakers, though otherwise identical to the front speakers, were used to produce the lowest frequencies.

Finally, during the fine-tuning part of the development process, the Bose experts listened to music over the system they had created to produce a "concert hall in a phone booth."

small crew with selected engineers from the almost completed F-car program. Fred and his team worked tirelessly to solve the structural problems and keep the test program on track.

Fred, and handling development engineer Rick Darling, thought that 1.0g cornering was within our grasp if we could keep the tires from cambering. Race cars are often set up with the tires initially cambered by one to two degrees negative, so that during hard cornering the outside tire is straight up. This is an accepted compromise for the racetrack, but for a road car which has to perform satisfactorily in the rain and even on ice, the resulting camber thrust experienced during straight driving and its accompanying tire wear would be unacceptable. For running straight down the road, the tire wants to be upright and roll straight ahead with as little toe as possible. To raise the handling limit without compromising straight-ahead running, Fred argued for increasing the roll stiffness so the car would roll less in a turn. To achieve this, he started raising the front and rear spring rates well beyond our original plan.

The Z-51 suspension option was the result. As it was developed, handling, acceleration and braking were wonderfully taut and precise, and maneuvers were conducted with a seeming absence of roll and pitch. There was no oscillation, no overshoot; the car simply did what was asked—immediately. On its new tires, the car was also very forgiving at full throttle, even when the throttle was released abruptly.

We drove the cars in the protected confines of the Proving Ground and could see no flaw in Fred's strategy. With security such an important issue for a new car—especially an all-new Corvette—and with Jim Dunne lurking at the edges of the Proving Grounds tying to photograph the car, it was suicidal to take the car off the grounds. Thus we drove the car only on smooth roads or on the brutally rough test roads of the Proving Grounds and missed the subtle nuances of frost-heaved real-world roads until after the press introduction.

The press introduction was scheduled for the fall of 1982 in southern California. We would start with testing at Riverside International Raceway and finish on the remote roads of the valleys north of the Los Angeles basin. But before we stood in front of the press, we had to decide on a model year and a price for this new car.

What had been approved as an 1983 eventually became a late 1983, with production starting just after the first of the year. And, because production started after the first of the year, the new car could be called an

1984 model. The federal government defines the model year by its emission certification rules, which state that the model year can contain only one January 1. We had lots of spirited discussions about uninterrupted Corvette tradition, but in the end we opted for the logic of building for 17 months and the attendant reduction in paperwork of not having to recertify for the 1984 model year.

INTRODUCING THE C4

None of us knew what the price was going to be, although we each had our own guess. Bob Stempel, who was back at Chevrolet as our Vice President and General Manager, planned to announce the price in front of the press at Riverside. We had set up several large tents, within the road course, which would be used for the press conference and for the extensive supplier displays. The night before the press conference, the area was hit with violent rain and winds in what later would be described as a "once in a 100 years storm" for the desert community of Riverside.

When we arrived at the track in the morning, the new Corvettes were fine, but the parts of the track that were not under water were covered with mud. The infield was a sodden mess and all the tents were down, with our displays underneath. While our support crew set about clearing the track, we salvaged the displays from under the tents and moved them to our hotel, where the hotel staff had rescheduled another event so we could use the ballroom for our press conference and supplier display. While members of the press were having breakfast, Stempel announced that we would hold our press conference at 10 o'clock and be lapping the track by 2 o'clock. We made our deadlines, thanks to the yeoman efforts of everyone who pitched in.

Stempel teased the press by announcing the price one number at a time. He put up a 1 in the ten thousands' place and then looked at it. "No, that's not right," he said, and replaced the 1 with a 2. And so it went until he had placed all the numbers to spell out $21,800. Reflected in this base price was the decision to make the P255/50R16 Goodyear tire standard equipment.

For the next two days the press flogged both manual and automatic Corvettes around the track. Then we moved our headquarters to the Biltmore in Santa Barbara and continued, with the press driving a one-day route that circled through the Sierra Madre Mountains. The route took them northwest out of Santa Barbara, over the San Marcos Pass, and across back roads to Santa Maria. Turning east past San Luis Obispo, the

route then took them over mountains and across desert to Taft, where they turned south through more mountains and canyons to Ojai, and then back to Santa Barbara. Jingles plotted the route, using short sections of expressway to connect together the most interesting high-speed mountain roads he could find. The press was ecstatic; the cars met their need for speed and exhilarating motoring. We would reap the rewards of a successful introduction with magazine headlines such as:

"Corvette, a Star is Born." *Motor Trend*, March 1983

"Corvette! Wherein America takes on all comers." *Car and Driver*

"One Classy Chassis: Behold the most ambitious array of high technology ever to roll down an assembly line on four wheels." *Car and Driver* Technical Analysis, March 1983

"The New Corvette: An American original, a world-class performer, and a job well done." *Motor Trend*, March 1983

"Formula One Chevy: A Technical Overview of the World's Best Handling Production Car." *Motor Trend*, March 1983

We were delighted with the response from the motoring press, and we were ready to put the 1984 Corvette into full production.

POSTSCRIPT

As we ramped up production, we started selling in California in January of 1983, and then went nationwide in March. The press hype over the first new Corvette in 20 years, and our having turned the corner on performance, caused a feeding frenzy. Finally, we could drive the cars anywhere without security being a problem.

The car had ridden beautifully on California's smooth roads, but driving in Michigan was a different story. The Z51 in particular was far too stiff for the typical frost-damaged roads. The car felt like it was launching itself over every bump. We began working on the problem by installing the lower-rate springs for which the car had originally been designed. The final solution came when we retuned the shocks for the lower-rate springs. The ride quality problem wasn't as much the high spring rates as it was the result of the higher shock-damping values that were needed to control the higher-frequency body motions that resulted from the higher spring rates. The shock absorbers (a misnomer because they actually transmit shock) that control body motions and wheel hop also introduced large impulsive forces when the car would go over a sharp vertical dis-

turbance, such as a frost-heaved section of pavement. The stiffer suspension increased the dynamic force input from rough roads, and the close frequency coupling between wheel hop and the first modes of the structure amplified this response, making the ride feel harsh and, at times, shaky.

Car and Driver, based in Ann Arbor, Michigan, also complained about the harsh ride after the magazine's staff had a chance to drive the cars on "Rust Belt" roads. We agreed with them, but couldn't say so. All we could do was wait until the 1985—with its lower spring rates—was ready, and try to discourage dealers from ordering the Z51 where its use was inappropriate.

NUCCIO BERTONE'S RAMARO

Every year, Nuccio Bertone challenged his designers to create a public display of the design capabilities of Carrozzeria Bertone S.p.A. Most of his show cars were mid-engine exotics, typically on a Ferrari platform, although one of the most famous was the Countach, designed by Marchello Gandini and later turned into a production car by Lambroghini.

We heard through Bertone's American agent, Bruce McWilliams, that the company was trying, without success, to buy an 1984 Corvette as the basis for their next show car. This was very flattering, yet I did wonder what Jerry Palmer's reaction would be to a competing Corvette design. I didn't wonder for long, though, because I asked Chevrolet if we could give Bertone a preproduction test car. With the General Manager's agreement we shipped Bertone a well-used red preproduction 1983 Corvette. We thought we were giving them the car until we heard that Chevrolet's financial manager, Jim Salarin, had sent Bertone a bill for $20,000. Thoroughly embarrassed, I volunteered that we would update the car to 1985 PFI engine specifications. We sent John Rice to Turin, Italy, to oversee the engine installation and to completely rewire the car as a 1985.

Bertone had not created a front-engine show car in years, and the Ramaro was an opportunity for his designers to give form and detail to a very different platform. They expressed themselves eloquently, although what they produced was not a "Corvette" in the traditional American sense. Their car was technically notable for its forward

sliding door (similar to a sliding mini-van door) and its rear-mounted radiator.

After its showing on the European auto show circuit, Bertone brought the Ramaro to the States. In a private ceremony at the Ponchatrain Hotel in Detroit, Nuccio Bertone presented me with a green 1/5 scale model of the Ramaro. In an effort to make conversation (his English was limited and my Italian was nonexistent), I told him that I would add tires and wheels so that the model would be like the real car. Mr Bertone looked at me quizzically, replying that the model was an expression of the design, and had no need for tires and wheels. So, I never added tires and wheels to the model.

Bertone's Ramaro was a dramatically different expression of the front-engine sports car.

Photo by Carrozeria Bertone

The C4 Matures and Spawns a Roadster

8

FINISHING UP THE ALL-NEW CORVETTE had taken all our energies for two years. We had largely ignored any future Corvette planning and had concentrated on delivering the 1984 model. When we had started this process in 1979, we had put every good idea we could muster into this car and had brought it back to a state-of-the-art sports car. Near the end of the process we were short of fresh ideas. Though it may have just been fatigue; in any case it would take us a while to get back on track toward giving the Corvette a future beyond the 1984 model. In all ways, it was fortunate that we had a 17-month model year to recover our energies and get on with the future.

CHANGES FOR THE 1985 MODEL YEAR

While we were finishing up the car, Roy Midgley and his V-8 engine team had given up on Crossfire throttle body injection (TBI). After three years of trying, they realized that TBI would never give them the precise cylinder-to-cylinder fuel control they needed to meet the ever-climbing fuel economy standard.

With product cost a constant aspect of the decision-making process, Midgley's group probably had to go through the TBI step to prove to themselves and to Chevrolet management that they needed the more precise metering of port fuel injection, to meet the standards. Corporate politics also played a part in the decision—GM was making throttle body injectors, and not unit injectors. For the 1985 model year, the only source of unit injectors and their metering system was Bosch, in Germany.

For several years, Bosch had been supplying the European automakers with electronic pulse-width-modulated individual-cylinder (port) fuel injection that used a mechanical vane to measure airflow (L-Jetronic). The company was just about to go into production with a hot wire air meter (LH-Jetronic) that further improved the system's ability to measure the mass flow of air used in combustion. As a bonus, the tiny hot wire

in the air stream caused virtually no intake pressure drop as it made its measurement.

When Chevrolet finally gave the green light to go with port fuel injection, Midgley's engine team chose not to use the complete Bosch system, but produced a hybrid combining Bosch and Delco componentry.

While meeting tougher emission standards, and increasing fuel economy 11 percent through the use of the port fuel injection, Midgley's team still managed to raise horsepower by 12 percent, from 205 to 230 net horsepower (nhp) at 4,000 rpm, and torque by a whopping 14 percent, from 290 to 330 ft. lbs at 3,200 rpm. The engine team took full advantage of the dry manifold, using tuned length intake runners to raise the torque peak. Given the code designation "L98," this version of the Chevrolet small block was still a "tractor motor." It lacked the free revving high-rpm character of the LT1 Corvette small block, but it did take the 1985 Corvette a big step closer to recapturing the performance peak of 1970.

PORT FUEL INJECTION FOR THE CORVETTE

Once the approvals were given to proceed with a port fuel injection system, Roy Midgley and his team integrated the Bosch injectors and hot wire air meter with an AC Delco High Energy Ignition (HEI) and a collection of sensors that measured the various parameters that were needed for the control strategy. These parameters included throttle position, crank rotary position, exhaust oxygen level, spark knock (detonation), detection and engine coolant temperature. They helped manage the process of turning on the fuel injectors and timing the HEI spark.

The fuel system began with an in-tank high-pressure electric fuel pump that pumped gasoline to the injectors. A fuel pressure regulator on the end of the injector fuel rail maintained a constant pressure at the injectors, and sent excess fuel back to the tank. This continuous return of excess fuel also served to purge the system of air and vapor, and to cool the injectors. The eight injectors, located just upstream of the intake valves, were turned on in cadence with every crankshaft revolution. Their "on" time was calculated to deliver the correct amount of fuel. Known as "simultaneous double fire," the computer system interrogated the mass airflow sensor and calculated the fuel injector "on" time needed to produce a stoichiometric air-fuel ratio. The computer improved the precision of this calculation with the exhaust oxygen sensor's data. When enrichment was required for starting or accelerating, the computer increased the injector "on" time accordingly. Cold starting in extreme conditions (below −20° F) was augmented with a ninth injector. Called a "cold-start valve," it flooded the intake manifold with additional fuel.

Idle speed was controlled independently of the throttle by an idle-air motor that modulated an air bypass around the throttle blades. Knowing the current engine idle speed and counting the turns of the idle air motor required the idle air passage to be closed at engine shut-down, the computer reopened the idle air passage at each engine restart to reestablish the design-intended idle speed.

The HEI ignition used a permanent magnet, eight-pole-piece ring rotating at half crank speed, and a pickup coil, all crammed inside the distributor to give the computer the crank position reference signal it needed for ignition timing. Timing changes were all done electronically—there was no vacuum or mechanical advance. The ignition computer monitored the engine sensors and computed the desired spark timing based on previously established relationships between the sensor values and optimum spark timing.

One of the most interesting elements of the fuel system was the knock sensor, an accelerometer mounted on the engine block to detect the high-frequency ringing that was the signature of destructive combustion detonation caused by low octane fuel. The HEI computer could progressively retard spark as much as 20 degrees, to reduce the detonation to a level that was no longer destructive.

As a result of John Heinricy's development testing, spring rates were reduced by 25 percent with the standard suspension, and by 16 percent for the front and 25 percent for the rear, with the RPO Z51. Interestingly, this was accomplished without a loss in handling performance. After our mid-year 1984 introduction of Bilstein shock absorbers with the Z51, we found that the Bilstein monotube high-pressure gas shock also improved ride isolation with the base suspension. As a result of this finding, the Bilstein monotube was made available on all 1985 Corvettes.

For years, we had been relying on the car magazines to test and report Corvette performance, and the 1985 model was no exception. *Car and Driver* tested the manual and reported 0-60 mph in 6.0 seconds, the standing 1/4 mile in 14.4 seconds at 97 mph, and a top speed of 150 mph. The automatic was even faster, reaching 60 mph in 5.7 seconds, covering the standing 1/4 mile in 14.1 seconds at 97 mph, although its top speed matched that of the manual version. This was world-class performance and could be bested by only a few European exotic cars.

Unfortunately, because of certain truth-in-advertising requirements, the Chevrolet Sales Department could use none of the media's splendid performance results in their advertising. But, they really wanted to tout Corvette's world-class performance, so the folks in advertising put together a comparison test that would be run under United States Automobile Club (USAC) certification. USAC bought, at retail, a 1985 manual transmission Corvette, a Lamborghini Countach, a Porsche 911, 928S, and 944, a Ferrari 308 GTSi, and a Lotus Turbo Esprit.

Using professional race drivers as testers, during the winter of 1984, USAC wrung out each of these cars for acceleration, braking, slalom performance, and lateral acceleration at an independently owned test facility in the Arizona desert. Our Corvette engineers were not allowed within 200 feet of the cars, so there was no chance for cheating. For each data point, as many as 90 runs were made, using three drivers. The ten best results were then selected for averaging and reporting.

The acceleration runs were done with high-rpm "pop the clutch" type starts and, late in the testing, the Porsche 911 exploded its transaxle. But, USAC was out of time: Chevrolet needed the results by the first of the year for their advertising campaign. USAC couldn't repair the 911 in time, so the only option was to retire the car.

The test results were an absolutely honest record of the performance of these world-class sports cars. Many years earlier, Ralph Stein had written his prescription for the ideal world-class sports car. He had stipulated

John Heinricy has brought his competitive skills as a race driver and development engineer to two generations of Corvettes.
Photo by Jim Ward

USAC COMPETITIVE RANK AND PERFORMANCE FOR ALL THE COMPETITORS

	Corvette	Lamborghini Countach	Porsche 944	Ferrari 308 GTSi	Lotus Esprit Turbo	Porsche 928
Total Points	21	18	14	11	11	9
Acceleration 0–60 (sec.)	4 (6.00)	6 (5.33)	1 (7.95)	3 (6.43)	5 (5.95)	2 (6.66)
Braking 60–0 (sec.)	6 (129.2)	3 (135.7)	4 (135.2)	2 (143.1)	1 (144.7)	5 (135.1)
Slalom (sec.)	6 (6.13)	3 (6.38)	5 (6.33)	4 (6.36)	2 (6.40)	1 (6.62)
Lateral Acceleration (g's)	5 (.91)	6 (.92)	4 (.86)	2 (.83)	3 (.85)	1 (.82)
Price as Tested	$26,703	$103,700	$26,121	$60,370	$50,384	$49,495

Point scoring was based on an Olympic system in which a total of six points was awarded the winner of each event, five points for second place, and so on. The total points were then tallied for the overall winner, Corvette.

The USAC certified test began in mid-November and concluded January 1, 1985. All the cars were the latest models available in the U.S. at the time of testing.

that such a car would have a top speed of at least 150 mph, with acceleration of 0-60 mph in under 6.0 seconds, and a standing 1/4 mile time of 12 to 14 seconds. By 1985, this level of performance was being achieved by the Corvette as well as a few of its competitors.

ABS FOR THE CORVETTE

In the late 1960s, GM's brake division, Delco Moraine, pioneered a two-wheel antilock braking system (ABS) for the rear wheels of the front-drive Oldsmobile Toronado. The ideal front-to-rear brake balance for any braking system varies with changes in deceleration rate and with passenger and luggage load. Under braking, a car's front tires experience increased downforce, and the rear tires experience decreased downforce. When the car decelerates at 1.0g deceleration, the front tires are subjected to approximately 20 percent more downforce and the rear tires are subjected to approximately 20 percent less downforce. This is dealt with conventionally by using a proportioning valve that moderates the pressure to the rear brakes as the brake pressure is increased. Increased passenger and luggage load produces the opposite effect, increasing the weight on the rear wheels more than it does on the front. With more than 60 percent of its weight already on its front wheels, the Toronado tended to overuse its front brakes and, consequently, use too little of the rear braking capacity. Antilock control of the rear brakes allowed the brake engineer to increase

the use of the rear brakes without inducing rear-wheel slide. If the control system detected any tendency for rear-wheel slide, it caused the brake pressure in the rear wheels to be moderated until the wheels were rolling again. This two-wheel antilock system was little more than a sophisticated proportioning valve. Because it was optional and its value was never well understood by the dealers or the customers, it never sold well and was ultimately cancelled.

Kelsey-Hayes built a variation of this two-wheel system, and in 1975 experimentally combined two sets of ABSs into a four-wheel antilock brake system, which they demonstrated on a Ford police car. We evaluated this car and were impressed. Yet it was hard to extrapolate results from a servo-assisted sedan with drum brakes to a four-wheel disc brake Corvette. Under aggressive braking, the servo-assisted drums tended to be self-locking and made a slow recovery from a momentary lockup. Conversely, the Corvette disc brakes were linear and were much more quickly and easily modulated. We contracted Kelsey-Hayes to build the system into a Corvette, for our own evaluation.

The completed ABS-equipped Corvette test car was a maze of wires, relays, and solenoids and was managed by a pair of two-wheel computers tied together electrically and packaged into a one-cubic-foot box. The microchip-based onboard digital computer was still in the future, but the ABS computers, even though they were solid-state devices, functioned as analog computers; using resistors, capacitors, inductors, and amplifiers to modify input signals and produce a control signal. Only the simplest calculations could be made, and the test car's computers were unreliable and had no fault detection ability. The system required a test engineer to keep it running and to reprogram it for any variations.

We tested the car in a wide variety of road situations and saw the benefit of reduced wheel lockup, although the Corvette's foundation disc brake system was so linear, and easy to modulate, that much of the benefit could be duplicated within the foundation system using carefully modulated braking. We were lukewarm as to its possibilities, given the system's complexity, its poor initial reliability, and its intrusiveness in the car. With only weak customer acceptance of two-wheel anti-lock brakes and no major interest, Kelsey-Hayes ultimately abandoned the program.

In 1978, Mercedes-Benz and Bosch collaborated on a four-wheel antilock brake system, ABS-1, which was introduced on the German automaker's top-of-the-line cars. By 1984, Bosch was developing a second-generation system that would take advantage of all the intervening

developments that had taken place in engine controls after the introduction of the onboard digital computer.

As Chevrolet management was negotiating with Bosch to use its port fuel injection hardware for the 1985 Corvette, Bosch briefed them on their development of ABS-2. I first heard about this when Paul King, Chevrolet's Engineering Director, called me into his office and asked me to work with Bosch, to introduce ABS-2 on the 1986 Corvette. Paul sensed the potential value of ABS and, although we had no idea of the system cost, we knew that making technological advances in safety was the right use of the Corvette. As it turned out, the system cost for this first low-volume ABS application was more than 10 percent of the cost of the entire car. It did, however, demonstrate the benefits of ABS to a large audience and encouraged the broad application, which led to a dramatic reduction in the system's cost.

Bosch took almost a year to build the first ABS-equipped Corvettes and then put them through a test cycle in Germany and in frozen Sweden. When

HOW THE ABS WORKS

The antilock brake system takes advantage of the phenomenon that a tire slipping on the road but still rolling (short of a locked slide) exerts the maximum braking force and still manages considerable lateral force, which can be used for steering control. Bosch's ABS-2 began by measuring the instantaneous angular speed of each tire with a 72-tooth wheel. From this, the ABS computer calculated the tire deceleration. When tire deceleration reached a predetermined rate, the system would presume that the tire is starting to lock up. The computer would then open a solenoid valve in the brake line, and drop the brake pressure that was causing the tire to lock. As the tire began to reaccelerate, the solenoid closed and held the wheel's brake pressure. As the tire accelerated further, brake pressure from the master cylinder was reintroduced, to start the cycle over again. Continued cycling, and dumping of brake fluid, would make the brake pedal go to the floor, so a hydraulic pump repressurized the dumped fluid and returned it to the pressurized master cylinder.

If the system managed each corner independently it would keep the tires from sliding, and thus maximize deceleration and maintain some steering control. But, given sufficient capacity, the computer could compare the forces being generated at each corner, and manage them to maximize the braking performance and fully maintain the directional stability of car.

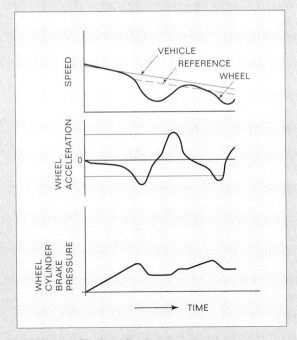

Time history of brake application.

Bosch was satisfied with the performance of the system, the company began involving us in the testing, first in Sweden and then in Michigan.

From our experience with the Kelsey-Hayes four-wheel ABS, we were still skeptical that the performance of the Bosch system could possibly justify the effort, or the cost. Jim Ingle (Jingles), who had done most of the testing with the K-H system, was the most skeptical of all, so he was picked to test the Bosch system.

Jingles first ran a comparison of dry-road straight-line stops from 100 mph. A locked slide from 100 mph was a spectacular sight, because of the tire smoke it generated. The tires were flat-spotted all the way to the steel belts, and were awful to drive on even at low speeds. Jingles started the sliding stop with the car going as straight as possible so that it would continue to slide in a straight line, unless it hit road turbulence. It was almost impossible to stop without some rotation. With no directional control during the slide, Jingles simply had to wait it out. He learned not to release the brakes until the car stopped completely, otherwise the tires would regain rolling contact and send the car shooting off in whatever direction it was pointed. The locked-wheel stops showed a consistent 0.75g average deceleration.

Driver-modulated stops were much better. With practice, several drivers were able to achieve 1.0g stops, although their average stops were in the 0.90 to 0.95g range; their worst stops were no better than the locked-wheel stops. When it came to the ABS-controlled stops we found that they were essentially equivalent to the best driver-controlled stops, but they were much more consistent and required no practice to achieve.

What really blew us away was being able to brake hard under limit cornering or during a violent evasive maneuver, without sliding. We set these driver tasks up on the Proving Ground's Vehicle Dynamics Test Area (VDTA), otherwise known as "Black Lake" because its quarter-mile square of asphalt gave us safe runout room no matter what we did with the car. We found that during high-speed cornering we could now bang on the brakes at any time during the maneuver, and still stop hard. For example, at 100 mph we could enter a 0.9g turn, bang on the brakes, and be stopped within 4.5 seconds. As a car with ABS decelerates in a constant-radius turn, the lateral acceleration falls away with the square of the speed, and the car quickly trades lateral acceleration for longitudinal acceleration and stops under complete control with very little steering correction needed. A 100 mph double lane change, or evasive maneuver, behaved in much the same manner. If you could negotiate the maneuver

without braking, you could now bang on the brakes at any point in the maneuver and come to a controlled stop in 4.5 seconds.

For the driver, this was a heady leap forward in dynamic control. For the passenger who had no experience with ABS, and was now being subjected to a violent maneuver that was previously impossible, this was sheer lunacy. All the passenger knew was that the car came to a stop after 4.5 seconds of violent maneuvering and it was still pointed in the right direction.

Mike Kimberley, President of Lotus Cars and of their engineering consultancy, visited us at the Proving Grounds while we were doing the ABS testing. He expressed some disdain for antilock brakes, particularly for a car as controllable as the Lotus Esprit. So I took him for a ride on Black Lake. As a result of the controlled violence I put him through, he gained a new appreciation for the possibilities of ABS.

One of the more difficult situations for ABS to control was hard braking with the left wheels on dry asphalt and the right wheels on the gravel shoulder. In this instance—called "a split mu encounter"—the braking forces are much more effective on the paved side and the car will tend to yaw if a steer correction is not quickly applied. In addition, because of its large steering scrub radius, the Corvette fed these differential forces into the steering so that the driver had to deal with a large torque tugging on the steering wheel.

Bosch had a solution. If the brakes were applied rapidly and the right wheel, which was on gravel, went quickly into ABS control instead of allowing the left wheel to continue ramping up, the control system took charge of the pressure to the left brake and ramped it up at a controlled rate. The highest useful rate was established by driver reaction time, so even if the driver banged on the brakes, the yaw buildup was slow enough that the driver could correct for it. Through testing, we found that drivers could react to this situation if the left front brake pressure was ramped up within about one second. Ramping up faster presented no loss, in terms of reduced stopping distance, because it was not a controllable maneuver anyway. Bosch called this strategy "yaw control." With its addition to the system, it was beginning to dawn on us that the car's limit of control, which contained many instabilities as we combined cornering with braking and acceleration, could be stabilized using system-wide microprocessor-based control.

However, even this early yaw control did not come without a price. As we went back and reviewed braking in a high-g high-speed turn, we found we had lost the marvelous stability we had before. The tire slip

behavior above 0.8g looked the same to the control system as a split mu straight-line stop. The control system was ramping up the heavily loaded outside front tire, reducing the initial deceleration enough that more time was being spent at the limit and making the path control, which had previously been so easy, more difficult. No sooner had we discovered this instability than Bosch had a solution for it. They would add a lateral accelerometer that would allow the control system to discriminate between the two situations. Yaw control would apply in all maneuvers below 0.6g, and above 0.6g lateral acceleration the control system would ignore yaw control.

One day during ABS development, handling development engineer Rick Darling came in from a test ride all excited. He had been hot-lapping the Proving Ground's ride and handling loop. On the long straight section, which contains a series of high-amplitude waves that can make a car go airborne, Rick had been running about 110 mph, letting the car fly across the troughs. At the end of this series the road makes a sharp 75 mph right-hand turn. Rick braked for the turn and nothing happened for what seemed like an eternity. The brakes did finally kick in, and Rick made the turn, although he didn't enjoy the experience. We finally figured out that the control system had interpreted the application of the brakes while the car was airborne as if it were braking on wet ice, where there is virtually no traction. In the case of wet ice, the system would apply the brakes with great care to avoid wheel slide, allowing for a long recovery time to get the tires rolling again. A time delay was programmed into the system that would not allow another heavy application of the brakes for at least one second.

If you have ever tried to walk on wet ice, you know that it can be so slippery that it is difficult to simply stand up. Our ABS was actually quite capable on wet ice, giving the car a level of stability and control we had never known before. We obviously didn't want to lose this, but we also didn't want drivers to have to wait a second for a full brake application, after hitting a large bump in the road. At 65 mph, the car travels nearly 100 feet in one second, and any braking delay could be critical. Bosch started working on the problem, but couldn't solve it immediately because everything they did affected everything else, and they required a winter test cycle to verify that no other attributes of the system had been compromised. Eventually, Bosch was able to safely reduce the time delay to half a second. Given the unusual nature of the situation, this seemed like an appropriate balance of requirements.

While we were working with Bosch, the teams that were running the Corvette in SCCA showroom stock racing provided an excellent testing opportunity for the system. And ABS was included in our 24-hour endurance track testing. One of the racers we were testing with, John Powell, also ran an advanced driving school on the track at Mosport, in Ontario, Canada. We supplied him with 1985 Corvettes and learned a great deal from watching his students react to the car. This became a confirmation that the car was well behaved yet fun to drive for the amateur as well as for the skilled driver.

We asked John to work with us on our ABS development and gave him ABS equipped cars for his school as soon as we could. We wanted to be sure that we weren't missing something, as we turned the car over to our own civilian customers. We recognized that, with the amount of testing we did, we tended to be expert drivers, accumulating tens of thousands of test miles a year, with many of them on the racetrack. Would our customers react to ABS the same way we had? Could ABS be introduced without extensive driver training? How would civilian drivers react to the pedal pulsations encountered in braking on low-coefficient surfaces, as the ABS pump returned fluid to the master cylinder?

We learned that the Corvette could be the same capable car even in the hands of a novice. But, we also learned that the full benefits of ABS were not going to be achieved unless drivers had at least minimal training in its use. ABS benefited from an aggressive approach to brake application. Banging on the pedal and staying hard on it was the best approach. This activated the ABS quickly, for increased stability and rapid deceleration, both of which are important first steps in response to any emergency situation. Unfortunately, this approach was diametrically opposed to everything most people had ever learned about applying brakes. Drivers are taught to bring brake pressure up gradually until wheel slide is detected and then modulate the brakes to maintain them as close to wheel slide as possible. People are also taught never to apply the brakes under hard cornering and certainly not during an evasive maneuver, because doing so will upset the balance of the car and probably cause a spin. All of this knowledge went out the window with ABS; Corvette drivers would somehow have to learn about the new capabilities attached to their brake pedal. They also had to learn not to pump the brakes, which just wasted precious time and distance and was totally unnecessary with ABS.

Having become accustomed to it, we treated the pedal pulsations as useful feedback. They told us that the ABS was activated and that the car

was at or close to its control limit, which was vital information on wet or potentially icy road surfaces. Some drivers, when being exposed to ABS for the first time, were startled by the pulsations, thought that something was wrong, and backed off the brake pedal. We concluded that the pulsations, as useful as they were for feedback, would have to be minimized for use by the general public. Otherwise, the antilock brakes seemed to be a well-adapted system, limited only by the driver's willingness to apply the brakes.

CORVETTE SALES SUCCESS

Sales of the 1984 Corvette had gone very well, and based on Chevrolet's continuing strong sales forecast, management thought they could sell even more Corvettes in 1985. Through the 1984 model year, GM's Assembly Division (GMAD) had been building 15 Corvettes per hour with only one shift at Bowling Green. Chevrolet asked the corporation to increase the plant's output by changing its assembly rate to ten Corvettes per hour and then operating the plant on two shifts.

Chevrolet management never asked anyone at Bowling Green about the details of the proposal. (Management had a habit of not listening to the plants anyway.) When the Bowling Green people were finally told about the plan, they counterproposed that the plant stay running on one shift but increase the line rate to 18 cars per hour, and then use overtime to achieve the equivalent of 20 jobs per hour. Chevrolet and the corporation rejected the idea of building cars on overtime and instructed Bowling Green to go ahead with the hiring and training that was needed to bring on a second shift. So, GMAD ran the plant on two shifts, building ten Corvettes per hour for about six months. Then the market slumped and Chevrolet had too many Corvettes in dealer inventory. GMAD ended up laying off the newly hired second shift and reverting to one shift production at 12 cars per hour.

CORVETTE DROPS ITS TOP

Chevrolet estimated that Corvette demand was going to fall even further in 1986. How much it would have dropped, we'll never know, because Lloyd Reuss intervened with a new model which would make up a third of Corvette production. Lloyd had seen a custom-made convertible version of the 1984 Corvette at Heinz Precter's American Sunroof Corporation (ASC), and he was so intrigued that he asked us if we could get a convertible into production within the next year.

The original ASC Corvette convertible was built by hand from a 1984 targa.

ASC Inc. file photo

Lloyd knew better than we did that the odds of getting the convertible designed and released during 1985 were slim to none. The expertise from the last Corvette convertible, which Bob Vogelei had designed in 1968, was long gone. And Fisher Body, the organization that had designed all other GM convertibles, hadn't designed a new open-top car in over a decade, and the original people who had worked on those projects were themselves long gone.

If this weren't enough of an impediment, Lloyd, our Group Vice President by this point, was working on a complete reorganization of the company. On January 2, 1985, the motor divisions would be transformed into marketing entities. In addition, Fisher Body would be eliminated altogether, and a new integrated car design and manufacturing entity called the Chevrolet Pontiac Canada Group (CPC) would be established.

With all this change, and the resulting chaos, we probably couldn't have designed and released a convertible in three years, solely from within GM. I suspect that the 12 months goal was ASC blowing in Lloyd's ear, just to get a design contract. Our integrity was too important for us to promise such an impossible schedule just to get the project going. We finally committed to working to get it done in 18 months, as long as we could design the convertible at ASC and keep it out of the GM releasing system until the very last moment. We accepted the risk that we might not have given ourselves enough time for unexpected problems.

Lloyd reluctantly agreed to our 18 month proposal, and the work was soon underway with ASC. We gave project management to a capable young body engineer named Phillip Rezanka, who was under the direction of our new chief body engineer, Paul Huzzard. That Lloyd wanted this done was a marvelous advantage when it came to getting priority and money. CPC Purchasing Staff assigned Ben Siragusa to the project. Ben contracted with ASC for the design, and almost immediately began using his clout to line up suppliers.

American Sunroof had a small cadre of convertible experts who had put together the Corvette convertible proposal on a 1984 coupe. The ASC prototype featured a completely redesigned rear end and a convertible top that stowed underneath the deck lid.

ASC's original concept vehicle had a lot of things right about it, but also had a number of things that had to be reengineered for it to become a production car. Taking out the rear roof post structure had a surpris-

ingly negative effect on the structural performance of the car. The targa car was soft enough in torsion with the roof out, but with both the roof out and the rear upper bow structure removed, we judged it to be unacceptable, so we knew that structural work was needed. When folded, the top mechanism interfered with the seat back so the seat couldn't slide all the way back. So, the bow system had to be completely redesigned to articulate and fold farther back. Additionally, the deck lid was too flat, so the Design Staff's Corvette studio cut the rear end off one of their Corvette armatures and clayed up an all-new deck lid and convertible top.

From the clay, we produced a 1:1 wooden model of the entire rear upper panel and top lid. In order to save time, Bill Weaver cut up the wooden model, expanded it with inserts, and glued it back together again, producing the 3-percent-oversized patterns from which we would cut the steel tools that molded the rear end parts. This saved us several months and was a key element of the strategy that got us to an 18-month program.

Two primary requirements were established for the convertible: It should be built in the plant, as a normal part of production; and it should not weigh significantly more than the coupe.

ASC was known in the industry for building a lot of the "chop shop" convertibles. We were opposed to this kind of manufacturing, and when we explained the options to Jack Gerbick, Bowling Green's production manager, he quickly agreed that building a complete coupe, throwing away the rear end, rebuilding it as a convertible, and then repainting it would be a total waste. Even though he didn't yet know how to do it, Gerbick volunteered that Bowling Green would support the convertible program and build the car on its production line. This was a monumental decision, because it gave us a convertible that we could build in a controlled process.

In order to manage weight, we specified that virtually all of the bows and mechanisms of the top system would be made of aluminum. And, in order to make the convertible an acceptable all-season car, we specified that the convertible top would be lined and insulated. We didn't know how to fold down and safely store a glass window, so we accepted the flexible plastic back window that was common to most convertibles of the period.

When Bill Weaver and ASC settled in to produce the convertible, they realized that they had to literally remove the entire rear end of the coupe, above the frame. The seat belt upper anchorage and the rear-end cross-car structure had to change, and, of course, all the surface panels were new. The rear fascia, however, was common with the coupe.

That we could get the design done and the parts tooled and approved in time for production was always a cliffhanger. A number of key sources that had participated in the 1984 coupe program bailed out of the convertible, because they couldn't see us getting the job done in the time allowed. They reasoned that late delivery would hurt their performance scorecard with GM. But, Ben Siragusa and ASC ultimately put together an acceptable group of suppliers, and we were under way. We initially released everything for production through ASC's system. And then, just before actual production was to begin, we rereleased everything into the GM system, so that Bowling Green could order production parts.

At the Proving Grounds, Dave Mash—under Doug Robinson's guidance—went to work on studying and fixing any structural deficiencies that we had caused by taking the rear roof bow out. He ultimately came up with a package of reinforcements that would include a new front rail inner reinforcement and a major increase in the cross-car structure behind the seats. He also found that a local vibration problem in the seat and floor pan could be significantly reduced by adding an under-floor X-member. So we made that part of the program as well.

We ultimately got everything sorted out and produced the final pre-production cars in the summer of 1985. We scheduled these cars for a press preview in October 1985. Production would start in early 1986 for a spring delivery of the first Corvette convertible in ten years.

Years before all this, I had toured Yosemite National Park in a convertible. Even though it was October and the mornings were misty, every mile that I drove was with the top down, sometimes with the side windows up and the heater going full blast. Driving through the vastness of this fabulous place in an enclosed car just wouldn't have been the same experience. The smells and sights of autumn were enchanting. To be

The 1986 convertible returned open air motoring to the Corvette.

Drawing by Dave McLellan

able to drive, while still feeling connected to the scenery, was a reminder of why the convertible has such a special allure.

As we thought about presenting the convertible to the press, I remembered that drive through Yosemite, and I proposed to Chevrolet Public Relations' Ralph Kramer that we introduce the Corvette convertible in this same setting. It was purely coincidental, though, that we would introduce the convertible during the same cool days of autumn.

All summer long Yosemite and its environs were crowded with tourists, but by October virtually everybody had disappeared. We set up our base of operations at the Railroad Inn, just outside the park on the Fresno Road. We let the press explore the roads around the park, where they could get up to speed, and then went into the park to experience its incredible scenery. The base of Yosemite is at an elevation of about 6,000 feet and is surrounded by sheer vertical rock faces that go up 3,000 feet or more above the floor. One of the roads through the park climbs to a height of over 10,000 feet before it peaks, over Tioga Pass, in crossing the Sierra Nevada Mountains. We let the press enjoy all of this, experiencing the car on all the winding roads. At these high elevations, the performance of the car certainly fell off, but our purpose was not to demonstrate its performance as much as it was to rekindle interest in the Corvette as a convertible.

We knew that, no matter what we said to some of the press, they would use this as an opportunity to drive like they were on a racetrack, so we did what we could to keep them reasonably sane. We also cleared our presence in the park through a Department of the Interior lawyer who was also, coincidentally, racing with one of the Corvette showroom stock teams.

One writer showed up at the Railroad Inn with a turbocharged Mustang, courtesy of Ford Motor Company, and proceeded to taunt us, claiming that this Mustang could beat the Corvette in a road race. (A not unreasonable expectation at 6,000 feet above sea level.) Ignoring the possible consequences of this boorish and inappropriate behavior, Jingles took him on in a match race with one of our Corvette convertible test cars and beat him handily.

Almost all the journalists were reasonably well behaved, and it was only on the last day that one of the members of the press was caught speeding by the park police and ticketed. It is my opinion that every Corvette convertible should be christened with a visit to Yosemite National Park. There is just no more delightful or exciting place to tour in a convertible.

Chevrolet decided to promote the 1986-1/2 convertible by making it the Indy Pace Car for the 1986 Indianapolis 500. When we had done the

1978 Pace Cars, Vince Piggins' product promotion engineers fussed over them, installing hot-rodded and blueprinted engines, just to be sure they could pace the field and that everything would go right. This time we told them to leave the cars alone: "Build your three pace cars at Bowling Green, mount the required special lights, and go pace the race." As it turned out, the stock cars worked just fine, and pioneer jet test pilot Chuck Yeager was the celebrity driver.

Pacing the Indy 500 was the perfect way to bring the Corvette convertible back into public notice. After a ten-year absence, it took remarkably little time for the open-top Corvette to catch on. Even though it was in production for less than a full model year, initial sales topped 7,000 units and constituted a quarter of all Corvette sales. By 1987, the convertible topped 10,000 units and constituted a third of all Corvette sales. And, to our surprise, the convertible opened a up an entirely new market, with significantly different demographics than the other Corvettes. Lloyd Reuss' decision was vindicated and Corvette had an ever greater appeal.

Chuck Yeager's skill and daring as a test pilot are legendary. He seemed to enjoy being an Indy 500 celebrity and the Pace Car driver. We certainly enjoyed his storytelling.

Courtesy Indianapolis Motor Speedway

The Crucible of Showroom Stock Racing 9

DOES RACING IMPROVE THE BREED? You bet it does, because racing forces you to optimize everything in the car. Improvements can then be passed on to the production car. However, in racing series other than showroom stock, I would give a much more abstract answer. Does the technology of Formula 1, CART, or NASCAR cars translate to production cars? At best, the link is tenuous.

As we were developing the 1984 Corvette, we thought it could be a competitive production-based race car. However, while we were busy designing, developing and testing it for the consumer, we didn't have time to deal with it as a race car. By the time we introduced it to the automotive press at Riverside Raceway, in the autumn of 1982, we knew we had a car that at least felt good and performed well during racetrack demonstrations, especially the Z51 configuration. We, somewhat naively, assumed that all the testing we had done on the Proving Ground, to build reliability and robustness into the car, would translate to the racetrack.

We were further encouraged, later that year, when Kim Baker took his 1984 manual transmission Corvette and won the SCCA SSGT national championship. Even though he was down on power, the fact that he had superior braking, car preparation, and driving skill, allowed Kim to beat out the favored 300 ZX turbo. We had also heard that John Greenwood was racing a 1984 Corvette, but was having wheel bearing problems.

CORVETTE GOES ENDURANCE RACING

In the summer of 1984 we learned that the SCCA was planning to expand its Playboy-sponsored Showroom Stock Endurance Series for 1985 to include the Corvette, Porsche 944, and Nissan 300 ZX turbo. We also learned that several racers were planning to prepare Corvettes for this series. We reviewed what we knew with Don Runkle, Herb Fishel, who was responsible for managing Chevrolet's racing programs, and Ralph Kramer, head of Chevrolet Public Relations. They agreed that Corvette

Doug Robinson, Corvette's development manager, supporting the Morrison-Cook number 88 IMSA GT class Corvette. With additional modifications, the production Corvette was capable of competing far above the level of showroom stock.

Tommy Morrison Collection,
Watkins Glen, NY 1986

Engineering would provide technical support for the racers. Quite simply, we knew a lot more about the production car than anyone else, and stood to gain the most from GM's involvement.

Our Corvette Development Manager, Doug Robinson, added racing support to his assignments. And, with the help of the entire Corvette product team:—powertrain, chassis, body, and electrical—we were off to the races. Since the 1985 series consisted of 3, 6, 12, and 24 hour races, we immediately recognized that we needed to know more about the car in an endurance racing environment. With a road car you may wear out three or four sets of tires during the vehicle's lifetime, but a day in the life of a race car on a 24-hour track is significantly more stressful for the tires. Half a dozen sets may be worn out entirely. Quite simply, endurance racing puts extreme and unusual stresses on the whole car.

Doug's strategy for 1985 was to work directly with the team that showed the best potential. He chose the Tommy Morrison, Jim Cook, and Dick Guldstrand team. Doug started by supplying the team with a 1985 manual transmission Corvette, and a plan to thoroughly test the car in a simulated 24-hour race. We wouldn't let them take it out for competition until we were satisfied that we had sorted through and solved all the problems that occurred in our simulation. The involvement of Morrison, Cook, and Guldstrand in the testing gave them an edge over the other Corvette competitors, but since these were our tests, we would also share the results with all the other Corvette teams. Our group also managed the relationship with SCCA, and provided special parts as soon as the SCCA approved them. The objective was to beat the non-Corvette competition, and having several capable Corvette teams competing with one another made it even more difficult for the non-Corvette competition.

Our racetrack test program used experienced team managers, drivers, and mechanics, who were all focused on preparing the car for the racetrack. From the start, the 1985 Corvette already differed from the 1984— the new car had a 230 nhp port fuel-injection engine and stronger wheel bearings. The rules in showroom stock racing required that the car run on street tires, although not necessarily the OEM tire, so Goodyear pro-

duced a sport compound "S" version of the Gatorback, which most of the cars ran on in 1985. Girlock, our brake supplier, developed improved racing pad compounds and a quick change strategy for replacing hot brake pads.

The test vehicle, from which we developed the 1985 race car, ran at about 275 hp with an open exhaust system. Test sessions were used to develop camber and toe settings that were tailored to racing conditions. These adjustments were allowed by the SCCA as long as we stayed within production tolerances. Probably the most significant thing we learned in testing was the importance of synthetic lubricants, as a way of extending the life of all lubricated components under racing conditions. Before we were finished, we were using synthetic oils in the engine, the power steering system, the manual transmission, and the axle. The power steering system was a good example of what happened with conventional lubricants in racing conditions. The continuous hard driving and dithering of the steering wheel would continue to heat the power steering fluid until it reached temperatures where it tended to break down, causing premature wear of the steering components. With synthetic power steering fluids, the same system ran cooler and exhibited a much longer lifetime, before wearing out.

John Powell's number 50, under development on the track at Mosport for the original Playboy SCCA Showroom Stock series.
Photo by John Powell

Everything we learned in these test sessions was shared with all of the Corvette racers. Armed with this information, they built up their 1985 race cars. These cars were developed to the best of our ability, in the time available and within the showroom stock rules. The Corvette racers were racing against Porsche and Nissan drivers, as well as against each other. So, starting from our basic specifications, each team continued to develop its car, independently, to be the fastest and most reliable car they knew how to put on the track.

The 1985 season opened with a 24-hour race at Riverside Raceway, east of Los Angeles. The Morrison-Cook team was well prepared, from their test sessions. They had developed a fueling rig, and practiced tire and brake pad changes. The team prepared three Corvettes, and assembled a bevy of experienced race drivers and mechanics to support them.

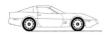

Top: A routine pit stop for Powell's car number 30 took less than a minute and included fuel, tires, and even brake pads.

Bottom: You can see the tension in their faces as Doug Rippy and his crew try to sort out a problem while the pit stop clock is ticking on them.

Photos by Rich Chenet (both)

Success in endurance racing is all about preparation and pacing the car on the racetrack. The last thing you want to do in a 24-hour race is go flat-out. As we learned from all our testing, and our years of competitive racing, as the car is pushed harder and harder, its reliability decreases and the chances of mechanical failure increases, while the consequences of driver error become more severe.

Our strategy for a 24-hour endurance race was to establish a lap time, or pace, that we were reasonably confident we could maintain for 24 hours. We would then adjust the pace during the race if other competitors demonstrated that we were too conservative. With three cars, the Morrison-Cook team could play the tortoise and hare game by assigning one of its cars to be the rabbit and the other two cars sticking to the planned pace for the race, adjusting as the race progressed to stay within striking distance of the lead. The rabbit car was there to push the competition into driving as hard as they could. Going as fast as possible is the natural response for race drivers, so the hardest thing for a race driver to do is to slow down to a managed pace and drive the car smoothly to minimize the wear and tear on the car.

These 24-hour races were boring to watch. The cars just seemed to go on endlessly with little competitive racing. After many hours it was hard to keep track of who was really in the lead without consulting timing and scoring. It was imperative for the teams to have their own timing so they could manage their strategies. Working in the pits and trying to stay alert for some 30 hours means you have to put up with periods of tedium when the cars are simply lapping the circuit. However, that can quickly turn to sheer panic when you discover that one of your cars is missing.

The Morrison-Cook Corvettes continued to lap the Riverside track through the night and into Sunday morning. As the finish of the race approached at noon on Sunday, we were all incredibly awake and excited—as we had stayed up all night worrying. In the end, the Morrison-Cook team finished first and second overall, and won its class. The

third car in the team came in several places down, but was at least able to finish, despite problems it experienced during the night.

Including the season finale at Atlanta, the Corvettes won every 3, 6, 12 and 24-hour race; an almost unheard of accomplishment for any car, and certainly for one in its very first year of competition. The competing Porsche and Nissan competition teams certainly didn't expect this outcome: They came back race after race, trying even harder. But so did we, and we were able to continue to keep just ahead of the competition. As a result, we helped develop capable Corvette teams that would put us in the best possible position to start the next season.

SECOND SEASON SAME AS THE FIRST

In 1986, Porsche upped the ante by bringing the 944 Turbo into the fray. SCCA continued the showroom stock series, and created a new GT Class for the Corvette, 944 Turbo, and Nissan 300 ZX. With this new class, the other cars running in class A at least had a chance at a victory, although the Corvettes, Porsche 944, and Nissan 300ZX would surely dominate the overall wins. As in 1985, Corvette engineering continued to support the major teams, building test mules and sponsoring test sessions that would develop chassis, suspension, brake, and powertrain components to the highest possible state of reliability.

When we introduced anti-lock brakes on the production Corvette, we also encouraged the use of ABS on the Corvette race cars. We were satisfied that ABS was suitable for the race car and would make a big difference during the races, particularly on a wet and slippery track or in emergency avoidance situations.

Four-wheel ABS was new to the automotive scene, as well as to racing. The generation of race drivers who were driving Corvettes had never driven with ABS, so they approached it with a great deal of suspicion. Because the ABS is so driver-interactive, we finished its development at John Powell's driving school on the Mosport race track near Toronto.

John Powell and his race drivers developed anti-lock brake training that would be useful for all the drivers competing in showroom-stock Corvettes. During the early races of the 1986 season, John conducted

Although not part of the SCCA Showroom Stock series, several of the Corvette teams also participated in the 24-hour, Longest Day of Nelson Ledges. In this June 1986 race, the winning Morrison-Cook Corvette, driven by John Heinricy, Don Knowles and Bob McConnell finished 13 laps ahead of its nearest competitor.

B. F. Goodrich press release

ABS driving schools before each race, in order to give the drivers familiarity with the capabilities of the braking system.

We still had a number of drivers who wanted the system turned off, but we encouraged them to drive with the ABS engaged. Toward the end of the season, drivers learned to use it to their advantage. We even had instances of drivers pulling into the pits during a race because their ABS light was on. The good news was the drivers were using the ABS effectively; the bad news was that we couldn't fix a malfunctioning ABS during a race.

For the 1986 season, Porsche returned with a showroom-stock version of the 944 Turbo. In a typical race, the best Corvettes, and the quickest 944 Turbos, would qualify very close together—sometimes the 944s took the pole position, other times Corvettes qualified on top. Even in endurance racing, there are advantages in starting from the front. The first benefit is that any spins or crashes in the early minutes of the race occur behind you. The second advantage is psychological. Being on the pole tells your competitors that you're faster than any of them. However, this could also be a disadvantage if the governing body of the series tries to balance the competitors by adjusting the rules mid-season. As a result, hammering the competition in qualification could very well lead to a weight penalty being imposed for subsequent races.

The tight competition between the Porsche team and the several Corvette teams continued all season long. The Corvettes had the advantage in numbers. Even though this was supposed to be endurance racing, the competition became so heated that there was often wheel-to-wheel racing, with Corvettes and Porsches taking each other out with spins and crashes.

Corvettes won all of the races coming into the event at Portland, Oregon. But Porsche came to each race determined to win, and the team certainly had a good chance at Portland. The fastest German car started from the pole, and was able to maintain an unassailable lead on the best Corvette. About a half hour before the finish of the race, it started to rain. Charging to stay ahead, the leading Porsche spun on the drenched track. The driver of the following Corvette saw the plight of the Porsche and was able to slow down in time, using the anti-lock brakes. Slipping past the spinning Porsche, the Corvette took the lead and stayed there to the finish. The Corvette team finished out the year by winning the subsequent races and established a two-year record of winning every race in the SCCA Showroom Stock Endurance Series.

For 1987, Porsche was rumored to have bought a 1986 Corvette and to have thoroughly tested it on the company's Weissach test track in Germany. From this comparison, they developed a 944 Turbo racing package, featuring more power, bigger brakes, and ABS.

Porsche had developed the 944 Turbo as a serious race car for European competition. For the SCCA Showroom Stock Series, the company was only mildly constrained by the rules. It brought whatever it needed to the track, whether it was in production, about to be produced, or experimental.

SCCA bent over backward trying to help Porsche get into the winner's circle. Even though we would complain about the concessions made for Porsche, it was the right thing to do for the racing series. For SCCA and the spectators, having Corvette and Porsche each winning half the time would have been just right. SCCA also had a received assurances that the Nissan 300 ZX turbo would return, and that Mazda was also considering entering the series.

Given the concessions that SCCA had made for Porsche, and that the 944 Turbos were as fast or slightly faster than the Corvettes on a straightaway, Corvette felt it had the right to petition SCCA for more freedom in engine preparation. With the improvements that were agreed to, the Corvettes would run at 350-375 hp, which was still down in power from where we expected the turbocharged Porsches to be. But, with the Corvette's excellent torque curve and the better fuel economy of the naturally aspirated engine, we felt this was a reasonable balance, particularly for the longer endurance races.

At full power, the production Corvette's engine management computer is programmed to run rich, to protect the engine from the extremes of the ambient environment. Very high temperatures, very low humidity, and low-octane fuel can cause detonation that a somewhat-richer full-throttle mixture will avoid. A production car spends very little of its time at full power. You'd have to be driving in excess of 140 mph continuously to get into the full-throttle enrichment system. So, this enrichment protection is invisible to the average customer, however, under racing conditions it dramatically increases fuel consumption, because the car is running at full power up to 40 percent of the time.

One of the real secrets to successful endurance racing is to maximize fuel economy. At the track, we know what the ambient temperatures are going to be. We know what the humidity is. We have good control of the fuel that's being used. As a result, we can run a fuel calibration much closer to stoichiometric, without concern for detonation or over-heating.

Top: Baker Racing's number 4 car on the starting grid for the Escort 24-hour race at Mid Ohio. The 944 Porsche Turbo is lurking right behind, hoping to out-drag the Corvette.

Middle: In this 1987 race, Baker Racing's cars number 4 and 5 lead a bevy of Corvettes sandwiching a lone 944 Porsche Turbo.

Bottom: Baker Racing's number 4 takes the flag to win the 1987 24-hour race at Mosport in Ontario.

Photos by Rich Chenet (all)

The ideal mixture, combined with a driver trained to maximize smoothness at a calculated pace, could literally double the racing fuel economy (and halve the pit stops). The Corvettes were regularly achieving as much as 7-1/2 mpg while winning.

THIRD YEAR'S A CHARM

When it was time for the 1987 racing season, our 1988 chassis was almost in production, so the new chassis changes that would benefit racing Corvettes were introduced. These changes included a modified rear suspension and big brakes on all of the cars. Late in the season, we also introduced the six-speed ZF manual transmission that was being developed for the 1989 Corvette and the ZR-1.

The 1987 season developed much as SCCA had planned it. Porsche was very competitive, and took most of the pole positions. Nissan showed up at a couple of races with what looked like it could be a very competitive car once it was developed, but it never went anywhere. Mazda never showed. Porsche typically fielded three cars with a team of internationally respected endurance drivers. They had every chance to make it into the winner's circle but, with crashes, mechanical failures, and the extreme competitiveness among the Corvette racers, this was not to be. In the end, twelve great races from 3 hours to 24 hours in length were all won by Corvettes, and Kim Baker, with his number 3 and 4 Corvettes, won the series and clinched the manufacturing championship for Corvette.

SCCA must have been bombarded with complaints from the racers in the other classes, about being overrun by the Porsches and Corvettes, and never having even a chance at the overall win. It was not unusual for competing Corvettes and Porsches to blow by on each side of a competitor from a different class. So for 1988, both cars were kicked out

of the series. Corvette was out for winning all the time, and Porsche was barred because the 944 Turbo was still so much faster than any of the other cars that they would have dominated the series without the Corvettes. Needless to say, the series lost much of its interest that year. Meanwhile, with the momentum we had built up with the cars and racing teams, we went off to play on our own for the next two years, in what became known as the Corvette Challenge.

THE CORVETTE CHALLENGE

The Corvette Challenge was the dream of John Powell, who had run one of the Corvette teams in the SCCA Showroom Stock Series. These races, held in conjunction with a major SCCA Trans Am event, were one-hour, no-holds-barred, sprint races which typically fielded 15 to 20 Corvettes which were, essentially, identically prepared. These races produced some of the best wheel-to-wheel Corvette racing ever seen.

Several of the automotive journalists who wrote for the major car magazines were also amateur race drivers and were part of the scene at the Showroom Stock endurance races, getting rides from competitors in various classes. We looked on this as an opportunity, and encouraged Corvette competitors who had a third car running to include the journalists among their drivers. This gave us the opportunity to train the journalists on anti-lock brakes in a racing environment, and also for the journalists to get a chance to experience driving Corvettes in the heat of battle. From this experience they got to know the car—and us—much better. The writers also gained first-hand knowledge of the car's robustness. The car could take pretty big hits before serious damage was done. Even

Twenty Corvette Challenge race cars line up for their one-hour race.
Photo by John Powell

157

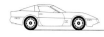

damaged, the cars were often repairable and could be sent back out on the track to continue racing.

By the mid 1980s, FM radio communication with the drivers was common, but data telemetry was still very unusual. We began by telemetering the digital instrument panel data from the car back to an instrument panel set up at trackside. From there, we went to telemetering more data as required. With a computer interface, we could watch the driver on the track to make sure the car stayed within rpm and temperature parameters. In this way, we could detect problems long before the driver could, and recommend corrective action where possible. Relieved from having to watch the instruments, the driver could concentrate on racing.

We also experimented with the G-Analyst to study the lateral and longitudinal forces being generated. Drivers could profit from observing each others' detailed performance, and learn how to go faster everywhere on the track.

These five years of racing were incredibly important to Corvette. With the help of the teams and the drivers, including Tommy Morrison, Dick Guldstrand, Kim Baker, John Powell, and Doug Rippy, we took the Corvette from a 1984 car, that had potential but no pedigree, to a 1989 car that was world class as a production sports car and was capable of no-holds-barred competition. We would next drop in the 375 hp LT5 engine and turn loose the press—and Corvette enthusiasts—in the fastest production sports car on earth.

Handling Dynamics and Active Safety in the Corvette

10

MUCH OF THE THOUGHT THAT WENT INTO the 1984 Corvette's suspension design was our engineering estimate of characteristics that would best take advantage of the not-yet-developed Goodyear 50 aspect ratio performance tire. The first Goodyear Eagle P255/50VR16 tire was developed and evaluated against this suspension. Over the next several years, this suspension design was retuned, as the tire evolved in both its street and "S" compound racing version. Throughout this process, the suspension and the tires were developed simultaneously. So today, it's impossible to separate the Corvette suspension from its tires and fully attribute the aspects of the vehicle handling—control and comfort—to one or the other.

THE INSEPARABLE TIRE AND SUSPENSION

At each step along the way, we thought we had taken the basic concept as far as it could be developed. But, over time, we taught ourselves that there was no end to this process of improvement. Even though the steps were small, continuous improvement was possible. As for the big steps, compare the 2001 Z06 Corvette with the late C4s and then with the 1984 C4. In those 16 years, tremendous leaps forward occurred in tire, suspension, and control technologies, including ABS, traction control, and yaw control. Similarly, these comparisons can be made between the 1984 Corvette and the C3 Stingray Corvettes. This period also saw the introduction of the radial tire, with its dramatic improvements in ride and handling.

The inseparable nature of tires and suspension reflects the fact that the tire is the car's connection with the road. Nearly all of the forces acting on the car—cornering, braking, and accelerating—involve the tire-road interface. The tire acts as an air spring, filtering any bumps in the road; and the suspension serves to position and steer the tire, introduce braking and accelerating forces, and act as a secondary ride filter. And, ulti-

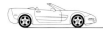
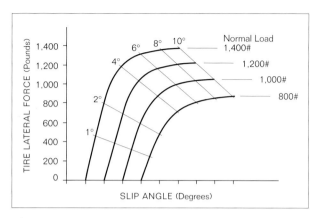

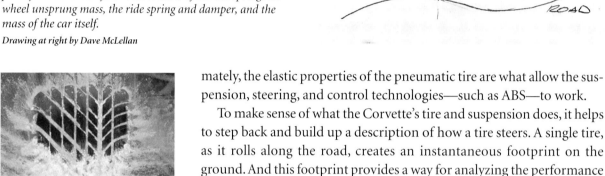

The tire isolates the vehicle from road disturbance, yet precisely controls the tracking and handling of the vehicle. It is part of a mechanical filter that consists of the tire spring, the wheel unsprung mass, the ride spring and damper, and the mass of the car itself.

Drawing at right by Dave McLellan

A Corvette tire is being tested in colored water over a glass road. The clearly defined portion of the tire is in contact with the road.

Courtesy Goodyear Tire & Rubber Co.

mately, the elastic properties of the pneumatic tire are what allow the suspension, steering, and control technologies—such as ABS—to work.

To make sense of what the Corvette's tire and suspension does, it helps to step back and build up a description of how a tire steers. A single tire, as it rolls along the road, creates an instantaneous footprint on the ground. And this footprint provides a way for analyzing the performance of the tire.

It is the angle of the tire with respect to its path that we call the "slip angle." And, it is the deformation of the tire, running at this slip angle, that generates the force that gives the tire the path control that directs the car. The tire deforms elastically up to about 0.6g, in what is characterized as the linear range of the tire. As the slip angle increases further toward the ultimate 1.1g cornering limit of the tire, the contact patch begins to slip progressively from its rear edge forward. But even at 1.1g the tire does not slide. At the point when the tire does start to slip, the lateral force no longer increases linearly with slip angle. Ultimately, at about 1.1g there is no increase in lateral force with increasing slip angle. The tire is said to be "saturated," or stalled if we use the analogy with the airplane wing. Braking and accelerating forces also exercise the tire elastically, with the ultimate limit being a skidding or sliding tire.

Because of the way the cornering tire instantaneously plants itself on the road and is then stretched progressively as it traverses the footprint,

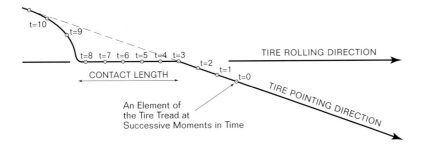

As the tire tread comes in contact with the road (t=3), it is progressively deformed elastically as it stays planted on the road, and then (t=8) leaves the contact patch and relaxes back to its neutral state.

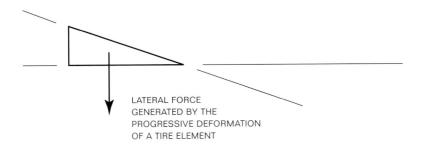

The tread element is deformed progressively as the tire rolls, giving the contact patch a triangular lateral force distribution.

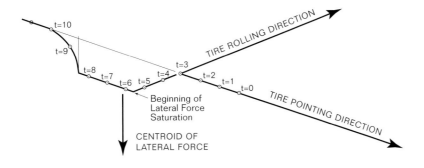

Once the tire contact patch element is deformed to the limit that the coefficient of friction can support, it begins to slip (t=6).

the center of lateral force occurs at the two-thirds point along the contact patch. This force is typically resolved into a lateral force at the geometric center of the contact and a self-aligning moment about the contact patch. As the tire saturates, the centroid of the lateral force moves forward. This is conventionally interpreted as a falloff in the self-aligning torque.

The footprint patch of the modern radial tire is stiffened by the tire's steel belt lessening the "squirm" that was characteristic of the bias tire footprint. The steel belt gives the radial tire its unique sense of stability and dramatically longer tire life. The stiff footprint is contrasted with the

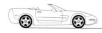

greater flexibility of the radial tire's sidewall. The radial tire gets its name from its radial sidewall cord construction. Radial tires typically have a low camber coefficient, reducing the effect of camber on handling. Early radials, when they reached their cornering limit, tended to fall off in lateral force, resulting in an instant spin if the rear tires saturated first.

The chassis engineer considers all four of these tire footprints in developing the handling characteristics of the car. Four footprints give the car static stability in the vertical direction and in roll. A motorcycle or bicycle, on only two wheels, does not have static roll stability. It achieves roll stability through its dynamic interaction with the rider, and gyroscopic motion. Dynamic stability is not guaranteed, and there are any number of situations where a two-wheeled vehicle can fall or flip, as its dynamic stability is overwhelmed by other forces.

STEERING DYNAMICS

Steering a car is a very natural process for the driver. What occurs technically is a little more complicated. Imagine a car traveling a straight path. If the driver quickly turns the steering wheel, the rolling front tires travel about a foot before they adjust to the imposed steering angle. The front tires are now at a slip angle with respect to the instantaneous path which is still straight. This slip angle generates a lateral force acting on the front of the car and starts the whole car rotating. As the car rotates, the rear tires begin to develop a slip angle and consequently a lateral force acting at the rear of the car. The front slip angle and its lateral force increase further as the car rotates. As all this is playing out, the steer-generated forces building up in the suspension are causing secondary compliance steering effects. And, the inertial acceleration of the car is causing it to roll, which introduces roll and camber geometry steering effects. It takes as little as 0.3 seconds for this steer transient to settle into steady-state turning.

The nonlinear behavior of the tire imposes three handling regimes on the car. In a sports car, the "linear region" extends to about 0.6g, before the "nonlinear region" begins. At this point, the tire begins to slacken off in its response to increasing steer angle, ultimately saturating at about 1.1g.

The third region is "on center." In this region, the car's straight-ahead tracking ability is considered. Very few roads are truly straight, even though they may look as though they are. Road irregularities such as parallel edges and road camber tend to pull the car away from the straightahead. Excess lash and friction can make precision control more difficult, although

some friction and viscous damping is desirable in the steering system to reduce the need for constant steering correction.

As the car is driven to its limit of control, the driver is forced into a fine balancing act. The sum of the lateral forces generated at the front and rear contact patches gives the car the lateral acceleration of its center of gravity. However, it is the difference of these forces—like the action of a teeter-totter—that rotates the car about its center of gravity, directing it along its path. This small delta can be affected by many things, such as front-to-rear weight transfer, the change in camber of a tire, or lifting off of the throttle. As the limit of control is approached, the driver's ability to rotate the car is reduced.

One of the chassis development engineer's chief roles is to develop a car to give the skilled driver the control capabilities he or she needs, and at the same time make the car forgiving for the untrained driver. These competing requirements are almost impossible to satisfy at the same time. It is a testament to the chassis engineer that foundation handling was as good as it was before we started to apply digital ABS, traction control, throttle-by-wire, and yaw control to the car's limit behavior.

The perfect example of the difficulty of the chassis engineer's job is the phenomenon of dropped-throttle steer. If a driver corners hard near the limit of control and then closes the throttle abruptly, the car may spin out of control faster than the driver can turn the steering wheel to apply a correction. Closing the throttle, particularly at high rpms with a manual transmission powertrain, applies an abrupt and substantial drag on the car through the rear tires only (in rear-wheel-drive cars). The deceleration causes a corresponding load transfer from the rear to the front tires. This is akin to applying the rear brakes by themselves, and is guaranteed to spin the car. It even has a name: It's called a "bootleg turn."

The chassis engineer uses toe-in under braking and tire selection to mitigate dropped-throttle steer. Toe-in under braking is difficult to accomplish in an existing suspension. The suspension needs to be designed kinematically and elastically to get all of its coefficients pointing in the right direction at once. Tire selection is the more common solution to the problem—if there is a solution at all.

PITCH AND DIVE

Acceleration and braking forces react against a car's inertial mass, causing the car to pitch. In Corvettes with independent suspension, acceler-

MILLIKEN'S MOMENT METHOD

Vehicle handling guru Bill Milliken developed a method for depicting the stability of a vehicle at the limit of control. Note that as the limit is approached, the moment available to rotate the car diminishes. If this moment at the limit is zero, the car drifts and the driver has no ability to rotate the car. A slight positive moment leads to excess rotation—a spin. A slight negative moment leads to underrotation—a plow. This static analysis does not take into account the driver's ability to further manipulate handling with brakes and throttle, nor does it tell us anything about the rate at which the car begins a spin and the driver's ability to dynamically intervene. We worked with Milliken using this technique to optimize the handling characteristics of the 1984 Corvette.

What causes a car at its limit of control to spin or to plow? While the tires may be generating sufficient force to corner the car at 1.0 g, it is the small difference in the front-to-rear tire forces that, at the limit, determine the rotation of the car.
Dave McLellan Archives

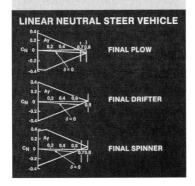

163

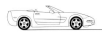

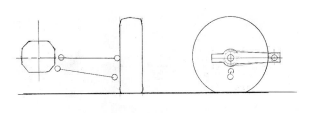

The 1963 Corvette's rear suspension was an excellent independent suspension except for its lack of anti-squat under acceleration, anti-dive under braking and compliance steering toe control.

Drawing by Dave McLellan

ation forces react on the wheel spindle and cause a nose-up pitch of the car. Braking forces react through the suspension and produce a nose-down pitch. A short-long arm (SLA) front suspension and a complex multi-link rear suspension (essentially a rear SLA) provides an opportunity to design the side-view suspension geometry so that the suspension itself introduces the countering moments that tend to reduce the pitching of the car. This is technically known as "anti-squat" for acceleration and "anti-dive" for braking.

The modern Corvette's front and rear suspensions introduce just enough of these countering moments that the car brakes and accelerates with only minimal pitch excursions. Excess pitch uses up the limited ride travel that is needed to absorb ride bumps.

The 1963 Corvette's independent rear suspension used a horizontal trailing arm whose thrust line was below the center of gravity. As the car was developed to higher and higher power levels, the only way to minimize the pitching of the car under acceleration was to use very stiff springs. But stiff springs reduced the suspension's ability to isolate the car from road inputs, and ultimately caused the driver discomfort as the vibration level increased. Good control under cornering conditions on a rough road demands that the tire move up and down with as little lateral force variation as possible, to minimize the change in cornering force with ride excursion.

Managing the vertical forces and body height was carried to its logical extreme in the Formula 1 Lotus of the 1990's. Its high-bandwidth active suspension maintained the vertical load on the tire as constant as possible and managed vehicle ride height and pitch attitude against the aerodynamic down force that, at high speed, would have otherwise smashed the suspension into full jounce. A suspension in full jounce (or rebound, for that matter) is no suspension at all.

Ride is the other dimension of the tire-road interface that is controlled by the tire and suspension. The vertical ride force acts through the contact patch as a normal force which, with the coefficient of friction, defines the shear forces (cornering, braking, and accelerating) that the tire-road interface can sustain. Before the introduction of digitally-controlled ride management, any improvement in ride quality generally worsened handling.

THE FINE BALANCE OF DAMPING

Ride isolation is necessary because of the human body, as well as the car, has limited tolerance to vibration. "Ride" is all about isolating the human body from the frequencies and amplitudes that characterize the road, and that one's body finds annoying, discomforting, and even nauseating. Many cars, including sports cars, have suspensions which vibrate at approximately 1Hz. High aerodynamic downforce race cars are suspended at upwards of 4Hz, in order to be stiff enough to prevent their suspensions from bottoming. They can be driven only on very smooth roads and still beat up their drivers unmercifully. Off-road race vehicles, in contrast, are suspended at about 0.5Hz, with upwards of 30 inches of ride travel, in order to be able to absorb the high amplitude "road" in a controlled manner.

Dampers are key to any controlled ride strategy. Hydraulic dampers have been the norm for years, with the best of them operating at high internal pressures to avoid cavitation and loss of effectiveness. The microprocessor has now invaded the damper world, giving us computer-controlled dampers, including a magnetic-fluid damper that offers almost infinitely variable damping control.

A road car needs dampers to control the resonant mode of the tire and wheel (hop and tramp) and the resonance of the body on its suspension (heave, pitch and roll). In the interest of minimizing the variation in vertical tire-road interface forces, the suspension system is better off traversing a bump with almost no damping. Damping is needed to stop the natural frequency ringing of the wheel and of the body.

The final function of the dampers is to pick the car up over vertical rises that are greater than the car's limited suspension travel. Springs do a very weak job of picking the car up so that it doesn't crash into its jounce bumpers. For the brief instant they are called upon to act, the dampers are programmed to deliver several times the force of the spring.

For dampers to be effective they need to react against a body structure that is itself rigid in the frequency range where damping control is required. For a car structure to seem rigid at wheel hop frequency (12-14Hz), it must have its lowest frequency structural mode at least 1.5 times wheel hop frequency.

The amount of damping required to control wheel hop (10-14Hz) is very different from the damping needed to suppress body motion (at 1Hz). As a result, all dampers are a compromise, using devices such as blow-off valves to vary the damping force nonlinearly with velocity. These modi-

Top: Tire handling-related forces and moments are measured to the limit of adhesion with a tire mounted on a fully-instrumented spindle rolling on a steel belt "road" that is coated with antiskid material.

Bottom: Tire testing in a large diameter drum approximates the effects of high-speed running on the road. Note the standing wave that the sidewall must pass through as it rotates.

Courtesy Goodyear Tire & Rubber Co. (both)

fications produce a damper (shock absorber) that better approximates the competing ideals.

TIRE DEVELOPMENT

Depending on the tread design and compound, the modern performance tire is capable of achieving lateral and fore-aft forces about 1.1 times the normal load acting on the tire. This is the same as saying the tire can achieve 1.1g cornering. This tire is capable of operating on either a dry or wet road, through snow, or under icy road conditions, although a tire that is fully optimized for all of these diverse requirements is not yet available.

The "Z" rated tire, used on the Corvette, is capable of operating under high ambient temperature conditions and performing to the top speed of the car. Corvette tires are now tested to guarantee that they will perform satisfactorily even at the car's top speed, of almost 190 mph.

Heat buildup is the tire's nemesis. Internal heating caused by the flexing of the tire, if it is not dissipated, will build up until the rubber degrades and the tire fails. As speed increases, the rate of heat buildup from tire-flexing increases. There is a speed and ambient condition where the heat dissipation is overwhelmed by heat generation. By careful design of the tread, the belt package, the radial carcass, and all the secondary elements that go into a successful tire design, the tire engineers are able to balance all of these requirements and produce an exceptional performance tire that can operate safely at high speed and has a life upwards of 50,000 miles.

This is an incredible achievement when you contrast it with the early years of the automobile, when flat tires were a routine part of any trip. Even though early pneumatic tires were prone to failure, they were used because the alternative provided a ride too harsh for either the human body or the vehicle to withstand.

Persistence paid off, bringing tire compounding and design from a black art to a sophisticated, analytical process. Computer models simulate the layered radial and belt construction of the tire, including the material properties of the fabric cords and the steel belts in their rubber matrix. And, they simulate the elastic properties of the tread itself. From

these models the tire engineer can even analyze the tire for the subtle rolling-resistance forces that influence fuel economy, and for the miniscule squirm of the tread that determines the life of the tire. The tire can also be loaded laterally and fore and aft to simulate the way it behaves when it is subjected to cornering and braking forces. A key control variable is the pressure distribution across the tread.

A tire engineer can even reverse-engineer a loaded tire. Using computer modeling, a tire can be lifted off the road, deflated, and taken off its rim. Only after an exhaustive simulation are molds created to build the tire. Then, when the tire is constructed, mounted on its rim, and inflated to the prescribed pressure, it is exactly the way the engineer wanted it. Up until a few years ago, none of this was possible. But now, computer modeling and simulation are causing a revolution in tire design. Tire designers still build and test experimental tires, but they are doing so more as a validation of their designs than as random experiments.

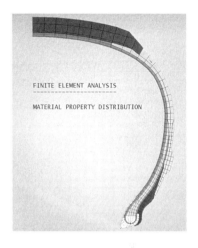

FINITE ELEMENT ANALYSIS

MATERIAL PROPERTY DISTRIBUTION

An accurate computer model of a radial tire allows the tire engineer to simulate tire performance.
Courtesy Goodyear Tire & Rubber Co.

A TIRE WITHOUT AIR

One of the first steps into tire design future has been the run-flat tire. Let the air out of a conventional automobile tire and it collapses on itself. Drive on the deflated tire and you will cut it and soon overheat it to the point where it is totally destroyed. In extreme cases, even slowing the car after a high-speed deflation can generate enough heat to damage the tire beyond repair.

By carefully adding stiffness to the sidewall of the tire, and adjusting the stiffness distribution across the tread, Goodyear engineers have been able to produce a Corvette tire that can run successfully without air. Running without air, the tire looks soft because there's no air pressure shaping the envelope of the tire, but there is sufficient sidewall stiffness to support the car, and the stiffness in the tread helps the tire maintain good contact with the pavement. As long as speeds are kept under 50 mph when the tire is uninflated, the rubber compound can tolerate the heat. Cornering hard on a tire without air tends to make it want to roll off the rim, so the Goodyear engineers designed a wider, elliptical bead-reinforcement to keep the tire stable on the rim even under the most severe handling situations.

Since the term "run flat" is something of a misnomer because the tire never literally goes "flat," Chevrolet and Goodyear chose to officially call the tire an "extended mobility" tire (EMT). The sidewall of the EMT is actually so stiff that it is not appropriate for all cars. But the C5 Corvette

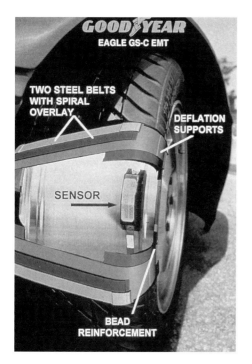

An extended mobility tire (EMT) uses extra sidewall stiffening to support the tire when it's running without air.

Courtesy Goodyear Tire & Rubber Co.

was a good match for the concept because it required a very low-profile, fairly stiff performance tire to begin with. The inherent structural stiffness of the car minimized the degradation in ride and isolation that the stiffer run-flat tire imparts.

While the EMT was a good choice for the standard Corvette models, the penultimate handling and traction requirements of the Z06 took the Goodyear engineers away from the EMT to design a no-holds-barred competition tire for the street. This Corvette's extraordinary performance—1g handling and 0 to 60 mph in 4.0 seconds—is in no small part due to this tire.

As we explored the attributes of the tire that made the car handle better, we also focused on the suspension that directs the tire. The first two years of showroom stock racing on some very hilly and bumpy racetracks, such as Mid Ohio, Sears Point, and Mosport, demonstrated that the Corvette handled better if there was less rear camber change. This was accomplished experimentally by lowering the inboard attachment points for the lower lateral strut, thereby lengthening the front swing arm of the rear suspension.

With our complex five-link rear suspension, the ride steer, roll steer, antidive, and antisquat geometry were thrown off just enough that all the other attachment points needed to be moved as well. The subtle geometry change of lowering the strut about an inch also changed the lever arm ratio for the spring and shock absorber, so we had to change the spring rates and shock absorber calibrations, too. All of these modifications came together as an entirely new suspension, which was introduced into production with the 1988 model year.

REAR SUSPENSION CONFIGURATIONS

The 50-year history of the Corvette spans rear suspension designs from the leaf-spring-mounted solid rear axle to the complex multi-link independent suspension of today. The Corvette bypassed the de Dion (other than the experimental SS) and swing axles and moved quickly to the multilink rear suspension designs that are characteristic of some of the best high-performance cars today.

The solid axle rear suspension had its good points. The axle kept the wheels pointed straight ahead, and there was no camber change in roll, so the lateral forces generated in cornering were as large as they could be compared to any other rear suspension configuration. Solid axles are still

used today, particularly in light trucks and in racing's NASCAR Winston Cup and Busch series.

The shortcoming of the solid axle is its dynamic behavior. On leaf springs, the windup of the axle, under accelerating and braking, can lead to dynamic wheel hop instability. Transmission output torque, reacting through the prop shaft at the pinion of the axle, tends to make the axle roll, increasing the normal force on the left wheel and reducing the normal force on the right wheel. Without a strong positraction (limited slip differential) or locked axle, a lightly loaded wheel spins at very low longitudinal accelerations. (A locked axle has no differential, and consequently, the car cannot be turned at low speeds without tire-scrubbing or "crow-hopping.")

The effects of the solid axle rear suspension are exaggerated as spring rates are lowered in an attempt to improve ride. Staggering, using more than two shock absorbers, is a solution to the dynamic power hop problem, but ultimately the solid axle requires a link control system in order to fully separate ride rates from control.

The de Dion rear suspension is an adaptation of the solid axle with the ring and pinion and differential chassis mounted, driving the wheels through two universal-jointed variable-length shafts. The de Dion rear suspension, like the solid axle, keeps the wheels pointing straight ahead, although they can be steered by the geometry of the trailing links. The bounce mass of the wheel system is reduced by moving the mass of the differential to the sprung chassis. It still leaves the left and right wheels coupled in tramp. The chassis-mounted differential isolates the axle system from engine-transmission output torque and eliminates the unloading of one wheel and the one-wheel spin that occurs at high torque.

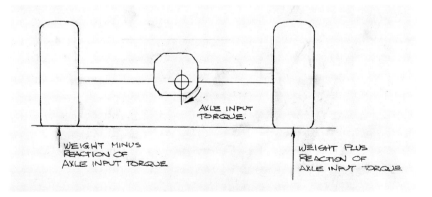

The solid axle rear suspension is inexpensive and keeps the tires running parallel and upright.
Drawing by Dave McLellan

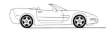

The de Dion rear suspension was the ultimate solution for the high-powered Grand Prix cars from Mercedes and Auto-Union just before World War II, and it was the suspension configuration used by Duntov in the 1957 Corvette SS and Sting Ray race cars.

Swing axles provide a supple independent ride through the rear suspension, and were used in a number of European cars and in the early Corvair. They reach their limit of usefulness as suspension rates are lowered and ride travel is increased to improve ride. Cornering on an undulating road can induce considerable camber steer effect. The swing axle, through its geometry, also introduces a lift force on the car which can, by itself, exaggerate the camber change phenomena. This is commonly referred to as "jacking."

Mercedes, an early proponent of swing axles, included them in the original 300SL Gullwing. When the 300SL was reconfigured as a convertible, the rear suspension was also changed to a low-pivot swing axle design. The low pivot point reduced the jacking forces but left the suspension with the same large camber change from bump to rebound. As raced, the original 300SL developed a reputation for being difficult to control at the limit. The later low-pivot swing axle design improved this situation.

The C4 Corvette's five-link rear suspension is an excellent design, with great flexibility for the chassis designer. It falls short only in requiring that the upper lateral link be positioned horizontally and that the tire operate at zero camber. The upper lateral link is the U-jointed shaft that supplies torque. This shaft was designed to operate with slightly off-zero angles, so that the needle bearings process as the joint rotates. This is also helped by the continuous up-and-down movement of the wheel as the car rides over the road. As U-joint angles are increased and camber is induced in the rear suspension, a two-per-revolution vibration is introduced into the suspension. This is an annoying limitation to using the U-jointed shaft as a suspension member. Zero camber is also required, not because of the suspension but because of road conditions. A road car has to be able to operate on ice, where even the smallest camber thrust can overwhelm the available traction and cause the tire to skid. On the racetrack, however, the car can be set up with an initial static camber of even two to three degrees. The only side effect is the minor half-shaft vibration, which the racers ignore.

The C5's multi-link rear suspension does not rely on the axle shaft for lateral location. It uses a separate upper link with a plunging drive shaft,

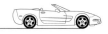

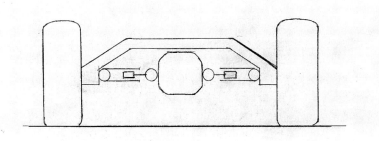

By mounting the differential to the chassis, the de Dion axle solved the prop-shaft torque reaction and wheel-spin problems of the solid axle before the days of limited-slip differentials and traction control.

Drawing by Dave McLellan

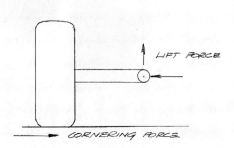

LIFT FORCE

CORNERING FORCE

The swing axle was one of the first attempts at an independent drive axle suspension; however, hard cornering could cause massive camber changes and difficult handling.

Drawing by Dave McLellan

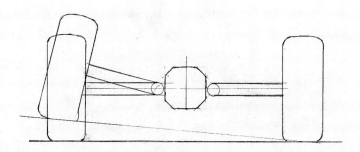

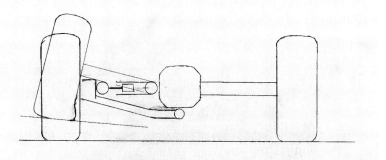

The low-pivot swing axle reduced jacking force but left the large camber changes of earlier swing axle suspensions.

Drawing by Dave McLellan

The Corvette C4 five-link rear suspension was similar to the 1963 Corvette independent rear suspension but used trailing arms to control squat; it also employed a stiff rear link for toe control.

Drawing by Dave McLellan

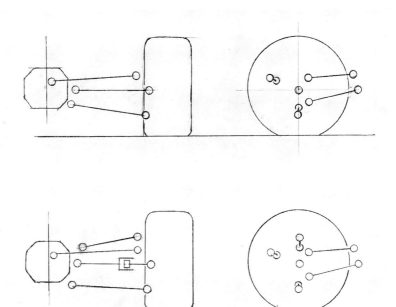

The Corvette C5 rear suspension replaced the fixed length drive shaft with a sliding and articulated shaft and added an inclined sixth member to control camber.

Drawing by Dave McLellan

which means that differential isolation is no longer compromised by handling requirements. The C5 suspension finally removes all the imposed geometry and dynamic constraints of the C3 and C4 rear suspensions, and allows the ride performance and steer effects to be precisely controlled.

DIGITAL CHASSIS CONTROL

What I've described so far in this chapter is the Corvette's foundation chassis system, which supports the tire-road interface and manages the performance and stability of the car under cornering, accelerating, braking, and in ride. As analog systems of springs, dampers, and links, these systems offer room for only small incremental improvements. However, thanks to the onboard microprocessor, the connection between tire and road is improving by leaps and bounds.

ANTI-LOCK BRAKING

We first introduced antilock brakes (ABS) to the Corvette in 1986. Then, in 1998, we made several changes to make the car work even better with antilock brakes. We introduced a zero-scrub front suspension so that braking with one wheel on gravel and the other on dry pavement, for example, would not induce a difficult-to-control torque in the steering system.

This was a significant ABS enhancement that allowed us to sharpen the response of the system when the tires were confronted with side-to-side variations in traction.

The 1992 Corvette added traction control to the foundation ABS. It took six years from the introduction of ABS for Bosch to develop the hardware and increase the computer capacity sufficiently to manage the more complex traction control task. Traction control manages the spin-up of the rear driving tires. It has to intervene very quickly and decisively, in order to avoid complete loss of directional control. In the Corvette's traction control, when a rear tire began to lose traction, the brake of the offending tire was applied and the throttle was reduced. The system required a high-pressure pump to apply the rear brakes separately and independently of the driver, and used a throttle-by-wire or, as Bosch proposed and implemented, a "throttle relaxer" to manage the application of power. Introduced in 1997, the C5 added throttle-by-wire to manage the engine and in 1998 added yaw control, or as Chevrolet calls it, "Active Handling," to control limit handling.

ABS, traction control and yaw control have their foundation in the longitudinal elastic behavior of the tire. A small, toothed wheel within each wheel hub produces 60 to 70 pulses per wheel revolution. The change in pulse timing is used by the chassis computer as a measure of the instantaneous tire velocity. The computer differentiates this signal to obtain an approximation of the tire's acceleration.

As a car accelerates or decelerates, the computer monitors each tire. (In physics, the term "acceleration" applies equally to the speeding up and the slowing down of an object, and I will use the word to describe both actions.) Only if a tire is accelerating at a rate higher than can be predicted by the highest mu (greatest traction) tire-road interface, does the computer intervene. An individual tire is presumed to be capable of accelerating at no more than 1.2g. If the tire starts to accelerate at more than this, the computer assumes that the tire is starting to slide or spin down, and goes into its control strategy. With the ABS, it releases brake pressure and watches for the tire to start reaccelerating. It then holds brake pressure and—depending on what the tire does next—reapplies or further dumps brake pressure.

The graph shows the tire characteristics that allow ABS, traction control and yaw control to work.

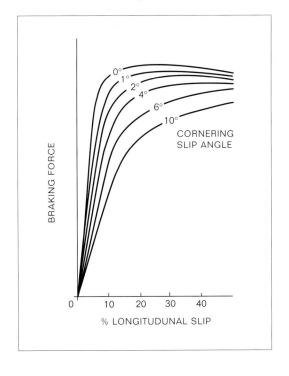

This cycle is repeated approximately 10 to 15 times per second in a dry road stop and is intended to maximize the deceleration of each tire.

Even though the early antilock brake systems did not have a sensor to measure the yaw state of the car directly, the systems were actually able to monitor all four tires and infer something about the stability of the entire vehicle. The control system managed the two front wheels independently and the rear wheels together, selecting the rear tire with the least traction as the controlling tire. This was conservative and gave good stability under braking, but gave away a slight amount of braking power in favor of dynamic stability.

This stability was demonstrated when we experimented with braking in a turn. The car was stable under hard braking on a straightaway, in a turn, and even in an evasive maneuver (which can be thought of as a series of consecutive turns). We found, even in a limit-handling racing maneuver, that if the driver was starting to lose control, the best strategy was to bang on the brakes and steer normally; the car would correct itself. We lost some of this natural stability as we modified the control system to deal with different levels of traction from left to right. But we regained the lost stability with the addition of a lateral accelerometer, which allowed the computer to switch from the split mu program at low lateral gs to the original program above 0.6 lateral gs.

The 1986 Corvette was the first application of ABS as standard equipment and followed Lincoln's optional introduction of their ITT-Teves system by only a few months. It was interesting to watch Paul King and our Chevrolet General Manager, Bob Stempel, sell this system to the Chevrolet Sales Department. This first-generation system was very expensive, costing us over $2,000 per car because of the very low production volume. Most of the Chevrolet sales people had never heard of antilock brakes, and certainly had not had a chance to drive one of the cars. Our customers also knew virtually nothing about antilock brakes, yet here we were adding thousands of dollars to the price of the Corvette by introducing the ABS as standard equipment. It was an act of faith for the sales guys to agree to all this, and I have to give them full credit for believing that the system would have the benefits that we, the engineers, said it would.

It took about five years for antilock brakes to be recognized by the general public as a real enhancement to active car safety. It took less than a year, though, for the drivers who were running Corvettes in the SCCA showroom stock series to learn that ABS could offer a real advantage. From then on, the racers demanded antilock brakes.

TRACTION CONTROL

Traction control is another use of digital technology to improve safety as well as performance. It operates to control the spin-up of the driven wheels in the same manner that ABS controls the spin-down of all four wheels. "Traction control" is another misnomer, because the traction itself isn't actually controlled, it's the longitudinal spin-up of the tire which is under control. Traction is the shear force between the road and the tire. Recognizing that we were controlling slip or the spin-up of the tire led us to a more technically correct name, Acceleration Slip Regulation (ASR). It took Bosch an additional six years to develop, which is a measure of how much more difficult it turned out to be to control the spin-up of the tire than it is to control the spin-down, as applied in ABS.

The introduction of traction control in the 1992 Corvette required using a much larger computer, yet it still did not have the capacity to do everything we would have liked. It required a complete redesign of the ABS, so that pressure could be applied to the rear brakes independently of the driver. It also required a motor system to intrude between the driver's accelerator foot and the throttle.

When the system recognized that a driven wheel was spinning up, it would momentarily apply the appropriate brake to regain control of the slipping tire. At this first level, with one tire slipping, it had the same effect as the positraction axle. If the system sensed that both tires were slipping, it would apply both rear brakes accordingly and also begin to close the throttle to keep the engine from overwhelming the system. So, on ice, for example, if the car was at a standstill and the driver stepped on the gas, the rear wheels would accelerate momentarily and begin to spin, but the ASR would recognize this as an out-of-control event, and correct for it. In such a case, the ASR would apply the rear brakes, reduce the throttle, and then manage both to keep the tires right at the threshold of spinning, thus achieving virtually maximum-acceleration takeoff. In an even more extreme situation, with one wheel on ice and the other wheel on dry pavement, the car could move out aggressively.

Driving any rear-wheel-drive car on ice has always been a tense proposition. The driver has to be on the throttle to maintain headway, yet it takes very little additional throttle to cause spin-up of the rear tires and a loss of directional stability. If the car crosses this threshold, the driver needs to back off the throttle and work the steering carefully to regain control of the car. On wet ice, however, closing the throttle can itself cause the wheels to spin-up due to idle torque. Driving on wet ice is an incredibly

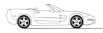

difficult task with a conventional rear-wheel-drive car. But, with ASR we found that driving under these most extreme conditions was dramatically less stressful. Driver fatigue associated with wet ice is significantly reduced with ASR, and a car can be a safe drive even under the worst circumstances. The important thing for drivers to remember in dangerous road conditions is to avoid drastic changes in speed or direction, in order to allow the system to maintain control.

The Corvette's ABS/ASR computer measures the spin up of all four tires. It knows the forward speed of the car, the torque output and the rpm of the engine. It can infer, from the difference in speed between the two front-wheel sensors, if the car is in a turn and how sharp a turn it is. It knows the lateral acceleration of the car. But the computer cannot answer the fundamental question: Is the car in or out of control? It can guess, with some degree of success, using the speed difference of the two front-wheel sensors, but it can't be sure. Therefore, the strategies it uses for control have to be tailored on the conservative side, so that the car is always stable, but this degrades the performance of the system to some degree.

As we developed ASR, we encouraged the engineers to make the system as aggressive as possible. But they determined that making it too aggressive could sometimes lead to an out-of-control event, rather than the stabilized condition we were trying to achieve. With the system programmed to be aggressive, the car seemed schizophrenic and unpredictable. We learned that we were far better off erring on the side that always gave stability.

As a result of this decision, there were a few conditions where ASR would activate inadvertently—at least from the driver's perspective. The latest versions of ASR are much less intrusive as a result of subsequent fine-tuning. However, one situation where a driver will want to turn off ASR is when negotiating deep mud, because wheel spin is actually useful.

Another form of traction control was developed to maximize the aggressive wheel-spinning standing starts in Formula 1 racing, and was used for a short time in the early 1990s, before being banned. It was subsequently reintroduced in 2001. With an automatic clutch, traction control could also be programmed to give the manual transmission Corvette maximum acceleration starts.

YAW CONTROL

Our first exposure to the power of controlling yaw or the angular rotation of the car was an experiment we set up for ourselves on Black Lake, one

of the testing areas at GM's Proving Grounds. Using cones, we established a curve that could be negotiated at about 70 mph. The question we were trying to answer was how fast could we safely approach the curve, if the car was braking as we entered. We tried the task without braking, with the full antilock brakes applied, and then with only the right front brake engaged. (The turn was to the left, so in the last scenario we were braking with just the heavily-loaded outside front wheel.) Without braking, our test car was quite neutral, but when the control-limiting speed was exceeded the car tended to spin. As we expected, ABS application on entry gave us a higher entry speed as well as stability under braking. Somewhat to our surprise, braking with the one outside front wheel (still under ABS control) gave us the highest entry speed, an aggressive turn-in, and good stability. This was as close to yaw control as we could get on our own.

A year later, in 1992, Bosch demonstrated a very early yaw control system. The system was so developmental that its computers took up most of the rear seat and the trunk of a BMW 5 Series test car. It also required a technician riding in the back seat to run the program. We didn't get as much out of this evaluation as I would have liked, but it was our first look at real yaw control.

So, what exactly is yaw control? At a first-order level, yaw control uses the ABS's slip control and the brake self-apply capability of traction control to make the car follow the driver's direction, even at the car's limit of control. Wherever the driver directs the car with the steering wheel the car will go, limited only by the laws of physics.

Technically, yaw control compares two actions: the driver's input and the car's response. When they diverge, the car is obviously not following the driver's direction. At this point, the individual wheels' braking forces

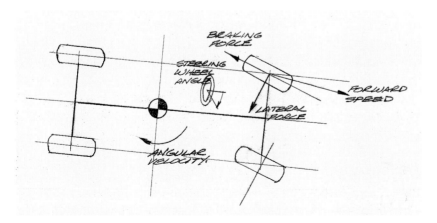

Yaw control combines electronic control of the individual wheel brakes and the throttle to improve the stability of the automobile.

Drawing by Dave McLellan

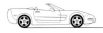

are used to make the car correct its course. The steering-wheel angle and forward speed, together, indicate the turning rate of the car, also known as the yaw rate. A yaw-rate sensor measures this quantity directly. If a car holds an actual yaw rate higher than the rate the driver is calling for, the car is spinning. If the yaw rate is less than what the driver is calling for, the car is plowing. An appropriate intervention is to apply either the outside front brake, to "unwind" the car and slow its yaw rate, or apply the inside front brake, to increase the car's rotation. The C5 Corvette uses a cadence of both front and rear brakes, to totally maximize the authority of its yaw control system.

The C5 lets the driver select strategies, recognizing that the driver is ultimately in control and that some circumstances are beyond the system's ability to discriminate. Remember that the "base" strategy is designed to work competently on all surfaces, but that it is impossible to program the system to give the driver both the slip-angle aggressiveness needed for a high traction run on a racetrack, and still provide for maximum control on wet-ice. Thus, the driver is given the opportunity to select the control strategy or turn the system off, depending on the situation at hand.

With the intervention of digital yaw control (Active Handling), the Corvette's limit-handling is completely stabilized. From here on, I expect only incremental improvements, as the system continues to be refined. An example of this refinement is the Conti-Teves tire, which has radial magnetic strips imbedded in its sidewall. Under braking, the shear strain distorts a tire's sidewall. In the Conti-Teves tire the magnetic strips are used to measure this distortion providing another indicator of the wheel's dynamic performance. The developer claims improved stopping performance, as a result.

As it is, the yaw control system is only as good as the driver's input. The driver can still overwhelm the system with too much steering input or underwhelm the system through too little input. There is work afoot to develop cars with situation awareness, such as the ability to recognize the trajectories of nearby objects and warn the driver, or even to take direct steps to intervene, in order to avoid a crash. The basic premise of this work is that cars shouldn't have to crash. Yaw control is an important underlying capability of such an electronic safety system.

RIDE CONTROL

Ride is also starting to be managed digitally. Our first effort with the Corvette was the Bilstein Selective Ride System, which was introduced in

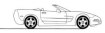

1989 for the ZR-1. This servo-motor-controlled shock absorber contained a range of damping values, which could be selected in increments as a function of speed and driver selection. The idea was to soften the ride at low speeds yet have a totally controlled ride at high speeds. It worked quite well.

The next leap forward is likely to be the electromagnetic shock absorber. Using a magnetic fluid and an electromagnet surrounding the shock orifice, control is instant, and a much wider range of forces are available. Driven by acceleration sensors, these systems will go a long way toward eliminating the sharp, sometimes brutal ride response to potholes and tar strips while still completely controlling ride.

ACTIVE SUSPENSION

Chevrolet R&D, under Jack Turner's direction, even experimented with full active suspension for the Corvette. In parallel with the development of the ZR-1, R&D worked with Lotus to integrate its high-pressure hydraulic active suspension into a variation of the car. Their car was a considerable departure from the contemporary Corvette chassis, and was distinctive for its unique hydraulic strut suspension at each corner, a huge 3,000 psi hydraulic pump on top of the engine, multiple accumulators, extensive hydraulic plumbing, and an elaborate electronic control system. We got as far as building several Active ZR-1s at Bowling Green. Ultimately, the complexity of the system, its considerable horsepower drain, and its strut-seal friction, which negated much of the potential ride qual-

An active suspension Corvette came close to reaching production but did not meet all of its objectives.
Courtesy The National Corvette Museum

ity benefit, all combined to kill the project. It turned out that the C4 Corvette was also a poor choice of platforms. The high-bandwidth active suspension system really needed a car with a very stiff structure to work to its capability. When active suspension will return to the Corvette is anybody's guess.

Just as electronic controls have enabled us to regain much of the power lost after the advent of emission controls, the future of better handling and increased ride comfort is in digital technology. And this technology, which is sure to improve performance, will have even greater value in making cars safer on the road.

Balancing Performance with Economy and Emission Control

11

THE FIRST CORVETTE ENGINE WAS A PRODUCT of the 1920s. Its inline six engine was originally conceived as a part of Chevrolet's strategy to use a six-cylinder engine to wrestle dominance of the low-priced field from Ford's four-bangers. The strategy worked, and Chevrolet overtook Ford and dominated the high-volume, low-priced automobile market from the late 1920s, through the 1930s and even after World War II. In the 1930s, the straight six engine was upgraded to aluminum pistons, inserted shell bearings, and pressure lubrication. By 1953, the engine was producing 108 ghp (gross horsepower) at 3,600 rpm from 230 cubic inches. This was hardly the starting point for a sports car engine, but it was all Chevrolet had to work with at the time.

For the Corvette, Chevrolet improved the breathing of the engine by almost 40 percent, opening up the intake with three Carter side-draft carburetors, using dual exhaust pipes and increasing the valve open time with a new camshaft. The result was a power output of 150 hp at 4,200 rpm.

The automatic transmission was a high-technology invention of the 1930s. General Motors, the industry leader in the development of automatic transmissions, began with the Hydramatic for Cadillac and Oldsmobile, and later introduced the Dynaflow for Buick and the Powerglide for Chevrolet.

The Hydramatic initially used a fluid coupling, where there had previously been a friction clutch. Planetary gear sets, with the attendant hydraulic controls and clutches to engage them, replaced the traditional geared transmission. The fluid coupling consisted of a pump and reaction turbine with sufficient slippage to allow the car's engine to idle in gear. The multiple planetary gear sets gave the car a selection of four forward speeds.

The Dynaflow and the Powerglide used a torque converter, which was like the earlier fluid coupling with the addition of a third element, a sta-

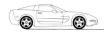

tor. The stator was a vaned wheel, which was connected to the output shaft of the transmission so that when the car was stationary, the stator was stationary, giving it maximum reaction as it redirected the oil flowing from the turbine back to the pump. The introduction of the stator multiplied the torque output of the torque converter by a factor of about two at zero mph. This multiplication effectively served as the first gear. With a planetary low-range gear set and a direct (1:1) high gear, this two-speed automatic transmission performed as well as the early Hydramatic with its four speeds. On the downside, the Powerglide torque converter had to be very "loose," for it to be able to operate with only two forward speeds. This gave the driver the sensation that the engine was only loosely connected to the road wheels, which was the antithesis of the kind of control the sports car driver expected of an automobile.

Despite the handicap of the Powerglide, the Corvette's performance was still exceptional for its day, and not far behind that of serious sports cars like the Jaguar XK 120. The Corvette could do 0 to 60 in 11 seconds, and reach the quarter mile in 18 seconds at 75 mph.

When the Corvette was introduced, Ed Cole, Chevrolet's Chief Engineer, was in the midst of turning Chevrolet around. Unfortunately, his new V-8 engine was still a year away from production. This forced Maurice Olley to develop the first Corvette around the old set of Chevrolet parts. It's not clear whether it was just the poor quality of the Corvette's fiberglass body, its cranky three carburetor variant of the L6 engine, its loose Powerglide automatic transmission, or all three combined, which virtually killed the Corvette before the public could experience it as a powerful V-8 powered sports car.

THE POWER GAME

Zora Arkus-Duntov was hired into Chevrolet Research and Development by Ed Cole, to do V-8 engine power development. Totally as an aside, Zora took the fledgling Corvette under his wing and began to develop it. From 1956 to 1974, Corvettes produced raw power, with only minimal regard for emissions, fuel economy, or noise. Corvette made its reputation on raw, unbridled, and ultimately big-block power and torque.

Many Corvette enthusiasts like to describe their engines in terms of horsepower and size, which makes for wonderful "code speak," but it largely misses the point. Power means nothing if is isn't applied efficiently, so the highest engine power rating doesn't necessarily ensure the best performance.

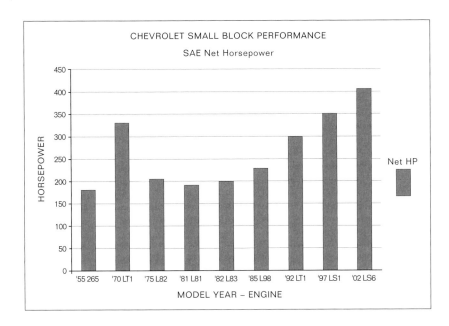

CHEVROLET SMALL BLOCK PERFORMANCE

SAE Net Horsepower

After many years of falling power ratings, the Corvette is more powerful than ever.

The engine produces torque over a range of speeds. The transmission multiplies this torque, as does the axle, converting the torque into the force which turns the wheels. The differential manages the torque distribution to the driven wheels which, with help from the suspension, push the car along the road. The magnitude of acceleration is a function of the thrust generated at the tire-road interface and the mass of the car. All the parts of the system need to be balanced and working together, to achieve maximum efficiency.

MEETING GOVERNMENT REGULATIONS

Our primal emphasis on producing raw power ended in 1975, as emissions standards reached levels that could only be met with the catalytic converter. And new standards for fuel economy were just five years away. In order to respond to these requirements, Chevrolet first eliminated the big block from all of its passenger cars. The "rat motor" would be relegated to low-horsepower, high-torque, heavy-duty truck applications.

The small block engine, the mainstay of the Corvette since 1955, would continue, but it would be manufactured only in configurations common to passenger car applications, because of the high cost and complication of certifying the engine to meet Federal emission standards. The emission control technology of the time could barely meet the higher standards, and we usually ended up sacrificing power for compliance.

By 1981 we were producing the lowest horsepower and slowest Corvettes since the six-cylinder days of 1954. This was a terrible marketing situation for a car that was defined by its engine and its performance. It was small comfort that all other car manufacturers were suffering this same difficulty of accommodating the new emissions standards.

Fortunately, for enthusiasts, the Corvette made a dramatic recovery in performance, starting in 1982. Today's Corvettes are faster accelerating and have higher top speeds than any production Corvette ever before, yet they meet all the emissions requirements, exceed the fuel economy Gas Guzzler threshold, and meet all the noise law restrictions (with the possible exception of Switzerland's). We can thank the emergence of digital electronic engine control technology for every bit of this.

GM had no intention of paying the Gas Guzzler Tax on any of its cars—certainly not by design. The corporation has, however, been caught a few times with a car that did not pass the Gas Guzzler threshold. When the Allante was introduced in 1990 with the first Northstar engine, the Gas Guzzler tax applied until the engine development engineers could find a way to improve the car's fuel mileage.

The seven-mode California emissions test cycle is the source for the fuel economy rating that applies to cars sold in the US. The city and highway parts of this test are combined with a 55 percent/45 percent weighting to determine an average fuel economy. What is notable about this test is that it is tailored to heavy-traffic driving, and is dominated by low-speeds and frequent-stops. This kind of driving never requires more than 60 hp from the Corvette's motor. So, how do we squeeze out the best possible fuel economy from an engine that uses less than 15 percent of its power capability in traffic? What emerged was a "dual engine" strategy. The best fuel economy was achieved by running the engine as slowly as possible—say 1,000 to 2,000 rpm—with valve timing optimized for these ultralow speeds. By keeping the engine speed low, throttling and friction losses, which are two of the major sources of reduced engine efficiency, were minimized. However, this being a Corvette, we still wanted an engine that maxed power output in the 4,000 to 7,000 rpm range. Optimizing the cam timing and intake tuning for both the high and low speed ranges required some effort.

TRANSMISSION FOR ECONOMY AND PERFORMANCE

So we needed a transmission that had a sufficient ratio spread for the engine to run efficiently and still provide full power on demand. The result

was a Corvette which uses a four-speed automatic transmission with the widest ratio range in the industry. Even with a 2.56:1 axle ratio, the 3.06:1 first gear and the 2:1 multiplication in the torque converter will cause the tires to chirp on acceleration, while providing a 0.7:1 ratio fourth overdrive at speeds as low as 42 mph.

There are five-speed automatics starting to show up in the marketplace, but so far, none has a ratio spread broader than the Corvette's four-gear transmission does. Rumor has it, though, that the C6 Corvette will have a five-speed automatic transmission, and that it will have an even longer wheelbase than the C5. This make sense, as the longer wheelbase is probably needed to accommodate the lengthier five-speed automatic transmission.

As for the manual transmission, designing an effective balance between fuel economy and power is much more difficult. And the way the EPA fuel economy tests are done complicates matters. The EPA stipulates that the one-two shift cannot be made below 15 mph; the two-three below 25 mph; the three-four below 40; and the four-five below 45 mph. As we were putting together our "dual engine" strategy, we discovered that these speed-gear couplings were inefficient for best fuel economy. It's actually OK to skip-shift when you're driving for economy; it's totally unnecessary to use each of the gears in sequence. A computer analysis of this approach, using a wide-ratio three-speed, indicated as much as a 2 mpg fuel economy improvement compared to a five-gear shifting strategy. We could always use a 2 mpg fuel gain, trading it off for more power with a bigger engine, or for a higher-numerical axle ratio.

Our first solution to the manual transmission problem, implemented with the 1984 Corvette and carried through the 1988 model year, was to add an overdrive to the conventional four-speed manual. Controlled by the engine computer, the overdrive sensed the acceleration level the driver was calling for. So, if the driver made a one-two shift under heavy acceleration, the transmission would shift into second gear. However, if very light acceleration had been called for, the transmission would shift to second overdrive.

This strategy worked reasonably well and gave the fuel economy improvement that was predicted, but it was, to be honest, an intrusion and an annoyance for the driver. As hard as we tried, we could never program the overdrive to avoid annoying the driver, at least some of the time. On the other hand, operating as a five-speed for performance driving, it provided an excellent spread of gear ratios for acceleration, and gave the

1984 car a top speed of just over 140 mph in fourth overdrive. In its last year of use, the 1988 Corvette with the manual overdrive transmission was able to reach 150 mph in fourth overdrive.

As we began planning the ZR-1, we recognized that we needed a manual transmission with a much higher torque capacity than the Borg-Warner four-speed, with its Doug Nash overdrive. This gave us the opportunity to rethink our skip-shift strategy. For 1989 and beyond, we took a totally different approach: We introduced a six-speed manual transmission. The first five-speeds were optimized for performance—first gear for launch, and fifth gear for running top speed. Sixth gear was purely a fuel economy gear. If the driver accelerated aggressively from a launch, the transmission was shifted into second at over 45 mph. However, if the driver launched using light throttle and shifted up at much lower speeds, the shift lever would induce a shift into fourth gear instead to second. This produced a one-four-five-six shifting strategy for fuel economy. This strategy also gave similar fuel economy results to the Doug Nash transmission, but without as much confusion.

AN ENGINE WITH TWO PERSONALITIES

The combustion process itself is at the core of designing any engine. Air—made up of 21 percent by volume of oxygen (the oxidizer) and 79 percent by volume of nitrogen (an inertent)—is mixed with atomized gasoline in a ratio of 14.7 pounds of air to 1 pound of fuel. This mixture, drawn into the cylinder and compressed, is ignited by the spark plug and burns rapidly, almost explosively. The products of combustion, mostly water vapor and carbon dioxide gas, dramatically increase the temperature and pressure in the cylinder and give up much of their energy to the piston as useful work as they expand and cool.

Both theory and practical experience demonstrates that increasing the compression ratio increases the useful work that can be extracted from the process. However, the tendency of the gasoline-air mixture to ignite prematurely gets in the way of raising the compression ratio and has led to the development of high-octane fuels that minimize this tendency. Due to the extreme temperature of the compressed mixture itself, self-ignition can occur at many points within the charge, leading to a premature and extremely rapid rate of pressure rise. This extremely rapid pressure rise and colliding flame fronts from more than one ignition source can quickly cause very high temperature and absolute pressure in the cylinder if not carefully controlled. Under these conditions, near top dead center the pis-

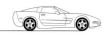

ton is nearly motionless and very soft (about 500 deg. F). As a result, the hot gases are easily capable of burning a hole in the piston top.

Until the compression ratio problem was well understood, and the slower-burning high-octane fuels were developed, engines were limited to compression ratios in the range of 4:1 or 5:1. These days, however, a compact combustion chamber with well-cooled surfaces and no hot spots can run successfully with compression ratios as high as 11:1. The octane tolerance of the chamber was further enhanced by closed-loop detonation control systems which use accelerometers to sense detonation even before it can be heard. Upon sensing detonation, the spark is retarded or the fuel delivery is increased to suppress any further detonation in the affected cylinder.

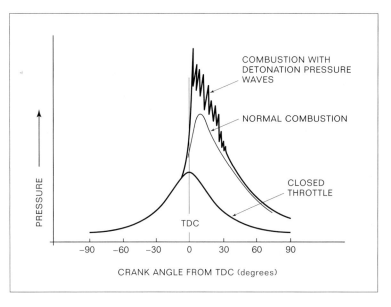

A mixture of air and fuel will burn successfully only over a limited range of air-fuel ratios. The stoichiometric ideal air-fuel ratio is 14.7:1, which is the point at which all the fuel is burned with no oxygen remaining. Decreasing the air-fuel ratio to 12.5:1 tends to increase power slightly by ensuring that all of the oxygen is consumed. Increasing air-fuel ratio to 15.5:1 tends to increase fuel economy by ensuring that all the fuel is burned. Further increases in air-fuel ratio, while they might seem to promise ever better fuel economy, will lead to combustion roughness, a too-long burn time, higher chamber temperatures and increased oxides of nitrogen in the exhaust. Ultralean burn engines, which overcome these problems, are just now being introduced.

It is difficult to see inside a cylinder and observe the combustion process at work, but some of the best insights have come from just this approach. Test engines have been built with quartz windows so that the induction airflow, the increased swirl of the charge during compression, and the combustion process itself can be studied visually. One of the findings of this research is that some of the finely-atomized liquid fuel droplets find their way into nooks and crannies of the combustion chamber and never participate in the combustion process. For example, fuel droplets have been observed migrating down the sides of the piston and onto the first com-

Pre-ignition occurs when the end gases reach their self-ignition temperature and burn instantaneously instead of burning in the propagating flame front.

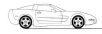

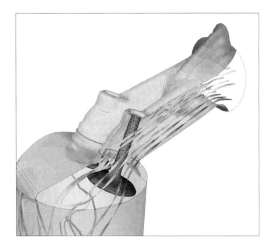

Computational fluid dynamic (CFD) modeling of the intake and exhaust flows and of combustion itself has become a normal part of the engine designer's tool kit.

Courtesy Cosworth Technology and Fluent, Inc.

pression ring. Being in such a protected and cooled environment, they never take part in the combustion process and, ultimately, exit with the exhaust products, as unburned hydrocarbons. Moving the compression ring closer to the piston top and tightening the clearances reduces the amount of fuel that can be trapped in this way.

When the air-fuel ratio is at its stoichiometric ideal, the production of hydrocarbons, carbon monoxide and nitrous oxides is minimized. As a result, all modern engines use sensors in the exhaust that detect residual oxygen. The computer, after sensing oxygen left in the exhaust, will adjust the fuel injection duty cycle, adding or subtracting small amounts of fuel, as appropriate. Today's Corvette engines use one oxygen sensor per cylinder bank. From an emissions standpoint, the V-8 is treated as if it were two, completely separate, four-cylinder engines. In the future, engines will very likely use one oxygen sensor per cylinder, as well as employing a newly-developed spark plug that contains a cylinder pressure sensor. The cylinder pressure data can be used with closed-loop feedback control to time the spark discharge so that peak cylinder pressure occurs just before top dead center (BTC). It is the precise control of the combustion process, for both its air-fuel ratio and for timing, that has led to the modern engine's ability to have lower emissions and improved fuel economy at the same time.

Catalytic converters have progressed from the original high back-pressure pellet beds to the much lower back-pressure ceramic or metal monolith designs. The ceramic or metal substrate is only the carrier, providing a large surface area that can be coated with minute quantities of the rare earth metals that comprise the actual catalyst. Platinum, palladium, and rhodium are typically used as the catalysts. In the converter, the minute quantities of carbon monoxide and hydrocarbons left over from the combustion process, react with oxygen to produce their fully-oxidized forms of carbon dioxide and water. The catalysts allow this chemical reaction to proceed at a much lower temperature than it otherwise would. The much lower back pressure of a well-engineered monolith converter not only improves power but also, through its configuration, lowers the car's noise level. It makes the job of developing discrete and separate mufflers easier to accomplish and, thus, contributes to lowering back pressure and improving performance.

KEEPING IT COOL

In some of the hottest parts of the engine, oil is the primary heat transfer medium. But for the rest of the engine a water-based coolant is used. Most early automobile engines used water alone as the heat transfer medium. Water has a very high specific heat, meaning that heat can be transferred to water more efficiently than to almost any other liquid. The problem is that water freezes and boils within the operating range of the engine. However, adding an equal amout of ethylene glycol to water lowers the freezing temperature to −34°F and, with the cooling system pressurized to 18 psig, raises the boiling point to 268°F.

The exhaust valve, its seat, and the exhaust port are the hottest parts in an engine, with metal temperatures reaching well over 300°F at higher horsepowers. This heat causes the nearby coolant to boil and creates steam bubbles which adhere to the exhaust port surface. If these bubbles are not removed, they act as a thermal blanket, retarding heat transfer and further increasing the metal temperature, and negating the cooling effect of the coolant. So, the coolant needs to be traveling at high velocity when it passes over the local exhaust surfaces, in order to scrub away the steam bubbles and maximize heat transfer. Careful attention to cooling helps to minimize octane demand and allows the maximum compression ratio, which in turn produces the highest-powered, most fuel-efficient engine possible.

The power available to an engine is a direct function of the fuel input. Because of gasoline's need to be mixed with air in order to burn, the power available becomes a function of the mass of air that can be crammed into an engine's cylinder. If it were not for the energy losses that come into play with increasing engine speed, running the engine faster would directly and proportionally increase horsepower.

Filling the cylinder with fresh charge is, first of all, a function of valve position and of time. If the engine speed is slow enough and the intake valve is open during the entire intake suction stroke, the cylinder will reach intake manifold pressure before the intake valve closes and the piston starts on its compression stroke. But as the engine speeds up, the valve takes time to open and the air column takes time to get moving, and by then the piston that had been going down starts back up again. All this forces

A CFD analysis of the heat flow into the coolant enables the design to be optimized for cooling effectiveness and reduced flow losses.

Courtesy Fluent, Inc.

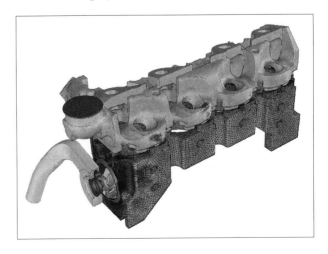

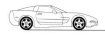

Top: Lotus devised a dual intake cam strategy for the LT5 Corvette engine.
Illustration by Dave Kimble

Bottom: Lotus' next approach was to switch each valve from the A to the B cam as a function of engine speed. This approach was ultimately used by Porsche in its new 911.
Reproduced with permission from Group Lotus PLC

the designer of the high-speed engine to open the intake valve before the power stroke ends, and to leave it open well into the return compression stroke, in order to compensate for the air's inertia. At high speeds, the opening and closing of the valves is limited by the stresses that can be withstood by the camshaft system. These limits can be stretched very significantly by using strong alloy steel cam lobes and lighter, higher-strength materials for the cam followers and valves. Cylinder filling can be improved by varying the valve timing with engine speed and load. Engine efficiency can be improved by varying both the timing and lift of the valves. But, these approaches are both costly and difficult to achieve.

How can the valve train support a dual engine strategy? Each valve has to open some 60 times per second, and almost a billion times over the life of the engine. Several mechanisms have been developed to perform valve control. Some are all-mechanical, some use hydraulics to control the mechanical system and some eliminate the camshaft and use electrical solenoids to move the valves:

• Use two intake valves, each with its own camshaft timing. This was the strategy developed by Lotus for the LT5 engine which was used in the ZR-1. The low speed valve, operating on the first cam, was active at all speeds. The high speed valve, operating on the second cam, had a secondary throttle valve in the port and was effectively closed at low speeds. This scheme worked well, and gave the engine excellent mid-range torque and over 400 hp at its peak.

• Considerably more power is possible if all the valves can be operated at high speed on the high-speed intake and exhaust cams. This was the next approach developed by Lotus, and is currently used by Porsche. At its heart is a dual-state hydraulic lifter which can pick up the low-speed cam with an inner element and then transition to riding on the high-speed cam on its outer ring. Since this scheme works on each intake and exhaust valve independently, it could also be applied to the current generation LS1 pushrod engine.

• A third method, which we never considered useful because it didn't give us the bandwidth we were after, is

to advance and retard the entire intake cam with a variable element on the sprocket drive.

- The penultimate strategy, if it can be made to work at the high speeds we are looking to run at, is to eliminate the camshaft entirely, and open the valve with a powerful electric solenoid or, as Lotus is proposing, with an electro-hydraulic actuator. The solenoid is, in effect, a giant version of the fuel injection pintle and solenoid. Its shortcoming is that it takes considerable electric power. (This may be less of a hindrance once the automobile industry converts to 42 volts.)

- A variation of the solenoid approach that reduces the electrical power demand is a shuttle valve scheme. The valve is spring-loaded so that its middle position (half open) is its default state. It is pulled closed against spring force by the first solenoid. When it's time to open, the solenoid unlatches the valve, and the spring and solenoid both give it a kick, sending it on its way to the open position. The open-position solenoid then catches and latches the valve. This cycle is reversed to close the valve. Just the right solenoid force is critical to bring the valve to a smooth stop at the end of its travel. If it can be made totally reliable, it should be the ultimate solution to valve control because:

  - It can operate on exhaust as well as intake valves.
  - Opening and closing the valve is totally under the control of the engine computer.
  - A much smaller starter motor is needed to spin up the engine if the valves are initially in their half open, neutral state.

Valves that open and close electronically provide an almost unlimited array of new possibilities.
Reproduced with permission from Group Lotus PLC

Below left: The electro-hydraulic camless engine is the Lotus response to its own experimental active valve control program.

Below: The electro-hydraulic valve at the heart of the Lotus camless engine.
Reproduced with permission from Group Lotus PLC (both)

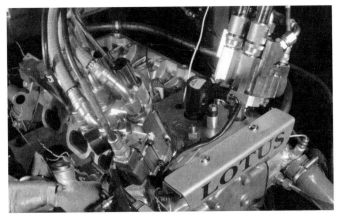

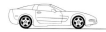

- The engine can be optimized for very low-power running by randomly shutting down individual cylinders or radically changing the engine cycle to, for example, the Miller cycle. (The Miller cycle uses early intake closure to reduce the air-fuel charge and a full exhaust stroke to extract the greatest possible energy from the process.)
- A pushrod engine with hydraulic lifters lends itself well to intake valve deactivation, which provides a virtual reduction in displacement. (GM has announced that it will apply this strategy to future truck engines.)

FORCED INDUCTION

The modern engine can handle higher thermal flux and mechanical stress than is typically experienced from a naturally-aspirated intake charge. This leads us to consider turbocharging or supercharging. Both approaches are being used successfully in emission-controlled engines at upwards of one atmosphere of boost. As boost pressure is increased, charge cooling becomes critical and the compression ratio must be adjusted in order to avoid detonation. Saab has introduced an interesting mechanical scheme to vary the compression ratio, it basically moves the crankshaft and lower block up and down, varying the compression ratio from a high of 11:1 to a low of 8:1 for boosted operation. Electromagnetically variable valves would have a similar effect on effective compression ratio.

A turbocharger gets its energy from the momentum of the exhaust gas stream. Higher back pressure on the engine is its "cost." Lack of power at low- and mid-range speeds is the downside of the turbocharger. Complex dual turbochargers and variable inlet turbochargers attempt to overcome these inherent disadvantages.

Mechanical superchargers are powered directly from the drive output of the engine. An engine that puts out 100 hp naturally aspirated, may be generating 180 hp supercharged. However, because the supercharger itself consumes 30 shaft-hp, there is a net of only 150 hp available to propel the car. Mechanical superchargers have another disadvantage in that they have no internal compression. They are only able to move the charge from inlet to outlet. Compression occurs—quite chaotically—through the backflow of pressurized air coming into the supercharger from its outlet port. Thermally, this is the most inefficient way to compress a charge, and it results in further elevation of the charge temperature and increased horsepower demand. A much more complex spiral supercharger, which

compresses the charge, is now in the automotive market. Both turbocharging and supercharging have their proponents, although currently turbocharging is much more common.

THE IDEAL CORVETTE ENGINE

If we were designing an engine today, we could put all of the new technology into an ideal Corvette. What might this ideal engine look like? Well, for starters, instead of using the standard 5.7 liter LS1, the racing version from the C5R would be substituted, to provide a more robust foundation. The engine would then be stretched to 7.4 liters, by taking advantage of the siamese bore castings of the racing engine. Both bore and stroke would be increased to 4.15 inches, and applying a Nikasil coating directly to the bores would give the same wear resistance as the aluminum liners of the LT5. This would be our foundation—a big block lurking in small block clothes!

We wouldn't want to give any horsepower away unnecessarily, so we would dry-sump the bottom end and create a vacuum instead of a whirlwind. We could choose to use the Lotus bi-state lifter for both intake and exhaust. Remember, this should be the engine that give us the best of all the conflicting elements—emissions, fuel economy, and power. If we were designing it a little more futuristically, we might choose the Lotus electro-hydraulic valves or the electromagnetic shuttle valves, and throw the camshaft away entirely. We would also want the deeper intake porting of a racing cylinder head. Note that we would still not be using a four- or five-valve head because it adds further, and so far unnecessary, complexity and bulk.

On the exhaust side we would need two very large catalytic converters and a suitably oversized exhaust system, because we would then have to meet the exhaust requirements of an engine with 750 horsepower.

Is this engine unrealistic? Not at all. Everything described is already available for inclusion in our ultimate Corvette engine. And, if 750 hp is not powerful enough, the electromagnetic valve system would accommodate supercharging or turbocharging very nicely. (The downside is that this would all mean an increase in the size of engine-bay, since the engine would have turbochargers, extra plumbing, and intercoolers protruding from it.) So, what is a reasonable power limit, if forced induction is added to our specification? The currently-available Lingenfelter 350cid

The Lingenfelter 427cid Twin-Turbo small block motor is rated at 725 hp and 650 ft.lbs torque.

Photo courtesy Lingenfelter Performance Engineering

Twin Turbo Stage II package, for the C5 Corvette, is rated at 650 horsepower. A 7.4 liter 427cid version of this motor is rated at 725 horsepower. Further gains are possible, but are limited by the intercooler's capacity. If we limit our peak-horsepower demand to periods lasting only a few seconds and employ suitable transient cooling strategies, we may be able to achieve 1,000 horsepower. These levels have already been achieved, with a turbocharged LT5, so this engine is clearly not a pipe dream. What would you get with 1,000 hp? One wild ride.

Since the tire-road interface is the limiting factor, with respect to the horsepower that can be transmitted through the tires, it is useful to understand the relationship between acceleration and horsepower.

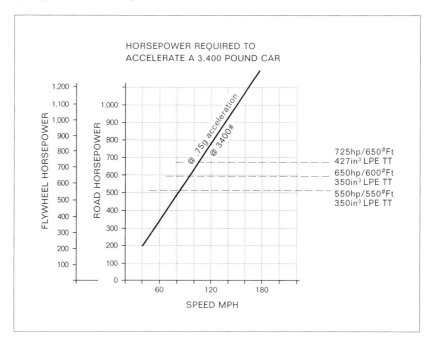

The ZR-1: How the LT5 Came About

12

ALL OF US IN THE CORVETTE GROUP liked to go fast, and by 1985 we had built twin turbocharged V-8 Corvettes that had well over 400 hp and 500 ft-lbs of torque. We met up with Lloyd Reuss during one of our winter test sessions in Arizona, and gave him a ride in all the cars that we were working on, including the turbo Corvette. Lloyd was so elated with the turbo's power and speed that he let it get away from him and spun off the road in a cloud of dust.

Performance was becoming a major factor by the early 1980s, but we still had to figure out the right way to go, and there were no maps to lead us along this path. By 1985, the production Corvette was rated at 230 horsepower, and we would soon reach 245 to 250 horsepower. Porsche had a road-legal 5-liter V-8 at about 250 horsepower, but it was uncertain if one could go much beyond that and still be able to meet the emission regulations.

All the important systems of the LT5 engine can be seen in this cutaway drawing.
Illustration by Dave Kimble

V-6S AND TWIN TURBOS

To his credit, Lloyd kept the pressure on the engine guys. Their first response was a turbocharged 90-degree V-6 for the Corvette. They reasoned that the smaller displacement was needed, both for fuel economy and to accommodate the turbochargers and auxiliary plumbing. But we rejected the V-6 engine, and so did the car. The engine caused problems in the driveline and rear suspension and made the car buzz and the mirrors shake. This unbalanced V-6 engine configuration was totally unacceptable when mounted in the Corvette, which had never been designed for such an engine. So, the engine guys finally got the V-6 out of their system, and we settled down to work with them to package a twin turbo V-8.

With high-octane fuel and the boost turned up, the twin turbo Corvettes were like rockets. They demonstrated the performance potential of the chassis and showed us what was possible if we were smart enough to figure out the emissions and fuel economy details.

All this euphoria was tempered by the realization that we did not have an automatic transmission with anywhere near 500 ft-lbs of torque capacity. Our manual transmission was also incapable of providing the torque requirements for this engine and would require total reengineering. Another obstacle to the turbo approach was that power would be drastically scaled back when the engine ran on unleaded gasoline. The real car would be a shadow of what we were demonstrating in these early prototypes.

A HIGH TECH SOLUTION

Up to this point, Lloyd hadn't discussed the issue of "high tech," but eventually he brought up his concern that the turbo motor would not be perceived as a sophisticated strategy for producing power. The cast-iron 350cid small-block V-8 of 1984 was not considered high tech at all, and turbocharging was already showing up on a number of small sedans. From a marketing perspective, the turbo motor was not promoted as cutting edge, even though it certainly was a high tech piece of machinery, and was composed of high-temperature, high-strength exotic alloy materials. And, at least in experimental quantities, we were seeing variable nozzle and variable waste gate designs that would broaden the working range of the turbo and promise virtually instant throttle response. Additionally, the twin turbo Corvette installation had such a high level of foundation engine torque that the lag of the turbos was hardly perceived—the acceleration was just one great rush of power.

We put this all into perspective when we demonstrated the twin turbo to Chevrolet Market Planning at the Desert Proving Ground. We started with our bright red Lamborghini Countach touring the track at a steady 120 mph. We parked the twin turbo at the side of the road with Jim Ingle (Jingles) at the wheel, and we stationed our team and the planners one mile down the track. When the Lamborghini went by Jingles, he launched the Corvette at full throttle. From our team's vantage point, both cars were just specks when the Lamborghini passed the Corvette. It seemed to be no contest; the Lamborghini quickly grew larger as it sped toward us. The Corvette didn't even seem to be moving. Then, as the Lamborghini nearly reached us, at 120 mph, the Corvette suddenly roared past going 180 mph.

Both cars had gone a mile in 30 seconds, but the Corvette had done it from a standstill. Yes, this show was set-up for the marketing guys, but still, it was an awesome demonstration of the performance of this remarkable car.

THE FOUR-CAM ENGINE

Lloyd Reuss 's high tech concern sent the engine guys off on a study of alternatives. That winter, Lloyd, Russ Gee, and Roy Midgley met with Tony Rudd of Lotus to share their thoughts about a four-valve-per-cylinder, double overhead-cam cylinder head on the Corvette short block. Sensing an opportunity, Tony was back within a month with an analysis of the proposal, and a proposal of his own. Tony argued that the engine would be octane-limited to about 350 hp. However, if the engine were designed from the ground up, controlling the piston cooling, cylinder wall cooling and head cooling could enable as much as 400 horsepower to be extracted from 350cid.

Roy Midgley bought Tony Rudd's technical analysis of the situation, and he agreed that we should consider doing the engine from the ground up. Roy insisted that the proposed engine be designed on the same 4.4-in. bore center as the Chevrolet small block, so that the cylinder head could conceivably be used in the Chevrolet at some point. So, we locked in on 400 hp and 400 ft-lbs of torque as a goal, but at that point we had no certainty that the engine could meet emissions or fuel economy requirements.

The engine group was responsible for emissions and fuel-economy certification, while the Corvette development group handled the noise-law certification. We didn't have the foggiest notion how we were ever going to get this engine to pass the noise test, which required a full-throttle acceleration past the microphone starting from 30 mph in first gear. This allowed the microphone to hear the full output of the engine from about 3,000 to 4,500 rpm. Taming the engine's roar would require radically restricting the power of the engine in first gear. If noise regulations had applied only in California, we might have ignored the test, gone ahead with a 49-state car, and then dealt with California as an exception. But, by the mid 1980s, the noise-test requirement had spread to almost half the states.

To usefully measure a car's real-world noise level, you have to have a car that is close to its final configuration. We were another two years away from that stage, so we made the conscious decision to keep quiet, and not burden top management with the risk that we might be designing a car that was not legal in half of the United States. As is so often the case, if

we had laid the whole story out on the table at the beginning, we'd have never been able to move ahead. Already, the engine guys had no idea where they were going to manufacture the engine or what it would cost. They made some honest attempts to estimate the numbers, but they were far too optimistic. In spite of all the initial uncertainties, Lloyd gave his go-ahead to the project. He ultimately supported us through the escalating costs and delays along the way to our ultimate victory of producing the LT5 engine and its ZR-1 car.

It may seem as if we had pulled Tony Rudd and Lotus out of left field for this project, but this was not the case. Tony and his engine design team at Lotus were in the process of designing a four-liter V-8 for their proposed Etna supercar, so they had gone through at least one iteration of designing a four-valve-per-cylinder, double overhead-cam V-8 engine. We also had arrived at Lotus at a just the right moment. Lotus had an entire team of engine design and development engineers ready to go to work, because a client had just canceled a program to develop a Formula 1 engine for the, then current, 1.5-liter turbocharged formula. When Formula 1 announced that it would phase out the existing engine and replace it with a 3.5 liter naturally-aspirated one, there was no point to continue with the project.

Larry Banning, the turbo Corvette project manager, was tapped to manage the engine group's side of the program. Meanwhile, our power-train system engineer, Jim Minneker, joined the program, and Lotus contributed Ian Doble as project manager and Dave Whitehead as chief designer. To support Lotus, our Corvette group set up a design shop at Hatal-Whiting in Lemmington Spa, England.

GM Designer Tom Peters contributed this sketch of what the LT5 engine should look like based on the emerging mechanical requirements.

Dave McLellan Archives

DESIGN AND MANUFACTURING

While Lotus was getting under way with the engine design and we were helping them to package it into the car, Roy Midgley set off on a quest to figure out how to manufacture the engine. The manufacturing process that built the Chevrolet V-8 produced more than 2,500 V-8 engines a day. Corvette needed only about 125 of these engines each day, so we only accounted for about 5 percent of the overall V-8 engine production. A specialty Corvette engine, at 25 per day, would only constitute a barely-perceptible

1 percent of the output of a traditional engine plant. However we decided to produce this engine, it couldn't be manufactured in the typical half-billion dollar process with which General Motors was familiar. This would only bury the program.

Roy looked around within GM and talked to the diesel engine people to see if they were interested, as they were already producing engines at fairly low volumes. He also looked at his own prototyping facility to see if it would make sense to build the engines there. Finally, he made inquiries outside the corporation, where there were a few low-volume engine manufacturers, principally in the marine field.

Roy sought an engine builder with computer-controlled machining centers, and a thorough grounding in statistical process control. He found a match for his requirements at Mercury Marine, a maker of two-stroke marine outboard engines and a remanufacturer of Chevrolet's and GM's four-, six-, and eight-cylinder engines for marine inboard-outboard drive applications. After an initial contact with their Vice President of Manufacturing Joe Anthony, Bud Agner, who was the Plant Manager at Mercury's Stillwater, Oklahoma, plant, was given the assignment to design and tool the manufacturing process and to produce the LT5 engine.

The precursor, Lotus' four-liter Etna engine, which was designed with very few packaging constraints, was so big that it wouldn't even fit into the Corvette. So, one of Lotus' first jobs was to tighten the package so that our engine, with almost 50 percent more displacement than the Etna, would fit into an even smaller space.

As a part of his thermal management strategy, Tony Rudd decided to use aluminum wet cylinder liners that were coated for wear with Nikasil, a nickel silicone flame-sprayed coating that was honed and grooved to a surface finish that would hold oil. The top of each liner was freestanding and supported the head gasket. This required slightly more space between cylinder bores than an all-cast-construction. With Roy Midgley's imperative that the bore centers be common with the Chevrolet small block's 4.40 in., Tony reduced the bore of the engine from 4.00 in. to 3.90 in. and lengthened the stroke to 3.66 in. to maintain the nominal 5.7 liter displacement.

Tony was concerned that the smaller bore would reduce the horsepower potential of the engine. That

The Lotus 4.0 liter V-8 Etna engine was the precursor to the LT5.

Reproduced with permission from Group Lotus PLC

the engine came into production at 375 hp, missing the 400 hp goal, was probably coincidental, but Tony always reminded us of his reduced estimate for the 3.90 in. bore engine. For 1993, it took little more than cleaning up the intake manifold and fiddling with cam timing to raise the output to 405 hp.

The Etna engine used two steel-reinforced rubber fabric cog timing belts to drive its four camshafts. The longitudinally staggered belts consumed about two inches of fore and aft real estate that didn't exist in the Corvette. Nor could we tolerate the large-diameter toothed wheels on the end of the exhaust camshafts, which made the engine way too wide for the Corvette. Tony proposed going back to the bicycle-chain style of cam drive which would be much more compact longitudinally and—because the chain could take higher tension loads—the camshaft wheels could be much smaller. Roy was concerned that this would be too noisy, so Roy and Tony went out and listened to an old Jaguar and decided that the bike-chain solution would work.

Several concessions were made to fit the engine into the space between the frame rails of the Corvette. The exhaust valve was straightened up to within 11° of the cylinder axis, and the cam bearings were made integral with the rocker cover, to minimize the width of the engine. Although the engine was still too wide to fit, Gib Hufstader devised a scheme to tilt the engine as it was being bottom-loaded between the frame rails and then tip it back into place. We were willing to accept almost any complexity in order to give Lotus the maximum opportunity to create a 400 hp engine.

If we had to, we were prepared to lengthen the wheelbase of the car,

The final engine faithfully executed Peters' design direction.
Dave McLellan Archives

change the frame rails, and commission a new hood, if that was what it would take to make power. Fortunately, as it turned out, Lotus was able to design an engine that fit into the Corvette's engine compartment. Part of Lotus' secret with this engine was a strategy to take special advantage of the two intake valves. At low rpms (below 3,000) only one intake valve on a fairly conservative cam profile was needed to achieve good low- and mid-range torque and to meet emissions and fuel economy requirements. Lotus developed this as the "A" cam profile. Running one inlet valve on the A profile with the second valve effectively closed off by an upstream throttle valve,

the engine would run out of power before 5,000 rpm, much like the standard Corvette L98. But then, the second valve, running on the "B" profile, would come in above 3,000 rpm and raise the power peak to 6,800 rpm. Each of the 16 intake valves had its own fuel injector, eight of which worked all the time. The other eight worked only when the second intake valve's throttle was opened. This intake valve scheme, with 16 injectors and an ignition timing map with detonation control, required a computer larger that anything that was in production at GM. It was fortuitous that Delco Electronics was working on a future engine computer that could be brought forward and adapted to our requirements.

Packaging constraints led to a very compact four-valve, two-cam cylinder head for the LT5 engine.
Illustration by Dave Kimble

A cooling system was developed to accommodate our requirements of high power output, high compression ratio, and high efficiency, using low-octane fuel. Cylinder head cooling, particularly around the exhaust valves, required high-velocity coolant flows to scrub the boiling vapor bubbles away. While the cylinder heads required very high-flow velocities, the cylinder barrels needed much less flow. Meanwhile, the radiator would have failed if we subjected it to the flow velocities required in the head. The very different cooling flow requirements of the cylinder head, the cylinder and the radiator led us to develop a bi-flow cooling system. The bi-flow system recirculated most of the coolant through the cylinder heads with only a portion of it going to the cylinder bores and an even lesser portion being bled off for heat exchange in the radiator.

THE LT5 LIVES

Lotus had the first engine running on the dynamometer in May of 1987, about a year after they started designing. When they ran the engine to 7,000 rpm for the first time, they found that the oil congregated in the four cam cylinder heads and wouldn't drain back into the sump, thus starving the bottom end of oil. With the crank and connecting rods whirring, and the pistons racing back and forth, the air inside the engine oil case was like a hurricane at 7,000 rpm. Consequently, to avoid extreme aeration and to get the oil flowing back to the sump requires a windage tray and drain-back passages that are isolated from the hurricane.

All the work that Lotus had done to make the engine compact had reduced the space available for drain back. The only answer was to stop the process and redesign the engine. This cost us six months of precious time while solutions were designed and tested. However, Lotus was able to start emissions testing with the defective engines by limiting their speed to 5,000 rpm, but the durability testing and power development had to wait.

Long before the engine was in its final configuration, Mercury Marine was designing a manufacturing process and ordering the tools and equipment, to machine and assemble our engines. By the end of 1987, Mercury Marine had built its first engine and shipped it to Lotus for durability testing. From then on, Lotus would be phased out of the prototype engine manufacturing business, and Mercury Marine would pick it up, building late prototypes in its developing production-manufacturing process. This made for a seamless flow between prototype, pilot, and production. It also gave us confidence that the production unit was every bit as good as the prototype and pilot engines which had been thoroughly tested.

GETTING THE CORVETTE READY FOR THE LT5

We wanted no compromise at all in our goal to put 400 hp and 400 ft-lbs of torque to the road. So, in conjunction with Goodyear, we began development of a special ultrawide rear tire which was 1.58 in. wider than the 275/40ZR17 tires that had been optional on the 1988 Corvette and became standard for the 1989. Unfortunately, the wider 315/40ZR17 tires intended for the rear of the ZR-1 model wouldn't fit within the bodywork of the Corvette.

To fit the big tire, Design Staff and Corvette Engineering looked at putting flares over the rear wheel openings. We all agreed that this was such an ugly tack-on solution that Jerry Palmer explored the alternative of flaring the entire rear of the car, to contain the wider rubber within the smoothly flowing bodywork. This approach worked, but it required completely new doors, rear quarter panels, and rear bumper fascia. We were already planning to change the rear fascia for the 1991 model year, giving it a more rectangular lamp design, so we decided to apply the new fascia look to the ZR-1.

About 20 percent of the total tooling cost of the project was for the body panel changes. To its credit, Chevrolet management gave us approval to change the body without our ever demonstrating that the wider rear

tires would outperform the standard tire. This was an indication of how fast we were moving on the project. We all had to trust that the tire would perform as well as we expected, until we had actual development tires from Goodyear that we could test.

PERFECTING THE PRODUCT

Base engine durability was taking on new interest at GM, as a result of recent four-cylinder and V-6 engines coming into production. Because these smaller engines spend significant portions of their duty cycle at full power, they were being designed to meet a 200-hour full-throttle specification. Roy Midgley applied this same requirement to the LT5 engine. This may have been overkill, but Roy didn't want any arguments from management about the engine's durability.

NEW FOR THE ZR-1

Many components for the ZR-1 were all new or extensively upgraded:

- A 450 ft-lb-rated, six-speed manual transmission replaced the 4+3 transmission.
- A zero scrub front suspension was designed to take full advantage of the ABS and to accommodate the new 11.5 in. heavy-duty brakes.
- The geometry of the rear suspension was changed to improve the driver's ability to get power to the road, even while cornering over bumps or undulations.
- Adjustable Bilstein shock absorbers (Selective Ride Control) were added.
- The wheel bearings were made more robust, to meet the rigors of racing.
- The spring rates were lowered, to give a lower-frequency ride without loss of handling control.
- The body was widened in the rear, by three inches, for the ultra-wide P315/35ZR-17 rear tires.

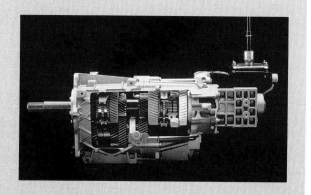

Top right: All gears in the ZF six-speed manual transmission were synchronized—even reverse.

Dave McLellan Archives

Bottom right: Using distinctly different tires for the front and rear gave Goodyear engineers an opportunity to develop a unique rear tire, suited to the performance demands of the ZR-1.

Drawing by Dave McLellan

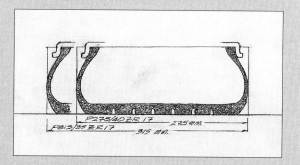

Cycling between the torque peak and the power peak for 200 hours, with multiple excursions into the red line, is quite a test for an automobile engine. Initially, the engine was good for only about 50 hours. The biggest problem was the formation of cracks in the crankcase bulkheads that support the main bearing ladder. In a series of steps, Lotus introduced cast-iron main-bearing-cap reinforcements into the aluminum ladder structure, and redistributed the crankshaft loads by increasing the number of bolts tying the ladder to the case until they were able to reliably achieve 200 hours. With the car capable of 180 mph and the LT5 engine's 200-hour durability life, the ZR-1 could theoretically go one and one-half times around the earth at its top speed.

In the spring of 1990, when we attempted a new series of FIA (Federation International de l'Automobile) speed and endurance records, we recognized that running the engine at 175 mph for 24 or even 29 hours straight used less than 15 percent of the life of the engine. With an engine this strong and reliable, the FIA endurance runs were really a test of the car and driver, not the engine.

We took a chance in doing something that no one at GM had ever done before, and our boldness showed up in the ZR-1's retail price. The design

THE LT5 OVERHEATING RUMOR

From the moment they heard about the LT5 engine, members of the automotive press expected us to be ready a year earlier than we were. The press picked up on a rumor that that the LT5 was overheating, and went with it as the explanation for the apparent delay. Our best guess is that this story originated with a mole in our organization who was just close enough to misread what was actually going on as we developed the engine and the car.

The real problem, which we were addressing, was the yellowing of the Arctic White body paint. This paint color was very susceptible to chemical attack. The problem occured relatively early in the life of the car and showed up first with a yellowing of the hood around the right headlamp door. As it turned out, a chemical emanating from the hot rubber coolant hoses was the culprit. The hood was sealed around most of its perimeter and, with the cooling fan blowing, a pattern of air circulation develops in the right front corner of the engine compartment. Acting as a chimney, the opening around the headlamp delivered the engine's contaminated air to the paint. We fixed the problem by eliminating the offending sulfur-based chemistry from the rubber compound. Our mole probably saw us testing with hot engines and changing hoses repeatedly, which required us to drain and fill the cooling system over and over again.

As a matter of policy, Chevrolet chose to neither confirm nor deny the story. As a result, the rumor gathered momentum and finally confronted us with a vengeance when the ZR-1 was announced to the press in France. Several of the publishers and press doubted that we could even run the cars with such a monumental overheating problem.

For us in the design department, it was annoying that someone within the company was leaking erroneous information, but it was amusing and instructive how the press could concoct such a story. The cooling system had been bulletproof from the start. It had been engineered not to just cool the engine, but to minimize octane demand and allow maximum compression ratio, so the engine could make its 375 hp even with low-octane fuel. When we finally gave the press the chance to drive the cars they loved the experience.

costs of the LT5 turned out to be at least as much as the design costs for other passenger car engines. Plus, the cost of tooling and setting up the special manufacturing processes, the special computer, the purpose-built catalytic converters, and a number of other unique and critical components left us with a staggering investment cost which had to be amortized in the price of the car. In the end, the pricing of the ZR-1 set a new record for the price of a GM passenger car.

The ZR-1 was launched in the spring of 1990 into a market ravenous for something new. But, by the third year, the recession of 1991 and the 10 percent luxury tax on cars selling for over $30,000 had taken hold and the market for the ZR-1 collapsed.

THE LT1 THROWS DOWN THE GAUNTLET

One of the unintended benefits of the LT5 engine was the impact that it had on the rest of Roy Midgley's V-8 engine Design Group. His staff watched from the sidelines, as the engine program unfolded, and they began wondering why hadn't they, themselves, been asked to design this engine? And, quite unexpectedly, they put together a proposal for a complete redesign of the Chevrolet small block that would dramatically improve its reliability, fuel economy, cost, and performance.

The engine group team, led by Anil Kulkarni, ultimately surprised themselves with 300 hp, when for years they thought that 250 hp was the

---

BRAKE TESTING AT 200 MPH

As late as the summer of 1988, the ABS had not been tested above 150 mph. Would the ABS software work correctly at 180 mph, the expected speed potential of the ZR-1? We needed an answer.

During the development of the ZR-1, we seldom had access to LT5 engines that could function at their full performance potential. When we did, we used them for high-priority, engine-specific vehicle tests. To solve this availability problem, we installed ZR-1 tires on a 500+ hp nitrous-equipped small-block Corvette. This excess power would make it possible to accelerate the car quickly to 180 mph, so we could run the ABS test and still have road left if the answer to our question turned out to be no.

After obtaining permission to run the ABS test at the GM Desert Proving Grounds, in Mesa, Arizona, Doug Robinson invited instructor and Corvette racer John Powell—who was in Phoenix doing driver training for Corvette dealers—to drive the test. We were hesitant to run just

a single stop where John would hammer on the brakes at 180 mph. First, he needed to become comfortable with the car, to have the best possible chance of maintaining control if his braking inadvertently induced a skid. It was decided that the safest path to take was a progressive series of brake stops. We would increase deceleration with each run until the tires slid or until the desired ABS action was achieved. We expected the final stop, from 180 mph, to produce an initial deceleration of about 1.5 gs that would fall off to 1 g by the end of the stop.

On his first test run, John touched 200 mph. Then, with the help of a decelerometer, he followed what he thought was the planned deceleration. To his surprise, the ABS activated immediately. To our chagrin, the decelerometer had been incorrectly installed. John had just run a full 1+ g ABS stop from 200 mph! Obviously, the ZR-1's entire braking system was properly interfaced to the ABS control system. End of test.

maximum they could ever extract from the small block while still meeting contemporary emissions and fuel economy standards. Continuing development revealed that 350 hp, and even 400 hp, was within reach. And extensive computer modeling of the engine verified that at least 350 hp could be achieved while meeting all the legal requirements. (The engine, in LS6 form, is currently rated at 405 hp.)

THE END FOR THE LT5

The LT5 engine was slated for another boost in performance for 1997, using a very complex, but elegant, rocker arm mechanism. Lotus had found a way to run both intake valves on the B profile for high rpm, which made 475 hp practical. But, it was not to be. The V-8 engine group's demonstration of a Generation III small block that was well in excess of 350 horsepower, and a growing commitment from management to retool the small block for the Corvette in aluminum, made it difficult to support the ongoing development of the LT5. In addition, the design of a completely new Corvette (later code-named the C5) was under way. With the recognition that this smaller, lighter pushrod engine would lead to a significantly smaller and lighter car, there was no logic in continuing the ZR-1. The LT5 engine ceased production at Mercury Marine in 1993 and the ZR-1's final model year was 1995.

THE CALLAWAY TWIN TURBO

It's a rare occasion when a major manufacturer decides to drop a project and then turn around and provide the project's technology and support to another company, thus creating a potential competitor. But that's exactly what happened when Chevrolet decided to pursue greater performance through a multi-cam engine and put its turbo project on ice.

VIEWED FROM THE INSIDE by Dave McLellan

The decision to build a naturally-aspirated four-cam performance engine ended all work on the fuel-injected turbo V-8. Don Runkle, head of Chevrolet Market Planning, suggested that we share what we had learned with Reeves Callaway. Callaway Cars had done a number of turbo-charged aftermarket-tuner projects on small cars, taking them through EPA certification and into low volume production. The success of these projects demonstrated to us that he knew how to manage the process. And a visit

to Callaway Cars in Old Lyme, Connecticut, was the beginning of a long-term collaboration.

We loaned Reeves one of our fuel-injected turbo Corvettes and agreed to support him in any way we could. The approach he finally took was different from our own turbo, but it was pragmatic for an aftermarket application that had to go through EPA emission certification. Instead of doing a scaled fuel-injection system, he left the production fuel system alone and added extra fuel with a pair of injectors ahead of the throttle. He found room for two turbochargers on the lower sides of the engine. The packaging of the engine compartment was so tight that they had to move induction air through the frame rails. They were also able to find enough room on top of the engine to add a pair of air-to-air intercoolers. The package went through EPA approval under the rules that allow changes that do not degrade the underlying already-certified emissions.

The benefit to this approach was that a small company like Callaway Cars went through a much simpler and shorter certification process than would a major manufacturer. The bad news was the turbo car had the same low-speed camshaft we were using in the production car. It seemed as if the turbos were barely kicked in before the gear gave out. The package just cried out for a high speed cam but the reality of certification made this impossible. Even so, the numbers were spectacular: 0-60 in 4.6 seconds and the quarter mile in 13.02 seconds at 108 mph. Assigned the Chevrolet B2K optimum designation, it carried a premium of $15,600, back in 1987.

We've often been asked why we encouraged a seeming competitor when we already had an LT5 engine coming along. The reason was simple. We pushed and shoved to get Corvette performance into the hands of our customers anywhere and anyway we could. If the four-cam naturally-aspirated project was killed along the way, we would still have something to show for our earlier efforts. On the other hand, if the four-cam project succeeded, we would have spawned a competitor. And competitors only make you stronger!

Chevrolet's support was invaluable, particularly when Calloway was given direct access to its dealer network. Reeves selected twenty dealers to offer his Callaway Turbo Corvettes. When a B2K option was requested, a standard model with minor production variations would be drop-shipped to Callaway for further modifications. The Turbo Corvette—including its warranty—was a transaction between Callaway and the dealer.

I think the Turbo Corvette was an elixir for Reeves. It stretched his desire to go faster and faster. We had already gone 200 mph with a C4 Corvette. Reeves wanted to go 250 mph. As we talked about it, I said he would need a sledgehammer to go that fast. So, Reeves, with the help of Chevrolet extreme engine guru John Lingenfelter, was soon building the SledgeHammer Corvette.

VIEWED FROM THE OUTSIDE by Reeves Callaway

In the fall of 1985, the phone rang. It was Dave McLellan, then Chief Engineer, Corvette platform. He started by explaining that there was a program running in-house [at Chevrolet] to develop a twin turbocharged Corvette and that the program had a lot of enthusiasm, and a lot of knowledge had been gained, but that it had been voted down in favor of giving the production go-ahead to the Lotus-designed LT5 engine package.

There was, in fact, so much support for this twin-turbo approach to performance improvement that he was calling to offer their knowledge and their assistance in making sure that a turbocharged version of the car would appear in the marketplace alongside, or slightly before, the ZR-1 debut. It was clear from our conversation that they were offering to work with us in the creation, support, and sales of an RPO [regular production option] twin-turbo version Corvette. This, of course, was the call that you wait for if you're a member of the automotive aftermarket. Let's look at the facts: America's largest corporation; America's only sports car; and being asked to do our own design program. Plus, have the result be sold as an official GM product with it's own RPO? What could be better? You would have thought we would jump at the chance. This is where someone could have blurted, "Does Dolly sleep on her back?"

I remember two distinct feelings going through my mind at that point. One was being very flattered that McLellan had called. The other was a certain reluctance to do the job. It later came out that the reason David had called us was that they had in their possession at the GM Proving Grounds one of the twin-turbo Alfas that we had done the year before, for Alfa Romeo North America. This little 2.5 L V-6, producing about 235 hp in a 2500- or 2600-lb automobile, made an impressive performance statement, and its raw numbers nearly equaled the performance of the standard 1986 Corvette! It was at this moment that the old axiom "you're only as good as your last job" appeared in golden letters in front of me. But, there was a big concern in those days: The Corvette did not have a superlative reputation; in fact, it was considered a cheap and cheerful, but

not very worthy, sports car. Remember, the car had been totally redesigned by the McLellan team in 1984, yet few understood the huge leap in sophistication, and the potential, of this fourth generation platform. This platform was the envy of all the other manufacturers who had ever tried to solve the equation of a front-engined, rear-drive, two-seat sportscar. Yet businesses such as ours had to be very careful with the company that they kept. We had largely been European in our product base and were, frankly, scared to death to associate with this workboot sports car. What we could not have possibly understood was the huge depth that the Corvette occupied as an American icon. And that meant an extraordinarily loyal owner base. And that owner base had one wish at the top of any focus group: more power. I feel foolish now in not seeing the opportunity clearly. But we caught on really fast....

Dave and his team wanted a car that was deliverable to the public in less than seven months. I believe they genuinely thought that their experience in building the twin turbo prototypes at SVI had brought the project close to production-ready. But this was far from the case. There were some 2000 individual parts that had to be designed and manufactured. There were emission considerations. There was the problem of setting up a small production line. And then there was the problem of how many to build. I remember one meeting with the Chevrolet marketing team when we asked them the question: "Gentlemen, how many are we going to build?" There were a lot of blank stares in the room at that point so they turned it around and asked us! "How many cars do you think?"

At that point we knew that this was going to be an expensive option because the production numbers were going to be small. A Corvette in those days cost $25,000. This engine option was probably going to double that. The marketing folks at Chevrolet had no experience trying to sell a $50,000 Corvette. And neither did we, so we both poked our collective fingers into the wind and said, "maybe 50 cars." So it was agreed that we would build 50 twin turbo Corvettes. What a mistake that was! When the first tiny one-page review in *Road & Track* magazine appeared showing a smokey burnout, all the lights on our telephone system in Connecticut lit up and didn't dim for a whole year.

For once it turned out that the focus groups were correct—almost every Corvette owner wanted a lot of power. In fact, too much was just enough. At that point the Callaway twin turbo Corvette was the highest performance American car ever released to the public. It only cost 50,000

bucks. It could turn better, stop better, accelerate better and get better fuel economy than any other car in its class, worldwide.

To produce that level of performance meant such a substantial reengineering of the engine that I am sure we did not make nearly as much money as we should have, even selling each engine option for $15,600 apiece (which eventually rose to $25,000 in 1991—the final year of RPO B2K production). First, Chevrolet had told us that we could turbocharge the stock engine. Well, the turbocharged stock engine lasted about three minutes on the dyno. Second, we had nanoseconds to develop a whole package, and even less time for testing. And since reliability was paramount, for both Chevrolet and ourselves, we could only do one thing: We threw the book at the engine in terms of every high-quality component and procedure that we knew. Those engines were really magnificent examples of how to build a small-block Chevrolet correctly. No expense was spared, no procedure was too time-consuming, and no car left our place unless it passed my personal driving inspection. It was as close to a hand-built automobile as anything that has ever borne the name Chevrolet. An early mistake we made was, in our enthusiasm for the product, that we gave two early prototypes to *Car and Driver* magazine. They blew them both up through abuse and were gleeful in doing it. My respect for the magazine evaporated. But the actual production cars had a real-world warranty record that was as good as or better than the standard car. And the owners loved them. All the subsequent press was superlative, and Chevrolet kept itself at the forefront of the enthusiast's mind as the ZR-1 gestated.

It seems that we did touch a nerve with the enthusiast. But, even with the Callaway Corvette on the cover of every automotive magazine each year, the phone calls started to slow down in the second year of production. I think we produced 187 cars in the first year, which was all we could humanly produce. In the second year we were able to make a much better car, but only sold 125 of them. Each year the vehicle got better, yet the demand decreased. To be sure, the ZR-1 had come onstream in 1989 and with Chevrolet's marketing muscle behind it, the ZR-1 pretty much superseded the Callaway twin turbo Corvette. Personally, I enjoy driving the twin turbo much more

The Callaway Twin Turbo Corvette would reach 60 mph in 4.6 seconds and run the quarter-mile in 13.02 seconds at 108 mph.

Courtesy Callaway Cars, Inc.

than its naturally-aspirated ZR-1 counterpart. There is nothing like the huge rush of manifold-pressure-assisted torque to launch a car down the road in a way that no other method of power generation, from an internal combustion engine, can do. It was sophisticated, on-demand power that had a real Jekyl and Hyde characteristic in that it was invisible when you didn't want it, and it was Front and Center, Right Now, and Hallelujah!! when you did.

By the time 1991 rolled around, five years of production and 500 cars later, we both agreed it was time to draw a line through the total. It was a wonderful run. It was a wonderful car. People who have them today are universally in love with them. We made just few enough to have them be super-exclusive and we made just enough so that a relatively large family of owners could exist. It was certainly a project that put us on the map.

Unfortunately for us, we supported the car so well in the field that we spent every nickel of profit on behalf of warranty and customer support. And when we went to Chevrolet for reimbursement there were, again, a lot of blank stares. It was, to say the least, a disappointing experience evaluating the Chevrolet view of what "partnership" meant. Ah, the price of glory.

Part of our responsibility was to promote the project through road tests at magazines. In those days there was an almost annual series of magazine top-speed shoot-outs. This version of the car was very good for that kind of event. And two things were learned: Always come home the winner; and winning was expensive.

How the SledgeHammer Got its Name

The SledgeHammer was a one-shot event vehicle prepared for top-speed testing by Callaway Advanced Technology with support from Chevrolet. In 1989, at the Transportation Research Center in Ohio, the car was officially timed at 254.6 mph, and to date is the fastest street-driven car in the world. To put a point on it, the car was driven comfortably from Connecticut to Ohio, tested to its top speed, and driven home.

The aerodynamic changes to the platform were incorporated into a body package, for the C4 generation Corvettes called the Callaway AeroBody. These body packages are available for general sale, and some of the production Callaway Twin Turbo Corvettes were fitted with this modification at the factory in Connecticut. Some confusion arises because the AeroBody package, fitted to a Callaway Twin Turbo Corvette, could logically be assumed to be a SledgeHammer. In truth, there is only one, and it may be found in the Klassix Museum in Daytona Beach, Florida.

The SledgeHammer used a Lingenfelter twin turbo motor to propel it to 254.6 mph on the Transportation Research Center oval track in Ohio before Reeves Callaway drove it back to Connecticut.

Courtesy Callaway Cars, Inc.

The SledgeHammer got its name from Dave McLellan. The Callaway Twin Turbo Corvette had just appeared on the cover of the most prestigious German car magazine, *Auto Motor und Sport*, with the title "Das is der Hammer!" When Dave saw this he was thrilled—to be called a "hammer" in German means to be a huge overachiever, a winner, or a top dog. And from a German magazine in Stuttgart—the home of Mercedes—it was a great compliment. So, when we proposed to Chevrolet that we build an event car, one that could always be the top dog in any speed contest, Dave said, "Fine, let's call it the SledgeHammer."

Chevrolet Introduces the ZR-1

13

IN THE SUMMER OF 1988, WORD FIRST LEAKED OUT through the press that the ZR-1 Corvette was about to be introduced. For once they were right, but how did they know? It wasn't until three months later that we in Corvette Engineering made the decision to build the first twenty production-level ZR-1s the following January. We planned to use fifteen of these cars for a ZR-1 press introduction and five for the final engine certification.

Built on the regular production line at the Corvette assembly plant in Bowling Green, Kentucky, these cars required the same planning and logistics that went into building a regular Corvette. The components that made this build unique came from all over: LT5 engines from Mercury Marine in Stillwater, Oklahoma; engine computers from Delco Electronics in Kokomo, Indiana; specially molded body panels from GenCorp in Marion, Indiana; and the giant P315/35ZR-17 tires from Goodyear's Lawton, Oklahoma, facility.

PLANNING THE ZR-1 INTRODUCTION

With the first cars being built, our thoughts turned to the ZR-1 press introduction and the myriad planning decisions that had to be made. When and where would we hold the introduction? How big an event would it be? Which members of the critical but clamoring press would we invite? How could we provide a safe, controlled environment in which to fully test the car, and still allow the press to experience its intoxicating performance? We were overwhelmed with questions.

Corvette Engineering was responsible for providing the cars and roads for the ZR-1 introduction. We also had to plan and arrange the activities in which these cars would be tested, and provide the parts (tires, wheels, brake pads, etc.). Additionally, we were responsible for staffing a pit crew with engineers and technicians, to support the cars on the racetrack and deliver the technical message to the press.

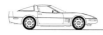

Press invitations and the other details (special activities, transportation, food, lodging, etc.) were the public relations (PR) department's responsibility. Needless to say, we all wanted to put the press in the best possible mood. If we expected the writers to write great stories about the car, we didn't want to feed them bad meals or put them up in fleabag hotels.

Because both Chevrolet and GM's NAVO (North American Vehicles Overseas) were to market the ZR-1, both PR teams met with us to plan press activities and to define our respective roles. In March 1989, Ralph Kramer, Chevrolet's Director of PR, planned to invite both the American and Canadian press to a major press evaluation for which he wanted all the ZR-1s he could get his hands on. Then Ray Koenig of NAVO PR threw us a curve: He also needed a ZR-1 in March for NAVO's display of US-built GM cars at the 59th Geneva International Auto Show, in Switzerland, and several weeks later he needed a few more for a European press evaluation.

The two events, staged simultaneously and 4,000 miles apart, would require more cars and personnel than we could muster. If we did not change our plans, the logistics of the ZR-1 introduction would be a nightmare. We needed to pinpoint the essentials of a successful ZR-1 introduction for Corvette Engineering and at the same time satisfy both Chevrolet and NAVO.

Designed as a road car, the ZR-1 needed great roads with an adjacent racetrack to fully show it off. Great roads are hilly, curvy, mountainous, and they give the driver a constant variety of challenging experiences. We also needed a racetrack if we wanted the writers, acting as test drivers, to safely and systematically explore the car's handling limits, and to be able to get the Corvette up to its impressive speeds.

As we sat there and racked our brains in the search for great roads and a contiguous road-racing track, Jim Ingle (Jingles), who was not only our development group trip captain but also a connoisseur of roads, whipped out his atlas. Together we reviewed all the roads of our past trips, but found that each one had its shortcomings. We looked at the great roads of the open range of the West. Nevada's long, flat roads were great for pure speed but had few turns to challenge the driver. Montana and Wyoming's spectacular roads were mile-high and subject to unpredictable snowstorms in March. What's more, the thin air at those altitudes would blunt the ZR-1's performance.

Every locale had its problems, and we hadn't even considered a road-racing track yet. Slowly, we realized that the combination of elements we

needed for the press to test the ZR-1 (good weather, high speed limits, challenging roads, excellent road-racing track), could not be found in the United States in March.

We knew that testing in Europe followed the seasons, just as it did in North America. Severe winter conditions are found approaching the arctic circle and more temperate weather is available farther south. Our minor introduction of the 1984 Corvette at the Goodyear proving ground in Luxembourg was brought up. Even though this introduction had been conducted with one Corvette and a single member of the press at a time, it was a positive experience and it led to outcomes we had not previously considered. From it, we gained working relationships with several European companies, who did considerable testing of Corvette components.

Suddenly, Corvette Development Manager Doug Robinson remembered Goodyear's new test track—once a road-racing track—on the Mediterranean Sea, near Montpellier in Mireval, France. We realized that the answer to our site problem was Europe. What an audacious idea. We would give the press a "no holds barred" European experience. The pieces of the puzzle finally began to fit together.

We, in Engineering, especially liked the plan for several reasons. The exhilarating roads of the French Alps north of Mireval would provide us with a superb mountain driving experience. They would be clear of snow in late March, and would still be free of tourists. This combination of roads and Goodyear's racetrack would guarantee the press a complete test of the ZR-1.

Chevrolet and NAVO also liked this plan. A single European car evaluation would make their jobs much easier, as the cars could be scheduled so there would be enough ZR-1s to go around. Engineering would work with the press invited by Chevrolet and by NAVO separately. Additionally, the press could enjoy superb European cuisine, as well as old-world lodging. Finally, having the ZR-1 at the Geneva International Auto Show would internationalize the introduction.

Knowing that a publisher's positive impressions and excitement for the car were essential for the extensive magazine coverage that leads to a successful introduction, Ralph Kramer decided to invite America's most important car magazine publishers to a special three-

Goodyear's test track at Mireval, high-speed autoroutes, and the mountain roads of the Gorges du Tarn are all within a day's drive of Montpellier.

©MICHELIN Bordeaux/Agen/Montauban No. 79 (1926). Permission No. 95-278

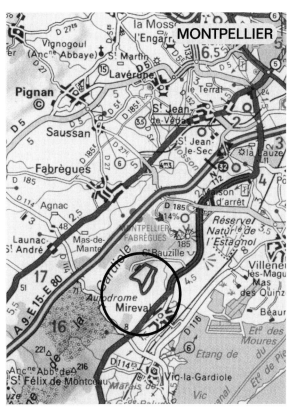

part ZR-1 introduction. The plan was to have the publishers attend the Geneva International Automobile Show, drive through the spectacular mountains of southern France for two days to the Mediterranean, and then drive the cars on Goodyear's track at Mireval to complete their evaluation. It was hoped that the two-day drive through the mountains would clinch the publishers' attendance. As a bonus, they would become the ZR-1's first critical test drivers.

The reason we worked so hard for the press was because they were imperative to the success of the car. Automobile magazines had become the natural conduit through which Corvette sent its technical message to its potential buyers and thirsty enthusiasts. Corvette ads, which were placed from time to time across the whole magazine spectrum, wonderfully conveyed the car's visual message, but could not relay the car's technical or performance message. Editorial material could. A road test of several pages did far more to describe the Corvette's cutting edge technology than did a Corvette pictured beside a sailboat. Sometimes the magazines printed things that we didn't like to read, but when these criticisms were weighed against the benefits, they were a small price to pay for the gold mine of information that these publications transmitted to their reader.

Although Bob Burger, Chevrolet's Vice President and General Manager, was upset with the high cost of the LT5 engine and with his boss, Lloyd Reuss, for having rammed the engine program down his throat, Bob still approved our plan. Soon afterwards, we heard that all our European component suppliers, including Bosch, Bilstein, and ZF, were excited to participate in the introduction. Goodyear management graciously offered their people and the use of their Mireval facility as our engineering base of operation. The ZR-1 introduction was a go.

Few knew the gamble we in Engineering took when we told Chevrolet that the ZR-1 would be ready for the press in three months. We com-

Goodyear's Mireval Proving Ground started out as a racetrack, but had been completely renovated to make it suitable for tire development testing.
Courtesy Goodyear Tire & Rubber Co.

mitted early to the introduction to allow time to work out the logistics. There was, however, a downside to this decision. The ZR-1 introduction was now driven by the date of the Geneva International Auto Show, instead of being driven by anything that had to do with the car itself. Delivery of the cars to Europe would push forward the build of the ZR-1 into mid-January, giving us even less time to finish our development work. If we stepped out in front of the press with a car that was not ready, we would suffer the consequences in print. Given the amount of hype the press had given the unseen car, it would be hard to live up to the expectations that they themselves had created. The pressure was on.

Normally an engine design cycle takes five years from inception to production, but Lloyd Reuss had pressed us to devise a new plan that would shorten this cycle by two years and have the LT5 ready by the fall of 1988. Dauntlessly, we accepted his imperative and addressed ourselves to the task. The only difficulty was that the new plan left us with no cushion if problems arose. Unfortunately, we had already lost six months due to the oil drain-back problem.

By the time we committed to the European introduction in November 1988, Lotus had solved the oil drain-back problem and successfully reached the 100-hour mark on the dynamometer—but with cobbled engines only. We had also finished our developmental testing on the high-banked oval at Talladega, Alabama, on the road course at Road America, and at several other racetracks. From this testing, we knew what the final configuration of the production engine had to be. Then, in a flurry of activity, Lotus introduced the last modifications into the engine design and produced the final production-level LT5. However, before we left for Europe, as a final check we would have to verify that all the design changes we had made had actually solved our problems.

Because the oil drain-back problem was on the critical path for engine production, our car testing and production schedules had been set back. If we had stayed on our original three-year timetable, we would have been building production LT5s at Mercury Marine in March, not December, 1988. To have the engine ready for Europe, the execution of the production engine design had to be completed without a hitch.

After one of our meetings with Ralph Kramer, Doug Robinson, Jim Minneker, our Corvette Powertrain Manager, and I agreed that if we spilled our guts to Kramer over the uncertainties associated with the production LT5 engine, he would probably cancel the whole introduction. Not that Ralph was averse to risk; it was just that his job and its pressures

were different from ours, and he had no control over the risks we were assuming. On the other hand, we were accustomed to the position we found ourselves in, and to us the risk was a calculated one. So, we decided not to share our uncertainties with Ralph. We would go to France and deal with whatever came up—4,000 miles from our home base.

EUROPEAN LOGISTICS

In the fall of 1988, four months before the ZR-1 introduction, Jean Phillipe Collow of GM France and Bob Lobell, European PR guru for Goodyear, joined Ed Lechtzin, Assistant Director of Public Relations for Chevrolet, and Doug Robinson in southern France to search for lodgings and roads. First, they drove to Montpellier and inspected La Grande-Motte, a health institute and hotel that GM France PR recommended as their favorite. Once Ed saw it, however, he immediately decided that it was too modern and antiseptic for the American automobile press.

Continuing their search, Ed headed the group west, out of the Rhone Valley and past Mireval, for Toulouse. Halfway there, they spotted a castle perched dramatically on a hilltop. Investigating, they found La Cite, an eleventh-century walled fortress overlooking the modern city of Carcassonne and, inside, the Hotel du Donjon. With Ed intrigued at the prospect of having Le Cite and this hotel as the base of operations for the press, and the hotel manager interested in business in March when the hotel was normally closed, it was not long before a deal was struck. The manager agreed to have the hotel ready for us when we arrived the next spring.

With roads to find, Doug Robinson then took charge. A typical European press evaluation, unlike an American one, is loosely run. It consists of sending the press off at the beginning of the day with a car and a road map, and asking the drivers to show up at a certain destination for dinner. We were told that Europeans did not like structured events, but we were about to give them one, anyway. If a driver did have a high-speed accident with a ZR-1, we wanted be on top of the situation.

Jean Phillipe Collow argued for the autoroutes and the coastal roads around Mireval. He stated that the European press seldom used mountain roads for their car evaluations and argued that coastal roads were less dangerous. Doug disagreed. He saw the numerous switchbacks north of Mireval on his map and was interested in connecting them together to make a route. To him, having the press drive mountain roads created no problem. All of the press members we intended to invite were very skilled drivers. Furthermore, the ZR-1's capabilities and limits were so exceptional

that the press could have the ride of their lives and still be safe. Driving these roads aggressively in ordinary passenger cars with an average journalist at the wheel was a bad idea, but attacking them in ZR-1s driven by skilled drivers was quite a different story.

After some time, it became obvious to Doug that he and Jean Phillipe could not come to an agreement, so Doug assured Jean Phillipe that he would use the main roads for the introduction. Then he sought out Alain Beauchef, the manager of Goodyear's Mireval facility. As an experienced European rally driver, Alain knew the mountain roads of France intimately. Together they searched for the roads we needed, and plotted the course we would drive in March. When the job was finished, Doug and Ed Lechtzin returned home to work out the details of the introduction.

GETTING TO GENEVA ON TIME

In December 1988, we built what was intended to be the production-level LT5 engines at Mercury Marine. A few of these engines were then shipped to England for Lotus to test for production durability. The rest went to the Bowling Green Corvette assembly plant to be built into our first twenty 1989 production ZR-1s.

In early February 1989, Jingles took a crew down to Bowling Green, to drive the ZR-1 press cars back to the Milford Proving Grounds. The Geneva show car, the only yellow production 1989 ZR-1, was transported on a truck, in order to keep it in pristine show condition. As it turned out, this trip provided Engineering with its only chance to road test the cars before they would be shipped to Europe. It is hard enough to stress-test a 180 mph ZR-1 on US roads, but this drive accomplished even less because of the ice and snow the drivers encountered. Contrary to our intentions, serious stress-testing would have to wait until we arrived in Europe.

Back at Milford, the fifteen new ZR-1s were given a brief checkout, put on pallets, and airfreighted to Frankfurt, Germany. Included with them was the Talladega test car, a prototype ZR-1 set up as a showroom stock racecar, as well as other interesting "toys" that a European press, which was unacquainted with the Corvette, might enjoy. These included a Corvette Challenge racecar, an L98 convertible with its optional hardtop, and a six-speed L98 coupe. Five production ZR-1s were left behind in Michigan, to be used for final durability testing and emission and fuel economy certification. From Frankfurt, the cars were trucked down to the Goodyear Proving Grounds at Mireval for a final general checkout that confirmed that they had survived the trip.

The Mireval racetrack activities were to be structured so that the press could use the outer track as a racetrack and the specialized inner track to experience wet handling and antilock brake control with the wide tires. As the press tested the cars and observed the computer-aided maintenance system (CAMS) in operation, they would be able to interrogate our own engineers as well as the engineers from key suppliers. We wanted to give the press every opportunity to fully test and understand the ZR-1 and all its components.

Most of the US press and nearly all of the European press had had no experience with the standard 1989 L98 Corvette, which introduced the new ZF 6-speed, the Selective Ride Control (speed and driver-adjustable shock absorbers), and the heavy-duty front brakes. And none of them had had any experience with the components that were unique to the ZR-1, or with the CAMS machine that had been developed as the diagnostic system for all new GM cars.

ZR-1 IN EUROPE

A week before the Geneva International Auto Show and our ZR-1 press conference, Doug and Jingles drove two of the ZR-1s, by autoroute, from Mireval to Geneva to get there quickly and do some video work with the Chevrolet camera crew. They also wanted to try out the route that the publishers would be taking through the mountains to Carcassonne, and to test the brakes and tires on these nearly untested ZR-1s. Even before their run back, Doug and Jingles were quite confident that little would go wrong with the ZR-1s. However, the cars were new and of a new generation of build, so there were no guarantees.

On the run back, they drove hard from dawn until after dark, covering in one day what the publishers would drive in two. Even though concentration on the road kept them from viewing the spectacular scenery along the way, they still thoroughly enjoyed their drive. The ZR-1s experienced only modest brake and tire wear and never let its drivers down.

There was good reason to expect that the ZR-1 would be reliable. From the 1984 to the 1989, and then to the ZR-1, the Corvette had undergone a transformation as a direct result of extensive testing on the racetrack. The benefits of this racing and testing had been systematically transferred to the components of the production car, first to its chassis and then, ultimately, to its ZR-1 configuration. From the 1984 Corvette to the 1989, the transmission, the front and rear suspensions and their

attachment points, shock absorbers, brakes, wheel bearings, springs, and axle were all new or modified.

In Mireval, Doug and Jingles collected their team of engineers and technicians and drove all twelve ZR-1s and a support truck up to Geneva to meet the publishers, who were already in attendance at the Geneva International Auto Show. The support truck had 12 sets of mud-and-snow (M+S) tires that Goodyear had molded especially for the ZR-1s. Although water runoff was all they encountered on the roads, a sudden snowstorm could always erupt in the mountains around Geneva in early spring, and we were prepared.

INTRODUCING THE ZR-1

On Tuesday March 7, 1989, the ZR-1 was introduced at the Geneva International Auto Show. Upstairs in the PALEXPO Exhibition Center, the Competition Yellow 1989 ZR-1 was poised with an unclad ZR-1 chassis. Spectators from all over the world jostled for position, while the press photographed the car and the chassis endlessly. Judging from the attention it was receiving, the ZR-1 was the hit of the show.

Downstairs, at 4:00PM that afternoon, we held our world press conference. GM President Bob Stempel, GM Europe President Bob Eaton, Chevrolet Chief Engineer Fred Schaafsma, and I, sat on an elevated platform at a long table with microphones. A crowd of more than 200 people sat at tables in front of us. Headphones were provided with simultaneous translations in French, German, Italian, and Spanish. Interest in the ZR-1 was so great that we had to delay the press conference until television monitors could be set up in the hall outside the room, for a spillover crowd.

At floor level, the yellow ZR-1 and its juxtaposed chassis separated us from the audience. Each of the speakers talked about the car from his own perspective. Stempel discussed the ZR-1's importance to the corporation; Eaton talked about the possibilities for the car in Europe; and Schaafsma discussed Chevrolet's plans for the ZR-1.

My presentation took me off the dais and into the chassis. For nearly an hour, I described the features of the LT5 engine and explained how we achieved its exceptional power while meeting the world's most stringent emissions, fuel economy, and noise standards. I told the press about the

GM President Bob Stempel (left), Dave McLellan (right), and Chevrolet public relations chief Ralph Kramer conferring before the Geneva Auto Show press conference.
P. H. Cahier Photography

The yellow ZR-1 and its cutaway chassis were displayed together on the show floor.
Dave McLellan Archives

Dave McLellan describing the ZR-1 to the group assembled for the press conference.

P. H. Cahier Photography

MEET THE PRESS

David E. Davis	*Automobile*
William Jeanes	*Car and Driver*
Thos Bryant	*Road & Track*
Leon Mandel	*AutoWeek*
Harry Hibler	*Hot Rod*
Joe Oldham	*Popular Mechanics*
Herb Shuldiner	*Popular Science*
Dave Smith	*Ward's*
John Dianna	*Motor Trend*
Bob D'Olivo	*Motor Trend*

MEET THE EXECUTIVES

Don Runkle	Vice President, General Motors
Arv Mueller	Vice President, General Motors
Tony Rudd	Engineering Director of Lotus

Twelve Corvette ZR-1s lined up to depart from the Hotel Intercontinental in Geneva.

Dave McLellan Archives

chassis and how it was developed through showroom stock racing. The press listened intently before we opened the floor to questions.

TURNING THE PRESS LOOSE

Having attended the Auto Show, the publishers then wanted to hit the road to do what they really came for—to test drive the ZR-1. Our group, including the publishers and our Corvette engineers and technicians, milled around the twelve ZR-1s that were lined up, causing a huge traffic jam in front of the Hotel Intercontinental. All were ready for the two days of aggressive driving that lay ahead through the mountains of southern France.

Most of this group was from the US, and they neither understood French nor were familiar with our Alpine route. As a consequence, we sent the cars off in small groups of four. Sending cars out solo, in unfamiliar territory, would have increased the likelihood of a driver getting lost. It is easy to miss a turn while barreling along a twisting road at 80 mph.

Before leaving the hotel, we divided the twelve ZR-1s into three groups and put an engineer/navigator, who had previously run the route, in the passenger seat of each of the lead cars. They had sets of detailed maps for the entire route. The remaining ZR-1s had the same maps in case they became separated from the lead cars.

With drivers and passengers in place, we were off for Carcassonne. Down Geneva's narrow, twisting back streets, we slowly headed for the autoroute to the south where the pace picked up dramatically. The publishers, not surprisingly, observed the 80 mph speed limit for only a moment as they accelerated past traffic. In no time we reached the French border, where our twelve (four bright red, four dark red, and four dark blue) ZR-1s caused quite a stir. The gendarmes, baffled by what they saw, motioned us off to the side of the road. The publisher driving the lead car spoke in English. The gendarme listened in French. The publisher then showed the gendarme the packet of legal documents for the car. The ZR-1s were owned by a US company, manufactured in Kentucky, licensed in Michigan, and brought in under temporary permits through Germany to France. Finally, after much confusion, we were waved on our way. Incidents like this one were to plague us many times, and we were concerned that the publishers would feel harassed. Our mission was to have them experience the cars, not to be continually annoyed. Sure, they would have a story to write from all this, but would it be the one we had in mind?

DRIVING THE ZR-1

The autoroute took us directly into Grenoble, where drivers swapped places with passengers as planned, and where the road became just another four-lane highway. Our route turned off to take us through the Gorges d'Engins. I was happy to be at the wheel as we turned into the gorge. The road centerline that snaked down into the canyon captured my full attention. I dawdled for a moment, to let the car ahead of me gain some distance then I braked hard for the first turn, snatched first gear, accelerated hard to 55 mph, and up-shifted into

The absence of front license plates drew the attention of the French gendarmes.
Dave McLellan Archives

VEHICLE INFORMATION CARD USED IN FRANCE

As the trouble we had experienced at the French border became a regular occurrence, Jim Ingle's (Jingle's) frustration grew. The gendarmes were invariably curious about our ZR-1s. Because they spoke no English and Jingles spoke no French, Jingles, in his usual thorough way, had an explanation for the cars written down in French. We just flashed a copy of this new "vehicle information card" (see below), and the gendarmes waved us on.

VEHICLE INFORMATION CARD

This vehicle is a Chevrolet Corvette manufactured by GM in Bowling Green, Kentucky, in the United States of America. The car is registered and licensed by the state of Michigan. Michigan registered cars use only a rear license plate, so there is no front license plate for the car. The car is the property of GM Corporation.

The car is being used for a press introduction in conjunction with the Geneva International Auto Show. Journalists are here to drive the car on French roads and at the Goodyear Test Center at Mireval (near Montpellier). The occupants of the car are either journalists or engineers from GM, Goodyear or other manufacturers who supply components for building the car.

The car was flown to Europe for this press activity and will be returned to the United States afterward.

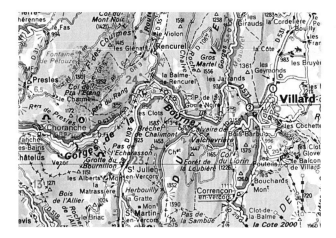

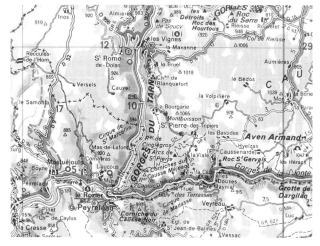

Top: French roads that were laid down over one hundred years ago follow the contour of the land and at their best snake down gorges like the Gorges de Bourne. We designed Corvettes for roads like this.

©*MICHELIN Valence/Grenoble/Gap Map No. 77 (1995). Permission No. 95-278*

Bottom: Great performance and great roads converge at the Gorges du Tarn.

©*MICHELIN Albi/Rodez/Nimes Map No. 80 (1995). Permission No. 95-278*

second. The next curve came up rapidly. I saw it, braked hard, down-shifted to first, turned in, cornered and, past the apex, accelerated toward second gear. The car was nowhere near its limit. As I gained confidence, I took greater advantage of the road. Finally, the road settled down for a few moments. Catching our breaths, my passenger and I took a moment to enjoy the scenery.

For the previous couple of months, I had been busy at my desk job as Engineering Director of the Corvette, and had not even driven a ZR-1 until the press launch. By the time I finished driving through the gorges, I reveled in what I had accomplished.

We turned off the highway just past Mende and headed down the D986 into the Gorges du Tarn. Thoroughly comfortable with their cars by now, the drivers plummeted through a series of downhill switchbacks, as the road descended precipitously toward the tiny village of Ste. Enimie, perched at the bed of the Tarn River. In the space of a mile we'd dropped 1,500 feet. We exited the gorge on the D995, and seven uphill switchbacks later, we gained back our 1,500 feet of altitude almost as rapidly as we had lost it. The ZR-1 climbs out of gorges almost as fast as it hurtles down into them.

Back on the N88, we headed for Rodez. The road gave us a chance to practice our passing maneuvers with local traffic. Several times we encountered streams of cars that we could only pass one or two at a time. When oncoming traffic cleared, I would downshift to second, accelerate hard, shift to third, brake hard to match the speed of the stream, activating the ABS, and while braking pull into the next slot. I have often wondered what those other drivers thought, when we so unexpectedly and quickly accelerated around them almost as if they were parked.

We traversed Carcassonne and headed for Le Cite, the eleventh-century walled fortress that would be our home for the next three weeks. Here we entered into a different world. We felt like knights of old on our trusty chargers, as we drove the ZR-1s across the drawbridge that spanned the castle's moat, squeezing through the gate, and up a steep, narrow cobblestone street. The going was slow. The road was barely as wide as the

car itself, and we had to share the space with pedestrians and bicyclists. We passed by tiny shops which were separated from the road by only narrow walkways and curbs. Finally, we found the Hotel du Donjon, and settled in to enjoy its medieval setting. After two days of great driving, we ate and rested well that night.

The following day, the publishers were in Mireval, at Goodyear's proving ground, overlooking the Mediterranean from its hillside perch. Originally a road-racing track, Goodyear bought it and rebuilt it to do controlled tire-testing. Goodyear had just finished the inner track, which could be watered to a controlled depth for tire-testing. Publishers and press could evaluate the ZR-1 on the outer track at speeds almost comparable to what they had driven on the road. And, on the wetted inner track they could explore the directional Goodyear tires, with their wet handling capabilities, and the ABS brake system, with its controlled stopping.

Over the next three weeks, we repeated the cycle with the American automotive press, giving each of them the chance to experience the ZR-1 on the high-speed French autoroutes, on the winding secondary roads, and on the wonderful mountain switchback roads of the Gorge du Tarn.

With twelve ZR-1s charging down French mountain roads and autoroutes for over three weeks, we were fortunate to have had only one accident. On the second day of the run from Geneva, one of the publishers felt drowsy. In searching for the window switch to give himself some air, he was momentarily distracted and drove straight into an embankment. Fortunately, the embankment stopped the car. On the other side of the embankment, 1,500 feet down, was the Gorge du Tarn in all its splendor. Driver and passenger suffered just a few bruises, while the car suffered more serious injuries.

After the last of the American automotive press had left, their European counterparts arrived. They experienced the road and track activities in the same order, but they had to cram their total ZR-1 time into one long day. Most of the Europeans were unfamiliar with the Corvette, although a few had tested recent models in the United States. Unfortunately, a number of the European journalists arrived with impressions gained from the popularity of 1970's Corvettes being used as pimpmobiles near the brothels of Hamburg, which was an unfortunate

Top: A ZR-1 as it enters Le Cite through the tower gate.
Dave McLellan Archives

Bottom: Goodyear's wet track was available for the publishers to test the ZR-1s in controlled wet conditions.
Courtesy Goodyear Tire & Rubber Co.

Top: On a break, the ZR-1s line up below spectacular French scenery.
Dave McLellan Archives

Bottom: Jim Ingle, better known as "Jingles," entertained the press with ZR-1 hole shots.
Photo by D. Randy Riggs

association for any car. By spending personal time with the journalists, and by thoroughly briefing them on the car and its capabilities, we hoped to send them away with the most positive message possible.

The Europeans have an even more hierarchical car magazine community than in the US—a real pecking order. At the top, were the premier magazines like *Auto Motor und Sport* (AMS) in Germany, *L'Auto* in France, *Car* and *Auto Car & Motor* in England, and then there was everybody else. The testers from some of the top magazines included exceptionally skilled ex-Formula One drivers. A thumbs-up or a thumbs-down, particularly from AMS, can set the tone for the rest.

Back at Mireval, Scott Allman, our ride and handling development engineer, had responsibility of supervising the outer track and keeping the press under enough control that they didn't collide with one another. He also scheduled rides for the press in the race-prepared ZR-1 and the Corvette Challenge car.

In between track driving sessions, Jingles entertained the press with ZR-1 hole shots and his smoke trick, earning him the nickname "Mr. Smoke." Jim would take the next ZR-1 in line for a run on the track and stage it in front of the press. Revving the engine against the rev limiter at 7,200 rpm, he would let out the clutch and quickly get on the brakes. With the rear tires already spinning, the front brakes would hold the car stationary. Within seconds the car—with its engine screaming and the rear tires spinning—would be completely enveloped in smoke, presenting a rare photo opportunity for the Europeans. As childish as this might have seemed, it taught the Europeans in one lesson what we couldn't convince them of in words: This was one tough car!

It was a letdown to have to pack up and go home after such a memorable exploration of a car that we had all labored so hard to produce. Now, we had to wait for the press reports in the magazines and the hoped-for feeding frenzy when the ZR-1 hit the Chevrolet dealer showrooms.

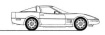

FIA ENDURANCE RECORDS

Jim Minneker was convinced that the FIA (Federation International de l'Automobile) 24 hour World Endurance Record was within reach of the ZR-1. Tommy Morrison then put together the proposal to actually go after the record. We took the proposal to Chevrolet management, whose reaction was, "We're selling all the ZR-1s we can build, why add to the hype." So, Chevrolet sat on the proposal. We finally said, "If you won't support the proposal will you at least not say no?" They reluctantly agreed they would not oppose the proposal but we would have to do everything on our own time.

This was enough for us. Tommy found outside sponsorship for the run and began building two cars: the ZR-1; and an L98, as requested by GM overseas marketing. Jim Minneker obtained a new LT5 engine, which had been rejected for car production because of cosmetic defects, and installed it into the ZR-1. We considered the L98 as a backup, in case the ZR-1 expired. The cars were configured, essentially, as showroom-stock race cars with 40-gallon fuel capacites. Goodyear recommended that the cars should be on racing slicks because of the continuous speeds we would be running. They then proceeded to make special tires just for our cars.

The track chosen for the record run was Firestone's 7.7 mile oval at Fort Stockton, Texas. And, during a test run on the track, John Heinricy hit 196 mph in a ZR-1. From this, they established a plan for the actual record run. They needed to average 175 mph for 24 hours, to comfortably beat the existing record, set in 1940 by Ab Jenkins in the Mormon Meteor III, at 161.180 mph. To average 175 mph, they would have to run in the low 180s, to make up for the time lost with pit stops.

In early February 1990, Tommy Morrison, his mechanics, drivers, the USAC observers, and a transport loaded with two Corvettes, spare parts, and all the communication and timing gear, headed for Texas. Once there, they had to sit and wait, as the weather in west Texas would not cooperate. Finally, on March 1, the weather broke enough for them to start.

Both cars got underway just before 10 am. For the first six hours, the L98 was assigned the class records, and then it was retired to be air freighted to the Geneva Auto Show for display. The ZR-1 forged on. It ran flawlessly

through the cold of night and, with Tommy Morrison behind the wheel, it set the 24-hour record at 9:56 am, having averaged 175.885 mph. The 5,000 mile record, set by the experimental Mercedes Benz CIII at 156.824 mph, was still within their grasp with only 5 hours to go. They went for it. Within 65 miles of the record, the unexpected happened: A coolant hose broke. The fan shroud had come loose and had been rubbing on the coolant hose, which finally wore through.

The FIA allowed the record car to carry a suitcase of repair parts, but required that any repairs be done by the driver. There was no coolant hose in the ZR-1's suitcase. Fortunately, the FIA rules considered the hose a "soft part" that did not have to be carried in the car in order to be used in repairs. So, the hose was quickly repaired, coolant was added, and the was car sent back out on the track. The repair held, and the ZR-1 went past 5,000 miles at 28 hours and 46 minutes, with a somewhat-reduced average speed of 173.791 mph. This was a monumental achievement by a team of dedicated Corvette operatives.

Our record-setting ZR-1 is now in the Smithsonian Institute, in Washington, DC.

FIA World Records Held by the ZR-1:

Distance or time	Average speed
24 hours	175.885 mph
5,000 miles	173.791 mph
5,000 km	175.710 mph (282.788 kph)

FIA International Records in Category A, Group II, Class 10 held by the ZR-1:

Distance or time	Average speed
100 miles	175.600 mph
500 miles	175.503 mph
1,000 miles	174.428 mph
12 hours	175.523 mph

continued on next page

FIA ENDURANCE RECORDS *(continued)*

FIA International Records in Category A, Group II, Class 10 held by the L98:

Distance or time	Average speed
100 km	172.843 mph (278.164 kph)
500 km	171.874 mph (276.604 kph)
1,000 km	170.487 mph (274.372 kph)
5,000 km	175.710 mph
1 hour	174.508 mph
6 hours	170.877 mph

Above: The 7.7-mile Bridgestone-Firestone track at Fort Stockton is notable for its desolation and its lack of guard rails.

Photo by Jim Ward

The drivers who made these records possible were straight from the Corvette engineering team at Chevrolet that had made the ZR-1 the rapacious car that it was, and from the showroom-stock group of drivers that had made the Corvette a winner for three years running:

Tommy Morrison*   Scott Allman*
John Heinricy   Kim Baker*
Jim Minneker   Stuart Hayner
Scott Legasse

*These drivers and Don Knowles are credited with the L98's International Records.

Below: A ZR-1 with a stock motor ran for 24 hours at an average speed of 175.885 mph, setting an FIA world record.

Photo by Jim Ward

Below: Tommy Morrison and this team of drivers and mechanics were responsible for the FIA records .

Photo by Jim Ward

Making the Chevrolet V-8 a Modern Engine 14

BASED ON SHEER NUMBERS, ITS LIFESPAN, and its incredible popularity, the Chevrolet V-8 must rank among the most successful industrial products ever made. The Chevrolet V-8 has been used in passenger cars and trucks for 47 years. It has been converted for marine and aircraft applications, and it has been a winner in all kinds of racing venues. During those 47 years, some 60 million engines have been produced, with more than a million of them going into Corvettes alone. More than any other single factor, this engine changed Chevrolet's image from that of a producer of stodgy low-priced cars to the leading producer of low-priced, yet exciting, cars. Indeed, the 1955 Chevrolet and its new V-8 engine brought youth and flare back to the Chevrolet name.

The Chevrolet V-8 benefited from a decade of research into fuels and combustion chamber design conducted by General Motors Research Laboratories. It also benefited from the new V-8 engines that preceded it at Cadillac and Oldsmobile. It was no coincidence that the dynamic Ed Cole came charging in from Cadillac to lead this Chevrolet renaissance.

One unique attribute of the Chevrolet V-8 was its ultra-compactness. Clever parts reduction and simplification were the forte of Chevrolet's design effort. For example, the intake manifold was designed to also act as the camshaft cover. The thin-wall iron casting was significantly lighter than any of the predecessor GM V-8 engines, and a unique shaftless valve-train rocker-arm simplified the valve-train hardware and made it lighter. This valve-rocker scheme was originally designed at the Pontiac Motor Division, but because it was first used successfully at Chevrolet, Chevrolet generally receives the credit.

When introduced in the 1955 Corvette, Chevrolet's new V-8 displaced 265 cubic inches and generated 195 gross hp. By 1970, as the 350 cubic inch, 370 gross hp LT1, it reached its first zenith of performance. This first high point came using all-mechanical analog engine controls. The 11:1 compression ratio, while it helped performance, demanded a diet of

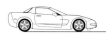

For its displacement and power output, the small-block Chevrolet engine was smaller and lighter than its Cadillac and Oldsmobile predecessors.

Illustration by Dave Kimble

ultra-premium leaded fuel, which relegated spark plugs to a useful life of just a few thousand miles.

Along the way, starting in 1965, Chevrolet produced an even larger displacement engine, which originally displaced 396 cubic inches. This engine took the Chevrolet stamped rocker-arm valve-mechanism one step further. With no shaft to force an alignment of the valves, the rockers could be oriented at whatever angle was optimum for the shapes of the combustion chamber and the valve port. This cylinder head was described colloquially as the "porcupine head." The new engine became known as the "big block" and the original Chevrolet V-8 as the "small block." They were also known, respectively, as the "rat motor" and the "mouse motor."

PERFORMANCE REACHES A LOW POINT

Ultimately, analog fuel- and spark-control doomed these big block engines, as emission control and fuel economy regulations began to tighten through the 1970s. By 1975, the small block was the only engine left in the Corvette. The passenger car version of the big block had been canceled because of the difficulty of certifying it with a catalytic converter, given the primitive emission control capabilities available.

By 1980, first in California and then nationwide in 1981, the carburetor's fuel metering under steady-state conditions, was controlled by a small computer. This computer sensed the partial pressure of oxygen in the exhaust and adjusted the air-fuel ratio to its stoichiometric ideal—the "sweet spot" where hydrocarbon, CO, and nitrous oxide emissions are at a minimum. But, even if the carburetor metered fuel precisely (which it didn't), the complex dual-plane eight-runner manifold introduced air-fuel variations of more than ten percent, from cylinder to cylinder—not the most efficient way to run an engine. The carburetor-manifold air-fuel distribution system was a hindrance to achieving optimal emissions, fuel economy, and drivability. The 1981 Corvette, with its oxidizing-reducing catalytic converter, had the highest back pressure and the lowest installed performance of any Corvette since the six-cylinder days. Its zero-to-60 quarter-mile acceleration performance was about equal to a modern Miata, at just under 10 seconds.

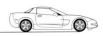

INJECTING NEW LIFE INTO THE SMALL BLOCK

The development of digital fuel control and digital ignition can be credited with bringing the Chevrolet small block back from its performance nadir, to the pinnacle the engine is at today. Digital technology is also responsible for giving the small block a bright future, which looks to extend at least two decades into the future.

In 1982 we finally replaced the four-barrel carburetor with a pair of unit fuel injectors. This system, with a fuel-wetted single-plane intake manifold, improved transient fuel control but left each cylinder with even more variability in air-fuel ratio. Most of the performance improvement in the 1982 system came from the much lower back pressure monolith converter that replaced the prior bead converters. With 200 net hp and a four-speed automatic transmission as standard, the 1982 car significantly outperformed the 1981, although top speed was not much improved.

The "all new" 1984 Corvette used essentially the same engine and transmission as the 1982. However, it now had 205 net hp and an automatic transmission that held in fourth overdrive. Not only was acceleration further improved, but top speed was raised to just over 140 mph.

By the early 1970s, individual cylinder injection developed by Bosch was available commercially. It used a microprocessor to control a pulse-width modulated injector at each intake port. This eliminated the air-fuel ratio variations associated with the wetted manifold, and allowed the manifold to be designed as an efficient air induction scheme.

Cadillac used the Bosch injection system starting in 1975 with the Seville V-8. Because of legal complications, Bob Stempel told us to keep our hands off. It wasn't until the 1985 model year that management acquiesced to the ultimate superiority of unit injection. Thanks to port fuel injection, the L98 was introduced in 1985 at 230 net hp; by 1990, it was up to 250 hp.

THE GENERATION II AND III SMALL BLOCKS

By 1985, the Chevrolet small block had been in production for 30 years. The people who had originally designed and processed the engine for manufacturing had long since retired. Over the years, the trail of process control had largely been lost. Production could only continue by carrying on with the current tooling and procedures. But changes would occur, sometimes inadvertently, and processing or durability problems would crop up as a result. It was camshaft wear that finally got the engi-

neers' attention. The wear was serious enough that the engine group felt as though they were losing control of the design, so they set about to rediscover how the engine was processed.

This revisit to the engine processing led to a general rethinking of the engine itself, with a focus on dramatically improving its reliability. At least part of the impetus for the reassessment of the small block was the LT5 project, which had been awarded to Lotus Engineering. The engineers made sure that they understood the parts that were working well, while those parts of the engine that didn't work well were slated for a major redesign. One area that was singled out for reengineering was the cooling system. Changes were needed to lower the octane demand of the cylinders and to allow for a higher compression ratio. By 1992, this work, under the direction of Anil Kulkarni, led to the first major reengineering of the Chevrolet small block. So much revision was involved that it was designated the "Generation II" engine. In addition to the revised cooling system, the new engine included the complete digital control of fuel delivery and spark timing, including detonation control. This engine had fewer parts and better reliability, and produced 20 percent more power than its L98 predecessor. The engine met the emission standards more readily, and improved installed fuel economy by as much as two miles per gallon. All this, and 300 net hp was quite a feat for a basic engine that was already 37 years old.

The research went beyond the Gen II to identify further changes that would take the engine to 350 and even 400 hp. This renaissance of the Chevrolet small block profoundly affected its future. The engine development was so promising that it prompted GM to completely retool its manufacturing processes, many of which dated to the original 1955 engine.

The Gen II small block generated 300 hp and was known as the LT1.
Dave McLellan Archives

With the opportunity to commission all new tooling, the Generation III small block was literally taken back to ground zero. The heads were reconfigured as a symmetrical design, with intake and exhaust ports equally spaced. This contrasts with the book-fold head configuration the small block had used since the beginning. With the book-fold design, the intake ports of the front two and rear two cylinders were adjacent. This asymmetry, along with the 90

degree firing order, was enough to unbalance the drawdown from the intake plenum for cylinder number 7 (which followed immediately after its paired number 5), leaving it slightly starved for air. Eliminating the asymmetry also spread out the exhaust ports and made it possible to cool the exhaust side of the head at higher heat fluxes. Intake and exhaust ports were increased in size and flow, for maximum performance. The valve train reverted to the conventional rocker-on-shaft design, to raise the maximum safe speed of the engine. The Gen III's bottom end looks more like that of the LT5, with a full ladder frame below the crank centerline. The result was 345 net hp in its LS1 configuration, and ultimately 405 net hp in the LS6 version, used in the Z06 Corvette. This contrasts with the highest-performance Gen II engine, which was the 330-net-hp LT4 that was used in the 1996 Grand Sport.

The Gen III engine, under the engineering direction of John Juriga, will likely continue to be used in passenger car and truck applications well into the twenty-first century. In the process of retooling the engine, the cylinder case and head machining were processed to accommodate both aluminum and iron versions, giving the Corvette its all-aluminum base engine. (The aluminum Gen III is also finding its way into experimental aircraft applications.) Corvette's Gen III is some 80 pounds lighter than the Gen II, as a result of its aluminum case and despite its ladder bottom end. It is two inches shorter than its predecessor, as a result of dispensing with the conventional distributor and oil pump drive. The engine is about the same height as the Gen II, which itself is almost two inches lower than the L98, which in turn was two inches lower than any carbureted Chevrolet small block. The net result of all this is an incredibly compact and muscular "power cube." In addition, the Gen III is mounted much lower than the older engines—low enough to keep the tuned intake plenum from obstructing the driver's view—finally solving the problem which had prompted Zora Arkus-Duntov to give the mid-engined Corvette a try.

Ed Cole and his engineers had it surprisingly right when they laid down the original small block, which now reigns in the Generation III, LS6 form.

Illustration by Dave Kimble

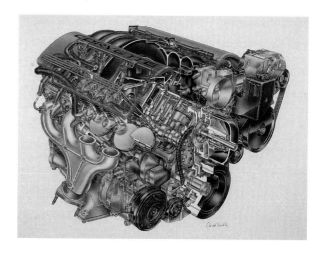

WHY THE GEN III DOOMED THE LT5

The contrast between the Gen III and the LT5 engine is striking. The LT5 is both taller and wider, as a result of its double overhead-cam cylinder heads and its complex intake manifold. It became apparent that the next generation Corvette, if it were designed solely

around the Gen III small block, could be significantly smaller and lighter than if it had to accommodate the LT5 engine.

Studies based on a large population of modern cars have given us the standard relationship between engine weight and total vehicle weight. Increasing an engine's weight by one pound means that the total car's weight will likely increase by two pounds. We estimated that taking 80 lbs out of the Corvette's engine would allow us to remove another 80 lbs from the chassis. In the case of the Gen III, reducing the engine's length would also contribute significant savings. Weight reduction of this magnitude is only possible when you're designing a car from scratch.

The planned future LT5 engine, with its even more complex valve train, would have been 205 lbs heavier than the aluminum Gen III. Thus, a Corvette designed around the Gen III aluminum engine would weigh around 405 pounds less than the same car designed to use the LT5. As a result, the LT5 engine would have had to generate 55 hp more than the Gen III, simply to compensate for the heavier car. With the Gen III generating 405 net hp and the future LT5 estimated at 475 net hp, the effective power gain would have been a mere 15 horsepower. And, given an estimated $25,000 price premium for the LT5 engine, the cost of this small increment of power is astronomical.

The Corvette had reached a crossroads. We could design the C5 around the LT5 engine or we could design a smaller, lighter car that was fitted like a glove around the Gen III small block. By opting for the smaller package, we could achieve ZR-1 performance at the price of a standard Corvette. This was too important an opportunity to ignore. As we explored it further, we convinced ourselves and Chevrolet that this was the right strategy for the next generation Corvette. This, however, left us with the conundrum that the far-superior Gen III might seem, to the consumer, to be low tech.

The Gen III uses computer management to control fuel and timing, providing smoothness, high power, and efficiency—a very high-tech feature But earlier forms of control—such as the four-valve combustion chamber—were what the public perceived as modern technology. We knew that the Gen III LS1 would do just fine without these older features, as they came at such a high price, in terms of size, weight, and complexity. Like the consumer, we had been accepting the notion that complexity was good. Yet, here was one case where just the opposite was occurring. The simple solution was almost as powerful, and it was smaller, lighter, cheaper,

and more fuel-efficient. Whether it was considered high-tech or not, the Gen III was the better engine. So, in the end, the only logical choice was to back the Gen III small block as the Corvette's engine of the future—even if its roots dated back almost 50 years.

RACING APPLICATIONS OF THE CHEVROLET SMALL BLOCK

The Chevrolet small block has been used in a number of racing series, from NASCAR to stock block Indy cars, to GTP cars. Each of these series regulated the engine differently. The NASCAR motor is a relatively simple, iron case 350 that was developed to produce in excess of 730 hp at 8,500 rpms. The GTP motors had similar performance but used port fuel injection and an aluminum case. The Indy rules were thought to favor a naturally-aspirated small block, but no one had ever taken advantage of this until Roger Penske and Ilmore Engineering came along with their pushrod Mercedes V-8, specifically designed to the stock block rule.

It is instructive to look across these engine applications and, even though many of the components that make up these engines are not stock, their horsepower output and rpm capability give some indication of what the small block can be stretched to achieve. Of course, the production engine is designed to be able to run for 200 hours at maximum performance, whereas the race engines typically have a life of 2 to 24 hours, which is all that is required to finish a race. 750 hp and 8,500 rpms put an upper limit on what's possible with the production engine using readily available materials. This represents a benchmark of what is possible, and is a useful goal for the continuing development of the Corvette motor.

Judd Larson drives the Chet Wilson Special to victory at Muskogee, Oklahoma, in 1963. It was one of scores of successful Chevy-powered sprint cars.

Photo by Leroy Byers

Breaking the Paradigm with the C5

15

THE INTRODUCTION OF THE ZR-1 put the Corvette in a new performance league. With 375 net hp and a chassis honed on the racetrack, this car could take on even the best of the exotic cars. It was also robust and reliable. Don Runkle, Chevrolet's planning chief, was so excited by the ZR-1 that he wanted to make all Corvettes ZR-1s. It was a great idea, but unfortunately we hadn't prepared for it. Mercury Marine could only build 18 of the LT5 engines a day. We would need seven times that many to put them in all Corvettes. And the cost, even at production level seven times higher, would have made the Corvette considerably more expensive—around $15,000 more than the base Corvette's price.

The small-block Chevrolet engine guys watched the LT5 engine program from the sidelines and said, "We could have done that—why didn't you ask us?" Embarrassed at what had been accomplished without them, they immediately set to work to develop the small block beyond 245 hp.

Showroom Stock racing and the introduction of anti-lock brakes had pushed us to a complete redesign of the 1984 Corvette chassis. Our experience in making the car a consistent winner on the racetrack was paying off. The foundation brakes were massively upgraded, the six-speed manual transmission was track-tested in the Corvette Challenge series, and engine output was increased to almost 400 hp in the racing configuration. The LT5 engine, with its 375 net hp, now catapulted the road car to racetrack performance.

But how could we give all Corvette owners the fantastic performance of the ZR-1 at a more affordable price? The only way we knew of was to start fresh and engineer an all new Corvette. Along the way, we would also attempt to solve the problems that plagued the Corvette convertible (and all other convertibles for that matter). It is preferrable, in any car, for the driver and passenger to have easy entry and egress, and to have room to stretch out inside the cockpit. As a convertible, a car should feel solid, not

shaky, yet it shouldn't weigh two tons. So the car's frame structure not only needs to be strong, but it also needs to be stiff.

We had been undone with the 1984 Corvette over this same rigidity issue. Originally conceived as a "T-top," to solve the structural stiffness problem, we had molded the car into a targa and then into a true convertible, making do as best we could with a compromised design. We weren't going to make this mistake again.

EXPLORING A STIFFER CORVETTE

There are very few designs that are truly new—everything has its roots, its antecedents or predecessor designs that show the way. The expression, "great engineers stand on the shoulders of those who came before" is operative in this situation. Surely, someone had already done what we were trying to do. So, in 1989 we began looking around again. Mercedes-Benz

---

WHY CONVERTIBLES SHAKE

Convertible shake and the corresponding feeling of looseness on rough roads can be understood if we consider the properties of vibration. The ride system of a car—tires, suspension, springs, dampers and structure—act as a tuned filter for the roughness of the road.

The first element of this "filter" is the unsprung mass (wheel, brake, and knuckle) bouncing on the spring of the tire. With a resonant frequency of 14 Hz, the wheel and tire begin to be effective as a filter above 20 Hz. This means that the rest of the car starts to become isolated from the destructive energy of the road at frequencies above 20 Hz. (The 14 Hz wheel-hop frequency in the steering wheel can be felt when driving at about 70 mph with an unbalanced tire.)

The second elements of the suspension filter are the ride spring and the mass of the car. Taken together, these two filters isolate the driver from road roughness down to about 1.4 Hz. There is a catch, however: The tire and wheel vibration at 14 Hz must be damped, or the system will experience destructive resonance. Tying the damper (shock absorber) to the ground is technically impossible, so the damper that controls body resonance is called on to do double duty, and control the wheel and tire resonance as well. In order for this to be effective, the body must appear solid to the damper at 14 Hz. And herein lies the dilemma of the convertible.

The convertible body is not solid; it is flexible. It wants to resonate, particularly in full body torsion, at about this same frequency. The consequence of this is reduced wheel-damping effectiveness and increased body shake on rough roads, driven by the damper trying to control tire-wheel resonance. The obvious solution to this dilemma is to raise the torsion frequency of the structure. Virtually all fixed-roof cars have their first body resonance significantly above 20 Hz for just this reason. To achieve similar results in a convertible, such as the Corvette, requires a four-fold increase in frame stiffness. To do this directly with the existing Corvette frame would require it to be four times as thick (and consequently, four times as heavy). A frame that started at 200 pounds would weigh 800 pounds, and still wouldn't have solved our entry/egress and roominess issues. So, some other solution needed to be found.

$$f = \frac{1}{2\pi} \sqrt{\frac{k}{m}} \quad \text{[cycles/sec.]}$$

Where: k = spring rate
m = mass

Basic frequency equation.

was about to introduce its all-new 500 SL convertible at the same Geneva Auto Show where we were introducing the ZR-1.

The German automaker's solution to the two-passenger-convertible dilemma was worth analyzing. They achieved entry, egress, and general interior roominess with a taller car. This allowed them to put their structural elements under the floor. They succeeded in raising the structure's first torsion mode to 18 Hz, just barely enough above wheel hop to control wheel-hop excitation. Unfortunately they did this at the expense of weight. The 500 SL weighed 4,127 pounds—even with its lightweight aluminum engine and magnesium seats—compared to the 3,400 pounds for a C4 Corvette. Most of the SL's greater weight went into "iron mongering" a very inefficient torsion structure under the floor. The solution was interesting, but it wasn't one that was useful for us.

We asked our friends at Lotus, who now had extensive experience driving ZR-1s, for a "white paper" on how they would do the next Corvette. In their response they included the need for a "torsionally-stiff backbone." As early as 1964, Chevrolet Research and Development had also proposed constructing the Corvette convertible with a backbone, although no detailed designs had ever been worked out. And Lotus was just finishing the design of the Elan, a front-wheel-drive convertible sports car, which was built around a steel backbone frame. The Esprit—a mid-rear engine rear-wheel-drive sports car—was also built around a steel backbone. What these cars had in common was that the engine, transaxle, and driving wheels were all at the same end of the vehicle. Neither car had its powertrain running through the middle of the car, which would compete with the backbone and passengers for precious space. The Corvette, in contrast, had its transmission, transmission support, driveshaft and exhaust all competing for the real estate that the backbone wanted to occupy. And, we were already trying to reassign some of this territory for the driver and passenger. It, simply, wouldn't all fit.

In the 1970s, Lotus had designed and built the front-engined rear wheel-drive Eclat, which used a cruciform (x-shaped) frame with a four-cylinder engine and manual gearbox. The Corvette, on the other hand, had to

The Lotus Elan backbone structure provided the required stiffness, but because it was for a front-wheel-drive car, it did not have the complication of the powertrain running through the passenger compartment.

Reproduced with permission from Group Lotus PLC

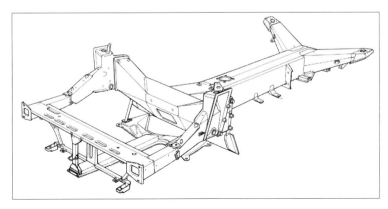

accommodate a massive automatic transmission, to provide the exhaust and power delivery of 400 hp.

The torsionally stiff backbone we were looking to package was roughly an 8-inch diameter round tube, or its rectangular equivalent, which would have to run the length of the passenger compartment. It would then need to connect to the entire structure to make the car stiff in torsion.

At the time, Lotus was building the Corvette Indy for Chevrolet. It was to be an ultra-sophisticated mid-engine active-suspension technology show car. In this car, the engine, transaxle, graphite composite central structural backbone, and suspension points were all an integral structural unit. The body was carried on this frame assembly on isolation mounts. We thought about using the engine and transmission as a stressed chassis system, similar to that used in the Indy, combining engine transmission, backbone, and suspension points into one rigid structure. But the engine guys, who had never used their engine as an integral part of the chassis structure, couldn't believe that we were serious. They nixed this approach as way too big a stretch. And, in my opinion, if we couldn't get our extended team to embrace a radical solution like the Corvette Indy, we would be walking into trouble. Even so, I pushed the idea pretty hard, in the hopes that the engine guys would get the idea that we were quite serious about rethinking the Corvette. So that they wouldn't reject the next, slightly less radical, solution.

The backbone concept was still a valid one, but if it were to work in the Corvette, the transmission would have to be moved to the rear and become a transaxle, in a unit with the differential.

I wasn't worried about the manual transmission. Here, we could do anything we wanted, as it was unique to the Corvette anyway. It was the complex automatic transmission that represented 75 percent of Corvette production that would be our stumbling block. It was also our major cost driver. Chevrolet R&D's Laslo Nagy laid out the design of engine, torque tube, torque converter, automatic transmission, and final drive and gave it to Hydramatic for a cost estimate of this unique torque converter housing and transmission case.

The car we were designing would look like no other Corvette ever. The transaxle solution moved the rear wheels back by 9 inches, giving the car a wheelbase of 105 inches. Weight distribution

In the Corvette Indy, the engine is integrated into the carbon fiber cruciform structure. The body, itself, is isolated from this structure.

Reproduced with permission from Group Lotus PLC

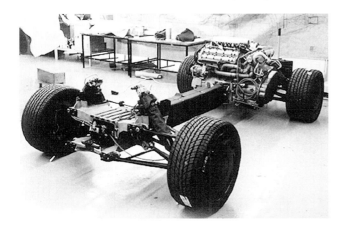

would not be affected; moving the transmission rearward was almost exactly canceled by the longer wheelbase.

But then, Hydramatic threw us a curve ball, coming back with a tooling cost estimate of $80 million. This was at least half of what we expected the entire car to cost, and was quite out of our league. However, we didn't quit. We simply set their estimate aside and planned to revisit the transaxle when we saw the overall requirements more clearly.

THE CORVETTE ENGINEERING TEAM

As we identified the powertrain issues, we began putting the team together that would engineer and package the entire car. Once again, we turned to Chevrolet R&D, where the first Corvette had been engineered 38 years before. This was the same Chevy R&D that, under Frank Winchell, had masterminded the highly successful Camaro Trans-Am effort and the automatic transmission Can-Am Chaparrals with Jim Hall. It was amazing that after all the reorganizations we had been through, Chevrolet R&D still existed as a "skunk works," although it no longer had any connection to Chevrolet, which was by then just a marketing and sales division. (Chevrolet R&D finally disappeared in the mid 1990s, a casualty of one more reorganization.)

Doug Robinson, from the Corvette Group, was named team leader, and Chevrolet R&D contributed transmission design specialist Laslo Nagy and two seasoned packaging engineers, Dick Balsley and Al Bodnar. Dick had been the lead engineer with Lotus for the Corvette Indy, and Al had designed the original powertrain concept for the C4. R&D also contributed senior designers, who laid out everything in three-dimensional detail. Critical to making this process work was the inclusion of a team of structural analysts, led by Steve Longo and Brian Deutchel. Computer analysis was now capable of calculating the stiffness of the complex metal structure as well as its strength. This was key to our task of defining the critical stiffness attributes of the backbone and its transition structures.

Jim Minneker, our voice with GM Powertrain, and a key player in the LT5 engine program, took on the transaxle cost problem. He discovered that Hydramatic (now a part of GM Powertrain) was also working with the full-size truck group to design a unique automatic transmission housing for their four-wheel-drive trucks. It turned out that the four-wheel-drive powertrain, consisting of engine, transmission, and transfer case, needed to be stiffened to solve a vibration problem. The solution required using a bolt-on bell housing for the transmission case, not unlike the one

we needed. Our problem was solved. Even if it cost $80 million to tool, the truck program was going to pay almost the entire bill. We were lucky to pull it off, because the truck group didn't need their new transmission case until the 2000 model year, three years after the C5 was introduced.

FUNDING THE CORVETTE

As the marketing division, Chevrolet wanted a new Corvette, but it didn't have the capital allocation to fund it on top of all its other programs. Capital allocations come from the corporation to buy the tools, equipment, and facilities needed to produce a new car. Though Design Staff and Engineering were budgeted separately, their work was directly tied to these major capital allocations. The capital available was based on cash flow expectations two to three years in the future and General Motors was losing tens of billions of dollars each year during this period. As a result, the Corvette had to wait, taking a back seat to the high volume programs that were Chevrolet's bread and butter.

Because of the unpredictable nature of future cash flows, the corporation had a history of starting, stopping, and then starting programs again. Management did this on all programs, and they continually changed their minds as to what they wanted and how many they needed and where they would be built and how much money they had to spend. The lesson that the corporation learned from this was don't start programs until you're ready. Mostly this meant having a plan and the capital allocated, to tool the car and equip the plants to build it, before Design Staff and Engineering start work.

Chevrolet management was always hopeful that they could find enough extra funding to do the Corvette as a 1993 model. We were on their financial bubble, and it could go either way. So, capital allocation became our biggest hurdle. We couldn't start the design until we had the capital. But an even worse scenario would have been if Chevrolet got the money from the corporation before we were ready to move out of R&D. Moving ahead too soon would have been a disaster, as we would have been designing, and ultimately tooling, the car before we had a workable solution to the structure problem. We couldn't afford to risk this and waste people, time, and money. But to even get the budget to start Chevrolet R&D working on the program, we needed a legitimate car program. Chevrolet came back to us several times with the discouraging news that they didn't have an allocation for the Corvette and had to slip the program to the next year. We thanked them for trying, knowing that if they

had given us the allocation we would still have had to drag our heels until we were ready.

Tom Wallace, who headed Chevrolet R&D, fully understood what was going on and did his best to protect our R&D budget from his many competing programs. It was to the credit of people all over the organization that, even though they didn't know what we were trying to do in detail, they had enough faith in us and wanted the Corvette to succeed, so they supported us.

STYLING THE C5

While we were trying to solve the convertible structural issues in Chevrolet R&D, Design Staff was busy producing competing styling themes for a new Corvette. Their Thousand Oaks, California, Advanced Concept Center, led by John Schinella, won the initial competition and was given the go-ahead to build their design, which became the Sting Ray III.

INSPIRING THE DESIGN STAFF

In early 1989, I flew out to California to meet with designers at the Advanced Concept Center. One of my objectives was to share with them what I knew about the future Corvette. I told them that the Corvette was:

- our dream car
- our vision of the future
- a statement of the best that GM is capable of in design, execution, and customer satisfaction
- a distinctly American vision—it's not a copy of someone else's vision
- a car that celebrates the pleasures of motoring— everything about it is tuned to be exhilarating to look at and to drive
- a car that wants to be a wonderful, positive, and joyful experience for its owner

I also told them the best cars in the world were like this— distinctive and joyful experiences for their owners. Their makers are saying, "We made this car to please ourselves and we would now like to build one just like it for you."

I also shared my view that the design of the Corvette has to say everything about it.

- it's fast
- it's sleek
- it's aggressive
- it's a car people want to be seen in and identified with

Engineering, manufacturing, and sales would have to execute the design and deliver the car to our customers in a way that fulfils the expectations signaled by the design.

- The design sells the car.
- The rest of us make it stick.
- We don't understand it very well, but design delivers powerful quality and reliability cues.

I told them that their challenge was to design a Corvette that would reach its mid-life in 1997—to envision the future but at the same time to retain a link with the present as well as Corvette's heritage.

- We can't underestimate the importance of our good name or our heritage, and we do want to sell Corvettes to customers. (That's why we have good jobs.)
- We can derive pleasure from our customers saying, "job well done."

I also shared with them the early conclusions from the market research that was being conducted on the Corvette. In short, I not only shared my views of what I thought the Corvette should be, I tried to challenge and inspire the designers of the next Corvette.

The car that came out of the Thousand Oaks studio, the Stingray III, was interesting thematically. It had a long 101 inch wheel base, an extremely low hood and a very forward cowl with a radically sloping windshield. Unfortunately, this left only enough room under the hood for a V-6 engine. (Later in R&D, we would shoe-horn in one of the developmental distributor-less small-block V-8s.)

The Stingray III had excellent cockpit roominess and a low door sill to facilitate entry and egress. Much of the increased roominess came from moving the small five-speed transmission from between the driver and passenger to the rear, and coupling it to the differential, forming a transaxle. Unfortunately, Design Staff ignored the structure completely. There was virtually no structure to this car, just a small rocker tying the front and rear together. The Sting Ray III was in no way a solution for us, although it unwittingly pointed us toward the solution. If Design Staff would do a 101 inch wheelbase Corvette on their own, they could be talked into a 105 inch wheelbase design.

Given the major changes we were contemplating in the powertrain, to make it compatible with a backbone structure, it became obvious early on that our quest for a rigid convertible was forcing a solution every bit as radical as the mid-engined Corvette, which Zora Arkus-Duntov had always pressed for as being the "technically correct" solution for a high-powered sports car. I had a private conversation with Jerry Palmer, then in charge of all the Chevrolet design studios, and told him what we had learned in Chevrolet R&D. I told him that this was his last chance for a mid-engine Corvette and that if he wanted it he would have to fight for it. I would support him, but the idea had to come from Design Staff. Jerry didn't take the bait. Not even Design Staff had the energy to fight for a mid-engine car. So, we kept working on the technically challenging but "conventional" front mid-engine car.

ZORA AND THE STINGRAY

For about two years after it was built, the Sting Ray III was kept tightly under wraps. Fitted with a V-8 engine, it was finally unveiled to the public and sent out on the Corvette show circuit. At a Corvette meet at Konner Chevrolet in Paramus, New Jersey, Zora Arkus-Duntov came face to face with the car for the first time. Always suspicious of Design Staff, he was immediately drawn to the car's unique three-spoke, three-bolt road wheel. His sensibilities as an engineer told him that this was wrong. He was appalled that a car masquerading as a Corvette would so violate engineering principles as to use only three bolts to hold each wheel in place.

When he was asked to sit in the car to have his picture taken, he refused. In no way would he sanction his association with a car displaying such disregard for engineering principles!

With a wheel at each corner and a 101-inch wheelbase, the Sting Ray III was a first step toward the C5.
GM Design Center

MARKET RESEARCH FOR THE CORVETTE

For the first time ever, Chevrolet decided to commission a market research project on the Corvette, to be conducted by Kenny & Associates. In the past, Chevrolet had always relied on Joe Pike and the instincts of other managers for direction. Research psychologist Charlie Kenny had developed a unique way of interviewing. His interviews were one on one, and they lasted between one and two hours. While they covered many specific questions, the interviewer could follow the subject along whatever line of questioning the conversation opened up. The interview was typically conducted in a dark, quiet room and during the interview the subject was even asked to use a sleep mask to totally eliminate outside distractions. Charlie saw this as a way to get his subjects totally focused and able to recall things that were tucked tightly away.

The subjects were chosen for the cars they drove and for their demographics. Chevrolet's marketing research people and our engineers were allowed to listen to the interviews from behind a one-way glass. At the end of the interview we could ask questions directly ourselves.

In typical interview fashion, it was not disclosed that Chevrolet was sponsoring the research, so that asking the subjects to bring their cars to the interview was viewed by some with suspicion. The purpose behind the request became evident at the end of the interview, when the subject was asked to take the interviewer for a ride in his or her car. This was one more chance to recall details that would otherwise be forgotten.

The interviews were conducted in Los Angeles and Washington DC. Cars owned by the subjects included Corvettes of all vintages, competing sports cars, muscle cars and luxury sports sedans.

What did we learn? Having traveled to countless Corvette events and having been involved with Corvette owners and enthusiasts for sixteen years, I already knew a lot about Corvette fans and what they expected of their cars. But it was interesting to see the owners' expectations through a different set of very professional and analytical eyes. I expected that the market research would validate what we already knew about Corvette owners and their expectations for the car. I also hoped that it would help us to articulate for Chevrolet and corporate management what we already knew intuitively.

Kenny reaffirmed that the Corvette owner was at the extreme end of the spectrum from the person who buys a car for transportation. The Corvette owner wants the car to project an image—a symbol of the owner's personality. Appearances, in the case of Covette enthusiasts, are everything.

Owners used their cars to experience power and control. They enjoyed the "on the edge" kind of control that their Corvette provided them. They wanted their car to be so powerful that only they could tame it. They also wanted their Corvette to be without defect. The researchers thought that flaws in the car may have reminded the owner of his or her own imperfections or even of the fragility of human life.

Kenny also uncovered important motivators as to why, and even when, people buy Corvettes. In their free-ranging interviews, Corvette owners talked about having been influenced by a Corvette in their youth—"a neighbor brought a new Corvette home and gave me the keys and said, take it for a drive." These impressions were often tucked away and forgotten until some trigger event reactivated them—such as a promotion, or a divorce. If somone had interviewed this person about their automotive preferences two weeks before this trigger event, they might not have even mentioned the Corvette. But after the trigger, they had their Corvette within days, often as a reward or as a an attempt to bring power and control back into their lives.

This research put the Corvette buyer into sharp focus for those of us who were listening. Corvette buyers had always demanded power, style, and perfection, but we couldn't articulate why. Consequently, the corporate mentality of "that's good enough" had beaten out the message that buyers were trying to send us.

Unfortunately, the Chevrolet market researchers didn't press Chevrolet management very hard with what they had learned. So, not surprisingly, Chevrolet management paid scant attention to the research and learned next to nothing. Certainly, management did not pick up that the Chevrolet dealer needed to treat a Corvette prospect in a very special way.

Chevrolet saw itself as a commodity car company. Chevy's solution to selling more cars was to strip the content and lower the price. Unfortunately, this approach was carried over into the Corvette. Chevy's ultimate solution to selling more Corvettes was to strip the motor, strip the content, and give the body a fixed roof. We code named this the "Billy Bob" Corvette. If you listened to the customers and believed the market research, the last thing Chevy should have done was sell a stripped Corvette.

I was so impressed with the insights this research methodology had given us that I talked Chevrolet into using the same Kenny interview process on automobile magazine editors and publishers, and even on GM executive management. Neither the editors nor the GM executives were

Corvette buyers, but the editors had a powerful influence on the market and the GM executives influenced what got built.

The editors were interesting. Some were Corvette enthusiasts, some were not. Some wanted a smaller, lighter, more nimble Corvette. Some wanted the perennial dream of a mid-engine Corvette. It's interesting how different their responses were from those of the Corvette owners and enthusiasts, who never mentioned a smaller car or the mid-engine Corvette. With all of the varied responses, there was no direction.

Chevrolet had no problem with my asking the GM senior executives for an interview, until we got to the chairman, Roger Smith. This was when Chevrolet panicked. I assured them it would be OK. Roger owned a straight-axle Corvette, so I was pretty sure we weren't sticking our foot in a bear trap. Just to be sure, I was asked to personally oversee the interview, which was to be conducted in a room at the GM Building. At the scheduled time, I went up to the fourteenth floor executive offices and brought Roger down for the interview. I had been hoping that this would be my opportunity for the classic "30-second elevator speech" with the chairman, and I had rehearsed what I might say. I also knew that Roger might use this as an opportunity to speak his mind to one of his chief engineers.

But, the elevator ride turned out quite different from either of my imagined scenarios. Roger wanted to talk—but he wanted to talk about his recent hunting trip to Mississippi. In the interview he continued to talk about his hunting experience until Charlie Kenny finally got him focused on the Corvette. Roger was no detractor of the Corvette, but it was clear that he was a consummate finance guy. We had to get the car right "by the numbers" or it was no deal.

THE VALUE OF MARKET RESEARCH

Market research should be used very carefully. I thought the Kenny research was valuable because it had shone a light on the customers and on their strong interactions with the car. As such, it was a valuable tool to continually reference as we conceived the next Corvette.

The next phase of C5 market research did not involve Kenny. It was highly specific, with questions about likes and dislikes of specific car design proposals and details. I had also done my own casual research with Corvette enthusiasts. Some of the Corvette owners I interviewed considered the solid-axle cars of the 1950s to be the last of the great Corvettes, and some still pined for chrome bumpers. This had led me to the con-

clusion that Corvette enthusiasts, in their own ways, were very conservative about their cars.

For me, the next question was how far could we stretch the Corvette enthusiast's imagination. Could we do a radical new Corvette, one that would attract enthusiasts from beyond the Corvette circle, yet still have the hardcore enthusiasts perceive it as a Corvette?

What's the point of asking current Corvette owners what the next-generation Corvette should look like when all they know is the past? To the extent that the Corvette is defined by its past, enthusiasts can tell you what they know and what they like. But, can they speak for the next generation of Corvette enthusiasts? Can they see into the future of the digital electronics revolution? Do they know what Active Handling is or that such a system is even possible? The answer is, probably not. Using market research alone to dictate to the designers and engineers what the car should be like severely hinders progress. It would be like driving down a road while only looking in the rear view mirror.

Unfortunately, this is exactly what happened next, as the future designs were picked apart in research clinics by well-meaning enthusiasts who "knew what they liked." The result was a predictable hodgepodge of yesterday's remembered details.

Early in this process we had a Corvette future-product show in the Design Staff Dome. Jim Perkins, General Manager of Chevrolet, addressed the assembled designers, marketers and engineers, challenging them to leap forward and design the C5 as the first car of the twenty-first century not the last car of the twentieth century. The show consisted of scale models, drawings, and clays that were part of the exploration toward the C5, as well as the Sting Ray III concept car.

Working from Chevrolet R&D's drawings, Corvette Chief Designer John Cafaro produced this first full-size fiberglass model of the next Corvette.

GM Design Center

Taking Jim Perkins' remarks to heart, John Cafaro, then the Corvette Studio Chief Designer, produced a design reminiscent of the Corvette GTP race car. This was Cafaro's first instinctive response to the next Corvette and it was a great design. It was my second favorite Corvette design ever, topped only by the double-ended Four Rotor Corvette. Unfortunately, it would be massaged in clinic after clinic until it lost its designer's edge.

Don't get me wrong, it was still a good design after the researchers got to it. John

Cafaro was a good soldier and integrated all the disparate cues wanted by Corvette enthusiasts into one package. But, knowing his initial design and knowing where it could have gone under his talented direction, I believe that a great Corvette was missed.

HOW WOULD BOWLING GREEN BUILD THE NEW CAR?

If our next Corvette program was to be successful, we would have to apply the process known as dimensional management, to achieve a precision that we had never before obtained. We had come from a C3, where the entire car was essentially custom-built. The St. Louis Assembly hadn't trusted anyone to give them dimensionally correct parts so everything had been slotted or made oversized and then ground to suit. Large parts such as the fenders had to be trimmed by hand, which produced gaps that looked rough and irregular.

Dimensional management was a strategy for assuring that all the various machined parts would fit together smoothly, without any need for adjustments. Ron Burns, our structures engineer, had applied the strategy to the original C4, but too few of the structure and body panel suppliers understood what we were trying to achieve and botched the effort. When we finally understood what had happened and why things were not fitting, we went to work retooling and regauging the entire structure and the exterior body panels of the C4 so that everything could be made to fit by design and process. We never quite finished the job because it took more time and money than we could muster. But we applied the process to enough of the car to know that the approach worked, and we resolved to be zealots for dimensional management on the next Corvette.

As the backbone structure concept began to take shape, Pete Licardello, our manufacturing process engineer, took on the challenge of studying how the car should be built to maximize the quality of the assembled product. He divided the assembly process into its major elements—the structure, exterior panels, chassis, powertrain, and interior with its instrument panel. With no preconceptions as to which was the right processing strategy, he explored all of the possible alternatives for assembling the car. His only assumption was that we would use dimensional management to precision assemble everything. Out of this study he concluded that the powertrain needed to be bottom-loaded, requiring a bolt-on bottom to the central backbone.

Given the paint processing problems that are associated with even the best quality plastic panels, Pete explored ways we could avoid paint defects.

The idea of processing the body panels through the paint, independently of the car, was born out of this study. This ultimately led to a complete reorganization of the Bowling Green paint facility, turning it into a state-of-the-art department with robot painting. The results in the C5's paint quality speak for themselves. Dimensional management also made possible the precision fit of the entire set of body panels and fascias to the car.

The other processing idea that came out of this initial study was the off-line build of the instrument panel. Implemented on the C5, the entire windshield frame and front of dash was built separately from the car. This frame was then used as a carrier to assemble the steering column, brake and clutch pedals, the HVAC system, all the dash electronics, and the airbags. This entire subassembly was tested as a whole and then installed in the car, with bolts to the hinge pillars and with sealant across the floor. This was in total contrast to the conventional assembly of instrument panels, which was done with the assembler awkwardly working on his or her back inside the car. Without dimensional management, the C5's innovative modular assembly process would not have been possible.

GM ultimately picked up on Pete's innovative approach of modular assembly, applying it to the problem of making small-production cars profitable. "Project Yellowstone," much maligned by the auto workers union for its seeming threat to lower the number of workers required to build a car, is alive and well on the Corvette.

The hydroformed side rail starts as a fifteen-foot-long, six-inch diameter round tube.

Drawing by Dave McLellan

CREATING THE STRUCTURE FOR THE C5

It was easy to move the transmission and define a two-rail, three-rail, two-rail structural strategy. The difficult part was designing the transition structures to connect the rails together while avoiding the engine, exhaust, transmission, passenger space, etc. This is where CAD (computer aided design), 3-dimensional models, and mock-ups came together to help the team visualize possible solutions.

Jerry Fenderson, our Corvette body Staff Engineer, took a big first step when she saw that the outer rails of the 2-3-2 structure could be combined into one continuous long rail. She committed to taking this on as a separate project. The rail would start as a steel tube that was 6 in. in diameter, 15 ft long, and 0.08 in. thick. It would then be transformed by hydroforming, at pres-

sures upwards of 10,000 psi, into a double-S-shaped rectangular-cross-section rail.

We had put an additional constraint on the front and rear transition structures. We wanted them to be formed from flat sheets of metal. We had hoped to use this concept of "origami design" to minimize the tooling cost of the structure, but ultimately this proved unfeasible.

To get the desired results, it was crucial to team the structural analysts—and their ability to predict stress and stiffness—with

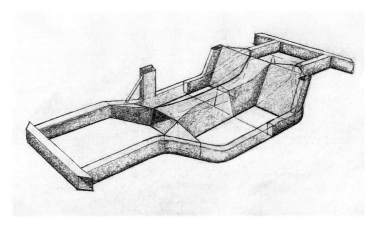

The C5 structure is four times as stiff in torsion as its predecessor.
Drawing by Dave McLellan

the designers and model makers—who could help us all visualize what was going on. Our team reviewed their work weekly, providing encouragement and direction. The analysis team, under Steve Longo and Brian Deutchel, had set their own goal—a first torsion frequency above 22 Hz—knowing that everything else would fall into place. I make all this sound easy and planned, but it wasn't. Nobody had achieved what we were attempting to do. We thought it was possible, but we could never be sure. In the end, it took many months of iterative activity to get just this one critical aspect of the design right.

When the structure was finally designed, we could move forward. We then put the entire car together as a wood, metal, and styrofoam mock-up for Chevrolet management's review. The powertrain, backbone and its rail structure, suspension with its tires and wheels, seating, and other key features were brought together in this first mock-up. We hadn't thought about where to locate the 20 gallon fuel tank at all, and we ended up plunking it on top of the structure behind the seats. Finally, we put the spare tire in an imaginary well behind the rear suspension.

Chevrolet marketing looked this all over very carefully, and Fred Gallash suggested that we find another location for the fuel tank—maybe

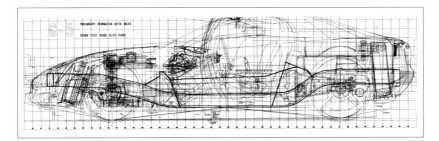

This side view drawing of the C5 Corvette dates from July 1992, before the spare tire was eliminated and the fuel tanks were moved to the rear transition structure.
Dave McLellan Archives

ALL CORVETTES ARE RED—REALLY?

Soon after we started on this latest Corvette, writer Jim Schefter talked Bob Stempel, then President of GM, into letting him become a "fly on the wall" at Corvette, so he could write a book about GM's new car-development process. Jim expected to be in and out, and have the book in short order—two to three years at most. But, Jim was forced to survive on his publisher's advance for six long years, because we delayed the car for three years before we even placed the project into the four-phase process that would take it to production.

As a fly on the wall, Jim never understood what he was looking at. It appeared to him that we were floundering, when we were actually working hard, behind closed doors in Chevrolet R&D, to define the critical attributes that would make the next Corvette a successful convertible platform. Jim did see the car finally starting through the four-phase process, and he saw the success and the accolades that it ultimately received. But, not having understood the initial design stages, he wrote about the first three years with disdain. He completely missed the brilliant crew that actually designed the car and laid the foundation for its ultimate success as a new paradigm in technical design.

GM, itself, also did this brilliant team a disservice by not recognizing and celebrating its accomplishments. I'm not even sure that the team who finally executed the car understood how much work had gone into the design that had been handed to them.

inside the rear transition structure. He wanted the trunk cleared out so it could hold two sets of golf clubs. This turned out to be an excellent suggestion, which we executed by locating separate smaller fuel tanks inside each rear transition structure.

We were ready to completely eliminate the spare tire but Chevrolet was reluctant to confront their customers with just a run-flat tire and no place for a spare. In the end, Chevrolet bought the extended mobility tire (EMT) concept developed by Goodyear. Tests proved to them that the stiffer sidewall of this tire, and its elliptical bead, made it possible to run the tire at speed and even on a slalom course with no air.

CHANGING OF THE GUARD

I retired officially as Corvette Engineering Director on August 31, 1992, which was the last possible day in my early retirement window. I agreed to continue to the end of the year to give an orderly transition to my, as yet unnamed, successor. There were two logical candidates from within the Corvette organization, either one of whom would have been an excellent choice: John Heinricy and Earl Werner. But, that was not to be. Management went outside the organization, and chose Dave Hill of Cadillac. Dave was well respected at Cadillac and had been the chief engineer of the Allante program with PininFarina.

By the end of 1992, we had defined the critical packaging attributes of the car and worked out the structural solutions. Computer analysis of the structure showed that we had gotten it right. We had a design that—amazingly—would meet all of our requirements simultaneously.

In early 1993, Chevrolet contributed enough money to build a structural backbone concept car to validate our design. Jon Moss, who built most of GM's show cars, built this car by modifying a C4 for wheelbase, powertrain, and structure. Management was amazed that a convertible Corvette could be easy to enter, roomy, and solid-feeling. We now had their enthusiastic support to move forward.

Engineering soon got the approval to move the program formally into the four-phase process that was now required for every new GM car pro-

gram. If the production team followed the road map, and they did, the car would be a complete success. A powerful, fast, structurally-solid, lightweight, V-8-powered convertible with excellent accommodations for two was the result.

BUILDING THE C5

Corvette's Bowling Green, Kentucky, assembly plant is where the car comes together. But first, the uni-frame side-rail is hydroformed in Michigan. The tubes are bent in preparation for being hydroformed to their

In early 1993, Chevrolet contributed enough money to build a structural backbone proof-of-concept car to validate our design.

National Corvette Museum

final shape. The bent tube is then placed in a strong, rigid tool cavity, the ends of the tube are sealed, and the tube is filled with water. At an internal pressure of 10,000psi, the water expands and shapes the steel tube as if it were putty to conform to the shape of the tool cavity.

At Bowling Green, the side rails, central tunnel (not closed on the bottom so I wouldn't call it a backbone, yet), its transition structures, and the front and rear cross-members are all welded together to form the uniframe. The frame is then chemically cleaned and dip-painted, to prevent corrosion and for bonded panel adhesion.

Using lasers, the welded steel uni-frame is then precision-measured at hundreds of control locations. This frame is the foundation building block for the entire car and it is crucial for every part to fit precisely with all of the other parts of the Corvette. To make these dimensional measurements, the uni-frame is pinned in a fixture which uses the frame's primary reference gauge holes as guides. A computer program records the data and compares actual readings to what the specifications should be. This determines if the uni-frame is within the required tolerance. If it is correct, the frame is then sent on its way to be built into a Corvette. The computer data is also used to plot dimensional trends, so the engineers can adjust the manufacturing process to produce a totally consistent product.

Next, door rings and the composite floors are bonded into place on the uni-frame. The entire front of the dash, complete with the windshield frame, is mounted to the uni-frame and bolted in place. The windshield frame is the starting point for all of the exterior panel fits. If it is misaligned, nothing that is put in afterwards will fit or seal properly.

The plastic body panels are primed and painted separately from the rest of the car. They are hung on racks in their ultimate car positions. They are dusted and thoroughly cleaned with deionized water, to eliminate any static charge that could otherwise bring contaminants into the sealed and pressurized paint shop. The paint is then applied by robots, which have been programmed to deliver a uniform quantity of paint to all surfaces, whether they are hard to reach or not. After painting, inspection, and any repairs are made, the painted panels are disbursed to the appropriate stations along the assembly line, where they are mounted and bolted in place.

The chassis and powertrain have their own mini-assembly line where the suspension and subframes are brought together. The powertrain, consisting of engine, exhaust, backbone and transaxle is assembled and added to the chassis. Even though there is no frame to act as a carrier, the front and rear suspensions and powertrain are fixed together in their final positions. The brake system is added, minus its brake pedal assembly, which is carried with the body.

At this point, all of the modular assemblages are brought together into a whole Corvette. When the car is complete, it is driven off the assembly line to have its front and rear suspensions aligned. In the next step, the car is driven on a dynamometer, where it sees speeds up to 70 mph and all driving functions are checked, including brake performance. Once the headlights are aimed, the car is washed and made ready for its final finessing and a white-glove inspection.

Finally, the Corvettes are delivered to the customer by Chevrolet dealers. Customers aren't allowed to pick up their new Corvettes directly from the factory, though for a nominal charge they can pick it up right across the street at the Corvette Museum in Bowling Green.

The Corvette Museum in Bowling Green, Kentucky, right across from the assembly plant, was the dream of Dan Gayle.

National Corvette Museum

THE FINISHED PRODUCT

What do I think of the C5 Corvette? The C5 is the sum total of everything we had learned about doing a great Corvette. Even in its first form as a 345 net hp sports car, it received rave reviews and met customer expectations to the tune of being a yearly sellout.

The Corvette has achieved the structural stiffness and passenger roominess we set out to achieve. The handling and performance are exemplary. If anything, the control efforts are too light and the engine intrudes too little. This efficiency is something even I would vote for when I'm just motoring down the road. But for a sports car, I would opt for firmness of control, driving precision, and for the intrusion of the engine at high revs and full power. Given the choice, I would give the car a dual personality, mating the more aggressive Z06 with the standard car. The car really needs a visceral "come alive" mode when you want to drive it hard.

SOME THOUGHTS ON THE CORVETTE'S FUTURE

Some things in the Corvette world are predictable. More power will likely sell more cars. The Generation III small block is an excellent base from which to move forward. We now know that 405 hp is possible with a naturally-aspirated small block. The Eaton supercharger, with intercooling, has given the Jaguar 4.0-liter V-8 almost 400 hp. There should be a similar 570 hp opportunity for a supercharged and intercooled 5.7-liter Corvette. When we were in the throes of making the decision to cancel the LT5 engine, supercharging the small block was Roy Midgley's suggested solution to more power. Conversely, a naturally-aspirated 7.4-liter Gen III based on the C5-R block and head should produce 525 net hp.

SHARING TECHNOLOGY WITHIN GM

As of the editorial closing of this book, a Cadillac-nameplate two-passenger car based on the Corvette C5 platform is a reality. On the show circuit it was called the "Evoq." On the market it will be called the Cadillac XLR and it will be built on a platform called the C6. This car will use a north-south version of the Northstar engine. The four-valve four-cam Northstar engine is physically bigger and heavier than the LT5 engine, though it produces less power than the smaller, lighter LS1 small block. The XLR will be heavier than the Corvette and, unless it is supercharged, it will be less powerful and, consequently, slower. This will be no competition for the Corvette although it has lots of Corvette enthusiasts annoyed.

In the past, Cadillac and Buick have both failed with their stand-alone two-passenger "sporty car" programs—Allante and Reatta. It makes sense for GM, and it protects the Corvette's very existence to put more product into the Bowling Green Assembly plant. I, frankly, don't understand why GM doesn't use Bowling Green for all its low-volume specialty-production models, including EV-1s and hybrids.

The existence of GM's full-size trucks also protects the Corvette. Without these trucks, the small-block V-8 engine and four-speed automatic transmissions would become much more expensive—if they remained available at all. Symbiotically, the truck group is the beneficiary of the R&D that produced the 345 net hp, fuel-efficient Generation III small block. In their first application of this engine, the trucks will use an all-iron LS1. Ultimately, as the trucks chase fuel efficiency, they will be introduced to the aluminum LS1.

In one very important way, Corvette's future is very solid. It has a worldwide fan club numbering in the millions. The only way to lose that support is for Chevrolet to screw something up, and I don't think they will. The market for sports cars is very small and is proliferated with numerous nameplates, all building excellent cars. The field is also littered

DRIVING FOR THE SHEER PLEASURE OF IT

Can driving be fun? Not where traffic is congested. It takes the open road to really enjoy a Corvette. The back roads of Kentucky, the sweeping roads of Wyoming, the autobahns of Germany, and the mountain roads of southern France beckon the Corvette driver. And the Corvette's limits are so high that it's nearly impossible to overdrive the car on public roadways. Would I argue for a return to sports cars like the MG TC where the driver can have fun, exhilaration, and even be confronted with a little fear without going very fast? Maybe for some people, but not for the king-of-the-hill Corvette driver.

If the Corvette enthusiast really wants to enjoy the car, and to experience it like the engineers intended, I would highly recommend driving school. The Chevrolet-sponsored Bragg-Smith Driving School in Las Vegas, Nevada, or the Justin Bell GT Motorsports Experience near Palm Beach, Florida, offer training on the racetrack behind the wheel of a C5. Other professional driving schools offer training in sedans or open-wheel cars. And, there are also local schools that let drivers bring their own cars. But, in my opinion, it would be more difficult for instructors to teach

when they aren't familliar with the car being driven. Any of these types of courses will provide a useful experience, but to be able to push the Corvette's active handling, ABS, and traction control to their limits is the real treat.

Dave McLellan at the Bragg-Smith Driving School, which uses Corvettes to teach high-performance and competition driving.
Dave McLellan Archives

with failed nameplates, many of which were good cars that never built a market. The Corvettes sold today will be spreading Corvette fever to potential buyers for the years 2020 to 2030.

CORVETTE MUSINGS OF A MARKET RESEARCHER
by Charlie Kenny

As I look back over the hundreds of brands and product categories we have worked on over the past 25 years, it strikes me that Corvette is one of the very few that stands out as exciting, memorable, and compelling. Just as we ask why consumers do what they do, here I ask myself why it is the case that Corvette is so compelling and exciting. Just what is it that makes Corvette so unique?

One reason that Corvette is so special, to a consultant, is the passion of the people who work on the car. It is the only automotive brand that we ever encountered where the engineers and design people are fanatically devoted to making the car as great as it could be. They endured some of the toughest times that any product team or any company has ever seen. Ultimately, the teams and the brand prevailed, despite lots of obstacles and even some internal opposition.

Another reason that consulting for Corvette is special is the way that the Corvette team involved us, the Right Brain team at Kenny & Associates, Inc. We were actually invited to participate in Corvette shakedown trips, called "caravans." So far as we could tell, and according to what some old hands shared with us, no consultant had ever been invited to participate. Naturally, we were touched by the honor, but had no idea what true excitement awaited us. Yes, it is almost impossible to believe that GM would ask us to join a 5,000 mile over-the-road trip that took preproduction 'Vettes on their first real outings. One thing that made this so exciting is that it was also the debut of the legendary ZR-1. Here I am, a guy who does not have any professional driving experience nor gasoline in his veins, as most of the engineers do, yet I was accepted as a valuable member of the team.

As I go back to the experience, in my mind's eye I am guiding this magnificent machine through its paces on a very rough two-lane highway in rural Arkansas—a road that time nearly forgot—and we are actually accelerating into a turn at 92 miles an hour—at the low end of the range

of second gear! This is a six-gear box, the first time it has been put through its paces! And four of the seven vehicles I am privileged to drive are the new ZR-1s, which are simply the fastest production cars in the world and could theoretically take me to 178 mph if the conditions were right—if we could find a road on which it was safe and if we could be sure that no other cars were in the area.

When in college, I had actually been in a Corvette that my friend pushed to 145 mph before I cried uncle, but that was just sheer speed. The experience on the caravan was a complete one. The chief powertrain engineer took me under his wing and gave me some driving tips, and I learned about the skill of driving a 'Vette, rather than just the thrill of the speed. I learned that the driving experience, especially with the manual six-speed gear box, is a different, but a far greater thrill than the raw speed I experienced when I was 25 years younger. So, I began to feel what the owners feel, and to appreciate why they are so fanatically devoted to this American automotive icon. Not surprisingly, all of this becomes an immeasurable help in analyzing all of the wonderful "stuff" that we get when we interview the owners.

Another reason for Corvette being so special is a rumor that Bob Bierley, at Chevrolet Product Planning, was arranging for us to interview the key executives at GM about Corvette, its role in the company, its role at Chevrolet and what its role should be in the future. I also had found out that there were those who were trying to phase this icon out—yes, that's right, some cost-minded folks actually wanted to put the "great American sports car" out to pasture.

So, there was some considerable trepidation and just a little fear inside me when it came time to interview Chairman Roger Smith. He was such an important person to interview, so I assigned myself to conduct the interview, something I had pretty much stopped doing because of the workload in our company. Roger's interview was remarkable in its own way, but the funniest thing is just how shocked and amazed many of our friends and colleagues inside the company were when they heard about the interview. We were surprised to find out that most of them had thought that Roger would be difficult, uncooperative, and maybe even would reject the interview. Of course, he was great—confounding his critics in the company yet again. This experience taught me one thing that has been invaluable—middle managers may think that they understand the top executives in the company, but in reality they almost never quite get there.

In subsequent years, I was able to get a great deal of traction with corporate executives by telling them that I had interviewed Roger Smith. Whenever they expressed doubts about how our trademark "right brain" methodology worked and how people would take to the idea of putting on the visualization mask and participating in the process, I would tell them about my time with Roger Smith and it truly would make a difference.

A fourth reason that Corvette became a special client for The Right Brain People® is the underlying psychological dynamic that moves people to buy the car in the first place. The owners are absolutely fascinating because their hot buttons are unique. These are a special group of people. They know that they are special because they have accomplished something in life that allows them to live their dream. All this makes them one of the most fascinating groups of people to meet and interview.

I often speak about Corvette in public meetings and conferences and can do so as a business-to-business project or as a consumer project because we had the chance to interview both segments of stakeholders. In fact, we also interviewed many of the writers who work for the automotive trade press, which really made it a special experience. The reason I speak about Corvette so often is that it is a wonderful example of how important understanding the intuitive "right brain" is to the marketer. And I am proud to have been associated with such a great brand, and with the people on the Corvette engineering team and those at Chevrolet who made it so great. I am especially proud of the contribution we made to saving the brand from the cost-cutters at GM.

As far as the future is concerned, I am sure that Corvette's best is ahead of it. The customer group is fanatically devoted to the car—to all of the versions: the old ones, the current ones and even the next one. They are like no other owner group in this way. We know this for sure because we have done our right-brain work on all segments of owners.

I am sure that the future can be even better for the brand. My only reason for not being entirely sanguine about the future is that the good folks in middle management at Chevrolet and at GM have never really understood how special the brand is. And, if they ever get their way—perhaps in a time of economic downturn—Corvette could still be threatened or at least might be watered down. And if that is done, the fanatic customer could be driven away and the brand would or could die. In my opinion, that would be a real shame. If anyone doubts that this is a possibility, just look at what has happened to Oldsmobile!! It, too, was a great brand at one time.

Understanding the Past to Build a Future

16

VERY FEW OF THE IDEAS THAT HAVE COME TOGETHER to make the Corvette what it is today are brand-new, although many of them are executed in unique and innovative ways. In fact, many of the engineering principles used in the C5 date back to the earliest days of the twentieth century. By the time Mercedes-Benz built its all-conquering W.125 Grand Prix cars in 1937, many of the basic design fundamentals we used in conceiving the C5 Corvette had already been brought together. The Mercedes employed a powerful eight-cylinder engine driving the rear wheels. That engine was mounted in the most rigid chassis that contemporary technology allowed, and the wheels were suspended in such a way that they were kept as close to upright as possible at all times, while also providing extensive suspension travel. Unlike other cars of the period, the chassis was strong and rigid, while the springs were soft. The W.125 was essentially an all-out competition car, and it embodied so much of what makes a superlative sports car today. What's more, the blistering performance—obtaining almost 200 mph in road-racing form—provided speeds remarkably close to the top speed of the modern C5 Corvette. However, the W.125 had been executed using the technology available at the time, which meant that the engine was a supercharged straight-eight (instead of a V-8) and the rear suspension was of the de Dion type (instead of fully-independent by transverse leaf spring), but the goals were still incredibly similar.

When Mercedes-Benz revisited sports and racing cars in the 1950s, the German company applied the same design philosophy of a rigid chassis with a supple well-damped suspension. Sports car makers in Europe, particularly in Great Britain, still allowed the chassis and body to flex

The Mercedes W.125—driven by Rudolph Caracciola in the Swiss Grand Prix at Bern July 22, 1937—pointed the way for all subsequent front-engined sports cars to this day. DaimlerChrysler AG

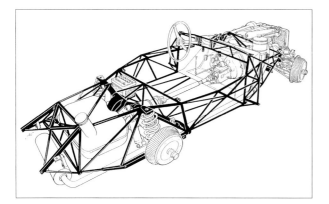

Top: The Mercedes 300SL space frame. Triangulation is the key to this stiff, yet light space frame.
DaimlerChrysler AG

Bottom: Mercedes-Benz continued to define the modern front-engined sports car with its racing successes with the 300SL—at LeMans in 1952—and later with the W.196 Grand Prix car and its sports car derivative, the 300SLR.
DaimlerChrysler AG

on a stiff under-damped suspension with little travel, and it was this model that the first Corvette followed. As a result, it neither handled particularly well nor offered its occupants a comfortable ride. But it was the start of a long journey through which the Chevrolet Corvette made gradual but steady progress.

THE MODERN SPORTS CAR

The first Corvettes fell far short of the definition that Mercedes had evolved for a sports car, and fell short of many other contemporary 1950s definitions as well. By the Stingray era, the Corvette was a sports car in every sense, and in the succeeding years it has contributed seriously to the modern definition of a what a sports car should be.

Three long-term players in the sports car market have helped define the contemporary sports car—Porsche, Ferrari, and Corvette. Porsche evolved its unique 911, and also contributed to the front-engine, rear-drive sports car with the 928 and 944. Porsche has now ended production of its front-engine cars and has returned to its roots by revitalizing the 911. The mid-engine Boxster is a further extension of this strategy. Ferrari is known for its magnificent V-8 and V-12 sports cars. It has now replaced its top-of-the-line road car, the mid-engine Testarossa, with the V-12-powered front-engine 550 Marenello, which has recaptured the spirit of the Ferrari road cars of the 1950s and 1960s. Ferraris make no pretense of being affordable and, consequently, have more freedom and flexibility to play at the top end of the market.

In the 50 years of the Corvette, sports car buyers' expectations for performance have changed little, however, owners have come to expect a much higher level of comfort and convenience. Even air-conditioning is a part of the highest-performance Ferrari models. Power steering and power brakes, anti-lock brakes, and traction and yaw control have all been accepted as important to good car control and the active safety of the sports car. Today, even sports cars enjoy the enhanced passive safety of both driver and passenger air bags.

The availability of wind tunnels, combined with high-speed race car development, has shaped the modern sports car to be much more aerodynamically stable. It has also made it possible to introduce deployable downforce devices that can make sports cars more stable at high speeds and provide substantial downforce in cornering.

Computer control of engine functions has brought performance back big time. What is amazing is the superb transient power and fuel economy—and that all this has been accomplished while meeting emission requirements. Today it is practical to give the sports car driver W.125 performance with a chassis that can safely manage this level of power.

The 550 Marenello—front-engined with a V-12—is a modern and elegant iteration of the classic Ferrari road car.

Photo by Harold Pace

WHAT IS THE CORVETTE?

The Corvette is just as much a dream car as it is a sports car. From the beginning, it was the personal expression of the designers and the engineers who created and built it. While the Corvette has evolved over these first 50 years, and changed with the times, it is still first and foremost a car that represents the vision of its creators.

The first Corvette missed the mark in some crucial ways that almost caused its demise. However, its creators persevered. They recognized and corrected their errors, and went on to produce increasingly better Corvettes with each subsequent iteration.

Many sports cars are the personal expressions of their makers. There are also many sports cars that have faded from the marketplace, or have never flirted with success. Although the car may embody its maker's best ideas and intentions, it also has to be a car that customers want to buy. This has been the legacy of the Corvette. Customers have bought into the dream to the tune of well over a million Corvettes in those first 50 years. These customers bought into the original vision of the Corvette as a front-engine, rear-drive, V-8-powered sports car. They did not buy Duntov, Mitchell, and Cole's vision of the Corvette as a mid-engine V-8 or Wankel-powered car.

Had the Wankel engine worked better, if it had not had technical difficulties in meeting emissions and fuel economy standards, and if Ed Cole—the Wankel's advocate—had not retired in 1975, we might be

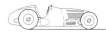

driving mid-engine rotary-powered Corvettes today. The visionaries of the Corvette were ready to make radical changes happen by fiat. There is no telling how readily the Corvette market would have accepted a mid-engine Corvette. Having talked extensively with Corvette owners and enthusiasts, I think the mid-engine car would probably have been accepted, but there are strong detractors among Corvette loyalists. In the end, the mid-engined layout probably would not have substantially increased Corvette sales. Today, even with the excellent Honda Acura NSX and a range of mid-engine Ferrari models, there seems to be no great aspiration among Corvette enthusiasts for a mid-engine sports car.

How did such a strong Corvette loyalty develop? Understanding this is crucial to a successful Corvette future. We know that enthusiasm for the Corvette starts at a young age, usually with someone's first significant emotional interaction with the Corvette. Yet it may take a decade or two for these enthusiasts to achieve Corvette ownership. Thus it is necessary for any new Corvette to maintain a conservative tie to its past. A strong resemblance between the Corvette that customers ultimately buy and the Corvette that first fueled their dreams is an important continuity link.

The median age of the buyer of a new Corvette is about 38 years old. That means that the person who will become the median buyer ten years from now is 28 years old today, and the median buyer of the Corvette of 20 years from now is currently 18 years old. The point is that the next three decades of Corvette buyers are already in this world. One can reasonably predict from a familiarity with their age groups what kinds of cars they are going to want when their turn comes.

If these future buyers are anything like today's Corvette owner, they will desire a sports car that promises excitement, speed, and power—in a styling package that complements the owner's lifestyle. If they're not concerned with these issues or have a different lifestyle, they're probably not Corvette intenders.

Today's Corvette buyer falls into the first of the computer literate generations. Like it or not, the current Corvette is powered and shaped by powerful digital computers. Looking forward, computers will be even more powerful, and they will be used to make the car more capable and more reliable. Future generations of Corvette buyers will have their lives shaped by computers and will be even more computer literate. Automotive computers will be increasingly interactive as well, and will give the driver the opportunity to customize the car in ways that we only dimly envision today.

The current regulatory environment still makes possible the high-powered V-8 sports car. However, as we saw in the late 1970s and early 1980s, regulation can force engineers to restrategize if impending legal requirements are not properly anticipated. It's also possible that powerful automobiles may become unfashionable or be seen as antisocial.

The safe course for Chevrolet to follow into this future is to first give their Corvette customers what they want, recognizing that it is risky to get too far ahead of the customer or to take the customers off in a direction in which they may not want to go. In doing so, Chevrolet can continue to keep the Corvette an excellent sports car value. The company should be able to improve the performance of the car and, as the technology evolves, continue to infuse the car with useful computer-controlled systems.

But is this enough? At what point should Chevrolet reinvigorate the designers and engineers to create a new generation of Corvette that represents not a finely-tuned formula, but instead takes us back to the Corvette's roots, where the designers and engineers, acting as visionaries, gave the customer a car that was not only unexpected, but exceptional?

At least for the short term, Chevrolet is likely to pursue a conservative course for developing the Corvette. I don't see a strong downside to this strategy, given that the current mid-engine sports cars in the marketplace are only marginally successful, and that the Corvette is broadly popular in its front mid-engine V-8 configuration. The most important thing that Chevrolet can do is to continue to improve the Corvette incrementally and, through style changes and performance enhancements, give future buyers the rationale for buying a new Corvette.

Chevrolet is using market research to ask its customers what they want and then giving it to them. While I agree that it is important to understand what the customer wants, Chevrolet also needs to recognize, with a car like the Corvette, that it was originally the vision of individuals like Mitchell, Cole, Duntov, and myself that defined what customers would find appealing. And, developing a product strategy around the last customer without a strong vision of the future could put them in a time trap of their own making. GM's success in the 1950s and 1960s, when they enjoyed as much as 55 percent market share in passenger cars, did not prepare them for the onslaught of competition in the 1980s and 1990s, which collapsed GM's market share to less than 30 percent. As difficult as it is to predict the future, companies that rest on their laurels and try to keep doing what they have always done best are leaving themselves open to rude awakenings.

The 1963 Corvette was almost too successful as a vision for the future of the Corvette. It directly defined the car through 1982. Even the C4 and C5 generations of Corvettes are simply an extension of the extraordinary 1963 car.

As I have noted, Duntov moved on with his vision for the Corvette, and by 1975, when he retired, he was convinced that the mid-engine Corvette was the right next step. Duntov, however, did not bring the Corvette marketplace with him, in spite of a great deal of press hype and publicity for mid-engine Corvettes. Nor was he able to convince Chevrolet that a mid-engine Corvette would sell.

The failure of the Wankel engine doomed the mid-engine Corvette, and put the front-engine rear-drive car back on center stage. The 1984 car gave the engine new life that would carry it forward for another decade. The C5 generation Corvette, although largely new in hardware detail, carried this same basic theme forward for yet another decade.

WHAT LIES AHEAD?

I see two big dangers ahead. The first is that the market for the sports car seems to be getting increasingly smaller. Although the Corvette can generate a profit at a volume of 25,000 units per year, this is only half of what the Corvette market was a little over a decade ago. The current Corvette's competition is experiencing the same situation, and the fragmentation of the market leaves each of the competitors with an ever smaller base from which to develop a profitable product line.

Porsche, the only other long-term player in the market, has been mauled over the last decade by competition, starting with Nissan. Porsche responded to the Japanese competition by moving upmarket in price, which made their existing owners happy as the value of their cars escalated with the price of the new cars. Unfortunately, this strategy collapsed Porsche's volume base and left it with a vastly diminished market. Porsche is finally making a comeback "down market" with the Boxster and—at ethereal prices—with the new 911. Corvette enjoys a market that is pretty much its own, giving extraordinary performance for the dollar.

Nissan and Mazda were originally situated below the Corvette in price and performance. Their strategies to compete with the Corvette have so far failed. Each company also has major corporate profitability problems that make it questionable as to whether they will even continue in the sports car market. With the NSX priced at Corvette ZR-1 prices, Acura

has seen a market trend similar to what happened with the ZR-1: an initially high demand followed by a much lower replacement sales rate.

Nobody really understands why the market for sports cars is so small and getting smaller at a time when the total market for new cars is increasing. My guess is that the many excellent sports sedans have taken a significant bite out of the sports car market. Many of these cars are gratifying to drive and offer performance equal to most people's expectations for sports cars. Except for the cachet of driving a sports car, these sports sedans offer most of the attributes that would-be sports car buyers desire, while providing a more practical and professional image. I also suspect that because, as sports car makers, we have settled into predictable middle age, we haven't been giving strong visceral incentives to buy the next new sports car. Here is where finding and capturing the right vision for the future is so critical to separating the market for sports cars from that for sports sedans. Potential customers must be given the incentive to spend their money on a true sports car.

Thanks to its large and loyal following, Corvette is somewhat protected from the short-term effects of a competitive sports car entry into its market. Nevertheless, if an exciting and stylish new sports car were to come to market, the newcomer could cause a great deal of mischief for all of the market's current players. And, if a new sports car were to take the market by storm, it would probably take a year or two for Chevrolet to assess that it was a real threat and that the company needed to react. Putting a response into the planning cycle adds another year, and then, even with quick design response, it would take another two years to bring the new product to market. In short, it would take four to five years to have a new car in place, in answer to a competitive threat. This long response time applies primarily to the architecture of the car. Much less time is required to ponder the installation of existing alternative engines, computer controlled chassis systems, and new tire configurations.

Defining the next Corvette by asking current owners what they like needs lots of careful interpretation. For example, Chevrolet has asked Corvette owners about their interest in racing. Too often the answer is, "I'm not interested in racing," which leaves Chevrolet's marketers confused. Along with this they've been told that many owners don't drive their cars aggressively, so they begin to wonder why Chevrolet is going to all the trouble of producing an ultra-high-performance sports car. If followed too closely, this logic might lead to the conclusion that Chevrolet doesn't need to give Corvette owners so much power.

This is a serious misreading of what the Corvette is all about. When an owner is as ego-involved with a car as sports car owners are, the car needs to be recognized as "King of the Hill." A Corvette with no performance and just a pretty face would soon be seen as a joke. I don't think this is what Corvette people want.

While any car company should certainly listen to their customers, they also have to understand what made a car great in the first place and attracted such a following. To the degree that the attributes that attract customers to the Corvette are technology-driven, asking customers what they want in their next Corvette is expecting them to be fortune tellers. It is highly unlikely that they could know what is technologically possible in the future. It is the job of the designers and engineers who shape the Corvette to know that. By their training and expertise, they are in the best position to bring what is possible to reality. Thus, I would argue that the engineers and designers working on the next Corvette need to be encouraged to develop their vision of the Corvette's future and hope that they are given the opportunity to make that vision a reality.

Where the engine is located may or may not be important to this future vision. What is important is that the designers, engineers, and planners understand what a sports car is, where the sports car has come from, and what has built the bond between the Corvette and its owners. With this knowledge, not as millstones around their necks but as guideposts, the designers and engineers can shape the future and bring it to reality for the next generation of Corvette enthusiasts.

THE IDEAL SPORTS CAR

Before we leap into the future, let me bring to mind automotive historian and writer Ralph Stein's prediction for an ideal sports car that was written in 1952, contemporaneously with the first Corvette. The best of the modern sports cars, including the Corvette, have pushed past anything Stein even dreamed of, in terms of performance, active safety (handling), and passive safety.

Acceleration and Top Speed Comparison

	Stein's Ideal Sports Car	1984 Corvette	ZR-1	LT4 (1996)	C5	C5/Z06
0–60 mph	< 6 sec.	6.9 sec.	4.3 sec.	4.7 sec.	4.5 sec.	4.0 sec.
1/4 mile	12–14 sec.	15.4 sec.	12.8 sec.	13.4 sec.	13.2 sec.	12.6 sec.
Top Speed	> 150 mph	142 mph	182 mph	171 mph	175 mph	171 mph

The Corvette's Future 17

THIS CHAPTER IS MY OPPORTUNITY to share my vision for the future of the Corvette. I will connect the Corvette with the rest of General Motor's future product line and argue that there is, or should be, a symbiotic relationship between the Corvette and GM. The Corvette is not just another product line; it is an opportunity for GM to work out its future technological and manufacturing strategies at low volume before committing its entire manufacturing base.

Today GM is struggling. It continues to lose market share as its products enjoy only mixed success. With few exceptions, and the Corvette is one of them, GM is not able to command a premium for its products. Premium prices exist because a manufacturer is producing a product that is so good that buyers are willing to pay extra for that product over its competitors. If GM is ever to learn how to extract a premium from the marketplace, it will, among other things, need to study the success story of its own Corvette.

Looking to the future, GM—along with the rest of the automotive industry—is faced with regulatory demands and market pressures that will inspire its engineers to produce technological miracles. Emissions could be driven to nearly zero, and fuel economy could be pushed to 80 mpg and beyond. How does GM protect its most profitable market segments in the face of this kind of future? Both luxury passenger cars and light trucks are vulnerable. And the pressure to make engines more efficient could too easily drive the engineers into solutions that might jeopardize the value of these vehicles to their customers. GM has been there before.

If this were not enough, the manufacture of cars and trucks is being reinvented. Car manufacture is becoming modular, and the space required to assemble a vehicle has been dramatically reduced. From top to bottom, the workforce is being challenged to work harder and smarter. Overall, this is not a great situation to be in for a company like GM, which is faced

with shrinking markets and old labor-intensive manufacturing and assembly plants.

The entire industry, including GM, has been pouring R&D energy (read dollars) into its product, technology, and manufacturing future. The PNGV (Partnership for a New Generation Vehicle) cooperation between the federal government and the domestic automobile industry is a visible example. This program has produced 80-mpg demonstration vehicles from each of the "Big Three." These five-passenger sedan concept cars are technological marvels with diesel-electric hybrid powertrains, ultra-slick aerodynamics, and exotic structures. This was all done to achieve the extraordinary efficiency and low weight needed to meet the fuel economy goal of using only 1.25 gallons of fuel per 100 miles, while also meeting today's standards for crash integrity. These cars are about as far from current manufacturing experience as Mars is from Venus.

DEVELOPING THE CORVETTE INCREMENTALLY

The Corvette presents GM with the unique opportunity to take several of the new ultra-efficient technologies out of the laboratory and use them to drive down their manufacturing process and cost learning curves. Having developed these technologies and their capable manufacturing delivery systems, GM is far better protected to meet future regulatory and market demands.

We also need to factor into our discussion the Cadillac Evoq—to enter production as the 2003 Cadillac XLR—which will be built on the next-generation Corvette platform. At its much higher price and lower volume, it will have to be a technological marvel to succeed at all. It could well be GM's first car with which to try new technologies and processes, although as a derivative of the Corvette it may not stand alone very well.

The first real attempt, by Chevrolet R&D, to develop a broad plan for the Corvette's future was brought to management in 1964. However, this plan made no attempt to connect the Corvette with Chevrolet or GM's future. It did lay out the broad-brush possibilities for the Corvette by itself. The plan proposed possibilities that ranged from carrying forward the then all-new 1963 Sting Ray, to an array of extraordinary ideas that included various mid-engine sports and racing cars. Zora Arkus-Duntov's hand was clearly visible in all of these proposals.

Through hindsight, we know that Chevrolet chose the least daring of the solutions, though the company did play with the mid-engine car for the next decade before eventually discarding it. The backbone front-

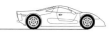

engine car, one of the intermediate proposals that would have made a better convertible, was not pursued until it was reinvented 25 years later and made practical for the current C5.

Through all this "future Corvette" discussion, I don't believe that the basic pattern for the Corvette will change: It will always be a two-passenger, V-8-powered vehicle. It should be powerful, lightweight, and structurally stiff, and it should give its passengers adequate space and reasonable entry. Everything else is negotiable.

With the C5, Corvette has the architecture to take the car to 500 hp with a curb weight of 3,000 lbs. This would be an extraordinary sports car in its own right. Its use of hydroformed tubular structure, with possible future variants in aluminum and the incremental application of magnesium, will serve GM well as the company looks to reduce the weight of passenger cars and trucks. Certified for emissions, the engine could immediately give trucks a new top-power option. There is hardly any risk in reaching for the 500-hp, 3,000-lb solution, however, the envelope can be pushed much further. In order to do this, GM needs to correctly evaluate its future regulatory and technology risks, and plan a strategy around them to avoid any pitfalls.

LESSONS LEARNED FROM THE MOSLER MT900

How far can GM push the Corvette without having to commit to major technological invention? With only development, the 500-hp, 2,500-lb Corvette is clearly possible. I know, because I've driven it. This level of power to weight would propel the Corvette to 60 mph in 3.0 seconds, with a quarter-mile time of 11.0 seconds at over 130 mph. The top speed for this Corvette projectile is more than 200 mph.

The car that is the basis for this extraordinary performance is the Mosler MT900. The "M" is for car builder Warren Mosler; "T" is for Rod Trenne, the car's designer, and "900" is the expected weight of the racing version in kilograms (900 kg equals 1,980 lbs). This car starts with the aluminum Corvette engine and suspension, and replaces the backbone structure with a composite honeycomb tub and tubular subframes in the front and rear that distributes the load and ties the front and rear suspensions into the honeycomb structure. This honeycomb structure has its counterpart in the almost indestructible tub structures of Formula 1 race cars that form the driver's compartment and tie the front suspension and engine compartments together structurally. They are light, stiff, and strong and protect the driver in a crash.

The Mosler MT900 is currently being developed as a road car.
Morrison-Mosler

The CAD layout and packaging of the MT900 under the skins.
Courtesy Rod Trenne, MT 900 Designer

To bring this level of performance to the Corvette is a technological and manufacturing challenge. It's certainly not the lazy route, but it could have real payoff for the corporation and give the Corvette a future that would be a clear winner over any of its competitors. In the process, it would set a new standard for even exotic sports cars. And 500 horsepower is not the upper limit; it's a step along the way, just as 2,500 pounds is an achievable step, but not the end.

The MT900 is a sleek and radical mid-engine car, but I don't want to get hung up in what it looks like and where its engine is located—at least not yet. What's important is the innovative use of slabs of preformed honeycomb composite and the way they pull the car together. These slabs are the building blocks of a structural solution. They are made in a linear manufacturing process that can have a high degree of automation, analogous to producing sheets of steel in a rolling mill. Composite honeycomb slabs can be made from a variety of materials, selected for their individual contribution to the requirements of the matrix. They typically have skins of woven graphite, Kevlar, or fiberglass. They may also have metal skins of aluminum or even steel. The honeycomb separator is typically paper or aluminum. The entire assemblage is impregnated and bonded together with epoxy resin.

Fundamentally, car bodies weigh what they do because the steel sheet they are made from is going along for the ride. Steel sheet can only be rolled, stretched, formed, and welded to a minimum of about

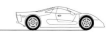

0.03 in. thickness. If it is much thinner, the sheet tears in forming and doesn't behave well, denting and buckling as though it were paper.

Honeycomb structures take their name from the structures that bees make. The honeycomb concept has also been developed as a structural solution for aircraft, which have the problem of producing very large, lightweight, stiff structures. A honeycomb core separates two surface sheets, giving the structure the ability to support bending loads. The honeycomb core supports the ultra-thin skins every eighth of an inch, which stabilizes an otherwise flexible sheet, allowing the skin to be very thin without buckling.

The rear subframe of the MT900 carries the engine and rear suspension loads to the honeycomb structure.
Morrison-Mosler

Advance composite aircraft and Formula 1 race cars use very complex shapes for their honeycomb structures. The key to applying this technology to a limited-production automobile is to avoid complex and labor-intensive shapes. As a result, intersecting flat composite plates are used to form the honeycomb structure. In the MT900, these plates are cut, tabbed for precise location, and bonded together to form the car's structure.

Major load-point attachments are accomplished with metal spools and local reinforcement of the structure. Due to their more complex shapes, the roof, doors, hoods, and other attached surface panels are much more complicated to build.

Honeycomb composite construction also brings with it the mass-efficient solution to crash management. Aluminum honeycomb blocks of somewhat higher density (known by the trade name Hexel) are used in race cars for crash attenuation.

APPLYING THESE LESSONS TO THE CORVETTE

Does the honeycomb composite structured Corvette have to be mid-engined? While that's the solution that has been demonstrated, it's probably not a requirement. But, as we saw in a number of engineering studies leading up to the C5, running the powertrain from one end of the car to the other through the passenger compartment compromises structural efficiency. The more the structure has to compete with the powertrain, the less efficient it is going to be.

Without a careful design study, one can only make an educated guess that the front-engine rear-drive solution, even in a honeycomb composite, is going to be 100 lbs heavier than a mid-engine version. This four per-

cent weight advantage of the mid-engine architecture is worth taking to the bank because the design is made up of many such solutions strung together. As a result, you need to have a powerful reason to reject any one of them. The corporation's need for developing a capable and cost-competitive ultra-light body is satisfied no matter where the engine is located.

As I discussed previously, the transverse mid-engine Corvette layout is capable of accommodating all-wheel drive. It would be nice to include this as an option in a future Corvette scenario that pushes horsepower well beyond the 500 mark.

MORE POWER FOR THE GENERAL

The engine is a prime case of a potential symbiosis between Corvette and corporate needs. In this case it is the light-duty trucks which need powerful, lightweight, yet fuel-efficient engines. Trucks are configured to carry a payload that approaches half the curb weight of the vehicle. If the payload takes the form of a trailer, the load can equal the weight of the truck. Consequently, trucks need a lot more engine, and have traditionally been the prime users of the Chevrolet big block.

The full-size-truck V-8 engine has already benefited enormously from the development of the Generation III, LS1 small-block engine. Variants of this engine are finding their way into more and more full-size-truck applications and can be expected to become the V-8 engine of record for all full-size trucks.

The Z06 Corvette's LS6 engine is already generating 405 hp and 400 ft-lb of torque. Race engine builders are now boring and stroking the 5.7 liter engine to as much as 7.4 liters (4.15 in. bore x 4.15 in. stroke). This much bore increase can only be accomplished by eliminating the iron liners and siamesing the aluminum bores in a unique case casting. The aluminum bores are treated to the same Nikasil wear-resistant coating that was used on the LT5's aluminum liners. The result is a reliable 650 hp engine that is winning races. If engine breathing is also scaled up by 130 percent, the larger engine will produce over 500 hp, in emission-legal street form. This would be a great truck engine, with both the power and torque to rival any big block. It is truly a "rat motor" in "mouse motor" clothes! With proper attention to breathing and the integrity needed to rev past 7,500 rpm, this would also be a great motor for future Corvette road cars.

Adding technology to this basic engine—particularly individual cylinder shutoff and the variable valve timing accomplished with electromagnetic valve-actuation—would give the engine improved fuel

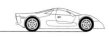

economy. Electromagnetic valve actuation, if it can be stressed to meet the high-speed demands of the Corvette application, would increase breathing and, consequently, horsepower beyond the 500 hp solution. As much as 600 hp is a rational possibility from a normally-aspirated engine, although more power will require turbocharging or supercharging.

Turbocharging is the second reason for considering the mid-engine solution. The mid-ship engine compartment is not as constrained by over-the-hood sight lines and the steerable front wheels. There is also more room to deal with engine compartment ancillaries, such as multiple catalytic converters and intercoolers.

Weight distribution is the third reason for considering the mid-engine solution. As the car's power-to-weight ratio climbs, the more rearward weight distribution of the mid-engine layout (40 percent front, 60 percent rear) becomes a distinct advantage that significantly reduces the power increment available for a car that uses four-wheel drive. With 60 percent of the weight on the rear tires, plus the rearward weight transfer under acceleration due to the center of gravity height, the actual dynamic "weight" on the rear driving tires is about 75 percent. Four-wheel drive allows 100 percent of the car's weight to be used for traction. However, its weight penalty—two additional differentials, drive shafts, and wheel half shafts—can be as much as 10 percent of the weight of the car. This additional weight reduces the overall power of the car by 10 percent, which reduces the effective power advantage for all-wheel drive to only 15 percent. Although this is too much of a performance gain to ignore, the added complexity is a high price to pay.

TWIN TURBOS FOR THE C5

John Lingenfelter has developed a twin-turbo package for the current C5 motor. In its mild Stage I form it develops 550 hp; in its more radical Stage II iteration it develops a hefty 650 hp. Even in Stage II, the engine idles smoothly and is as tractable in traffic as is the naturally-aspirated Corvette. First-gear acceleration, although limited by traction, offers a brief rush once the driveline is linked up. With boost regulated to 8psi by its wastegate, the acceleration in second gear starts out smoothly but ends in extreme tire squawk, as the peaking horsepower tries to break the tires loose between 60 and 70 mph. Third and fourth gears are a rush, not unlike the acceleration of a jet airplane as it approaches its rotation and takeoff speed. Lingenfelter's Stage II tuning, applied to a 427cid version of the C5 engine, produces 725 hp.

Can a 2,500-lb Corvette handle 725 hp? The car's acceleration potential is ultimately defined by the driving tires' ability to transmit horsepower. This limiting horsepower increases linearly with speed. Assuming a 40/60-weight-distribution load transfer to the rear driving wheels under acceleration and a tire coefficient of friction of 1.1, the car would be capable of accelerating at almost 0.9 gs for a quarter mile.

If our car could sustain 0.9 gs for the entire quarter mile, it would cover the distance in 9.5 seconds and achieve a trap speed of 180 mph. Ignoring aerodynamic drag, this car would need 1,450 hp to sustain its 0.9 g acceleration to 180 mph, at which point the aerodynamic drag on the Corvette would absorb about 400 hp. Aerodynamic-induced downforce is useful until it starts to absorb the limiting horsepower. Since the tire-road interface is the limiting factor, an acceleration of 0.9 gs cannot be sustained at these high speeds. Terminal acceleration is probably limited to about 0.7 gs, lengthening the time and lowering the trap speed somewhat.

John Lingenfelter runs a Pro Stock truck in the NHRA drags. The truck weighs 2,300 lbs, produces 950 hp, and runs the quarter mile in 7.45 seconds at 180 mph. It gets a big boost at the bottom end of the run from its 18-in.-wide slicks that generate an initial acceleration of 3.5 gs.

Can the output of the 427 twin turbo be increased beyond 725 hp? The performance of a turbocharged engine is fundamentally limited by the

The graph at right indicates the horsepower required to accelerate a car weighing 2,800 pounds. It clearly shows that reducing weight is just as effective in improving acceleration as is increasing horsepower.

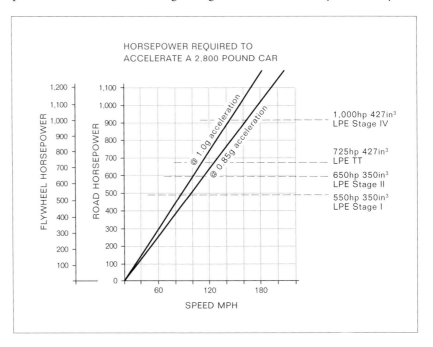

intake-charge heating that accompanies the turbo boost. The engine already uses a massive air-to-air intercooler in front of the radiator to cool the intake charge. The engine actually throws away much of the available turbo boost through the wastegates because of the limits imposed by charge temperature, octane demand, and the destructive detonation that occurs if the intake-charge pressure and the resulting charge temperature are increased any further. Lower the charge temperature and the boost pressure can be raised.

Modern electronic engine management includes direct detection of detonation and a controlled feedback loop around spark advance, which limits detonation to a barely detectable quantity. Use this in a modified form to control the wastegates and the boost can be raised without destroying the engine.

So, can the 725 hp 427 twin turbo do even more, and generate 1,000 hp? It can top this magic number if the charge is cooled sufficiently. This extraordinary charge cooling would only be needed for the six seconds of a 120-to-180 mph sprint. The additional transient cooling can be handled by an air-to-liquid-to-air heat exchanger, with precooled intermediate liquid being used to cool the intake charge during this short run. In fact, the capacity for this additional cooling is already on board, if the air-conditioning system is used to sub-cool the heat exchanger liquid. Managing such a system, with so many variables and the ever-lurking destructive forces of detonation and horsepower, require a totally computer-controlled approach. This is now a possibility, and I expect to see 1,000 horsepower available from Lingenfelter Performance Engineering sometime in the not too distant future.

HARNESSING BIG HORSEPOWER

The Corvette needs a transmission that can handle all the horses that Chevrolet and the aftermarket can throw at it. With the engine in the front, the current automatic and manual transmissions will suffice until they run out of torque capacity. With the engine behind the driver, Corvette would have to use a conventional automatic transmission as used in the transversely-mounted Northstar engine. This would not be an ideal solution, even though the car would be much lighter than other applications of this transmission, some of which weigh more than 4,000 lbs. This automatic transmission is heavy and bulky. Even though it is electronically controlled, manual shifting is accompanied by significant delay.

The light weight and consequent traction limit of the MT900 works in favor of being able to use existing automatic transmissions, even though the engine is transmitting considerably more horsepower. A far worse problem than transmitting power is the consequence of applying full power while the transmission is still shifting. This is the ultimate reason for automating the shifting process, whether starting with a manual or automatic transmission.

When we were exploring turbocharging, leading up to the LT5 engine program, we built several automatic-transmission V-8 turbo Corvettes. With about 500 hp on tap, these cars accelerated aggressively. With skilled drivers, the stock 700R4 automatic transmission transmitted this much torque without complaint. However, when we put inexperienced drivers in the car they burned up transmission after transmission until we figured out what they were doing. With the car stopped, the driver would step on the accelerator pedal and get an initial surge of turbo-boosted acceleration. The sudden surge would scare the driver into backing out of the accelerator, before immediately stepping on it again to resume acceleration. Easing off the throttle was a signal to the transmission that the driver wanted to upshift into a higher gear. But, while the transmission was executing this clutch-to-clutch shift, the engine was going back on boost and putting out 800 ft-lbs of torque, which was a level far beyond the capacity of the transmission clutches while slipping. The result was an instantly fried clutch.

When we did this work in the mid-1980s, we didn't have the advantage of electronic management we have today. Now, we can manage engine output, clutch actuation, and shifting to avoid destroying the system during the transient moments of a launch or a shift.

If the automatic transmission can be modified to achieve essentially instant shifting, I would use a paddle shift scheme such as has been applied in Formula 1 to provide a manual shift control option. However, if the shift delays cannot be made imperceptible to the driver (no automatic transmission has accomplished this so far), I would use a conventional manual transmission with automated controls.

There are now well-developed schemes to automate the manual transmission and clutch control functions. An automated manual transmission could replace the conventional automatic transmission and make the highest possible level of performance available in all Corvettes. A unique Corvette transmission would also make adapting an all-wheel-drive transfer case less costly.

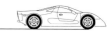
Why a paddle shift automated manual transmission? This is the only way to make the drivetrain able to survive 1,000 hp. With a manually-shifted transmission, it would be too easy for an overrevving downshift or application of full power before the drivetrain is hooked up, to cause grievous damage. On top of that, the conditions must be right: charge temperature, humidity, detonation, and so on. In the good old days, all the driver had for guidance was what we figuratively call "steam gauges." In a slow car, the driver has time to glance at the tachometer and the temperature or oil pressure gauges, but when the car is accelerating rapidly, the driver has no time to watch and manage gauges. This was certainly my experience driving the Lingenfelter Stage II C5 Corvette. As a passenger, I could watch the instruments over John's shoulder, but as a driver, my concentration was totally on controlling the car. At the end of a run I had no idea what the gauges had indicated.

CHASSIS ENGINEERING FOR THE CORVETTE SUPERCAR

I've now laid out the fundamentals of an extraordinary Corvette future—even making the Corvette an ultimate supercar in the process. I've done

GREAT CARS

What is a great car? It depends on the eye of the beholder. When buyers want a particular car so much that they are willing to pay a considerable premium over its "generic" competitor, something is going on. With the Corvette, we were always focused on meeting our customers' expectations. We didn't always succeed, but when we did we came very close to what I consider a great car.

In my mind, a great car starts as a vision that turns into a collaboration between styling, engineering, and manufacturing. The stylists contribute forms and lines that are a delight to the eye. By their organization of space and functional activities they make the car a pleasant and productive shape. When I climb into a strange car and find every function falling naturally to hand and operating as I would intuitively expect, I feel like I am in a space developed by the stylist working as an industrial designer. The engineer's contribution to the vehicle is to make the entire car work to perfection and to give it performance that exceeds expectations. Finally, a great car demands perfection in manufacture.

Under John Dinkel's leadership, Road & Track magazine ran an annual series on the "10 Best Cars in the World."

My boss at Chevrolet, Ken Baker, was planning to drive the magazine's top picks with all of his chief engineers in a test trip out of Phoenix. At the end of the drive, we would take a day to discuss what we had learned. I invited John Dinkel to join us for the wrap-up and to give us his insights into what made cars great. However, John instead talked about the process R&T used to select the ten best. John wasn't able to articulate exactly what made a great car but he could tell us that R&T used only its senior editors in its selection process. A couple of years later I encouraged Arv Mueller—CPC's (Chevrolet Pontiac Canada) engineering vice president—to follow up on this theme by commissioning a market research project with Charlie Kenny, which would help the engineers understand what made cars great in the eyes of the customers. The ultimate reward would have been customers who were delighted with their cars and GM would be able to sell more cars at greater profit margins. Unfortunately, corporate marketing saw Arv invading their turf and told him to back off.

The Chaparral 2E was one of the first cars to introduce deployable downforce. The driver controlled the angle of the rear wing to increase or reduce drag at will.

Illustrations by Dave Kimble

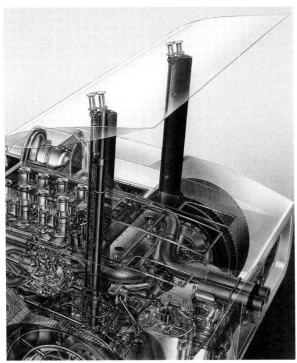

a reality check to be sure it is possible, and have considered some of the strategy of using common components, which might make such a proposal palatable to GM. There are a few more technologies that I need to talk about before the car is complete enough that it could be turned over to the stylists for its beauty treatment and aerodynamic development.

The chassis is key to getting the engine's power onto the road, to managing the road without beating up on the driver, and, of course, to effective cornering and stopping. And all of these functions depend on the most important chassis technologies: the tire, a variable-height spring, a variable damper, and a powerful brake.

The car is light enough that I don't have to go overboard on the tire. However, the current trend favors tall, wide, low-profile tires. I would select a 40-aspect-ratio 18-in.-diameter front and 20-in.-diameter rear tire to accommodate the suspension and brake requirements. This tire package will achieve 1.0 g cornering even before downforce is added.

An 18-in. front wheel will accommodate at least a 13-in. front brake rotor. Brake material technology for road cars is not up to the light-weight stopping power of Formula 1 carbon-carbon brakes, but it's getting close with the release of silicon-ceramic rotors and pads as an option on the latest Porsche Turbo Carrera. My super Corvette will need these brakes.

Even though the Corvette pioneered fiberglass springs, I'd like to move on and select an air spring system. Air springs are not quite active suspension, but they can give active height control and, as demonstrated by Daimler-Benz, semi-active roll control. Air suspension is not synonymous with soft suspension, though it is one of the best ways to create a soft ride. It can be tailored to give any vibration rate desired—even a variable rate—and by interconnecting the corners, the pitch, heave and roll rates can be tailored with some independence.

Height and pitch control are crucial for a modern sports car. Lowering the car is as advantageous for

directional stability at high speeds as raising it is for ride stability at low speeds on rough roads. Height control compensates for loading, and pitch control allows the car to be trimmed for minimum aerodynamic drag.

STYLING THE DREAM CORVETTE

My future Corvette would spend a lot of time with the stylists, first as they computer-modeled its aerodynamics and developed deployable downforce devices (wings). Downforce is extremely useful in cornering and under braking. The air suspension needs to be quick-acting enough that suspension height does not change as these devices are deployed. I would target 1.5 g braking and cornering at a speed of 60 mph. This would require the air spring to quickly accommodate a 50 percent increase in load.

Having sufficient power to be traction-limited at all but the highest speeds, the deployable downforce devices can also be used to increase the car's traction under acceleration. Thus these devices need to be deployed as a function of speed, cornering, acceleration, and braking.

The latest in damper technology is the electromagnetically-controlled magnetic fluid damper. Not unlike a conventional viscous damper, which generates its control force by flowing oil through a small orifice, the magnetic fluid flowing through the orifice is subject to a magnetic field that raises its viscosity and, consequently, the damping force. Damping force can be varied over a wide range, and controlled instantly from sensors and software. This kind of damper will offer the highest level of chassis control with the least disturbance to the driver.

Dropping into the enveloping driver's seat, I would want to find a very simple set of primary controls on the steering wheel, including paddle shifters. All of the secondary controls would be voice-commanded. Similarly, the instrumentation would be at an absolute minimum until the car was started (which could also be voice-commanded), then the head-up display (HUD) would energize. The HUD would provide functional information and situation-awareness feedback (obstacle or road-condition warnings). At night it would also include a superimposed

The magnetic control valve (shown) is the key to the magnetic fluid damper, which can be varied instantly over a wide range.
Drawing by Dave McLellan

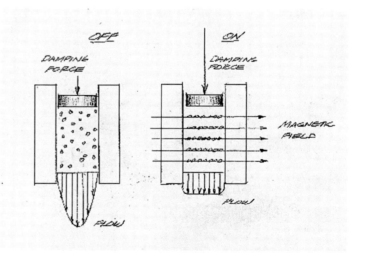

The first attempt to use night vision on the Cadillac LMP car at Le Mans.
GM Racing

infrared-enhanced image of the driving scene (night vision). Night vision allows a driver to see through fog and rain and at greater distances than headlights can illuminate.

All of this technology is currently available or in the development stages. So, has GM thought about its future in these terms? Does it have a role for the Corvette to help it develop this future? Is anyone aggressive enough to propose and carry through on such a radical future? Only time will tell.

Again I am reminded of Zora Arkus-Duntov's parting words to me, "Dave, you must do the mid-engine Corvette." With the demonstrated technologies at our disposal we can not only do this but we can do so much more.

Epilogue

As I settled into my retirement in 1993, I began working in earnest on the Corvette story. Soon, however, I received a call from Gerhard Frank, the head of Porsche's engineering consultancy. We had worked with Gerhard to develop the 1990 Corvette's driver's air bag system from a Porsche design. Gerhard asked if I would serve on the board of directors of Porsche's United States consultancy and help develop their business with the Detroit-based automobile industry. I agreed, and was formally interviewed by Horst Marchart, Porsche's Engineering Director. We agreed on what I would do, but then I heard nothing from Porsche for several months. When Gerhard finally called he was quite apologetic. Since we had last talked, Porsche had fired its manager in the United States and brought in Gerhard Koenig, from the parent consultancy in Weissach, Germany. But, would I still help?

I spent the next year working with Gerhard Koenig and serving on the board of directors of Porsche Engineering Services-Troy. This was an inside board as Porsche is a private family-held company. It gave me a taste for consulting and included several trips to Weissach and to the Porsche factory in Stuttgart. It also gave me the opportunity to occasionally sample Porsche's latest 911s.

Meanwhile, a friend, Joe Ziomek, who was himself an engineering consultant, brought me into a team that was forming under Mike Dudzik at ERIM in Ann Arbor. ERIM stands for Environmental Research Institute of Michigan, an institute that does mostly radar imaging research for the military. ERIM was spun off from the University of Michigan in the 1960s during the time of so much campus unrest and cloaked with this innocuous title. We bid on the engineering and construction of a software controlled, steer-by-wire and brake-by-wire car for the Federal Government's National Highway Traffic Safety Administration (NHTSA). Jet Propulsion Lab (JPL) had developed the specifications for the vehicle and would manage the project for NHTSA. We won the contract. ERIM's Tom

Blessing was responsible for the electronics and I handled the mechanicals and overall program management. Together, we put together an industry team that consisted of Milliken Associates for vehicle handling analysis, and several sources of by-wire experimental subsystems, namely, TRW for front and rear by-wire steering, Delphi for by-wire braking and Bosch for by-wire throttle. The electronic software system control was accomplished with a hardware-in-the-loop controller from dSpace. Roush Industries fabricated the physical vehicle and helped us wring it out. The purpose of the vehicle was to study driver response to a wide range of handling characteristics with the hope of reducing accidents.

This project led us to thinking about the possibility of using digital electronics to dramatically reduce accidents. With a study done by GM and the University of Michigan Transportation Research Institute called "44 Crashes" we found the footprint of accident scenarios against which we could test possible solutions.

We became convinced that what is essentially the same technology that lands an airplane without the pilot ever seeing the runway will also revolutionize the safety of the automobile. We have dubbed this "e-Safety." Basically, if the car knows where it is in space (GPS) and where the road is going (digital mapping), and the road to tire coefficient of friction, it can calculate the speed at which an upcoming curve can be negotiated without running off the road. The unknown is predicting the coefficient of friction. This prediction is being worked on but presents the most uncertainty. The driver has to deal with the same uncertainty. He may get clues from the car's handling or he can momentarily spike the brakes and gauge the car's reaction. (A momentary jerk response is reassuring. There is virtually no response to wet ice.)

Accidents with other cars will be predicted using sensors that can "see" (radar, visual and infrared). Knowing the road space, where other cars are and where they are heading, the car can predict collisions, much as the driver does. The key here is backing up the driver and giving him collision avoidance feedback. Driving in a space that is only a few seconds deep, the driver working at his best, recognizes potential accident situations in only the last moments to avoid a collision. Can a smart car communicate the imminent threat of a collision to the driver? Will the driver react in time with the right moves? The answer, yet to be proven, lies with head-up displays pointing the driver to the problem and, ultimately, to some level of autonomous braking and steering by the car itself. It will be hard to get over the hurdle of the car taking charge in these rare moments when an accident is inevitable if the driver does nothing. But, remember, the alternative is an actual collision.

At ERIM we also built off-road trucks for the army that demonstrate HMMWV (Humvee) performance from a pickup truck platform. This project took me to off-road driving school and on a ride across the Nevada desert in a well prepared (20 inches of ride travel) Baja chase truck.

The latest project I've been involved with, which became the basis for Chapter 17, is the Mosler MT900. I have already described the car, but there is another side to the story. The MT900 was designed in CAD (computer aided design) by one man, Rod Trenne, in about 6 months at which point it was released as computer files to cut molds and make parts. Compare this with the typical production car program that requires upwards of 3 years from styling to tooling and the efforts of hundreds of trained designers and engineers. While it's not a complete picture yet, it points the way to an all virtual, integrated design process.

Virtual areodynamics analysis (sometimes called computational fluid dynamics) is the latest piece of the puzzle to fall in place. A company called EXA—which I am also working with—has developed an anaylsis tool called PowerFLOW that can perform a complete aerodynamic flow analysis of a virtual car in just hours. This makes it possible to include aerodynamic performance as real time feedback in the design process.

I am also involved in consulting with Dr. Amar Bose of the Bose Corporation in Massachusetts. This connection came as a result of working with Bose to develop a high quality sound system for the C4 Corvette. Some day I hope to be able to describe the exciting work that is going on there.

In addition to working with a variety of companies related to the automobile industry, I remain very much involved with the Corvette world. Annually, I log tens of thousands of miles attending major events at the National Corvette Museum, Bloomington Gold, Corvettes at Carlisle, Mid-America's Funfest and others. Chances are that I'll see you at one of these events.

Bibliography

To read more about the Corvette, to enjoy it technically and to appreciate it as a car for the road and track, there are a number of books that I would recommend:

Burton, Jerry. *Zora Arkus-Duntov: The Legend Behind Corvette*. Cambridge, MA: Bentley Publishers, 2002.

Donohue, Mark, with Paul Van Valkenburgh. *The Unfair Advantage 2nd Edition*. Cambridge, MA: Bentley Publishers, 1975, 2000.

Frère, Paul. *Sports Car and Competition Driving*. Cambridge, MA: Bentley Publishers, 1963, 1992.

Friedman, Dave, and Lowell C. Paddock. *Corvette Grand Sport*. Osceola, WI: Motorbooks International, 1989.

Grinnell, James. J*ohn Fitch: Racing Through Life*. Oxfordshire: Bookmarque Publ., 1993.

Katz, Joseph. *Race Car Aerodynamics: Designing for Speed*. Cambridge, MA: Bentley Publishers, 1995.

Milliken, William F., and Douglas L. Milliken. *Race Car Vehicle Dynamics*. Warrendale, PA: Society of Automotive Engineers, 1995.

Probst, Charles O. *Corvette Fuel Injection & Electronic Engine Management*. Cambridge, MA: Bentley Publishers, 2001.

Rudd, Tony. *It Was Fun!: My Fifty Years of High Performance*. Newbury Park, CA: Haynes North America, 2000.

Sherman, Don. *Corvette 427: Practical Restoration of a '67 Roadster*. Cambridge, MA: Bentley Publishers, 2000.

Stevenson, Peter. *Driving Forces*. Cambridge, MA: Bentley Publishers, 2000.

Taruffi, Piero. *The Technique of Motor Racing*. Cambridge, MA: Bentley Publishers, 1958.

Van Valkenburgh, Paul. *Chevrolet Racing? 14 Years of Raucous Silence*. Warrendale, PA: Society of Automotive Engineers, 2000.

The classic book on the Corvette is still:

Ludvigsen, Karl. *Corvette: America's Star-Spangled Sports Car—The Complete History*. New York: Automobile Quarterly Publications*, 1973.

*To be reissued by Bentley Publishers. Contact publisher for more information.

Index

About the Author

Dave McLellan Archives

BORN IN MICHIGAN'S UPPER PENNINSULA, Dave McLellan was mechanically-minded from the start and learned by taking things apart. He first displayed his interest in cars by successfully participating in the future car design contest of the Fisher Body Craftsman's Guild.

After graduating from Detroit's Redford high school Dave studied engineering at Wayne State University. Although his father insisted he pursue a career in chemical engineering, within a year he was where he wanted to be—in mechanical engineering. While attending Wayne State, Dave edited the *Wayne Engineer*, a glossy 32 page magazine with feature stories written by the engineering students themselves.

Dave joined General Motors right out of college in 1959. His first assignment for GM was at the Proving Ground Noise and Vibration Lab. After working on the dynamics of cars, trucks and tanks, Dave was asked to manage the newly-completed Vehicle Dynamics Test Area (Black Lake) and its test programs.

Dave married Glenda Roberts in 1965, and the couple has two adult sons—David, who works for a Buick dealer, and Philip, who followed Dave's footsteps into automotive engineering. For 32 years, Dave and Glenda

have lived in their striking contemporary home designed by a former student and associate of Frank Lloyd Wright.

After his time at Black Lake, Dave's career next took him to Chevrolet Development where he led the team that finished the 70 1/2 Camaro. Moving to the GM Technical Center, he also managed John Delorean's unsuccessful attempt to marry the Camaro and the Corvette platforms. As chassis engineer on the Camaro-Nova, Dave learned the system at Chevrolet and in 1973 was picked to attend MIT as a Sloan Fellow.

On his return in the summer of 1974 he was assigned to Zora Arkus-Duntov. For the rest of that year he worked part time on the Corvette, chased problems uncovered with the application of catalytic converters and conducted a marketing feasibility study of a motorized scooter that was being developed in Frank Winchell's Engineering Staff. It was ultimately Dave's job to tell the aggressive, don't-take-no-for-an-answer Frank Winchell that his project made no sense for General Motors.

Appointed Corvette Chief Engineer in 1975, Dave would be indelibly linked with the Corvette for the next 17 years. The all-new 1984 Corvette was an outgrowth of his work, which continued to be developed with advanced electronics, and culminated in the 375 hp LT5 engine.

In what turned out to be his last development of the Corvette, Dave challenged an R&D team—led by Doug Robinson—to design a next generation Corvette capable of ZR-1 performance but at standard Corvette prices. Charged with the impossible task of making the Corvette faster, lighter, roomier and more rigid as a convertible, the team adopted the backbone architecture that would be the hallmark of the C5. Dave retired from General Motors in the fall of 1992 and turned the reins of the Corvette over to David Hill. Although Dave McLellan is no longer involved in Corvette Engineering, he remains extremely busy as an automotive engineering consultant and as an active member of the Corvette community.

Selected Books From Bentley Publishers

Chevrolet

Zora Arkus-Duntov: The Legend Behind Corvette *Jerry Burton*
ISBN 0-8376-0858-9

Corvette Fuel Injection & Electronic Engine Management 1982–2001: *Charles O. Probst, SAE*
ISBN 0-8376-0861-9

Corvette by the Numbers: The Essential Corvette Parts Reference 1955–1982: *Alan Colvin*
ISBN 0-8376-0288-2

Chevrolet by the Numbers 1955–1959:The Essential Chevrolet Parts Reference *Alan Colvin*
ISBN 0-8376-0875-9

Chevrolet by the Numbers 1960–1964: The Essential Chevrolet Parts Reference *Alan Colvin*
ISBN 0-8376-0936-4

Chevrolet by the Numbers 1965–1969: The Essential Chevrolet Parts Reference *Alan Colvin*
ISBN 0-8376-0956-9

Chevrolet by the Numbers 1970–1975: The Essential Chevrolet Parts Reference *Alan Colvin*
ISBN 0-8376-0927-5

Corvette 427: Practical Restoration of a '67 Roadster *Don Sherman*
ISBN 0-8376-0218-1

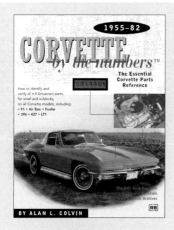

Camaro Exposed: 1967–1969, Designs, Decisions and the Inside View *Paul Zazarine*
ISBN 0-8376-0876-7

Chevrolet and GMC Light Truck Owner's Bible™ *Moses Ludel*
ISBN 0-8376-0157-6

Other Enthusiast Titles

Road & Track Illustrated Automotive Dictionary *John Dinkel*
ISBN 0-8376-0143-6

Jeep Owner's Bible™ *Moses Ludel*
ISBN 0-8376-0154-1

The Official Ford Mustang 5.0 Technical Reference & Performance Handbook: 1979–1993
Al Kirschenbaum ISBN 0-8376-0210-6

Driving

The Unfair Advantage *Mark Donohue*
ISBN 0-8376-0073-1(hc);
0-8376-0069-3(pb)

Going Faster! Mastering the Art of Race Driving *The Skip Barber Racing School* ISBN 0-8376-0227-0

Driving Forces: The Grand Prix Racing World Caught in the Maelstrom of the Third Reich
Peter Stevenson ISBN 0-8376-0217-3

A French Kiss With Death: Steve McQueen and the Making of Le Mans
Michael Keyser ISBN 0-8376-0234-3

Sports Car and Competition Driving
Paul Frère with foreword *by Phil Hill*
ISBN 0-8376-0202-5

The Technique of Motor Racing
Piero Taruffi ISBN 0-8376-0228-9

Engineering

Supercharged! Design, Testing, and Installation of Supercharger Systems
Corky Bell ISBN 0-8376-0168-1

Maximum Boost: Designing, Testing, and Installing Turbocharger Systems
Corky Bell ISBN 0-8376-0160-6

Race Car Aerodynamics *Joseph Katz*
ISBN 0-8376-0142-8

BMW

BMW 3 Series Enthusiast's Companion™ *Jeremy Walton*
ISBN 0-8376-0220-3

The BMW Enthusiast's Companion
BMW Car Club of America
ISBN 0-8376-0321-8

Volkswagen

Battle for the Beetle
Karl Ludvigsen ISBN 08376-0071-5

Volkswagen Sport Tuning for Street and Competition *Per Schroeder*
ISBN 0-8376-0161-4

Bentley Publishers also offers a comprehensive selection of Repair Manuals for Audi, Volkswagen, BMW and Porsche.